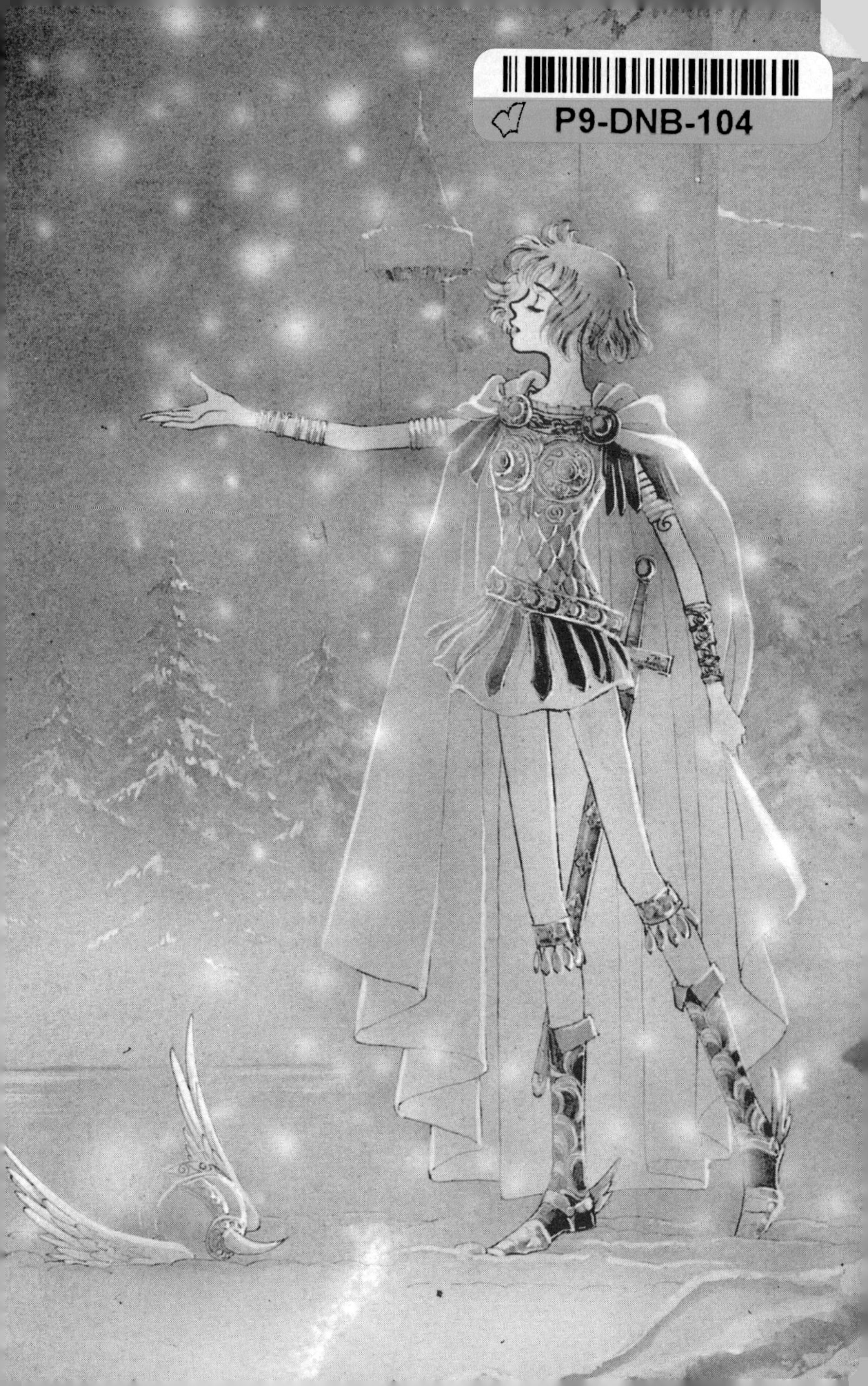

The Queen's Knight Vol. 2
Created by Kim Kang Won

Translation - Lauren Na
English Adaptation - Jeannie Anderson
Retouch and Lettering - Bowen Park
Production Artist - Vicente Rivera, Jr.
Cover Design - Gary Shum

Editor - Julie Taylor
Digital Imaging Manager - Chris Buford
Pre-Press Manager - Antonio DePietro
Production Managers - Jennifer Miller and Mutsumi Miyazaki
Art Director - Matt Alford
Managing Editor - Jill Freshney
VP of Production - Ron Klamert
Editor-in-Chief - Mike Kiley
President and C.O.O. - John Parker
Publisher and C.E.O. - Stuart Levy

A  Manga

TOKYOPOP Inc.
5900 Wilshire Blvd. Suite 2000
Los Angeles, CA 90036

E-mail: info@TOKYOPOP.com
Come visit us online at www.TOKYOPOP.com

ISBN: 1-59532-258-2

First TOKYOPOP printing: January 2005
10 9 8 7 6 5 4 3 2 1
Printed in the USA

THE QUEEN'S KNIGHT

VOLUME 2

BY KIM KANG WON

HAMBURG // LONDON // LOS ANGELES // TOKYO

LAST TIME IN...

THE QUEEN'S KNIGHT

DURING SUMMER VACATION TO VISIT HER MOTHER IN GERMANY, 15-YEAR-OLD YUNA LEE FALLS OFF A CLIFF AND IS RESCUED BY REINO, AN 18-YEAR-OLD KNIGHT LIVING IN THE MAGICAL LAND OF PHANTASMA. HE MAKES A DEAL WITH YUNA THAT IF HE SAVES HER LIFE, SHE MUST MARRY HIM AND BECOME HIS QUEEN. INDEBTED TO HER KNIGHT IN SHINING ARMOR, YUNA IS TORN BETWEEN HER FAMILY AND FRIENDS BACK HOME AND LIFE AS PHANTASMA'S QUEEN!

The Queen's Knight

Volume 2

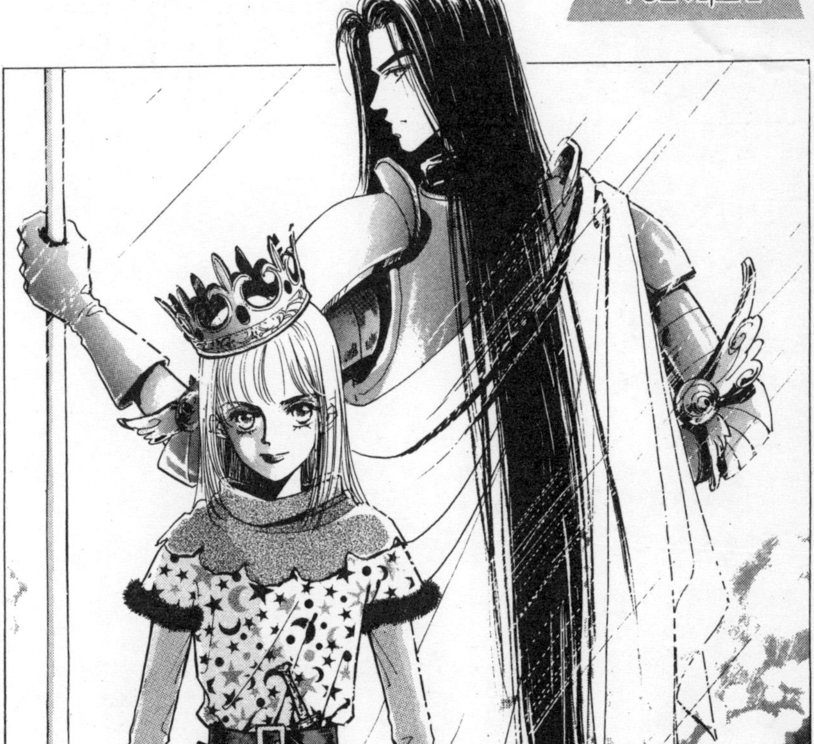

Kim Kang Won

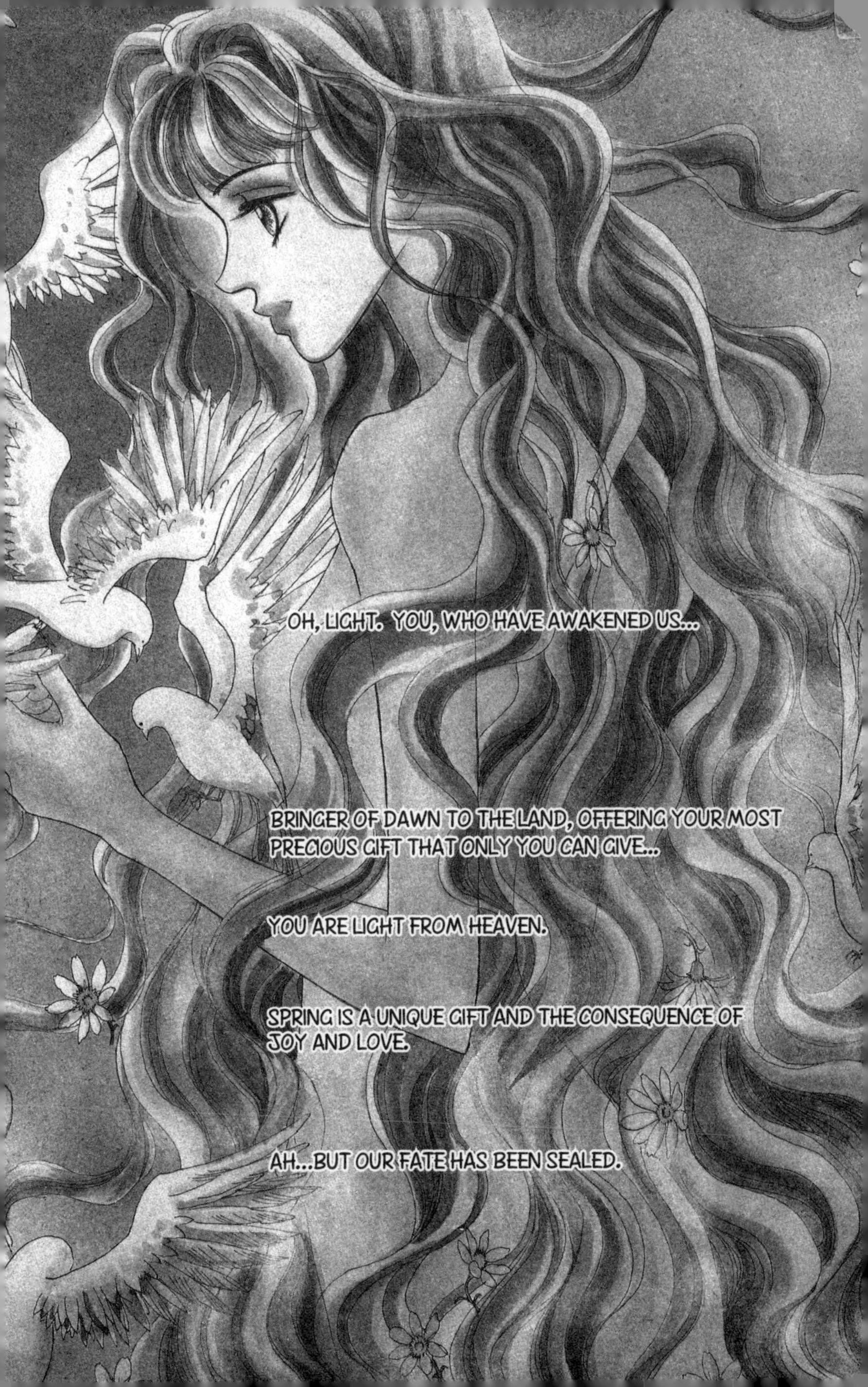
OH, LIGHT. YOU, WHO HAVE AWAKENED US...
BRINGER OF DAWN TO THE LAND, OFFERING YOUR MOST PRECIOUS GIFT THAT ONLY YOU CAN GIVE...
YOU ARE LIGHT FROM HEAVEN.
SPRING IS A UNIQUE GIFT AND THE CONSEQUENCE OF JOY AND LOVE.
AH...BUT OUR FATE HAS BEEN SEALED.

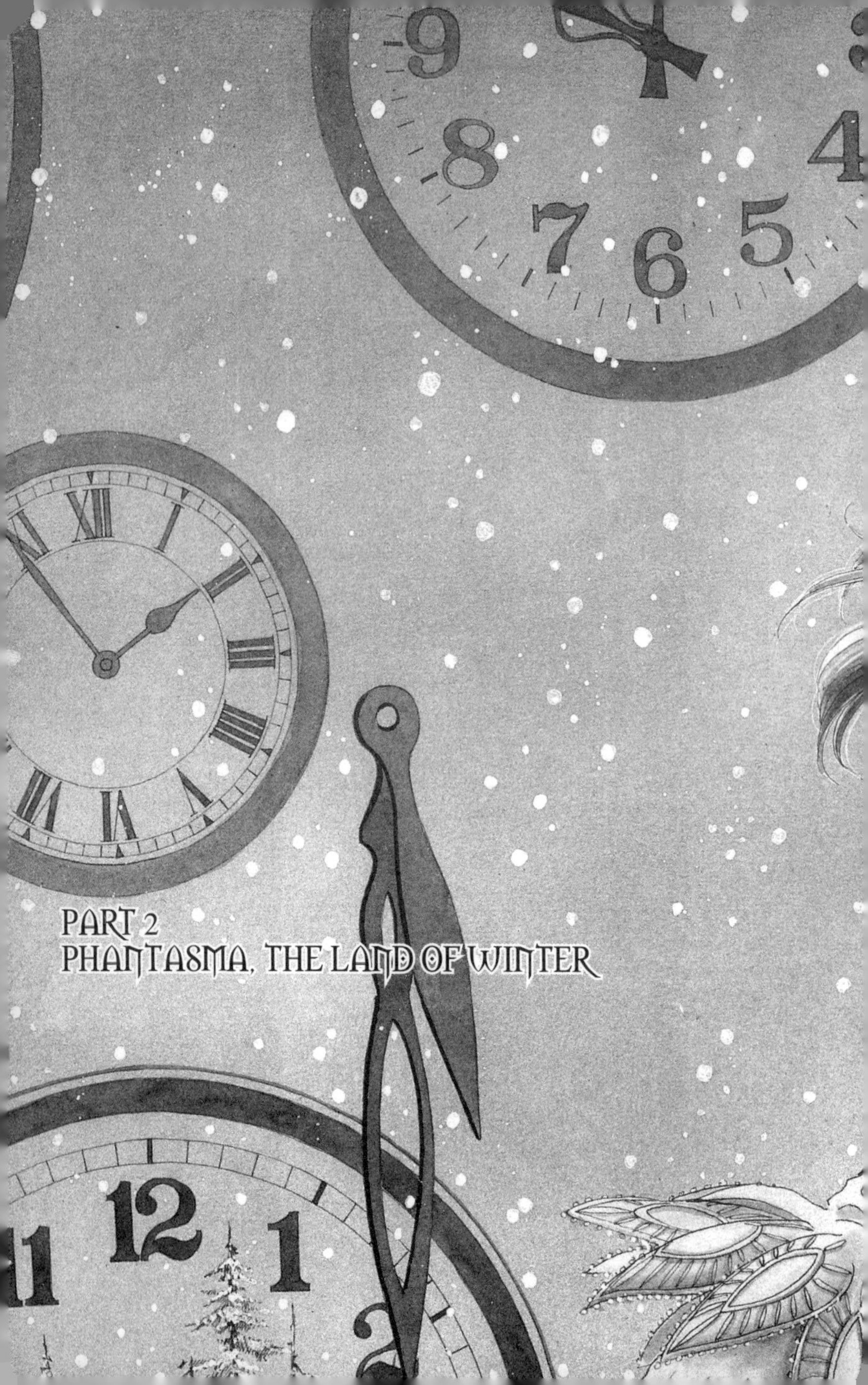

PART 2
PHANTASMA, THE LAND OF WINTER

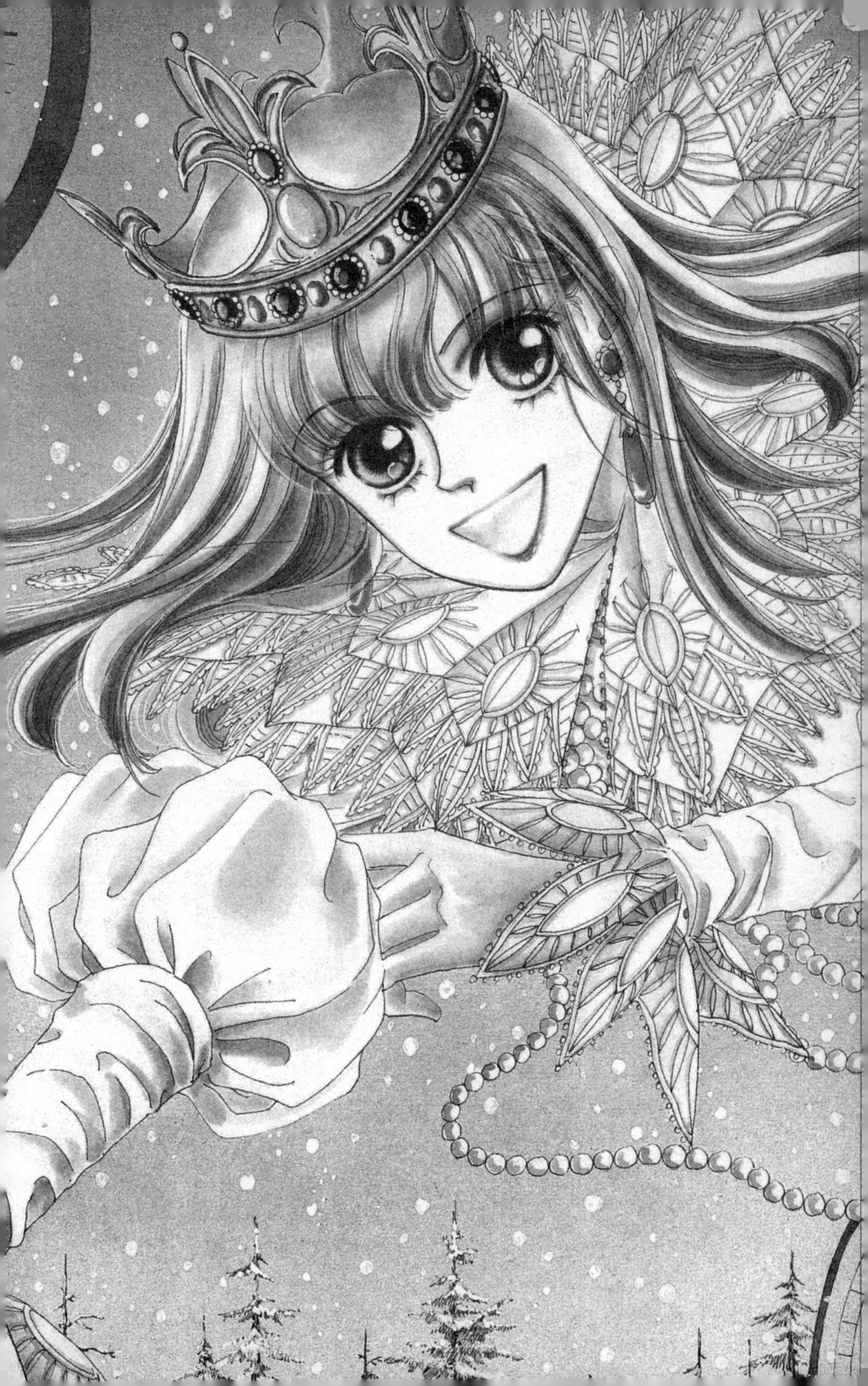

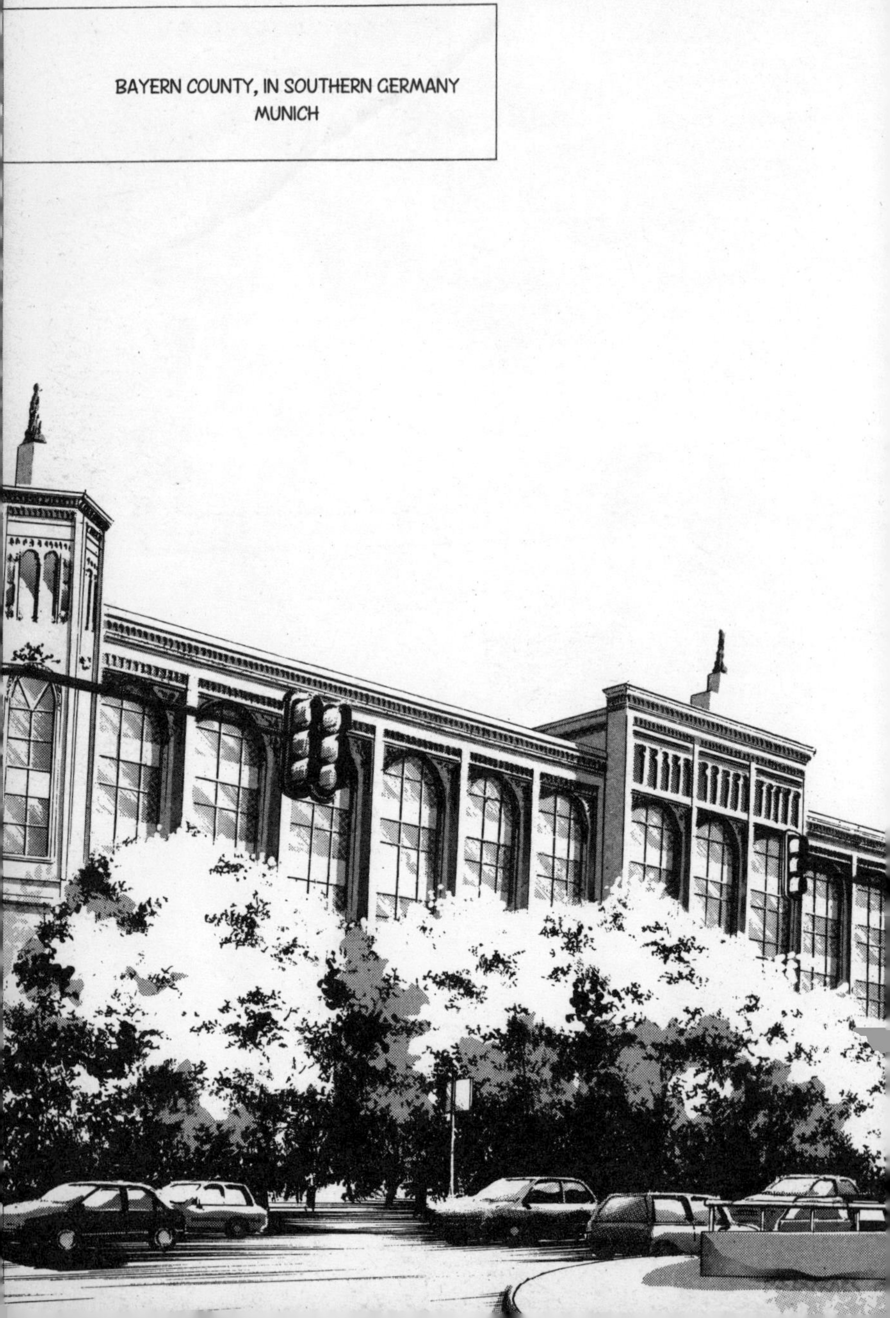
BAYERN COUNTY, IN SOUTHERN GERMANY
MUNICH

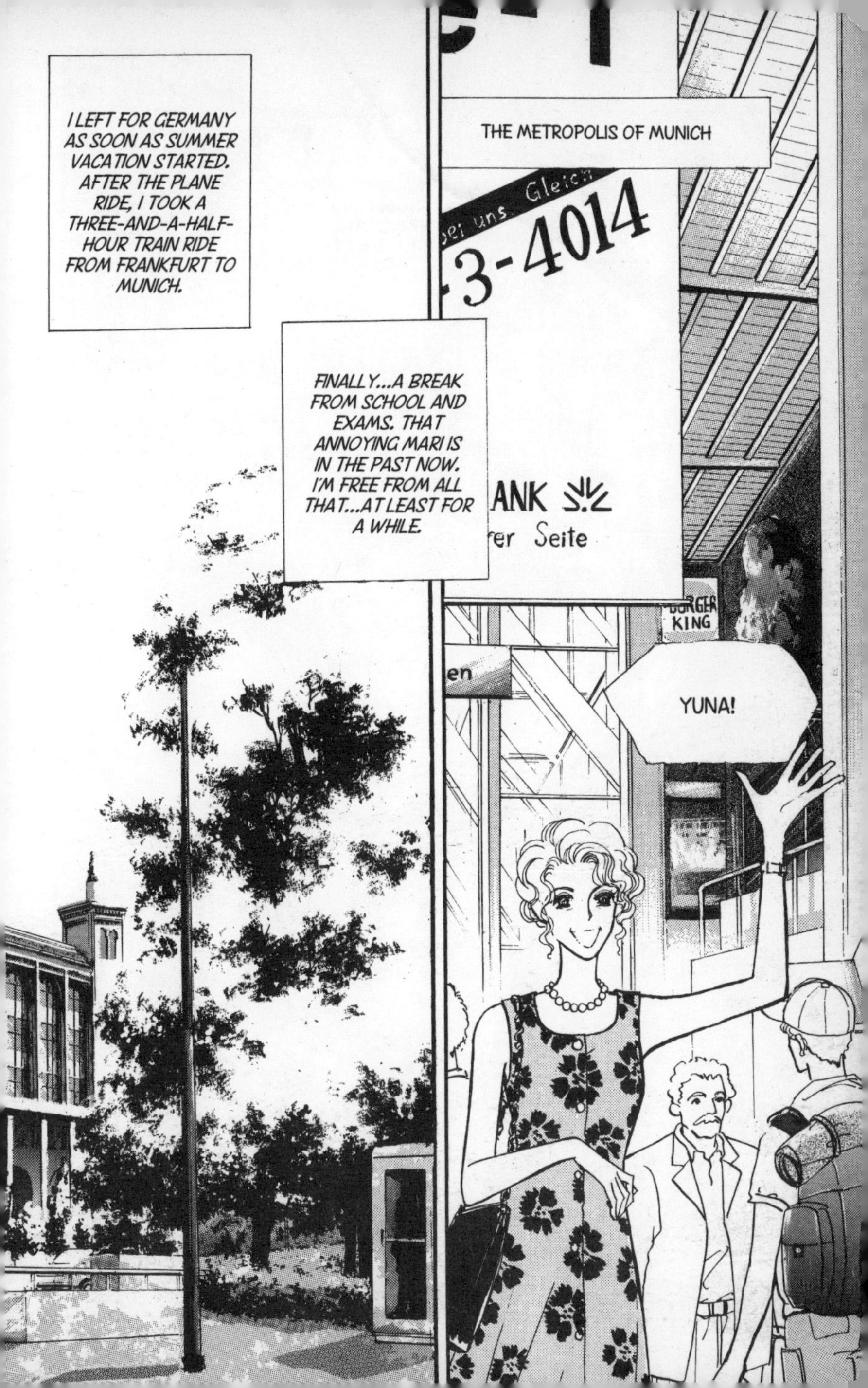
I LEFT FOR GERMANY AS SOON AS SUMMER VACATION STARTED. AFTER THE PLANE RIDE, I TOOK A THREE-AND-A-HALF-HOUR TRAIN RIDE FROM FRANKFURT TO MUNICH.
THE METROPOLIS OF MUNICH
3-4014
FINALLY...A BREAK FROM SCHOOL AND EXAMS. THAT ANNOYING MARI IS IN THE PAST NOW. I'M FREE FROM ALL THAT...AT LEAST FOR A WHILE.
Seite
KING
YUNA!

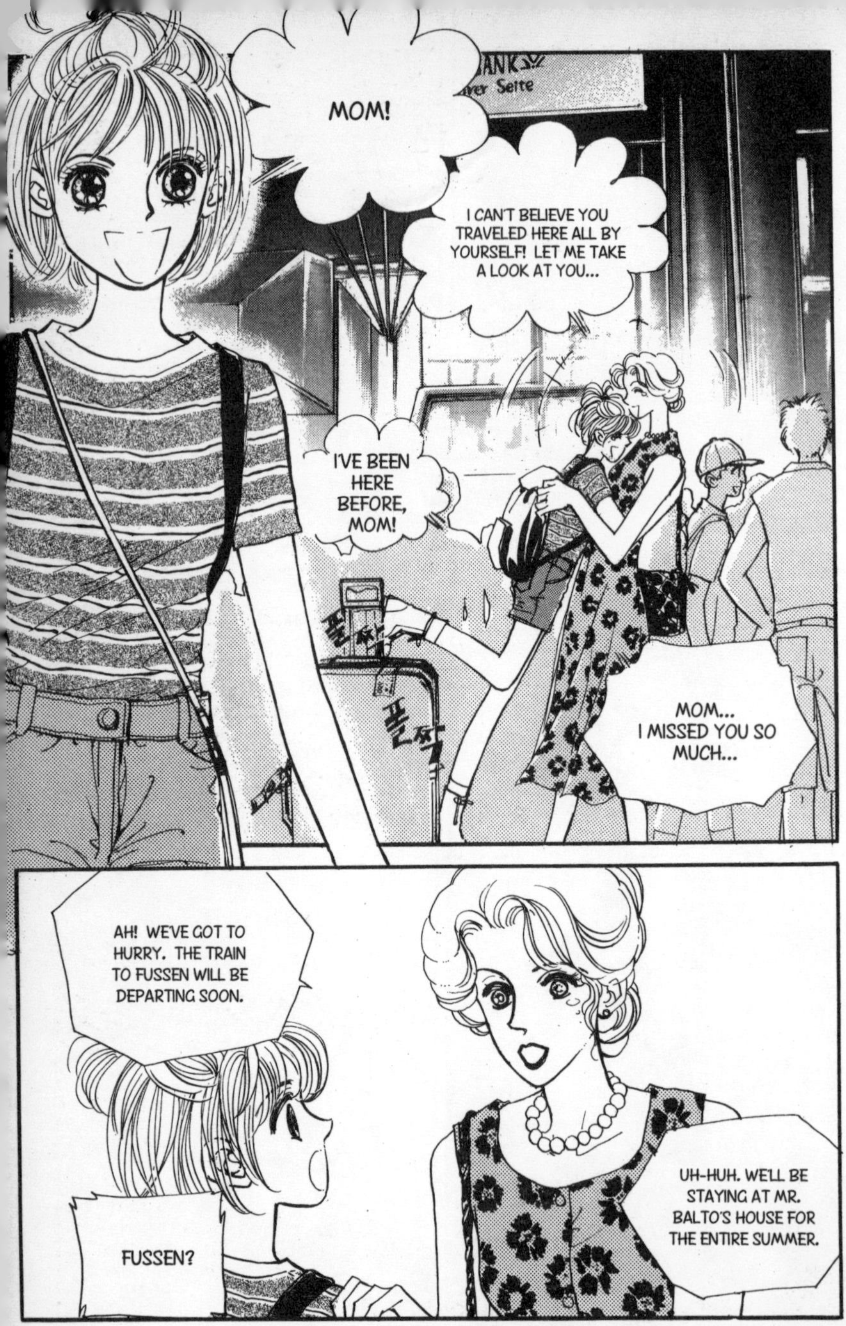
MOM!
I CAN'T BELIEVE YOU TRAVELED HERE ALL BY YOURSELF! LET ME TAKE A LOOK AT YOU...
I'VE BEEN HERE BEFORE, MOM!
MOM... I MISSED YOU SO MUCH...
AH! WE'VE GOT TO HURRY. THE TRAIN TO FUSSEN WILL BE DEPARTING SOON.
FUSSEN?
UH-HUH. WE'LL BE STAYING AT MR. BALTO'S HOUSE FOR THE ENTIRE SUMMER.

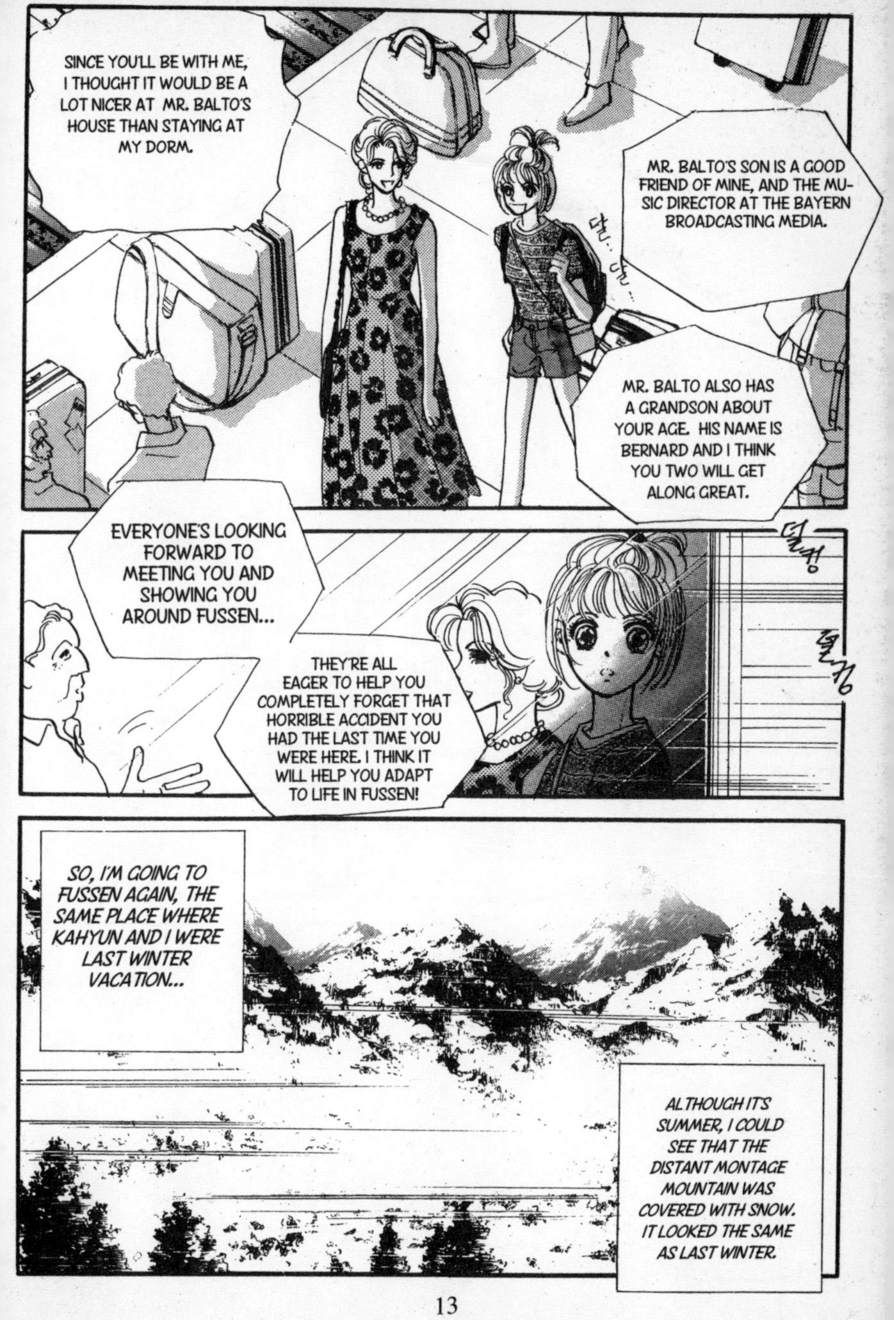

SINCE YOU'LL BE WITH ME, I THOUGHT IT WOULD BE A LOT NICER AT MR. BALTO'S HOUSE THAN STAYING AT MY DORM.
MR. BALTO'S SON IS A GOOD FRIEND OF MINE, AND THE MUSIC DIRECTOR AT THE BAYERN BROADCASTING MEDIA.
MR. BALTO ALSO HAS A GRANDSON ABOUT YOUR AGE. HIS NAME IS BERNARD AND I THINK YOU TWO WILL GET ALONG GREAT.
EVERYONE'S LOOKING FORWARD TO MEETING YOU AND SHOWING YOU AROUND FUSSEN...
THEY'RE ALL EAGER TO HELP YOU COMPLETELY FORGET THAT HORRIBLE ACCIDENT YOU HAD THE LAST TIME YOU WERE HERE. I THINK IT WILL HELP YOU ADAPT TO LIFE IN FUSSEN!
SO, I'M GOING TO FUSSEN AGAIN, THE SAME PLACE WHERE KAHYUN AND I WERE LAST WINTER VACATION...
ALTHOUGH ITS SUMMER, I COULD SEE THAT THE DISTANT MONTAGE MOUNTAIN WAS COVERED WITH SNOW. IT LOOKED THE SAME AS LAST WINTER.

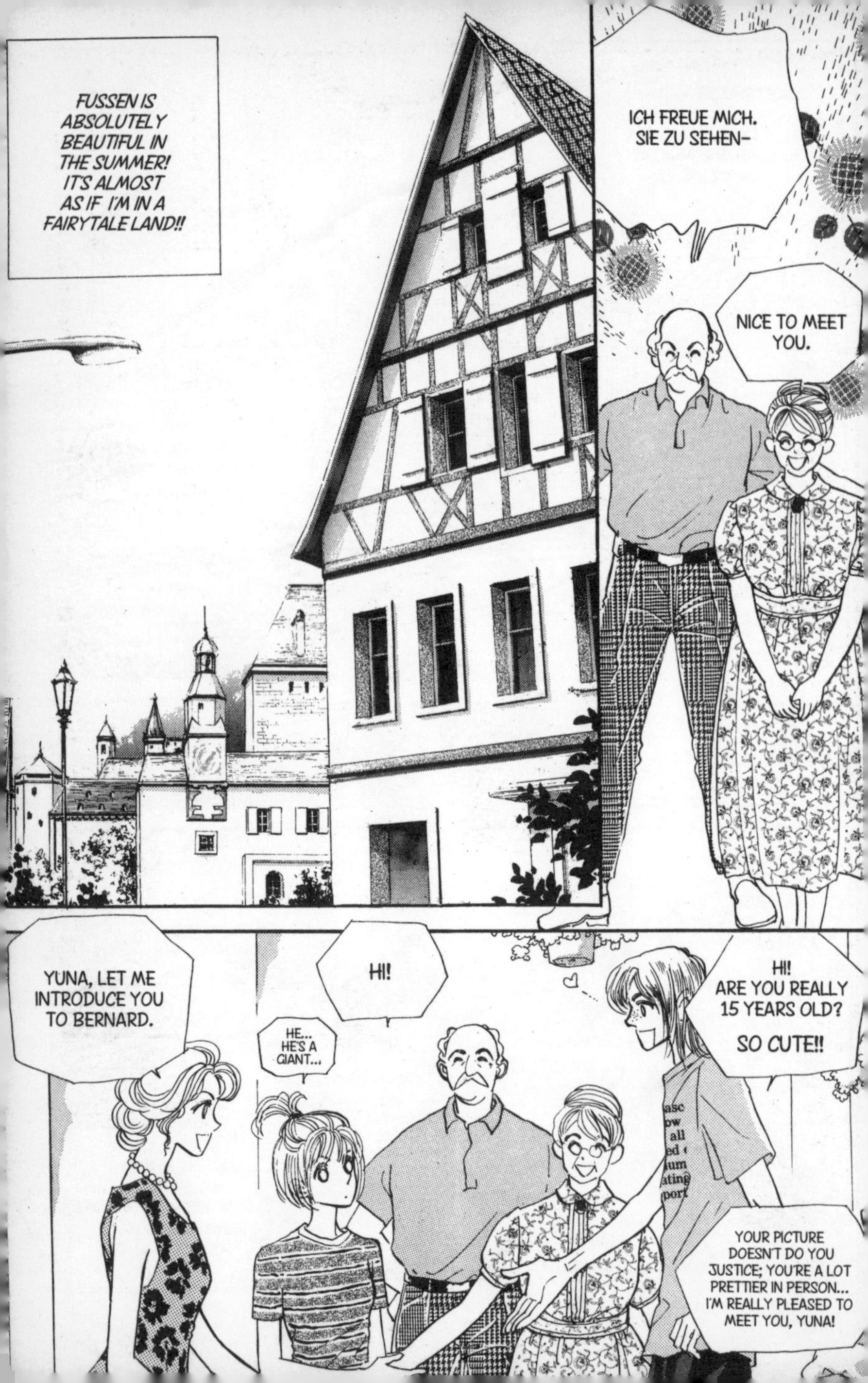
FUSSEN IS ABSOLUTELY BEAUTIFUL IN THE SUMMER! IT'S ALMOST AS IF I'M IN A FAIRYTALE LAND!!
ICH FREUE MICH. SIE ZU SEHEN-
NICE TO MEET YOU.
YUNA, LET ME INTRODUCE YOU TO BERNARD.
HI!
HE... HE'S A GIANT...
HI! ARE YOU REALLY 15 YEARS OLD?
SO CUTE!!
YOUR PICTURE DOESN'T DO YOU JUSTICE; YOU'RE A LOT PRETTIER IN PERSON... I'M REALLY PLEASED TO MEET YOU, YUNA!

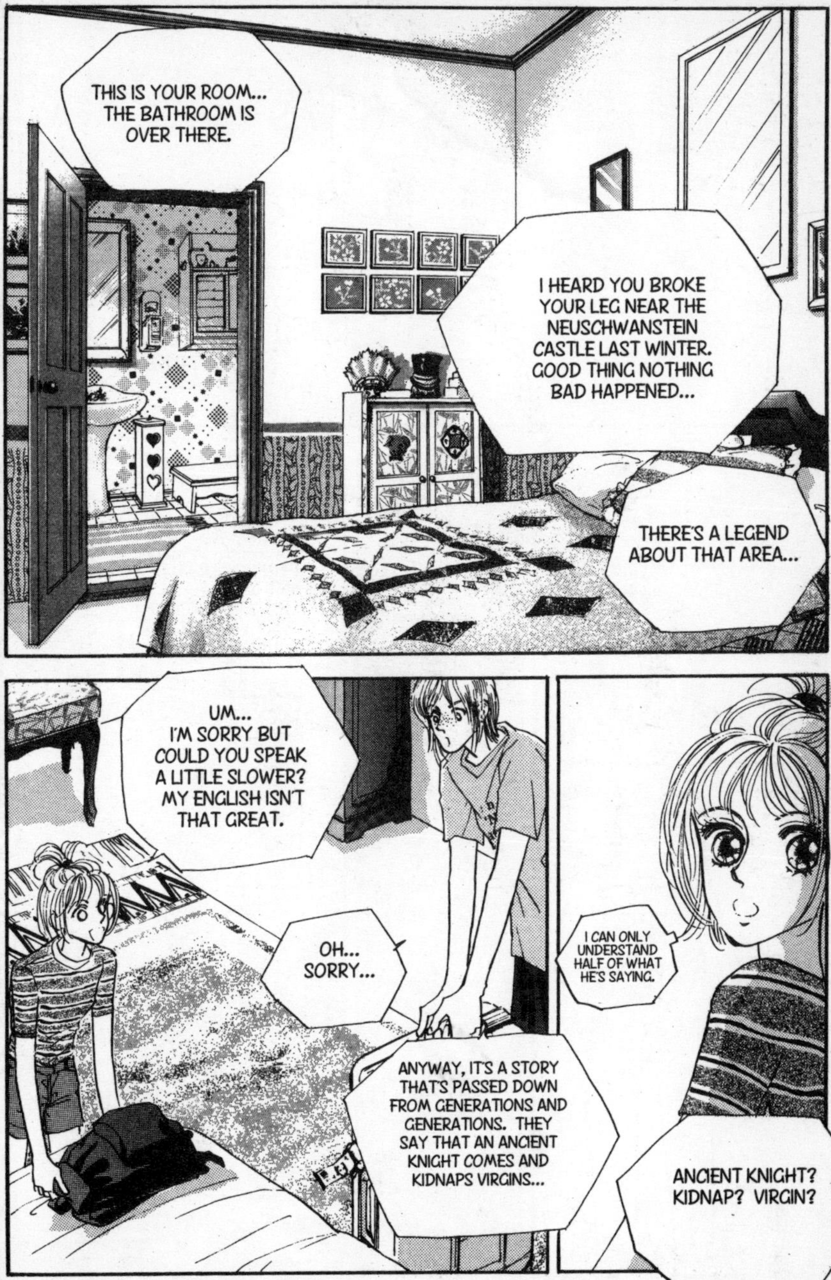
THIS IS YOUR ROOM... THE BATHROOM IS OVER THERE.
I HEARD YOU BROKE YOUR LEG NEAR THE NEUSCHWANSTEIN CASTLE LAST WINTER. GOOD THING NOTHING BAD HAPPENED...
THERE'S A LEGEND ABOUT THAT AREA...
UM... I'M SORRY BUT COULD YOU SPEAK A LITTLE SLOWER? MY ENGLISH ISN'T THAT GREAT.
OH... SORRY...
ANYWAY, IT'S A STORY THAT'S PASSED DOWN FROM GENERATIONS AND GENERATIONS. THEY SAY THAT AN ANCIENT KNIGHT COMES AND KIDNAPS VIRGINS...
I CAN ONLY UNDERSTAND HALF OF WHAT HE'S SAYING.
ANCIENT KNIGHT? KIDNAP? VIRGIN?

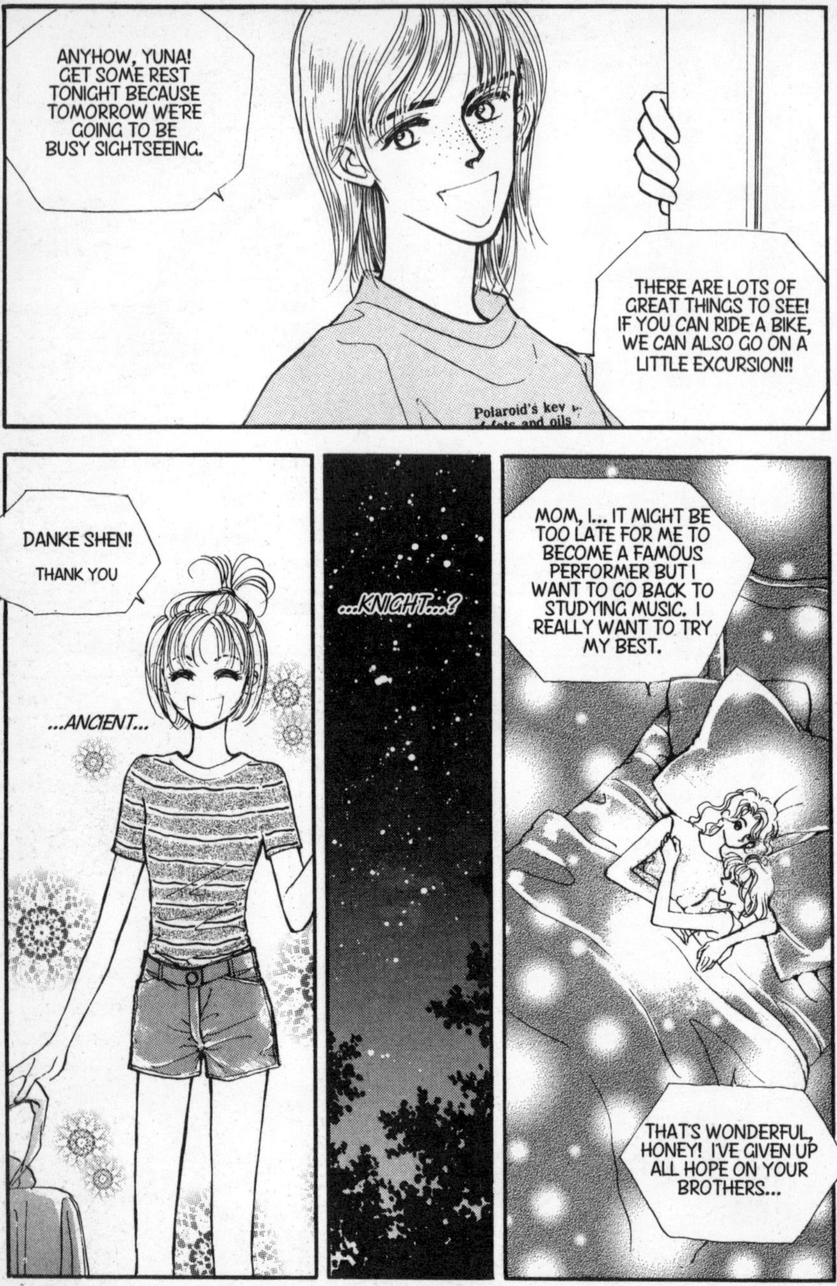
ANYHOW, YUNA! GET SOME REST TONIGHT BECAUSE TOMORROW WE'RE GOING TO BE BUSY SIGHTSEEING.
THERE ARE LOTS OF GREAT THINGS TO SEE! IF YOU CAN RIDE A BIKE, WE CAN ALSO GO ON A LITTLE EXCURSION!!
Polaroid's key
DANKE SHEN!
THANK YOU
...ANCIENT...
...KNIGHT...?
MOM, I... IT MIGHT BE TOO LATE FOR ME TO BECOME A FAMOUS PERFORMER BUT I WANT TO GO BACK TO STUDYING MUSIC. I REALLY WANT TO TRY MY BEST.
THAT'S WONDERFUL, HONEY! I'VE GIVEN UP ALL HOPE ON YOUR BROTHERS...

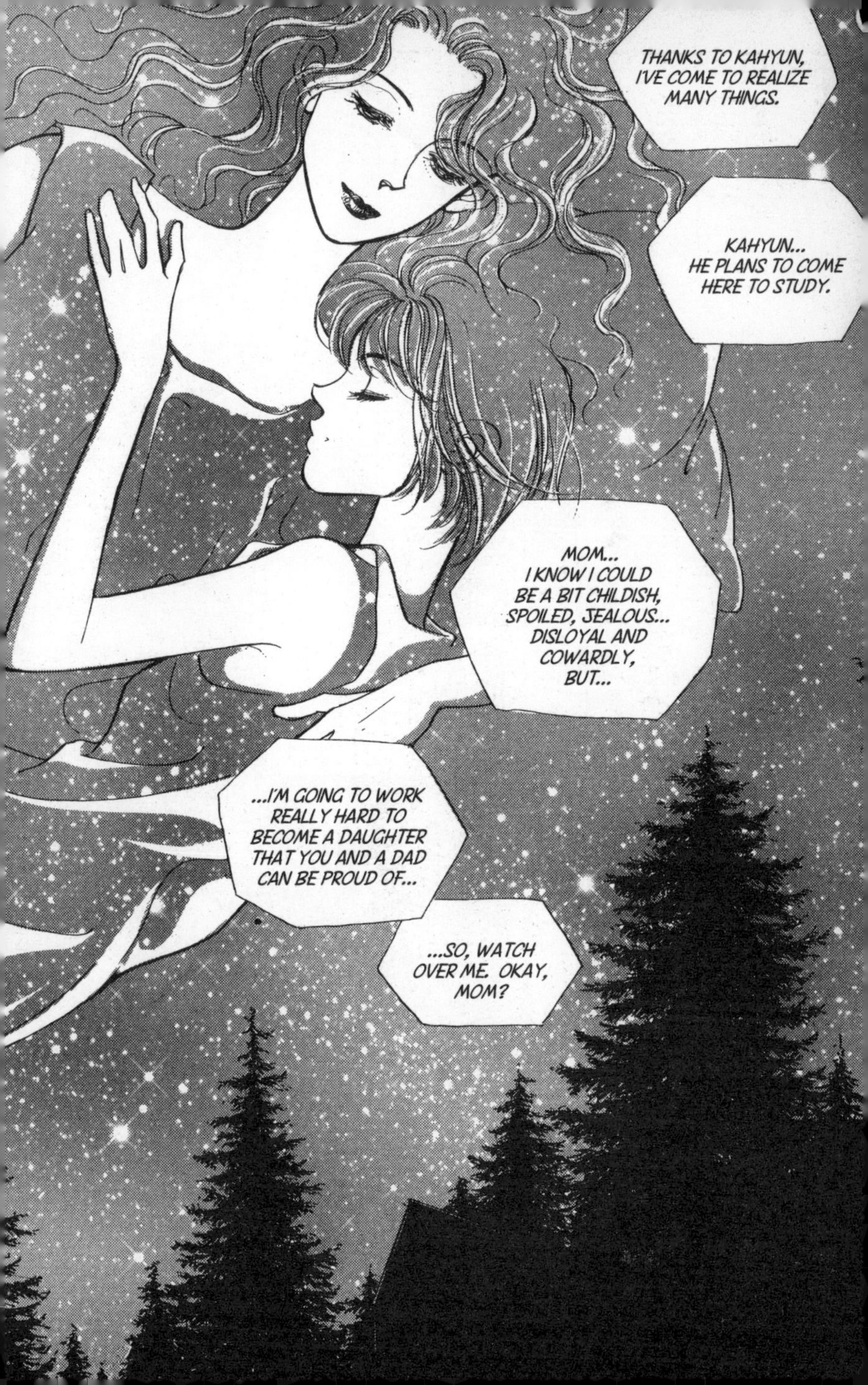
THANKS TO KAHYUN, I'VE COME TO REALIZE MANY THINGS.
KAHYUN... HE PLANS TO COME HERE TO STUDY.
MOM... I KNOW I COULD BE A BIT CHILDISH, SPOILED, JEALOUS... DISLOYAL AND COWARDLY, BUT...
...I'M GOING TO WORK REALLY HARD TO BECOME A DAUGHTER THAT YOU AND A DAD CAN BE PROUD OF...
...SO, WATCH OVER ME. OKAY, MOM?

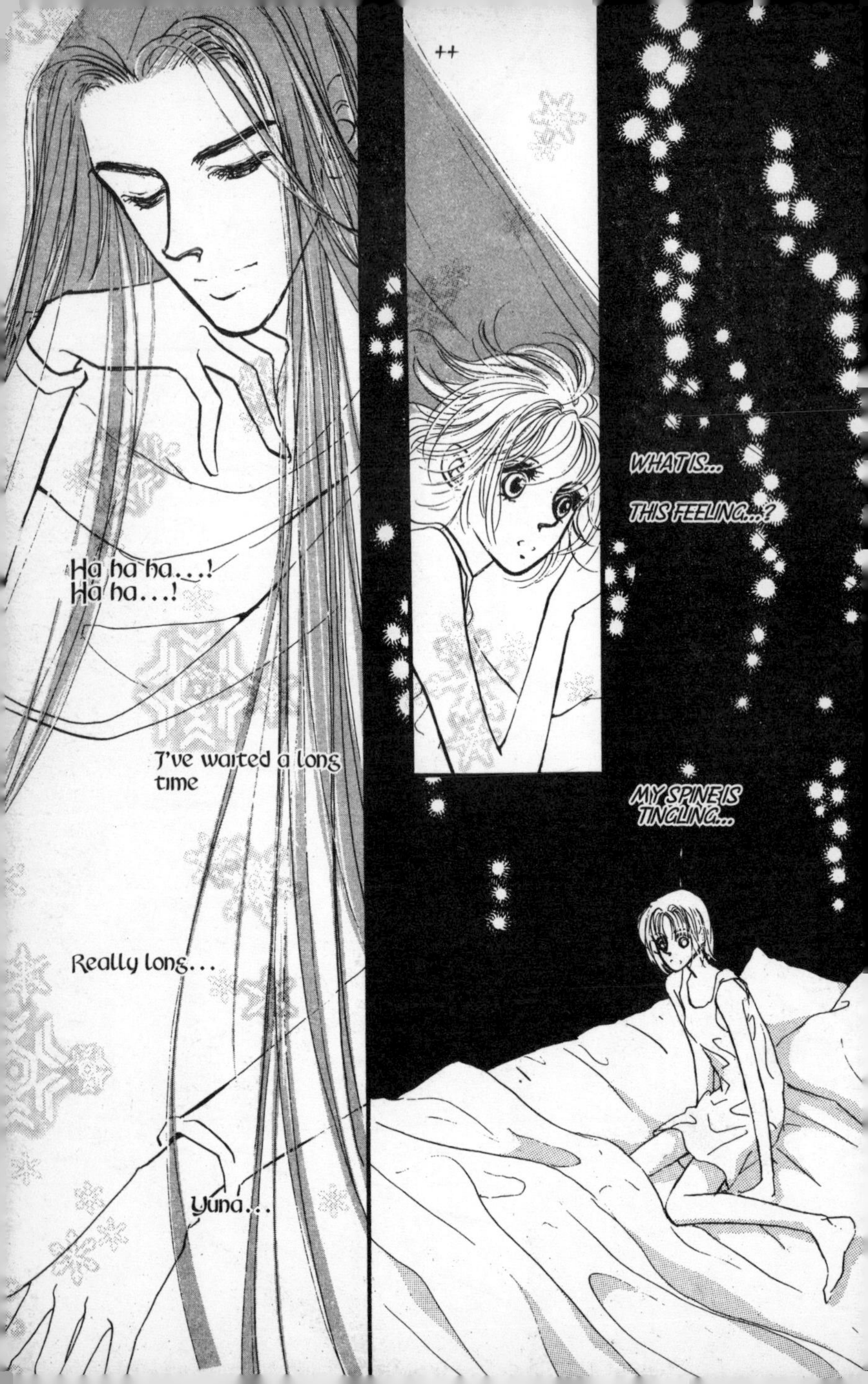
Ha ha ha...!
Ha ha...!
I've waited a long time
Really long...
Yuna...
WHAT IS...
THIS FEELING...?
MY SPINE IS TINGLING...

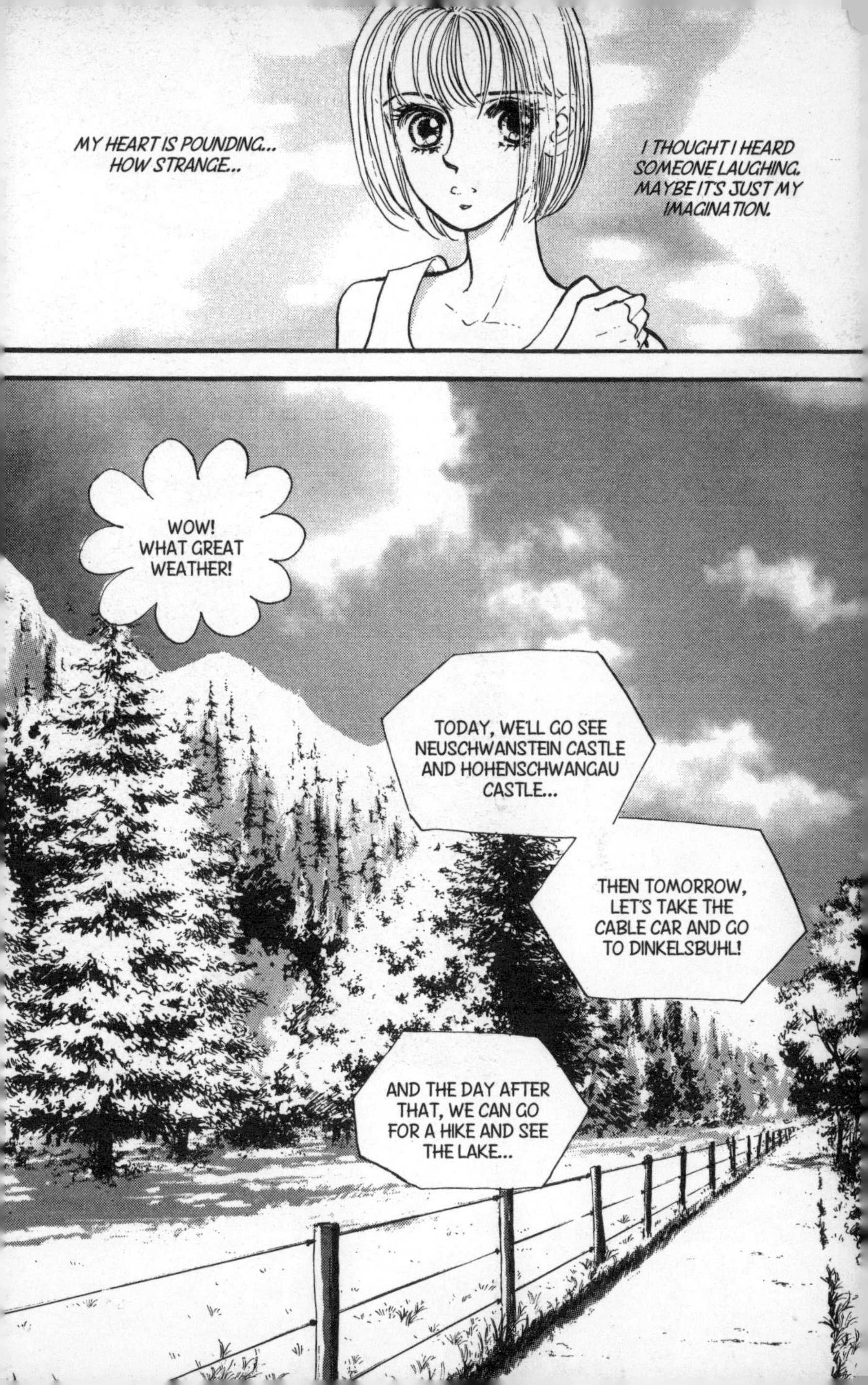

MY HEART IS POUNDING... HOW STRANGE...
I THOUGHT I HEARD SOMEONE LAUGHING. MAYBE IT'S JUST MY IMAGINATION.
WOW! WHAT GREAT WEATHER!
TODAY, WE'LL GO SEE NEUSCHWANSTEIN CASTLE AND HOHENSCHWANGAU CASTLE...
THEN TOMORROW, LET'S TAKE THE CABLE CAR AND GO TO DINKELSBUHL!
AND THE DAY AFTER THAT, WE CAN GO FOR A HIKE AND SEE THE LAKE...

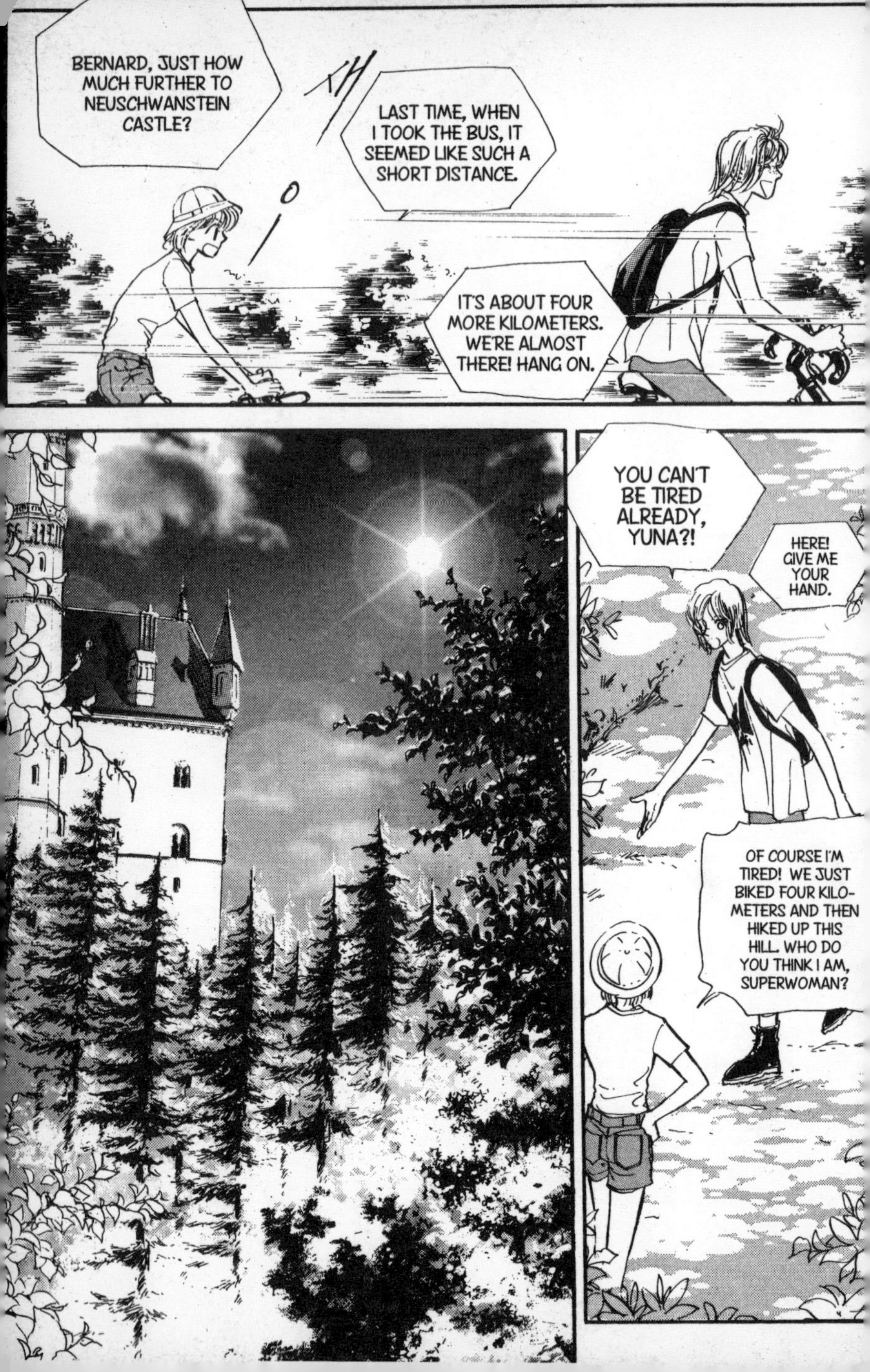
BERNARD, JUST HOW MUCH FURTHER TO NEUSCHWANSTEIN CASTLE?
LAST TIME, WHEN I TOOK THE BUS, IT SEEMED LIKE SUCH A SHORT DISTANCE.
IT'S ABOUT FOUR MORE KILOMETERS. WE'RE ALMOST THERE! HANG ON.
YOU CAN'T BE TIRED ALREADY, YUNA?!
HERE! GIVE ME YOUR HAND.
OF COURSE I'M TIRED! WE JUST BIKED FOUR KILO-METERS AND THEN HIKED UP THIS HILL. WHO DO YOU THINK I AM, SUPERWOMAN?

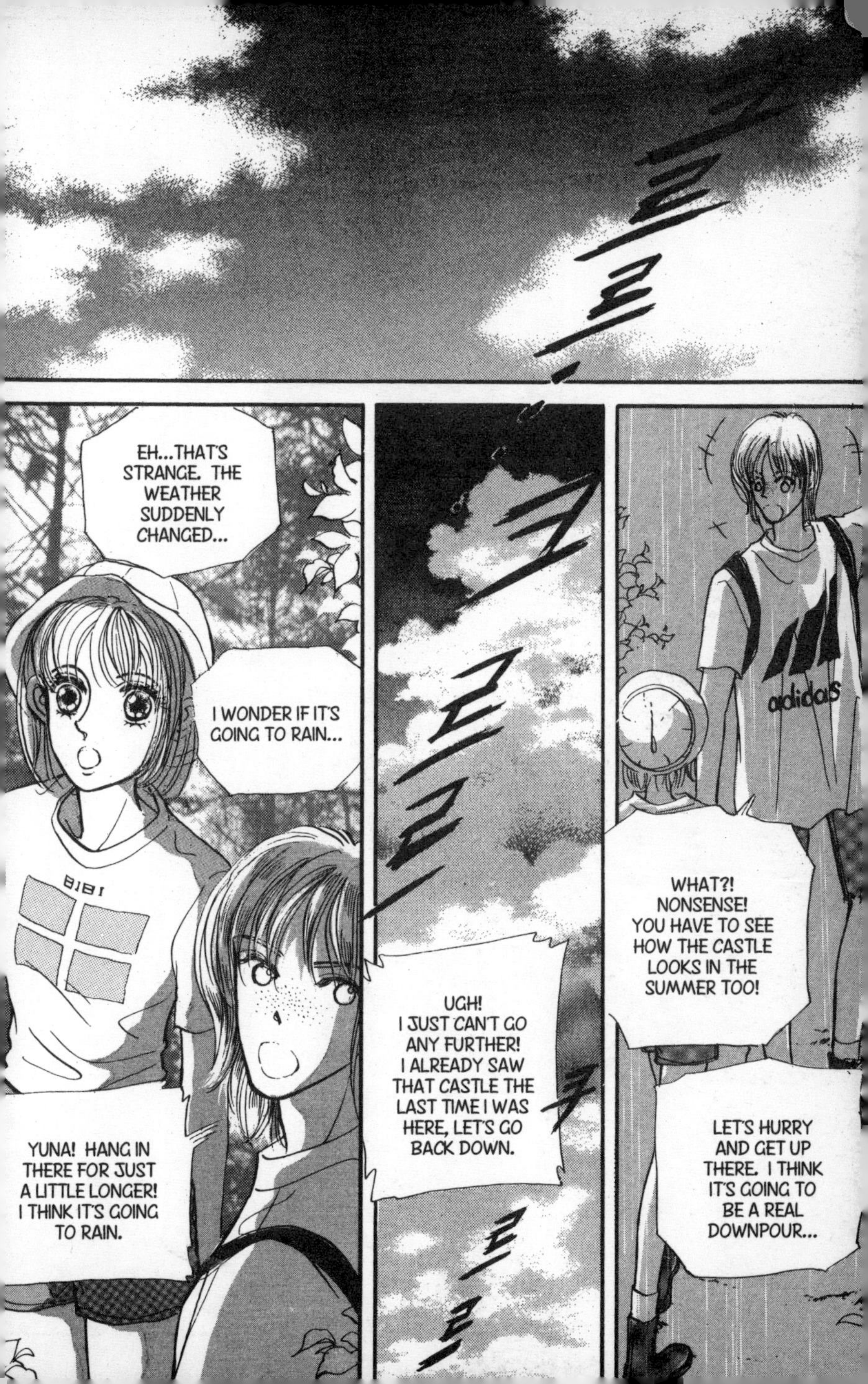
EH...THAT'S STRANGE. THE WEATHER SUDDENLY CHANGED...
I WONDER IF IT'S GOING TO RAIN...
BIBI
YUNA! HANG IN THERE FOR JUST A LITTLE LONGER! I THINK IT'S GOING TO RAIN.
UGH! I JUST CAN'T GO ANY FURTHER! I ALREADY SAW THAT CASTLE THE LAST TIME I WAS HERE, LET'S GO BACK DOWN.
adidas
WHAT?! NONSENSE! YOU HAVE TO SEE HOW THE CASTLE LOOKS IN THE SUMMER TOO!
LET'S HURRY AND GET UP THERE. I THINK IT'S GOING TO BE A REAL DOWNPOUR...

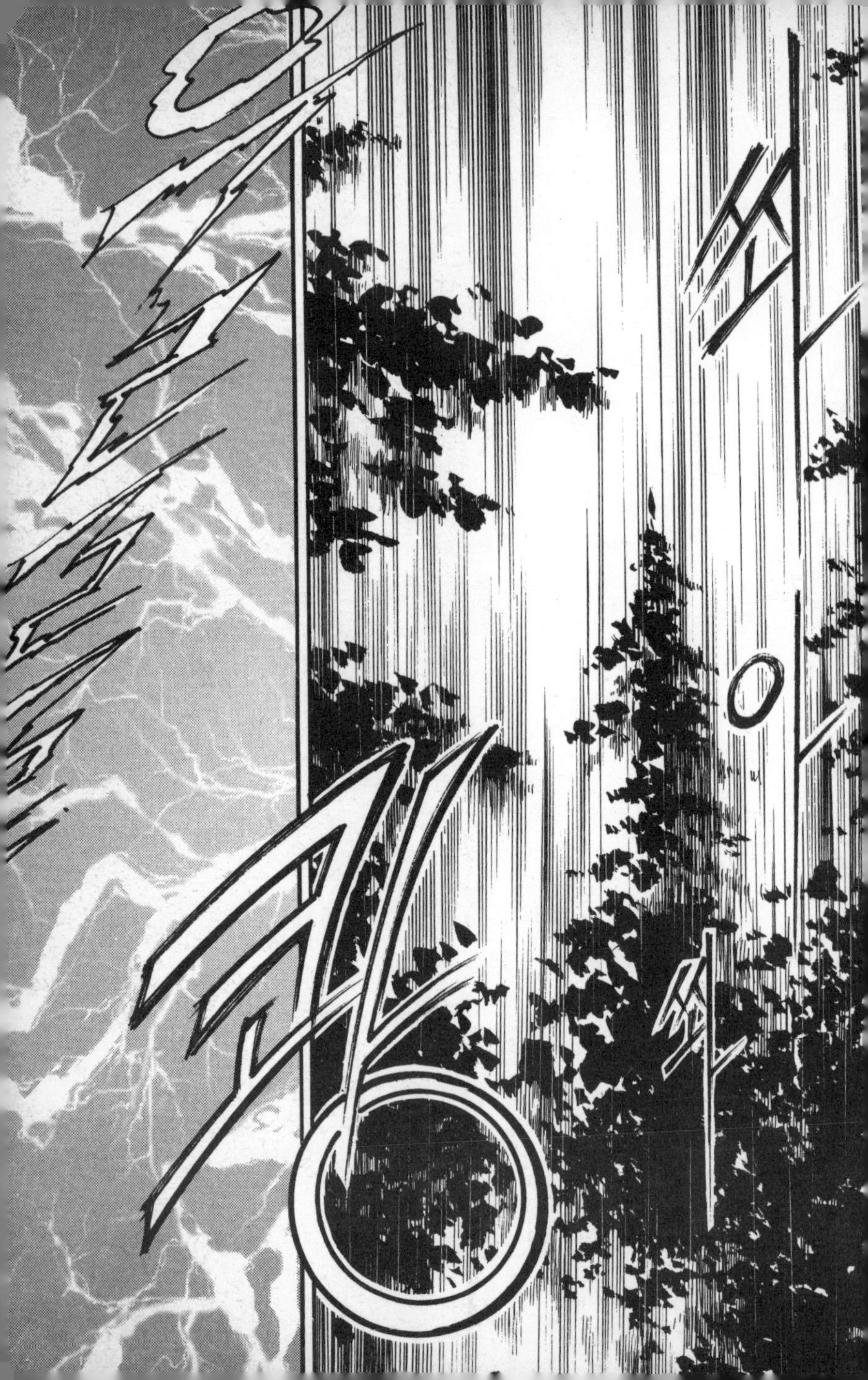

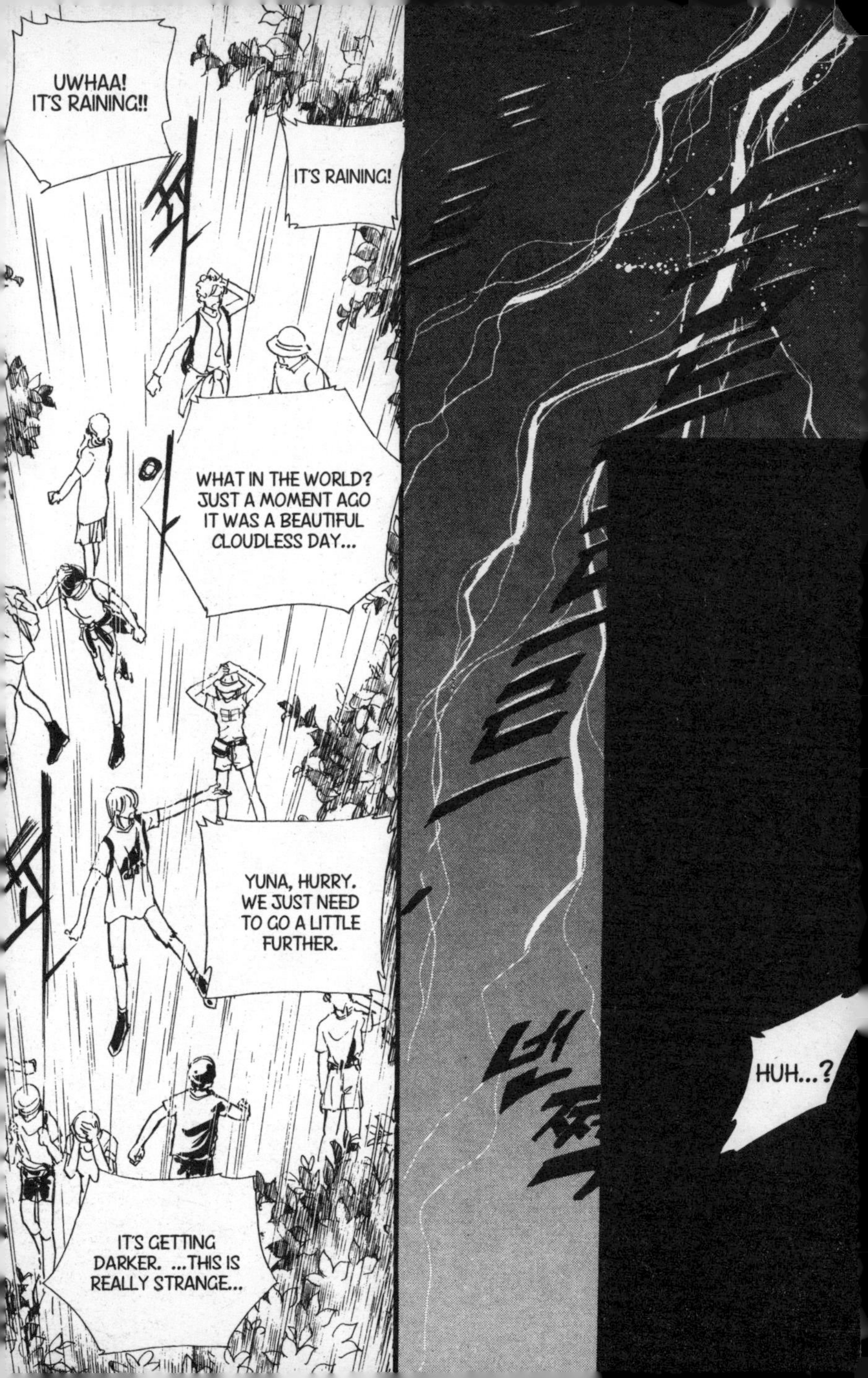
UWHAA! IT'S RAINING!!
IT'S RAINING!
WHAT IN THE WORLD? JUST A MOMENT AGO IT WAS A BEAUTIFUL CLOUDLESS DAY...
YUNA, HURRY. WE JUST NEED TO GO A LITTLE FURTHER.
IT'S GETTING DARKER. ...THIS IS REALLY STRANGE...
HUH...?

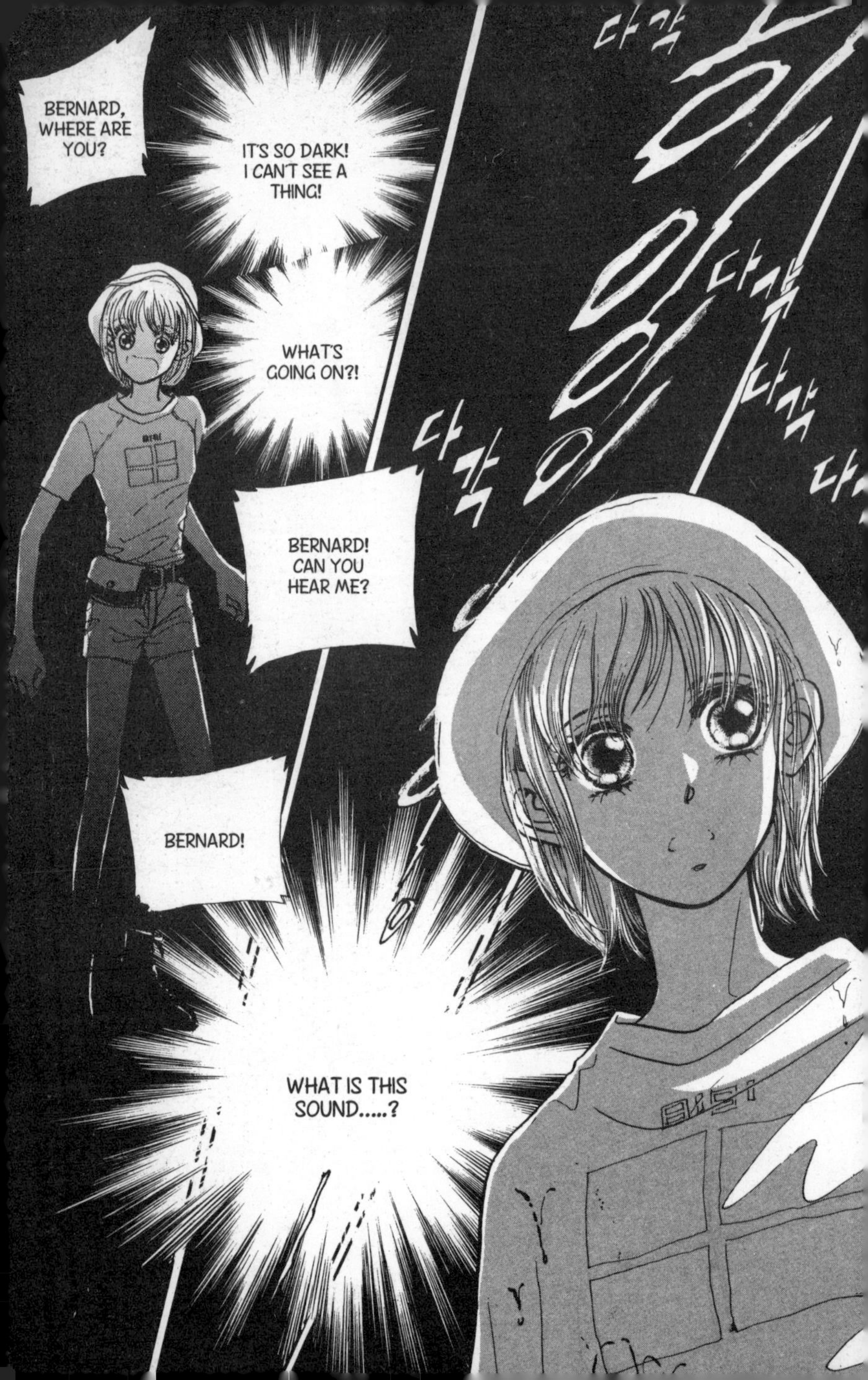
BERNARD, WHERE ARE YOU?
IT'S SO DARK! I CAN'T SEE A THING!
WHAT'S GOING ON?!
BERNARD! CAN YOU HEAR ME?
BERNARD!
다각
다각
다각
다각
WHAT IS THIS SOUND.....?

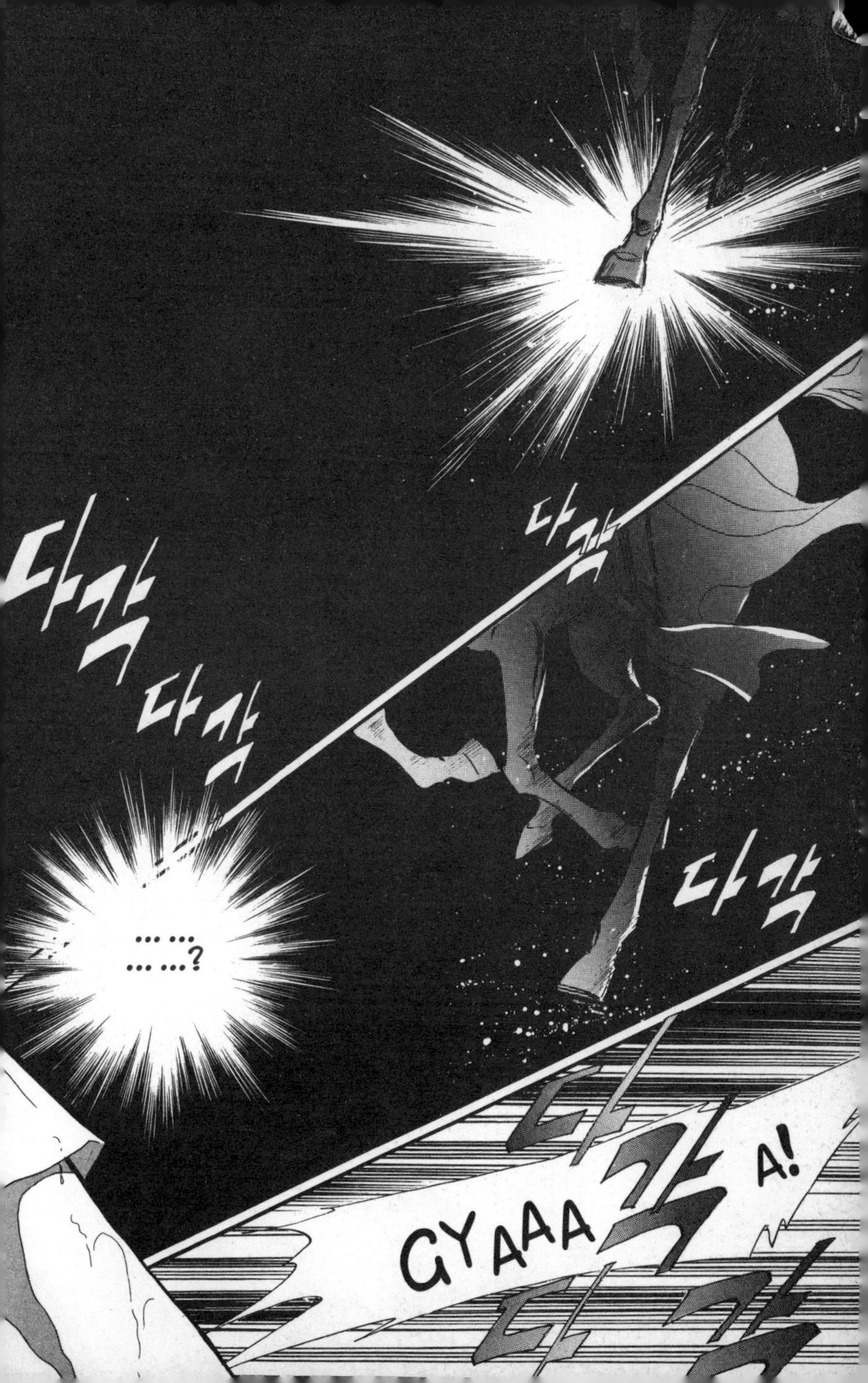
다각 다각
다각
... ...
... ...?
다각
GYAAAA!
다각 다각

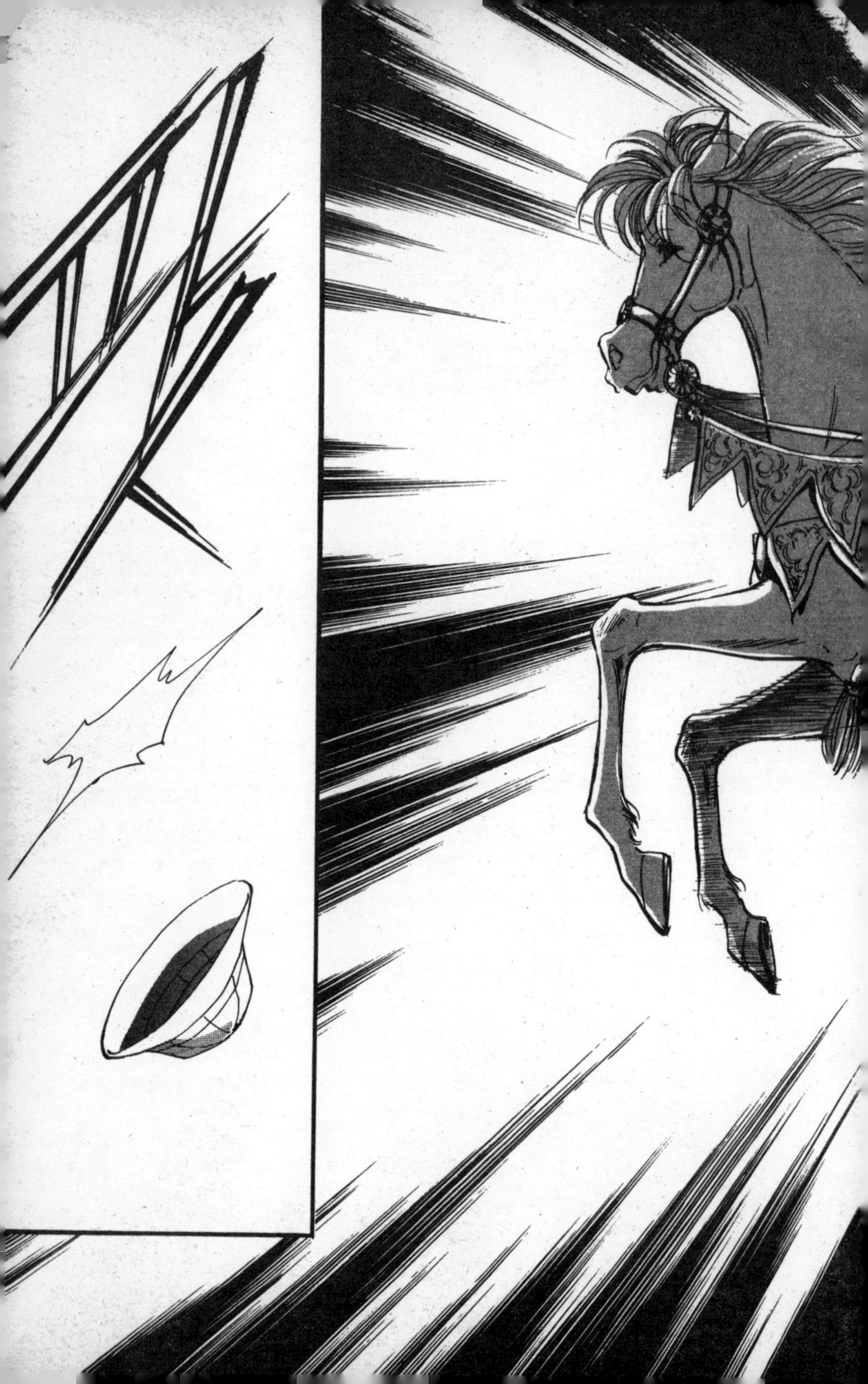

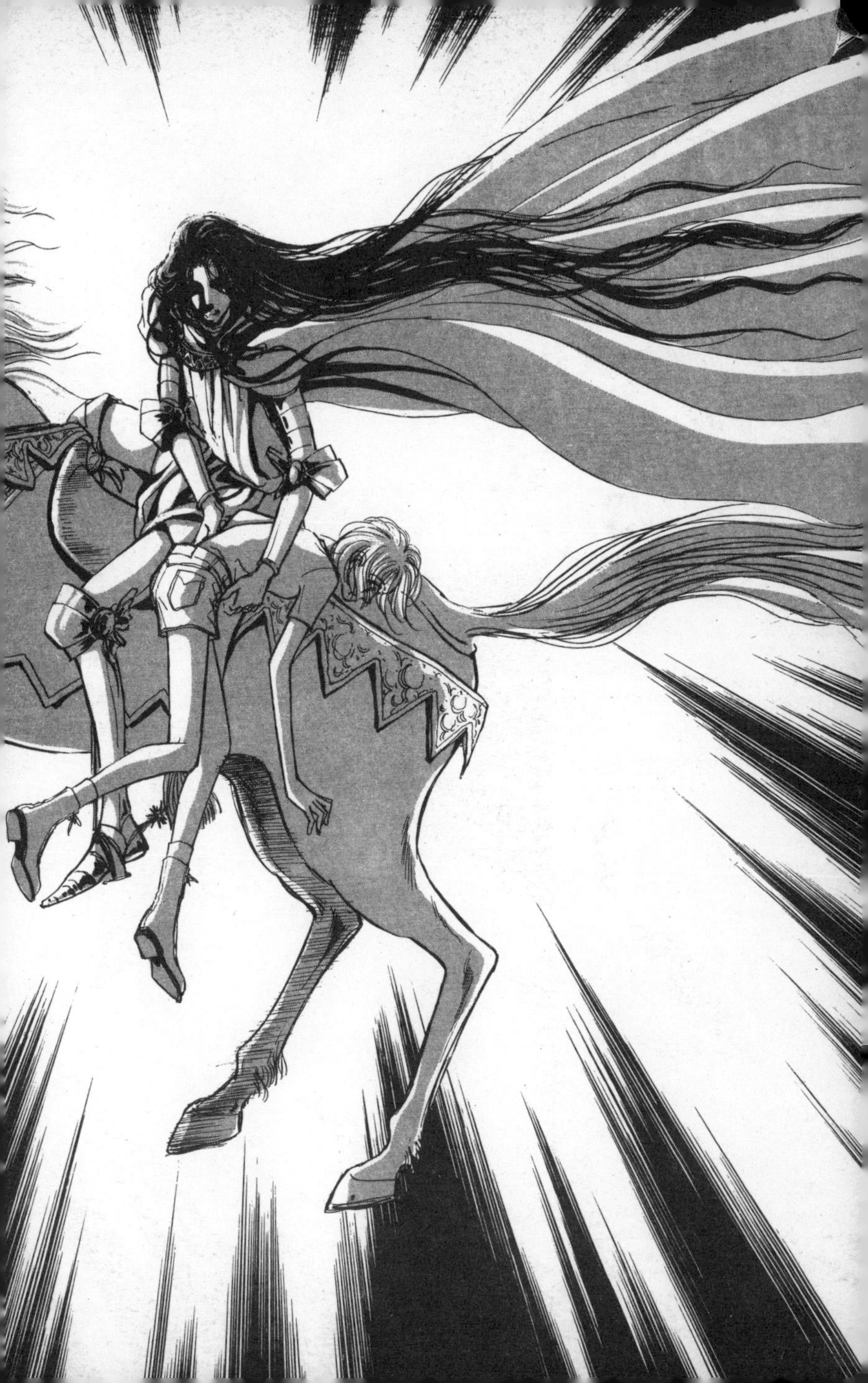

OH, LIGHT. YOU, WHO HAVE AWAKENED US...

BRINGER OF DAWN TO THE LAND, OFFERING
YOUR MOST PRECIOUS GIFT THAT ONLY YOU CAN GIVE...

YOU ARE LIGHT FROM HEAVEN.

SPRING IS A UNIQUE GIFT AND THE CONSE-
QUENCE OF JOY AND LOVE.

AH...BUT, OUR FATE HAS BEEN SEALED.

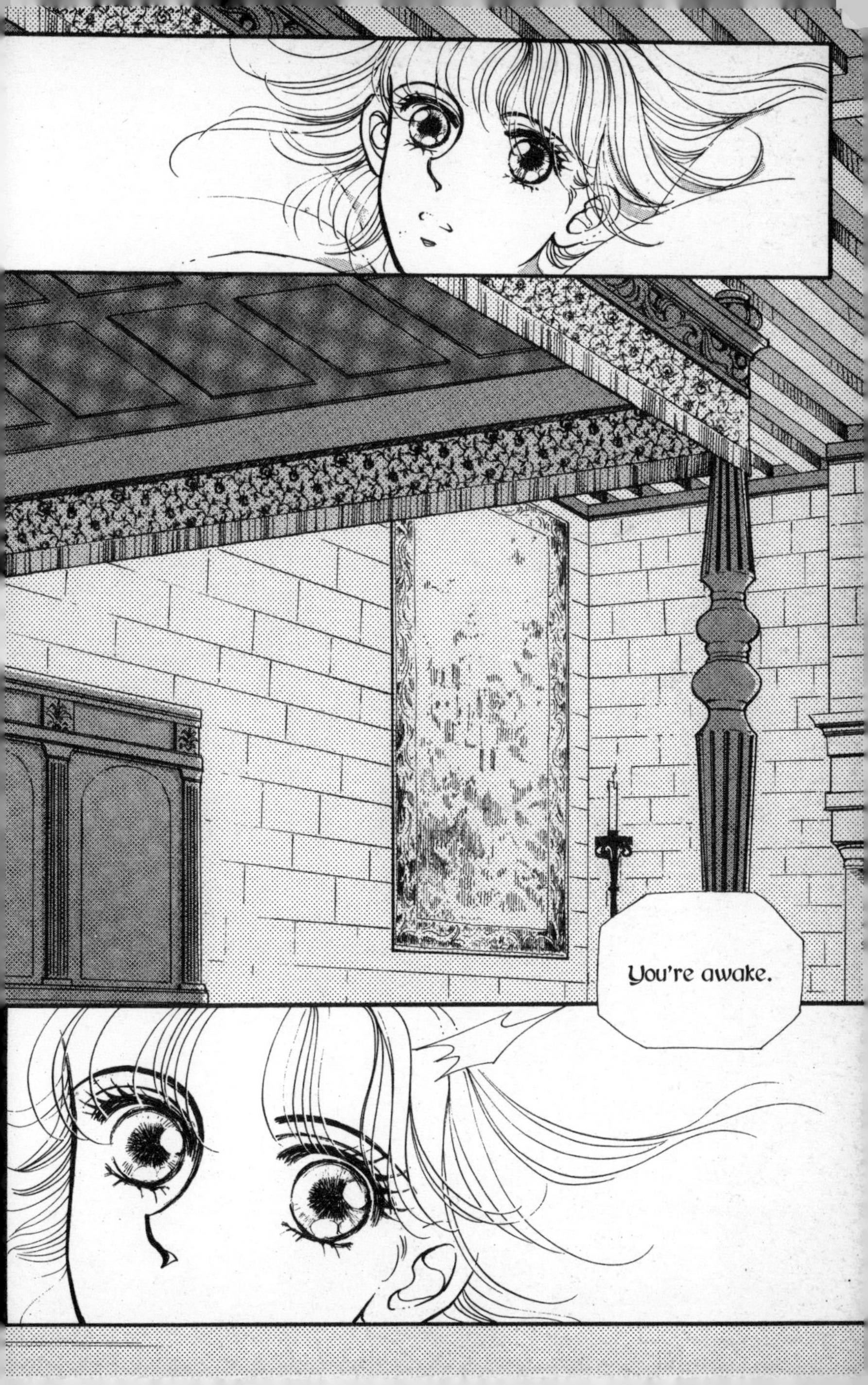
You're awake.

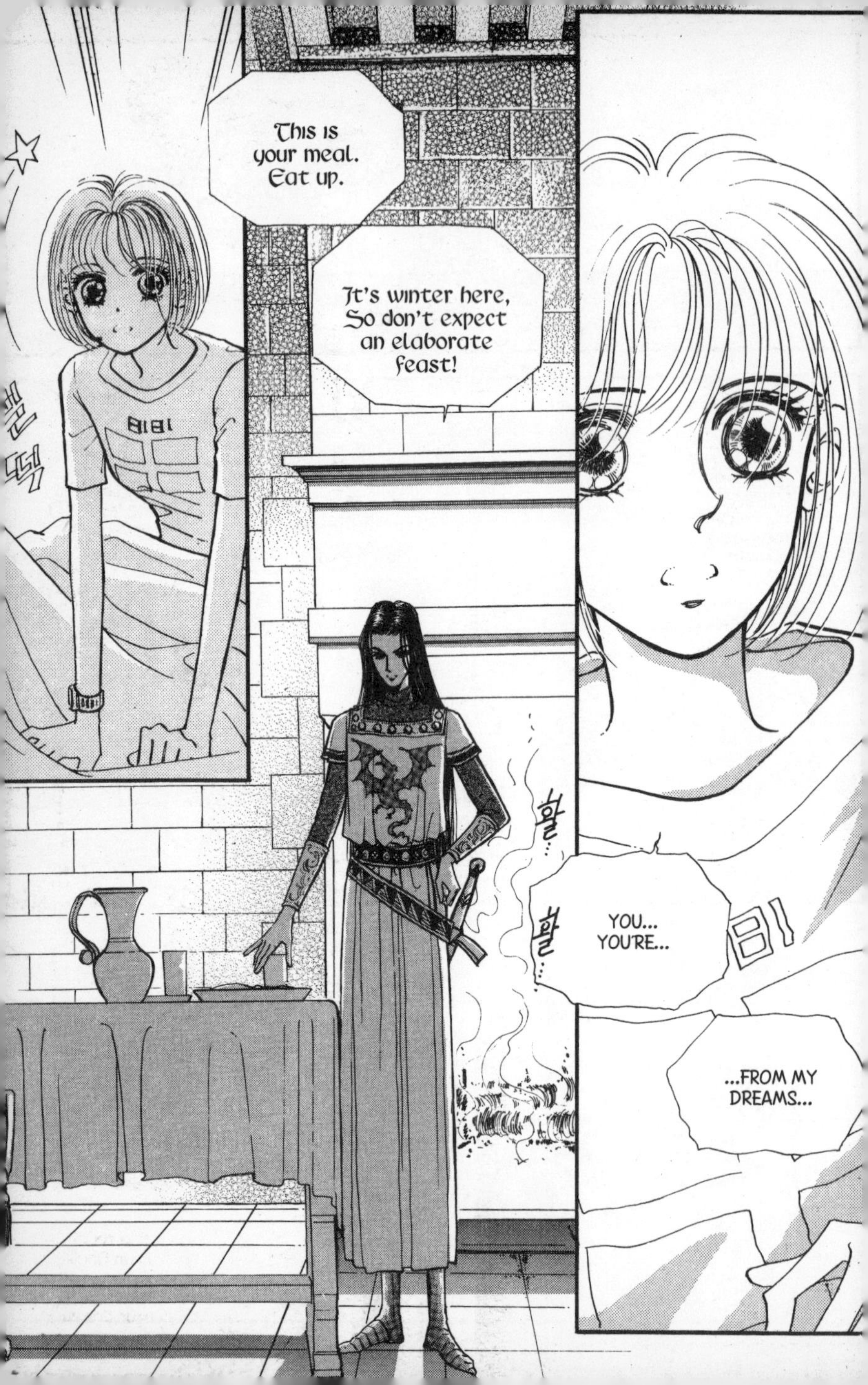
This is your meal. Eat up.
It's winter here, So don't expect an elaborate feast!
훨...
훨...
YOU... YOU'RE...
...FROM MY DREAMS...

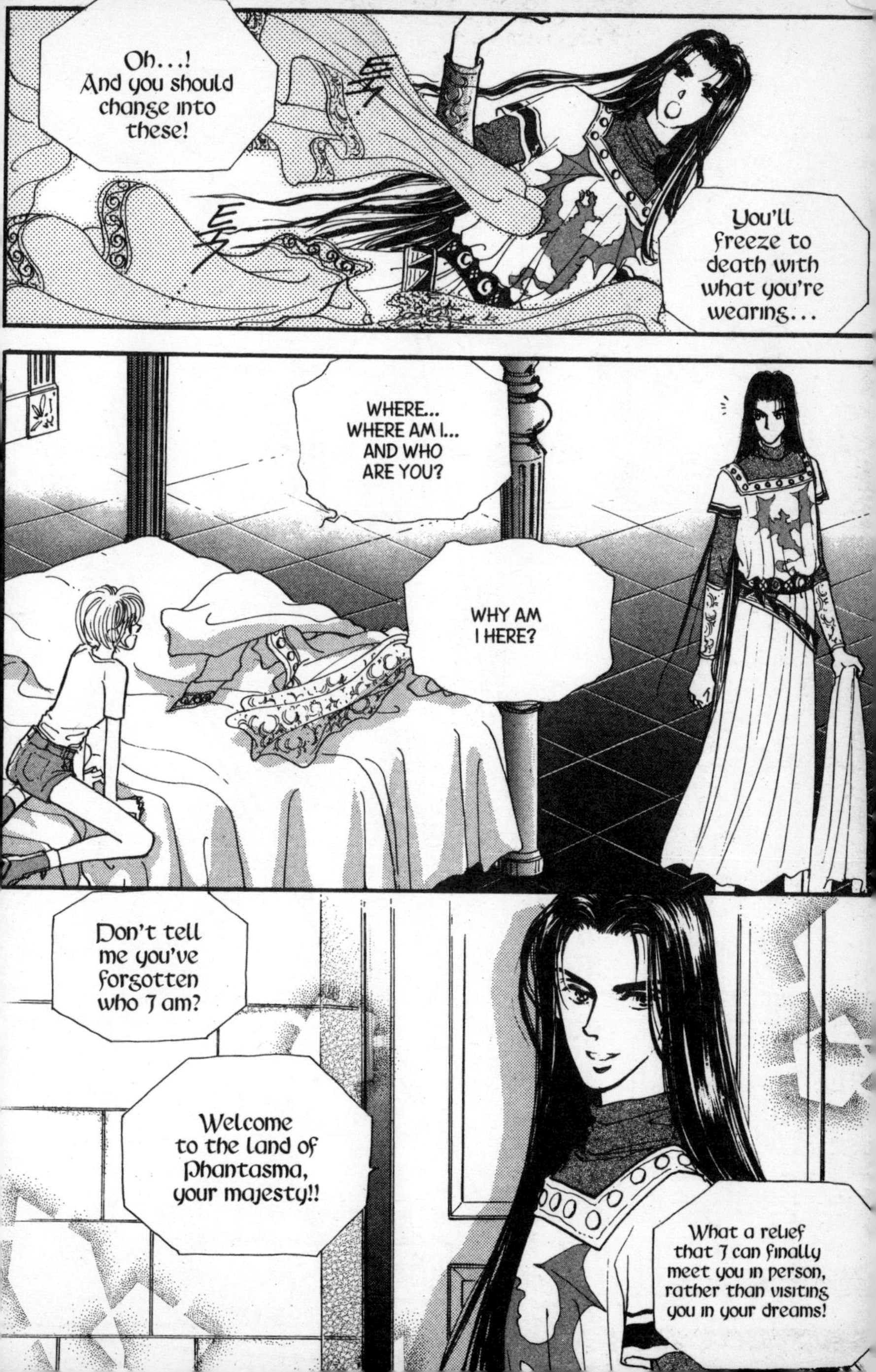
Oh...!
And you should change into these!
You'll freeze to death with what you're wearing...
WHERE... WHERE AM I... AND WHO ARE YOU?
WHY AM I HERE?
Don't tell me you've forgotten who I am?
Welcome to the land of Phantasma, your majesty!!
What a relief that I can finally meet you in person, rather than visiting you in your dreams!

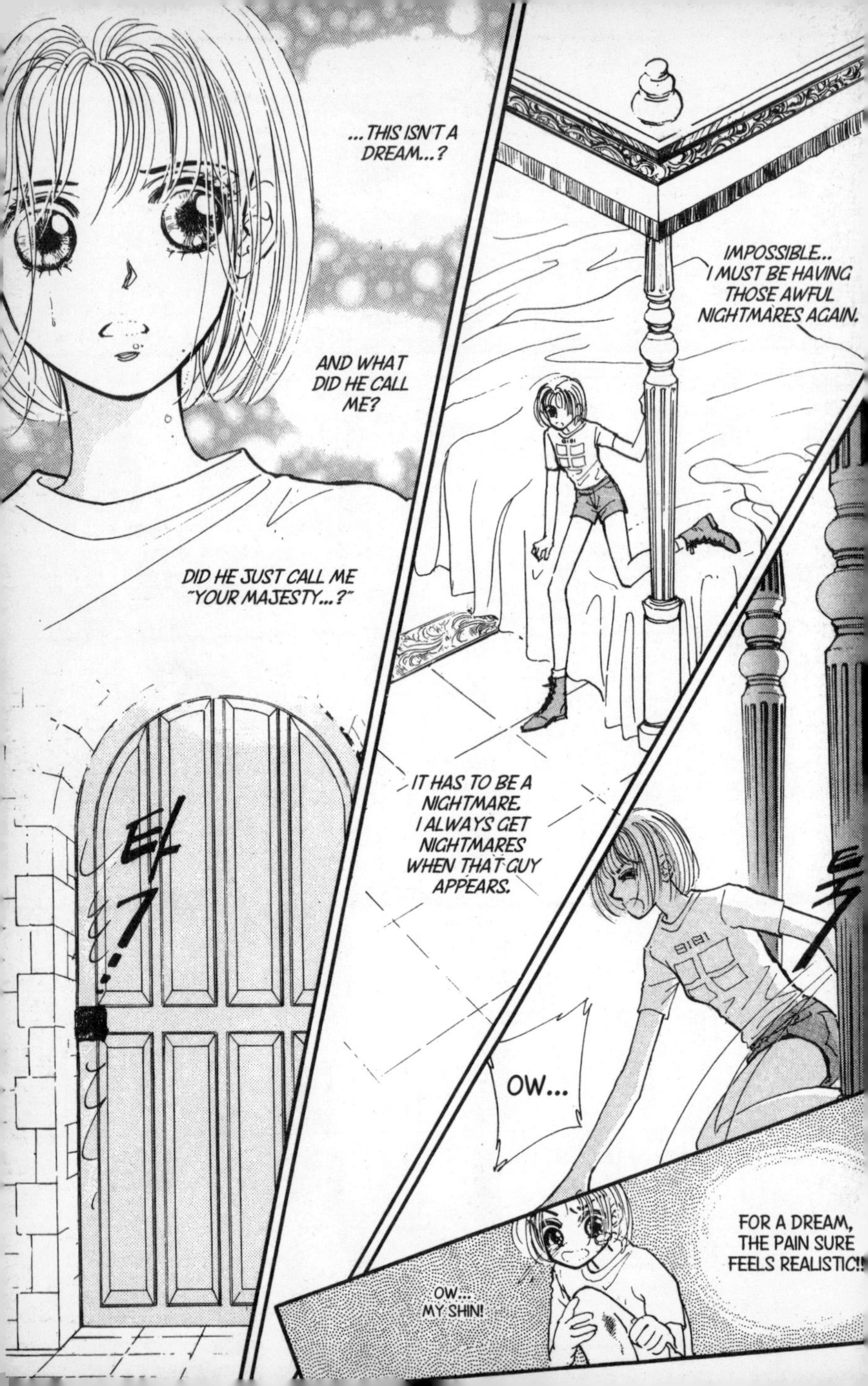
...THIS ISN'T A DREAM...?
AND WHAT DID HE CALL ME?
DID HE JUST CALL ME "YOUR MAJESTY...?"
IMPOSSIBLE... I MUST BE HAVING THOSE AWFUL NIGHTMARES AGAIN.
IT HAS TO BE A NIGHTMARE. I ALWAYS GET NIGHTMARES WHEN THAT GUY APPEARS.
OW...
OW... MY SHIN!
FOR A DREAM, THE PAIN SURE FEELS REALISTIC!!

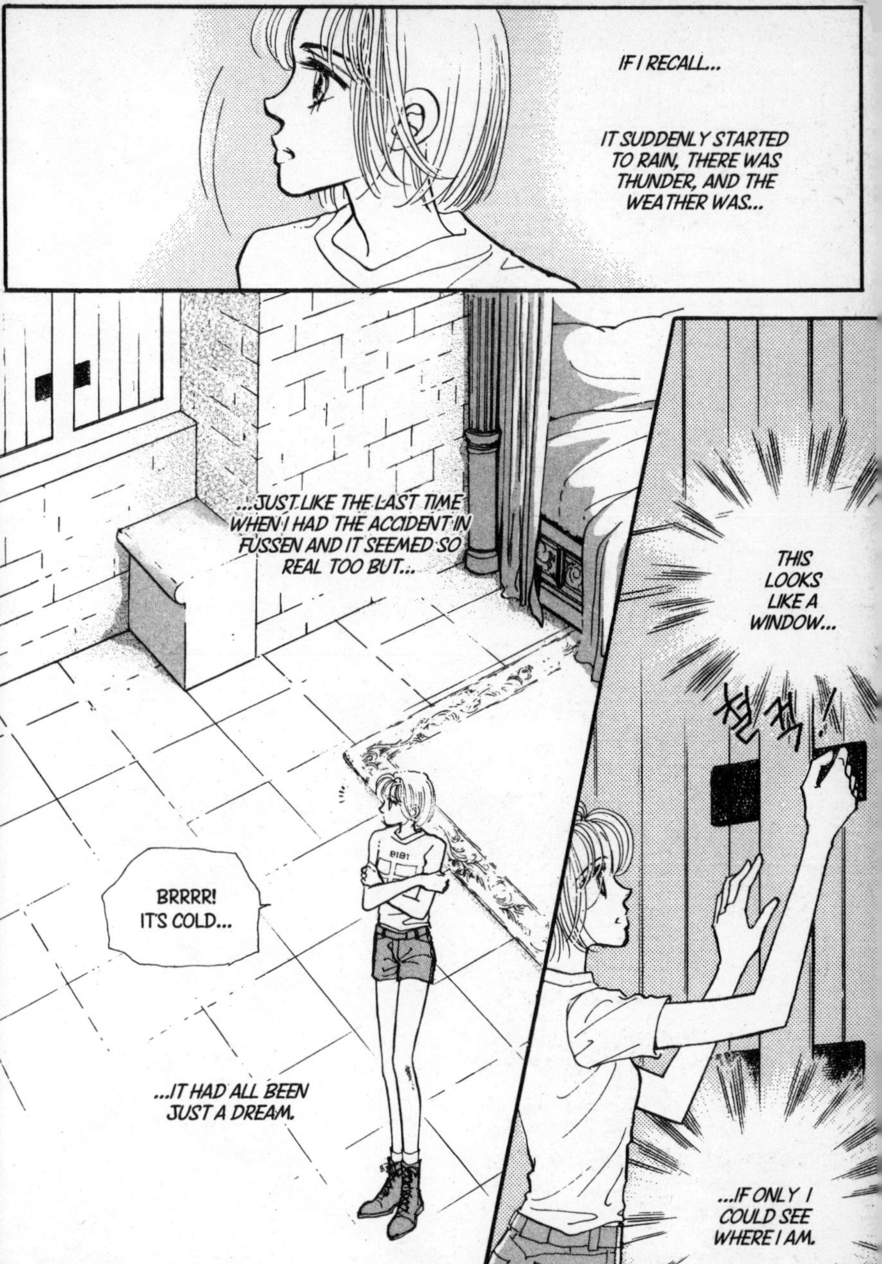
IF I RECALL...
IT SUDDENLY STARTED TO RAIN, THERE WAS THUNDER, AND THE WEATHER WAS...
...JUST LIKE THE LAST TIME WHEN I HAD THE ACCIDENT IN FUSSEN AND IT SEEMED SO REAL TOO BUT...
BRRRR! IT'S COLD...
...IT HAD ALL BEEN JUST A DREAM.
THIS LOOKS LIKE A WINDOW...
철컥!
...IF ONLY I COULD SEE WHERE I AM.

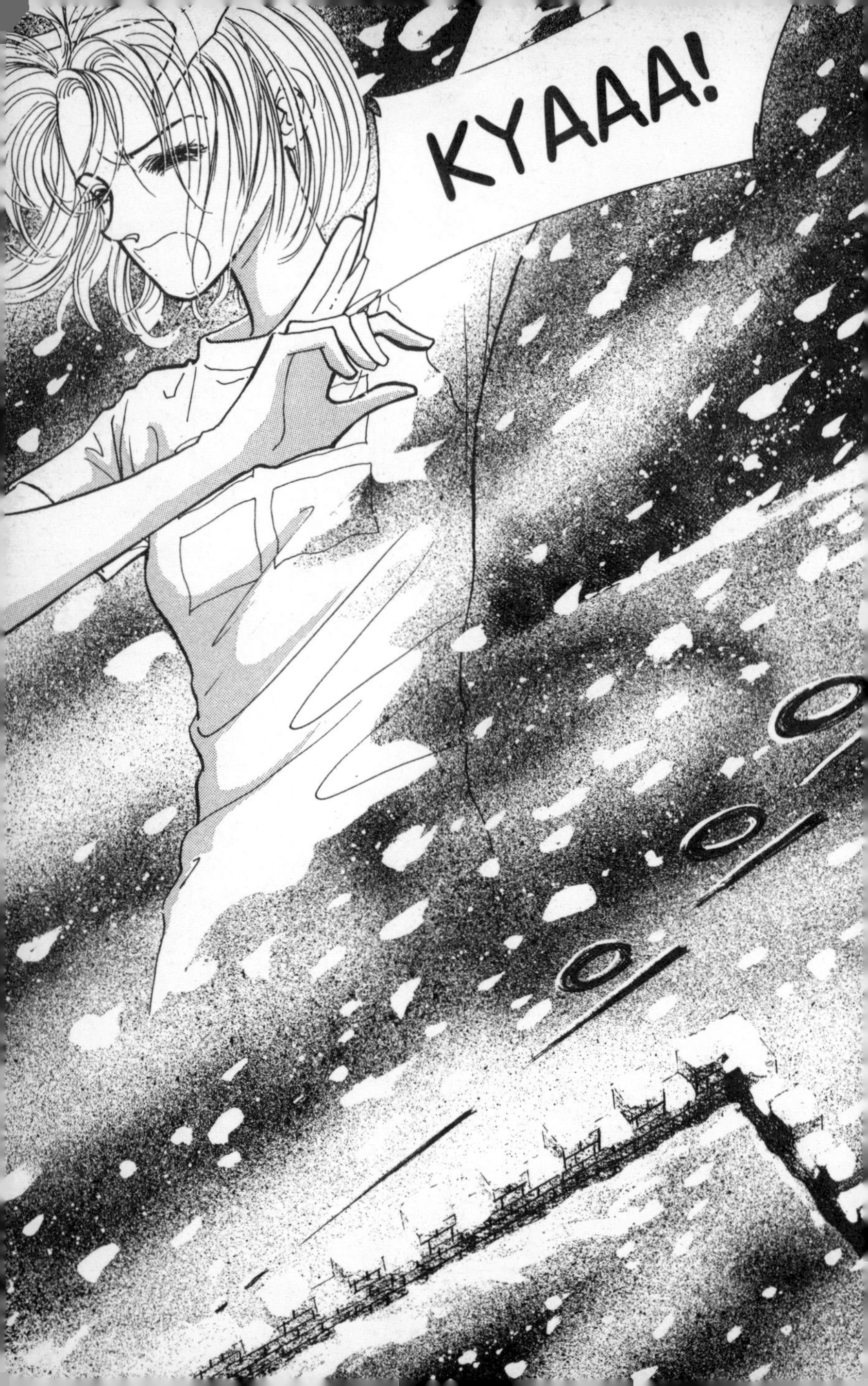
KYAAA!

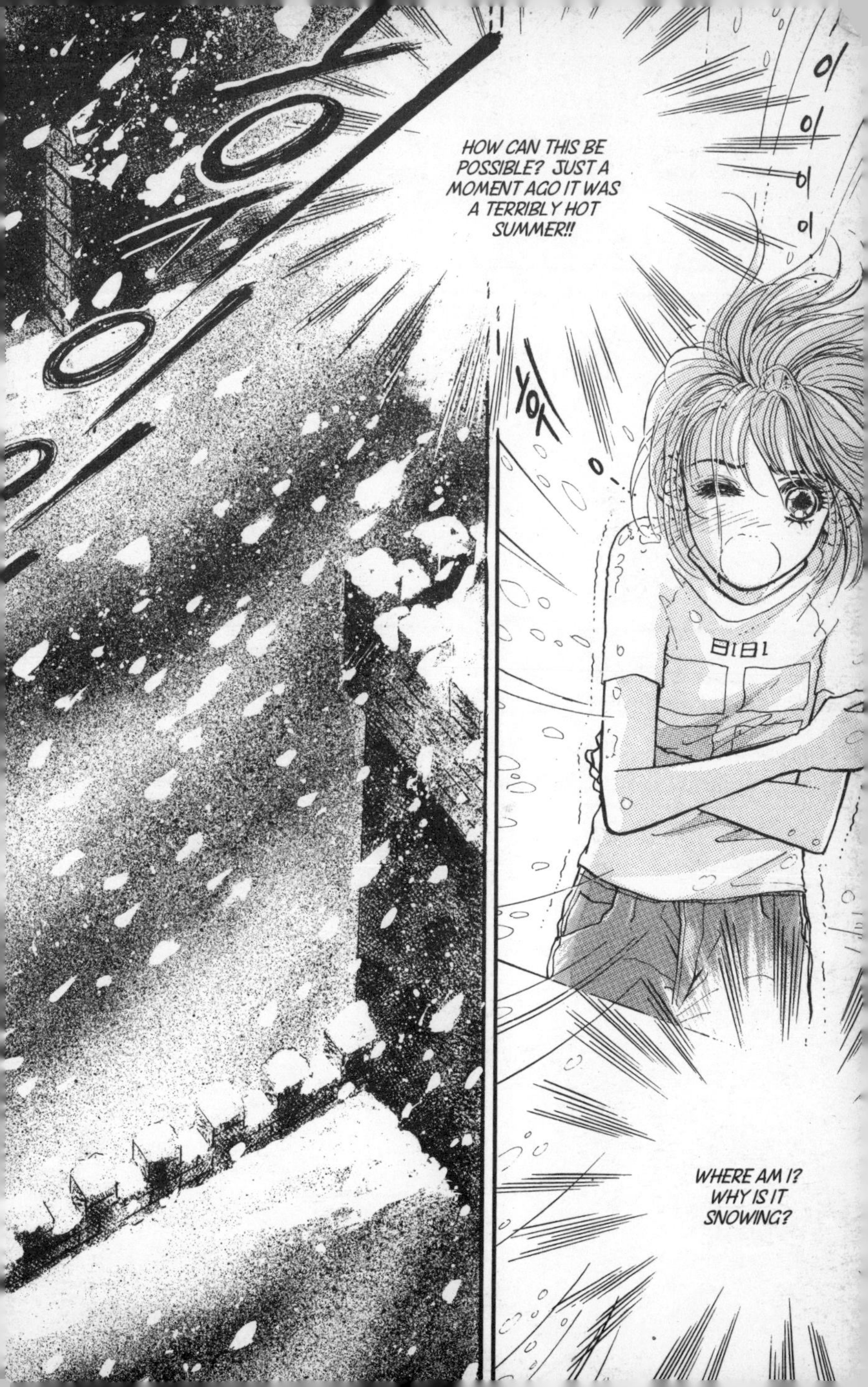
HOW CAN THIS BE POSSIBLE? JUST A MOMENT AGO IT WAS A TERRIBLY HOT SUMMER!!
WHERE AM I? WHY IS IT SNOWING?

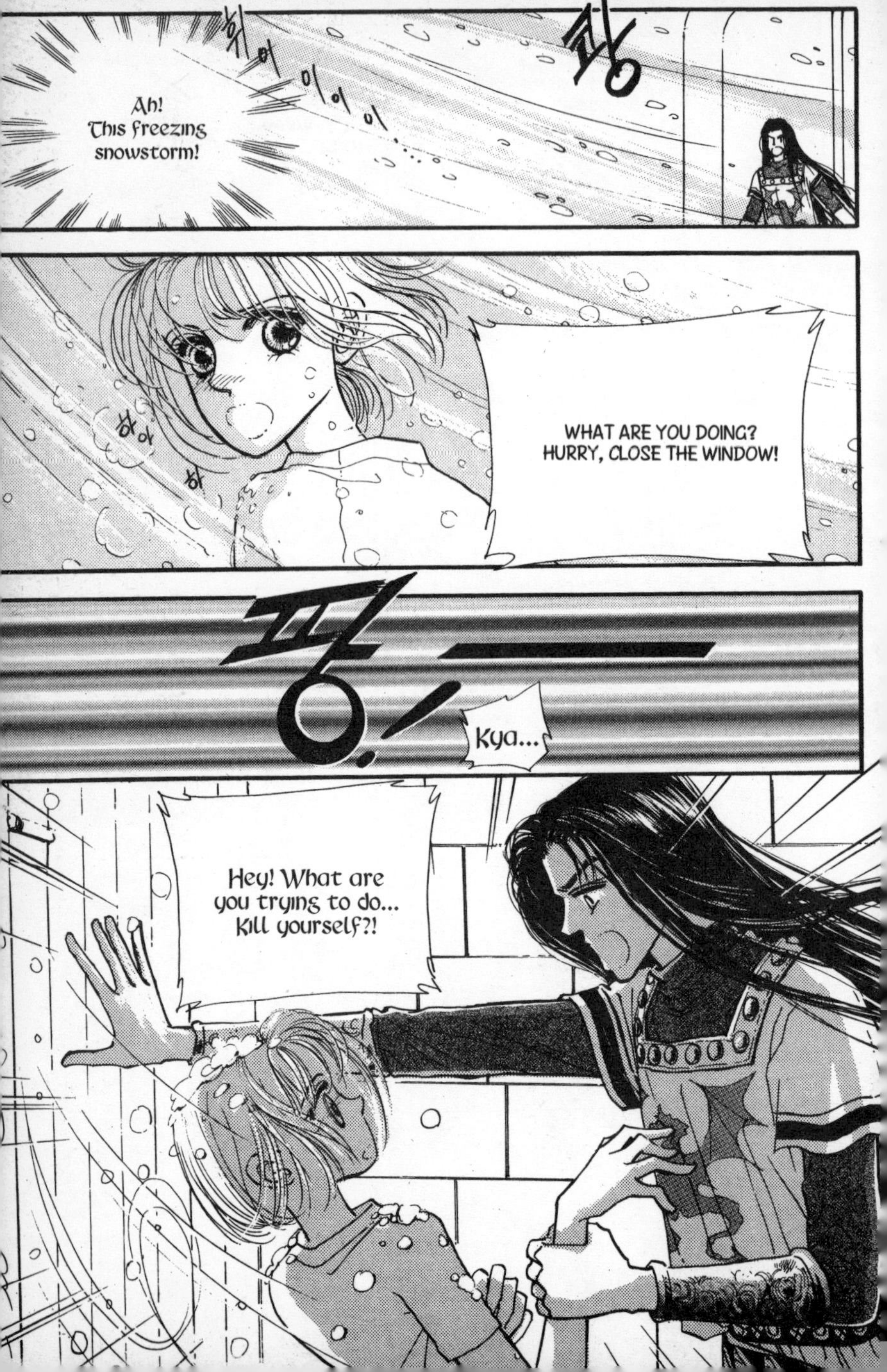
Ah! This freezing snowstorm!
WHAT ARE YOU DOING? HURRY, CLOSE THE WINDOW!
Kya...
Hey! What are you trying to do... Kill yourself?!

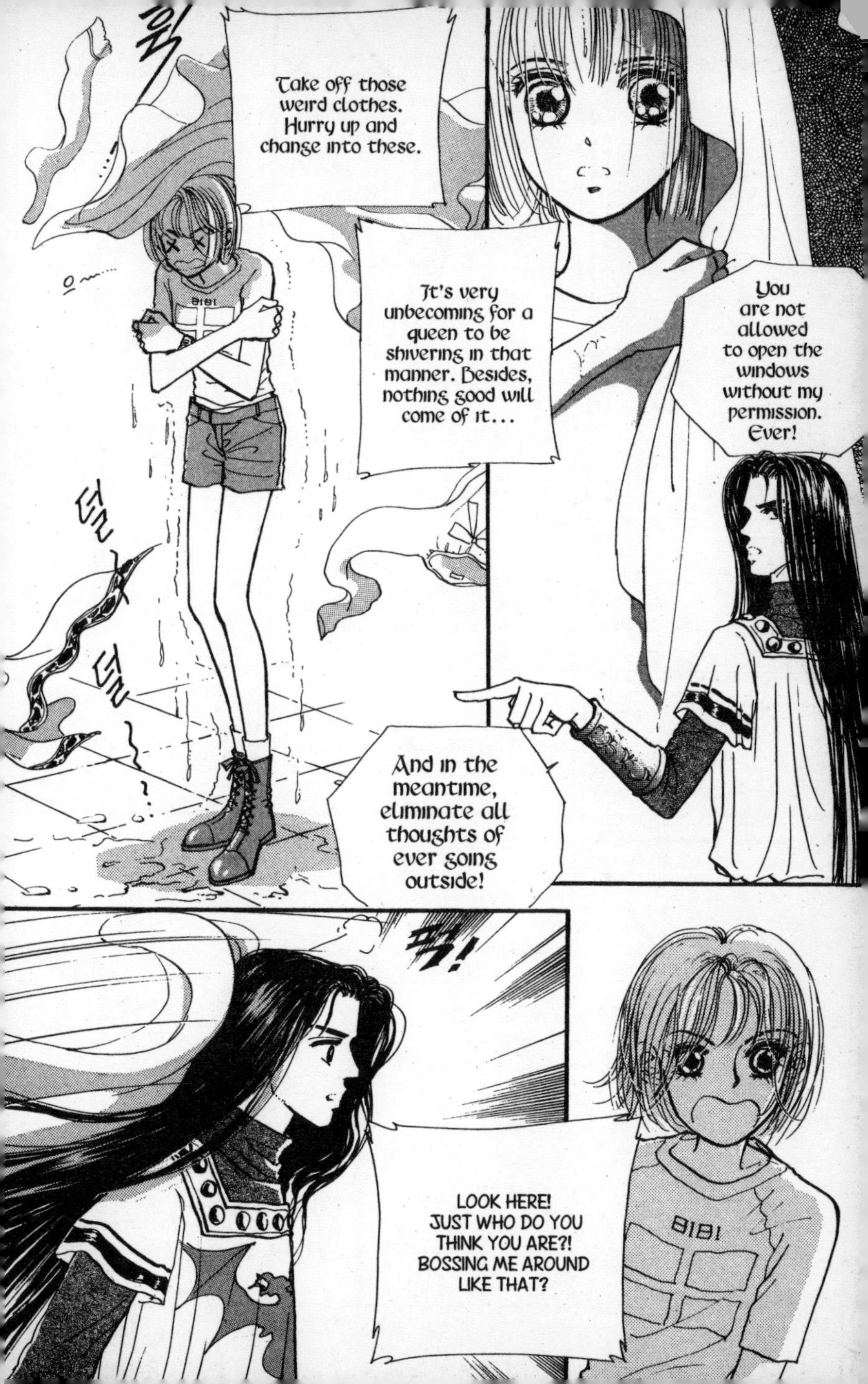
Take off those weird clothes. Hurry up and change into these.
으~
It's very unbecoming for a queen to be shivering in that manner. Besides, nothing good will come of it...
덜
덜
You are not allowed to open the windows without my permission. Ever!
And in the meantime, eliminate all thoughts of ever going outside!
LOOK HERE! JUST WHO DO YOU THINK YOU ARE?! BOSSING ME AROUND LIKE THAT?

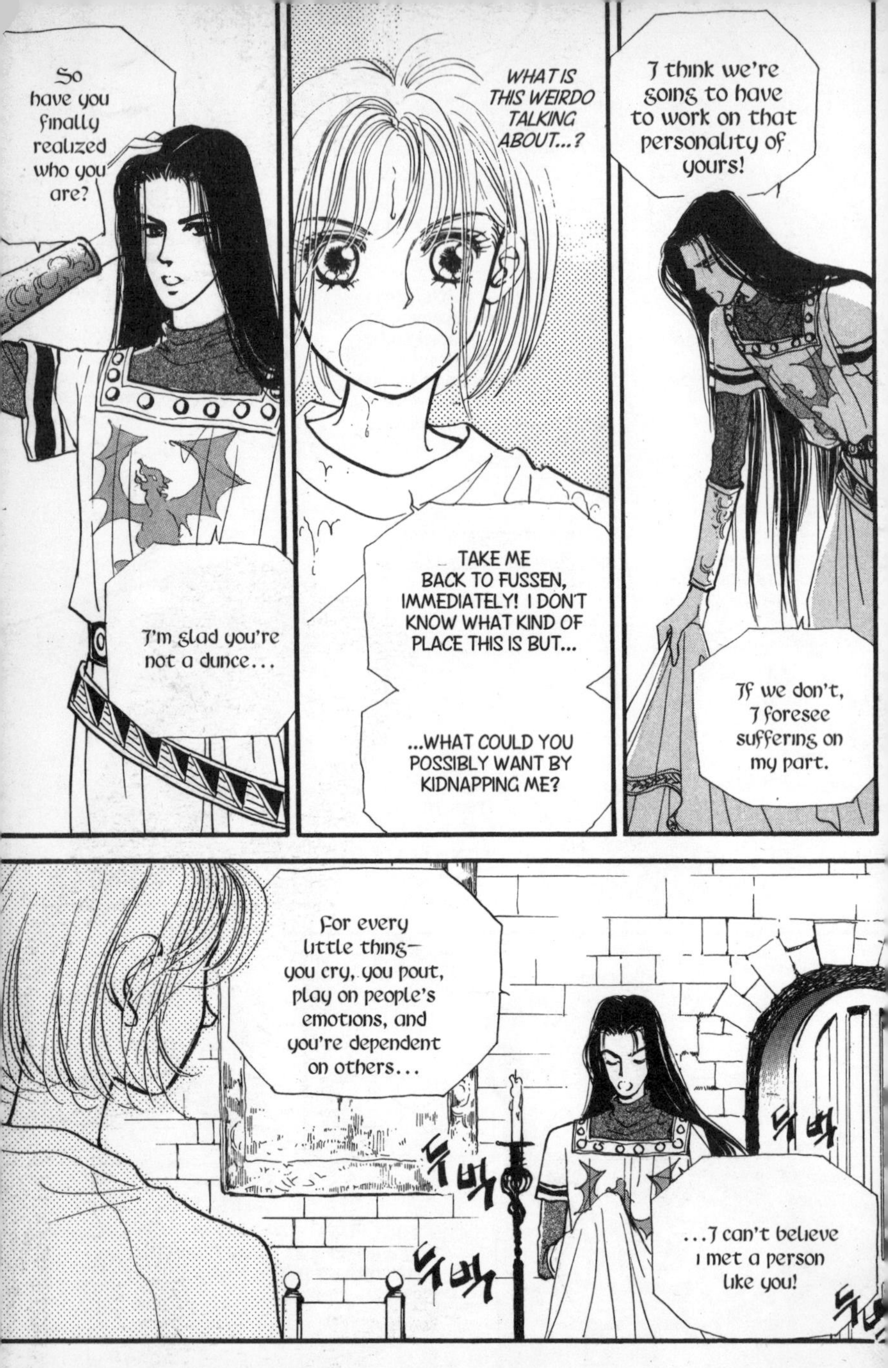
So have you finally realized who you are?
I'm glad you're not a dunce...
WHAT IS THIS WEIRDO TALKING ABOUT...?
TAKE ME BACK TO FUSSEN, IMMEDIATELY! I DON'T KNOW WHAT KIND OF PLACE THIS IS BUT...
...WHAT COULD YOU POSSIBLY WANT BY KIDNAPPING ME?
I think we're going to have to work on that personality of yours!
If we don't, I foresee suffering on my part.
For every little thing— you cry, you pout, play on people's emotions, and you're dependent on others...
...I can't believe I met a person like you!

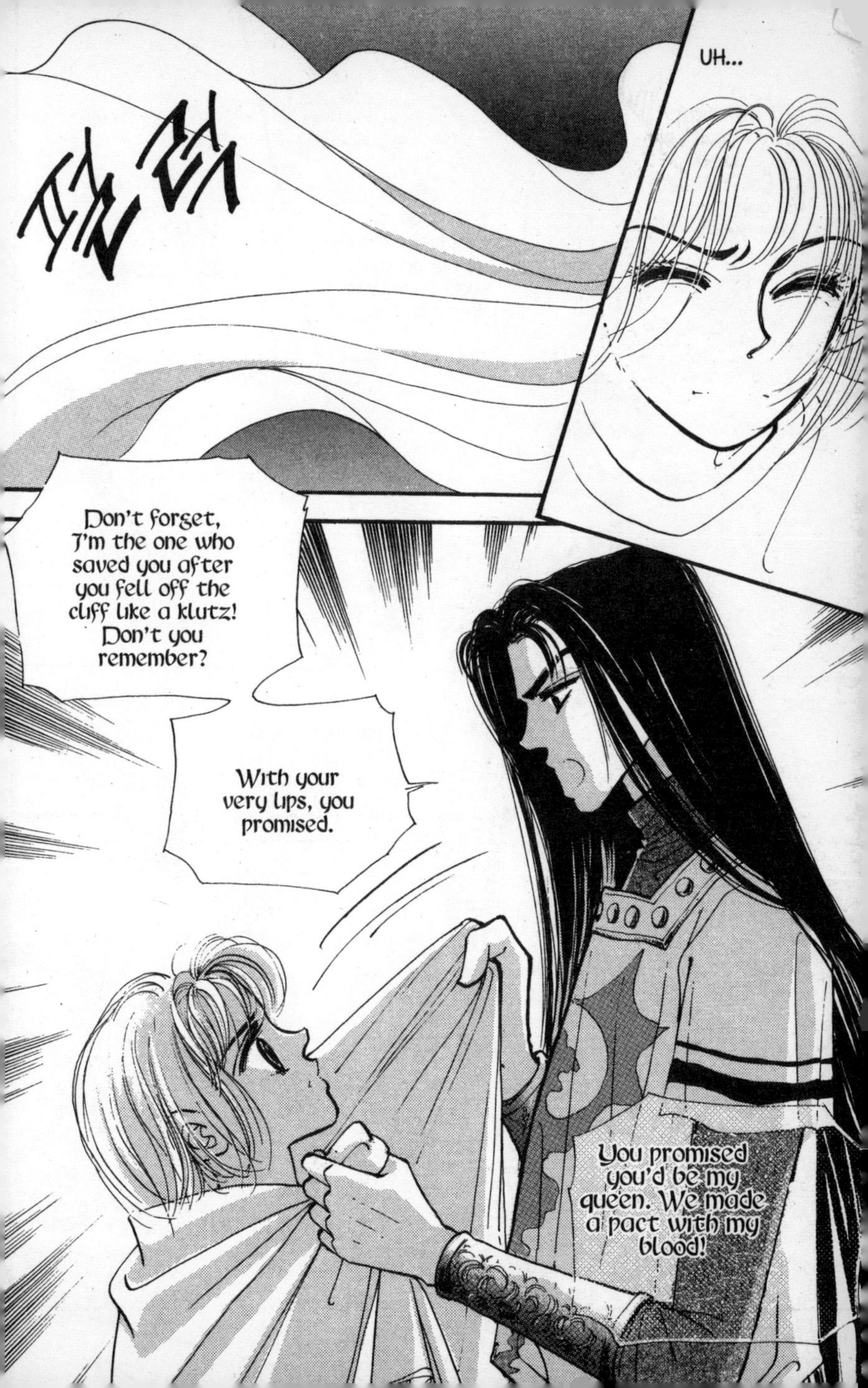
UH...
Don't forget, I'm the one who saved you after you fell off the cliff like a klutz! Don't you remember?
With your very lips, you promised.
You promised you'd be my queen. We made a pact with my blood!

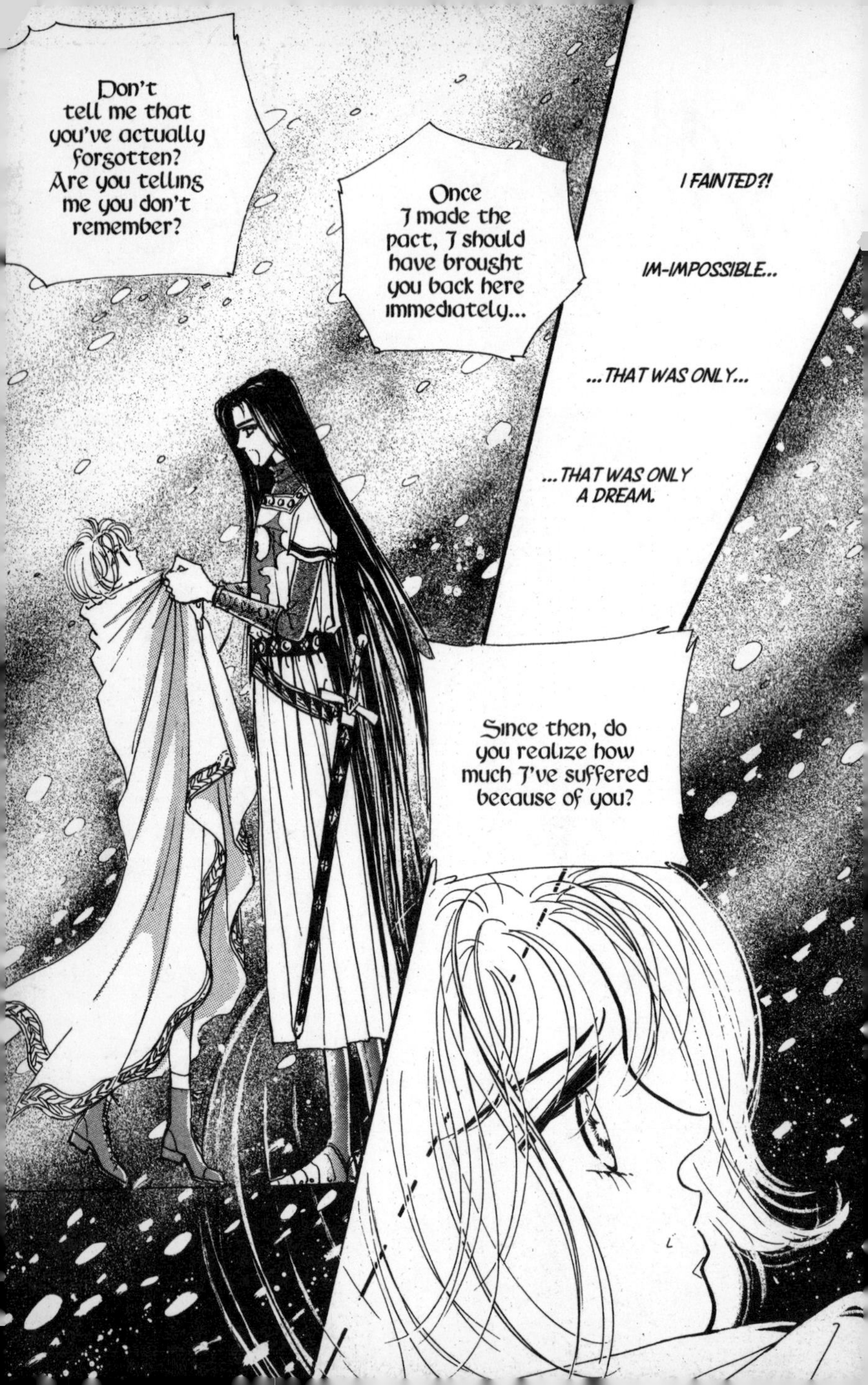

Don't tell me that you've actually forgotten? Are you telling me you don't remember?
Once I made the pact, I should have brought you back here immediately...
I FAINTED?!
IM-IMPOSSIBLE...
...THAT WAS ONLY...
...THAT WAS ONLY A DREAM.
Since then, do you realize how much I've suffered because of you?

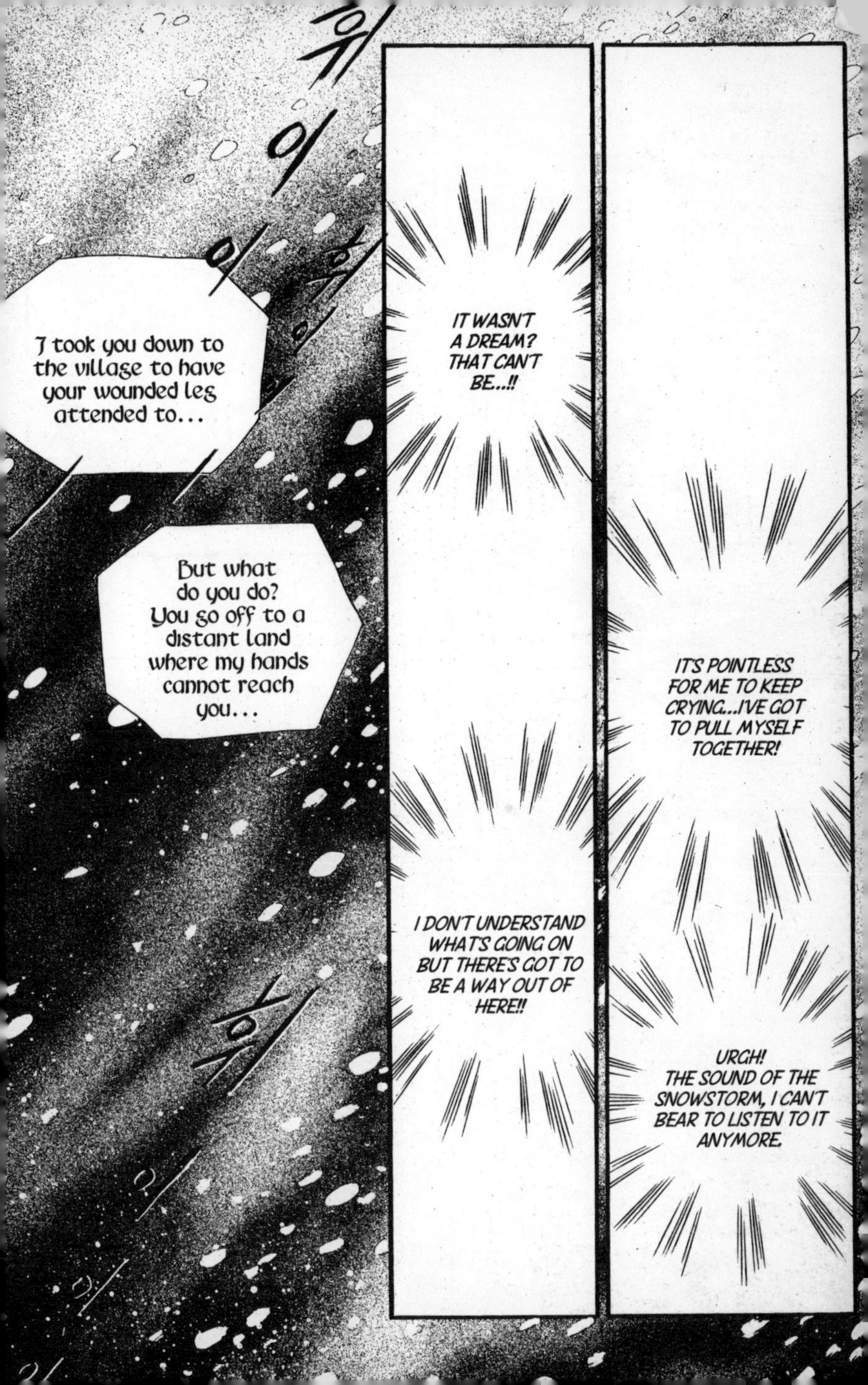
I took you down to the village to have your wounded leg attended to...
But what do you do? You go off to a distant land where my hands cannot reach you...
IT WASN'T A DREAM? THAT CAN'T BE...!!
I DON'T UNDERSTAND WHAT'S GOING ON BUT THERE'S GOT TO BE A WAY OUT OF HERE!!
IT'S POINTLESS FOR ME TO KEEP CRYING...I'VE GOT TO PULL MYSELF TOGETHER!
URGH! THE SOUND OF THE SNOWSTORM, I CAN'T BEAR TO LISTEN TO IT ANYMORE.

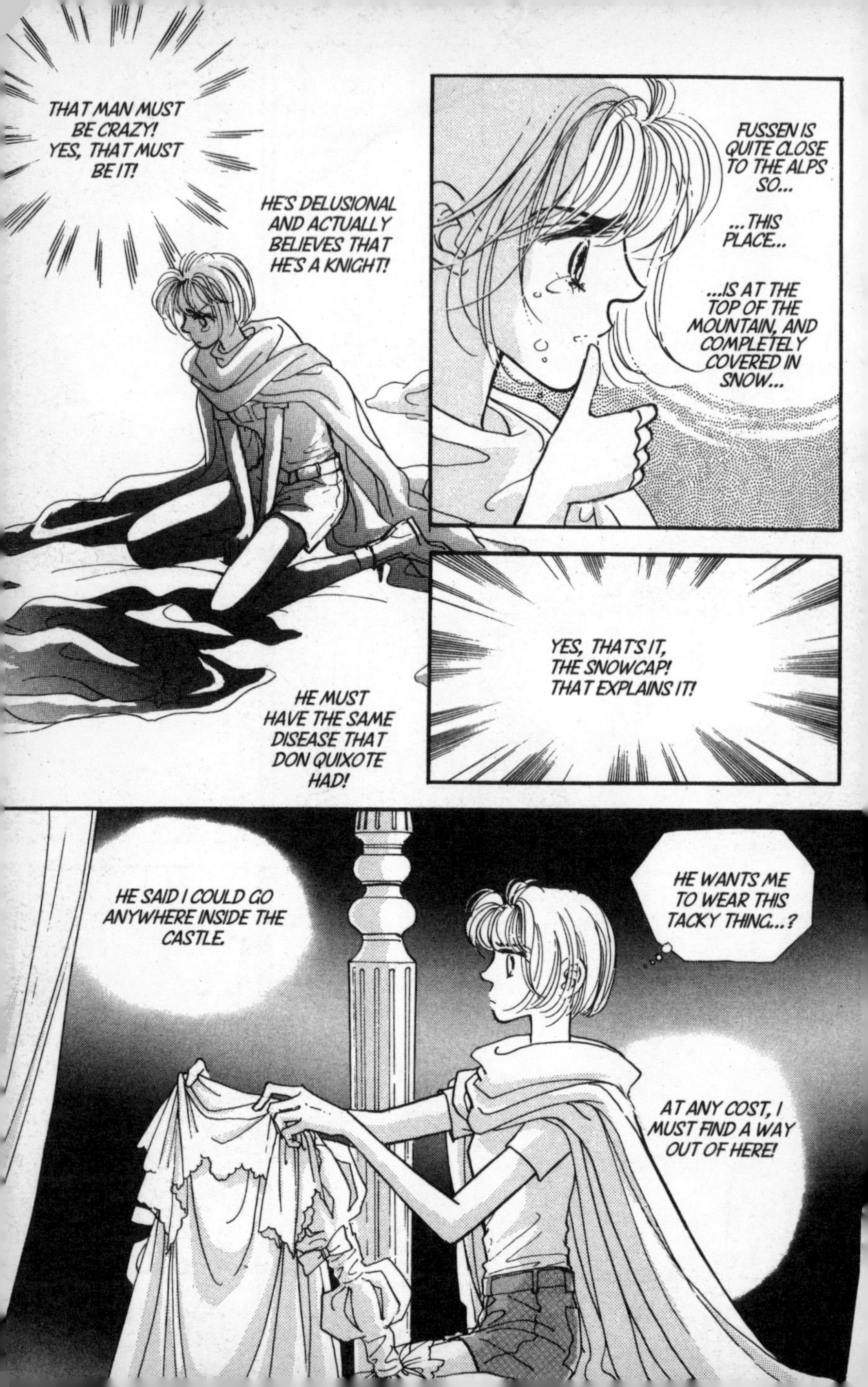
THAT MAN MUST BE CRAZY! YES, THAT MUST BE IT!
HE'S DELUSIONAL AND ACTUALLY BELIEVES THAT HE'S A KNIGHT!
HE MUST HAVE THE SAME DISEASE THAT DON QUIXOTE HAD!
FUSSEN IS QUITE CLOSE TO THE ALPS SO...
...THIS PLACE...
...IS AT THE TOP OF THE MOUNTAIN, AND COMPLETELY COVERED IN SNOW...
YES, THAT'S IT, THE SNOWCAP! THAT EXPLAINS IT!
HE SAID I COULD GO ANYWHERE INSIDE THE CASTLE.
HE WANTS ME TO WEAR THIS TACKY THING...?
AT ANY COST, I MUST FIND A WAY OUT OF HERE!

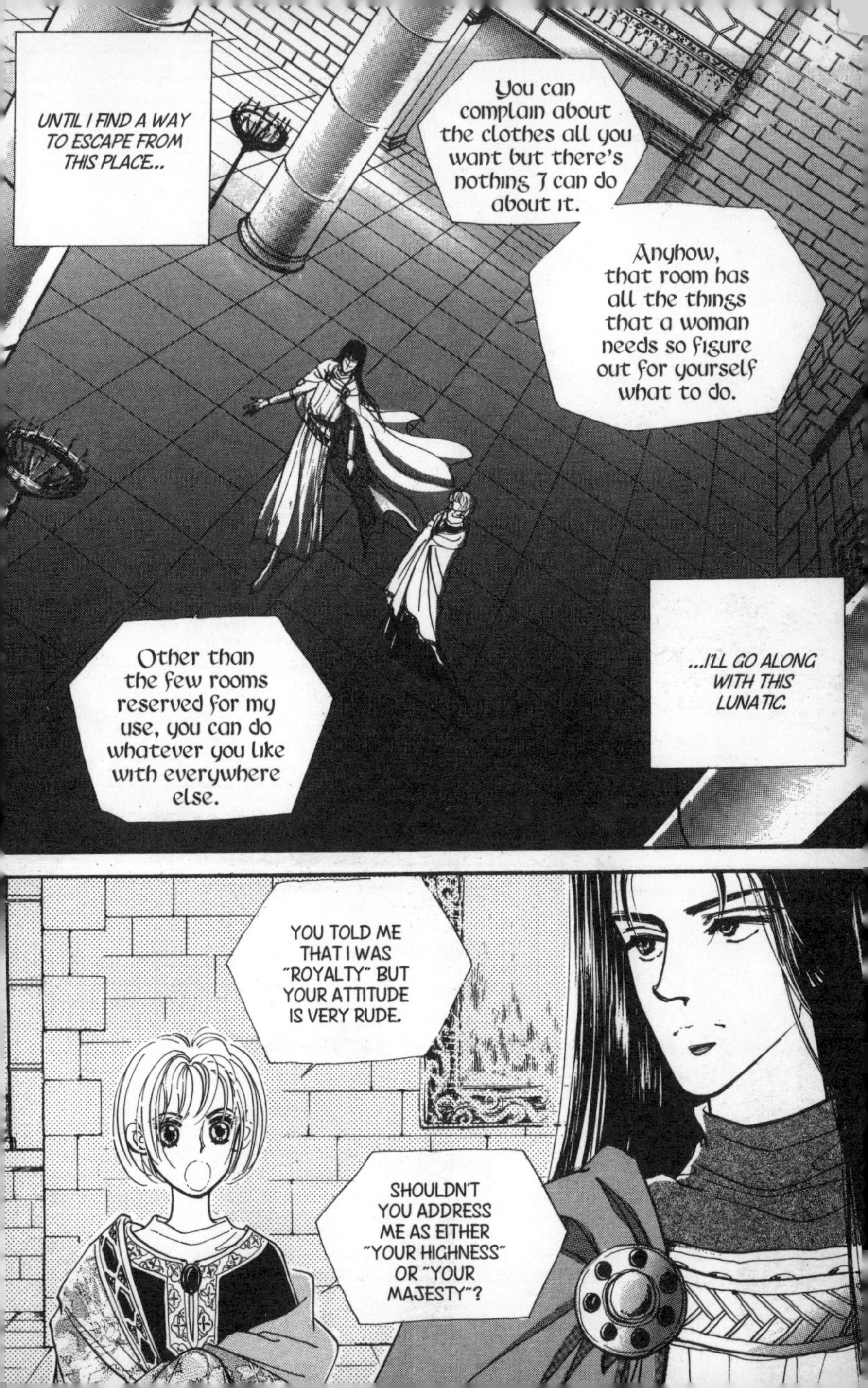
UNTIL I FIND A WAY TO ESCAPE FROM THIS PLACE...
You can complain about the clothes all you want but there's nothing I can do about it.
Anyhow, that room has all the things that a woman needs so figure out for yourself what to do.
Other than the few rooms reserved for my use, you can do whatever you like with everywhere else.
...I'LL GO ALONG WITH THIS LUNATIC.
YOU TOLD ME THAT I WAS "ROYALTY" BUT YOUR ATTITUDE IS VERY RUDE.
SHOULDN'T YOU ADDRESS ME AS EITHER "YOUR HIGHNESS" OR "YOUR MAJESTY"?

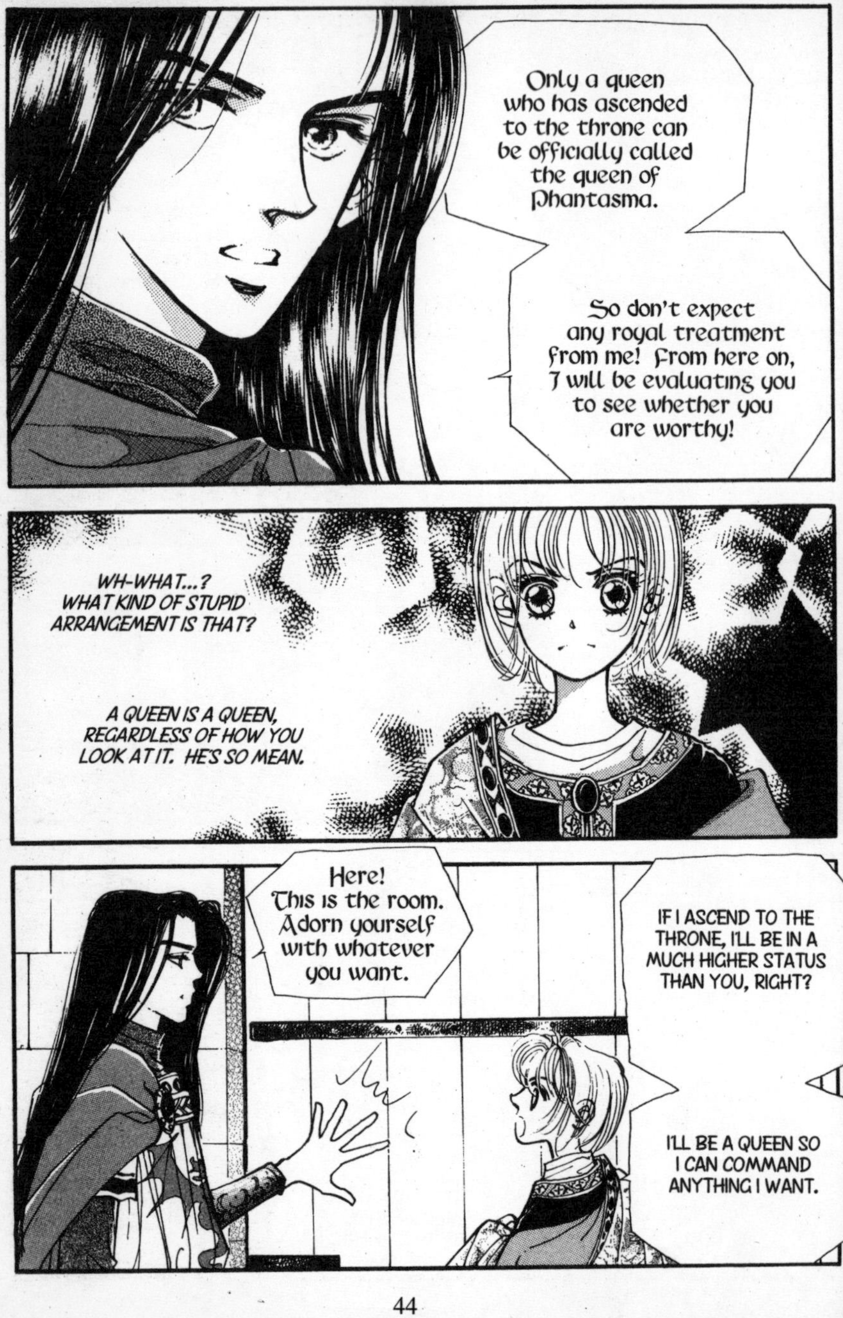

Only a queen who has ascended to the throne can be officially called the queen of Phantasma.
So don't expect any royal treatment from me! From here on, I will be evaluating you to see whether you are worthy!
WH-WHAT...? WHAT KIND OF STUPID ARRANGEMENT IS THAT?
A QUEEN IS A QUEEN, REGARDLESS OF HOW YOU LOOK AT IT. HE'S SO MEAN.
Here! This is the room. Adorn yourself with whatever you want.
IF I ASCEND TO THE THRONE, I'LL BE IN A MUCH HIGHER STATUS THAN YOU, RIGHT?
I'LL BE A QUEEN SO I CAN COMMAND ANYTHING I WANT.

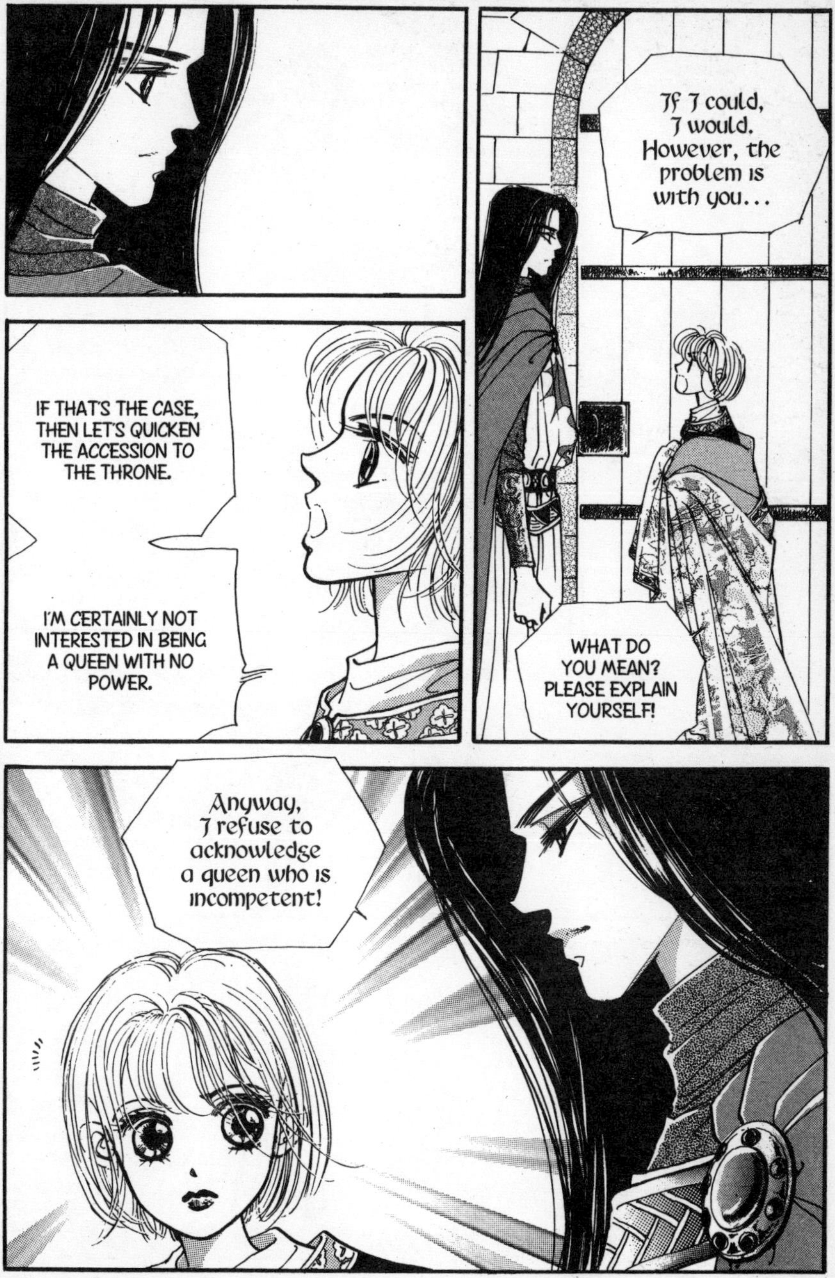
IF THAT'S THE CASE, THEN LET'S QUICKEN THE ACCESSION TO THE THRONE.
I'M CERTAINLY NOT INTERESTED IN BEING A QUEEN WITH NO POWER.
If I could, I would. However, the problem is with you...
WHAT DO YOU MEAN? PLEASE EXPLAIN YOURSELF!
Anyway, I refuse to acknowledge a queen who is incompetent!

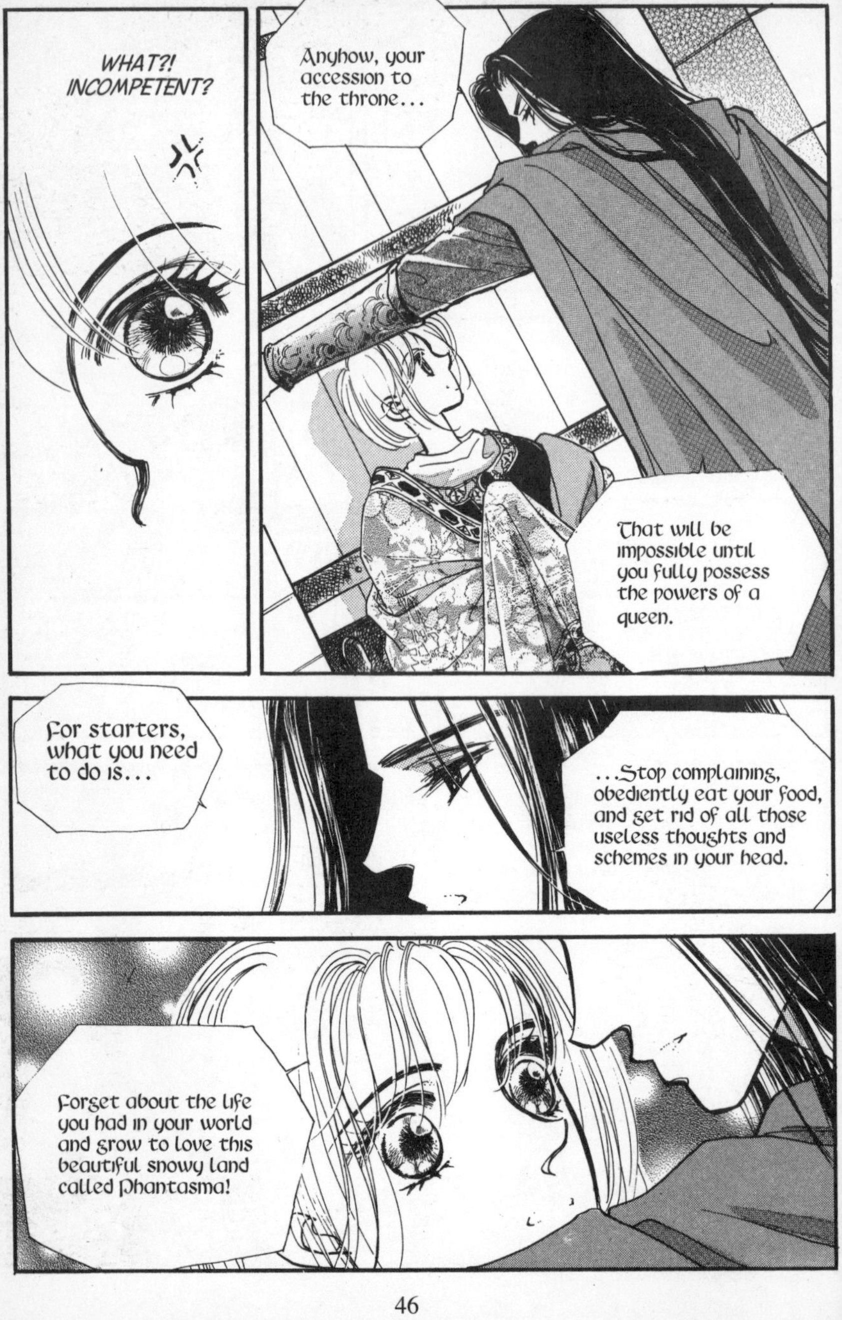
Anyhow, your accession to the throne...
That will be impossible until you fully possess the powers of a queen.
WHAT?! INCOMPETENT?
For starters, what you need to do is...
...Stop complaining, obediently eat your food, and get rid of all those useless thoughts and schemes in your head.
Forget about the life you had in your world and grow to love this beautiful snowy land called Phantasma!

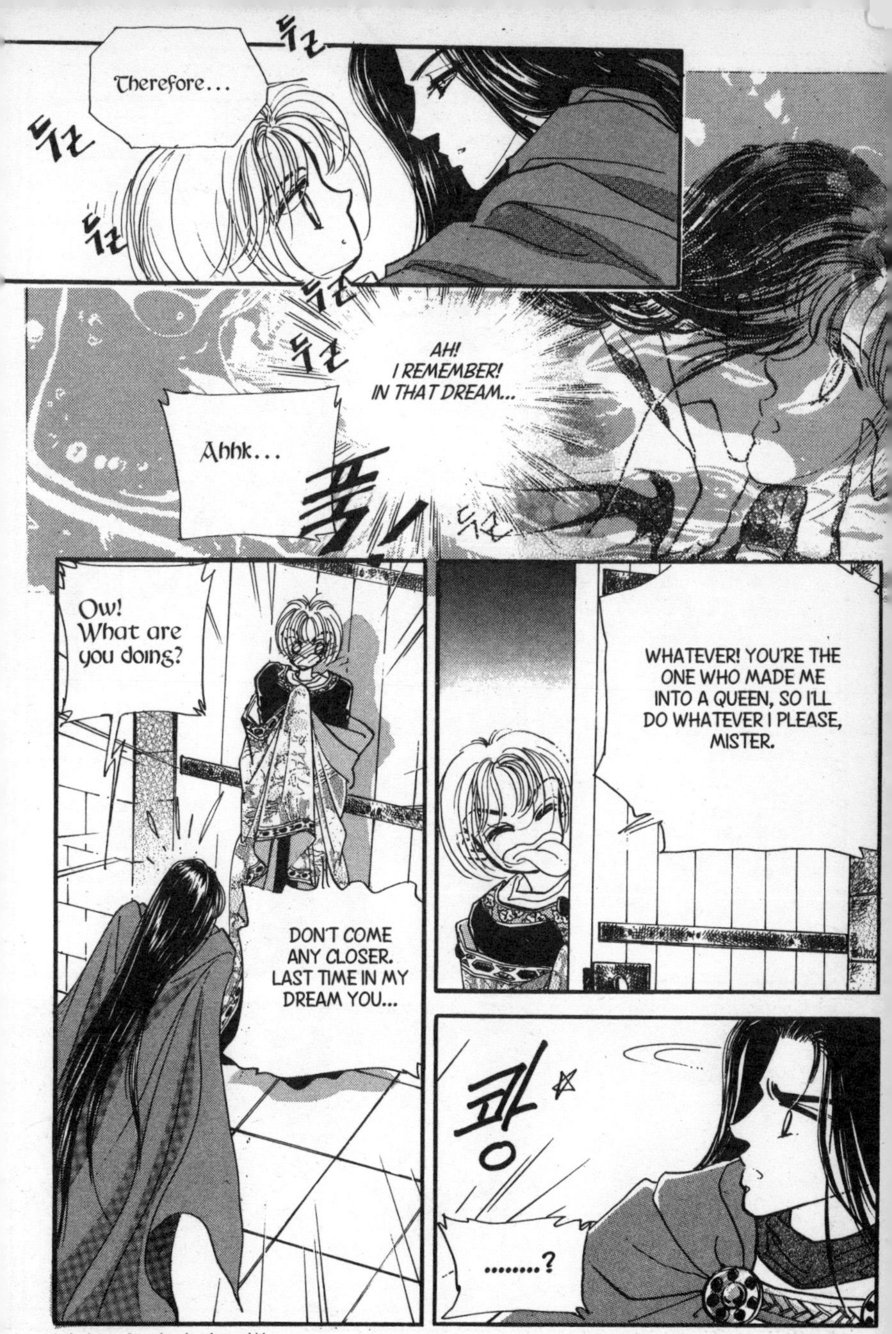
Therefore...
Ahhk...
AH! I REMEMBER! IN THAT DREAM...
Ow! What are you doing?
DON'T COME ANY CLOSER. LAST TIME IN MY DREAM YOU...
WHATEVER! YOU'RE THE ONE WHO MADE ME INTO A QUEEN, SO I'LL DO WHATEVER I PLEASE, MISTER.
쾅
........?

Author's note: I wonder where he was hit!

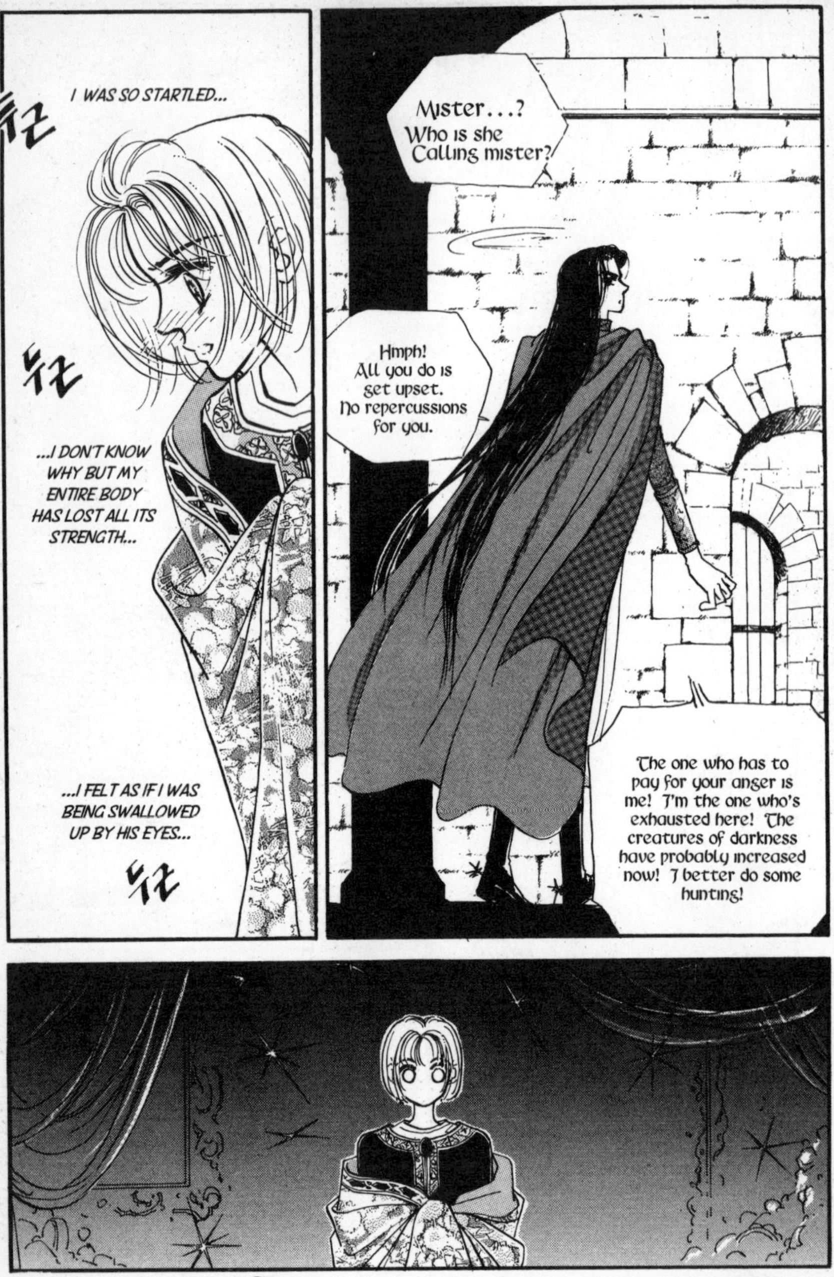
두근
I WAS SO STARTLED...
두근
...I DON'T KNOW WHY BUT MY ENTIRE BODY HAS LOST ALL ITS STRENGTH...
...I FELT AS IF I WAS BEING SWALLOWED UP BY HIS EYES...
두근
Mister...? Who is she Calling mister?
Hmph! All you do is get upset. No repercussions for you.
The one who has to pay for your anger is me! I'm the one who's exhausted here! The creatures of darkness have probably increased now! I better do some hunting!

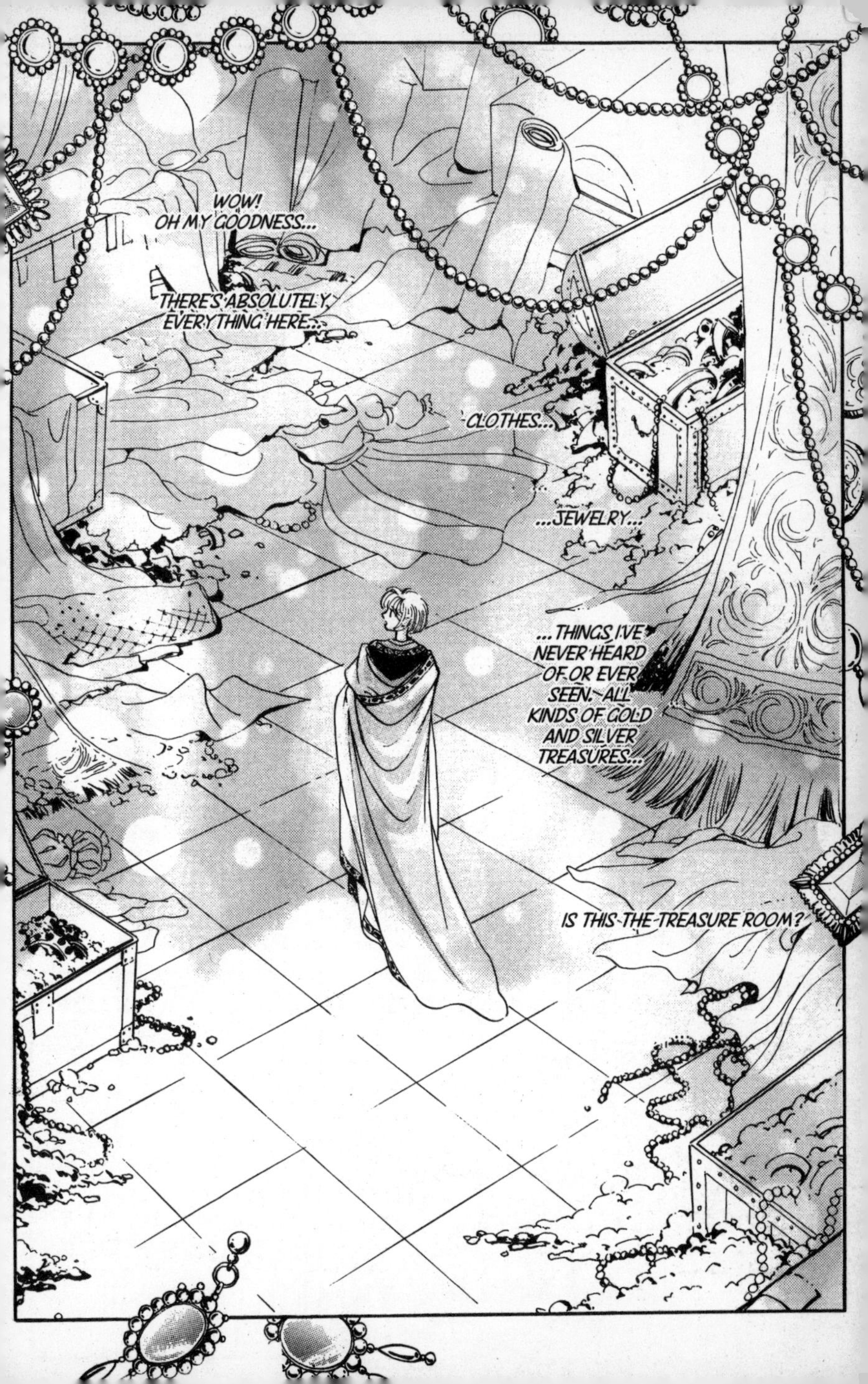
WOW! OH MY GOODNESS...
THERE'S ABSOLUTELY EVERYTHING HERE...
CLOTHES...
...JEWELRY...
...THINGS I'VE NEVER HEARD OF OR EVER SEEN. ALL KINDS OF GOLD AND SILVER TREASURES...
IS THIS THE TREASURE ROOM?

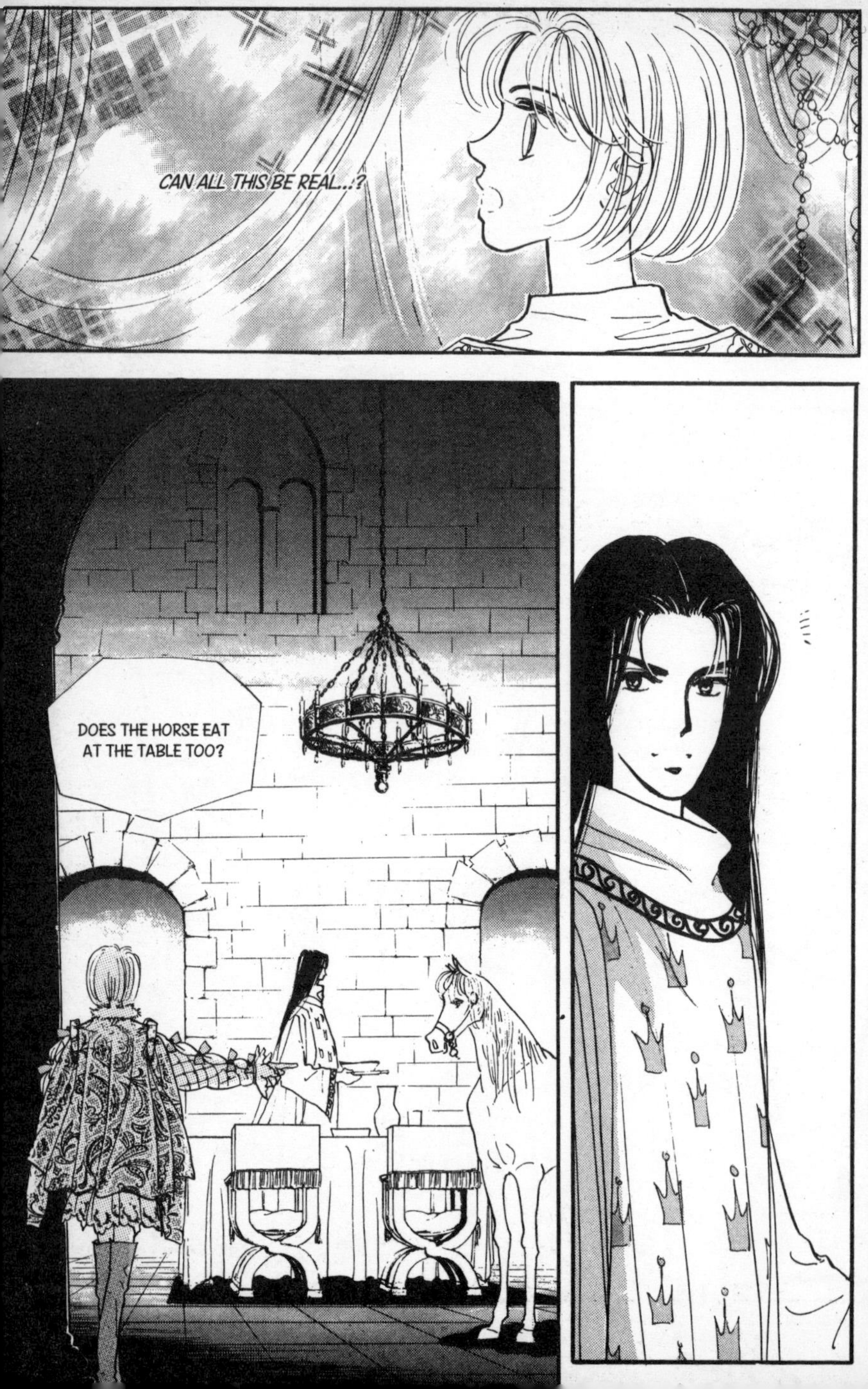
CAN ALL THIS BE REAL...?
DOES THE HORSE EAT AT THE TABLE TOO?

......

Those...clothes... Did you forget to finish dressing?

ALL OF THOSE DRESSES WERE ADORNED WITH LACE AND JEWELS. I HAD A HARD ENOUGH TIME FINDING THIS TO WEAR!

You have a pretty interesting fashion sense!

HUH? OH, WHAT'S THIS?

YOU EXPECT ME TO EAT THIS AGAIN? THIS IS THE SAME THING YOU GAVE ME EARLIER, MISTER.

My name is Rieno! And not mister!

THEN SHALL I CALL YOU MR. KIDNAPPER?

AN EXPLANATION OF YUNA'S ATTIRE

OUTER GARMENT

TIGHTS

WHITE BLOUSE (INNER GARMENT, MODERN DAY UNDERWEAR)

(WAIST AREA)

VERY LONG BOOTS

YUNA IS NOT WEARING A DRESS OVER HER INNER GARMENT (MODERN DAY UNDERWEAR).

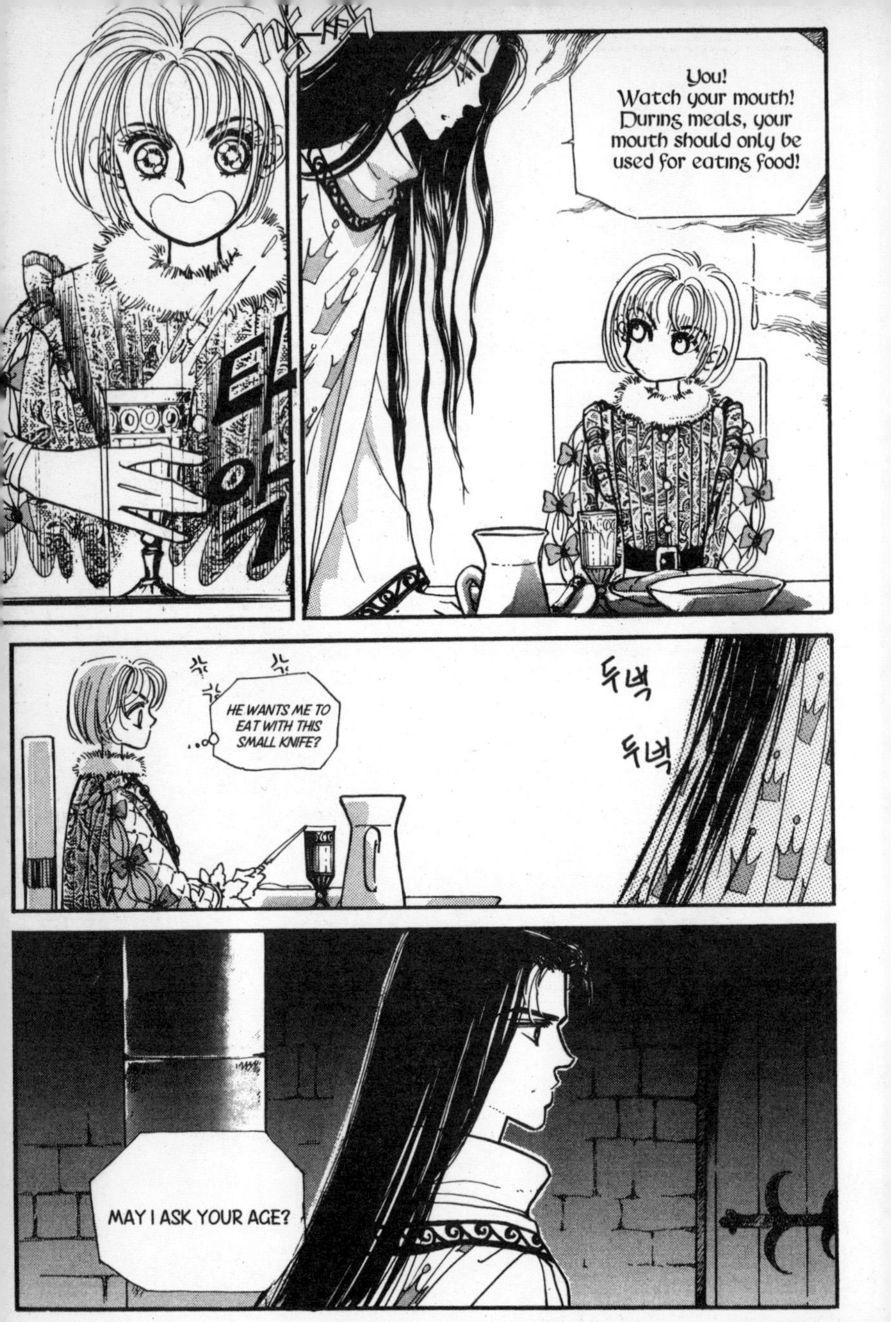
You! Watch your mouth! During meals, your mouth should only be used for eating food!
HE WANTS ME TO EAT WITH THIS SMALL KNIFE?
MAY I ASK YOUR AGE?

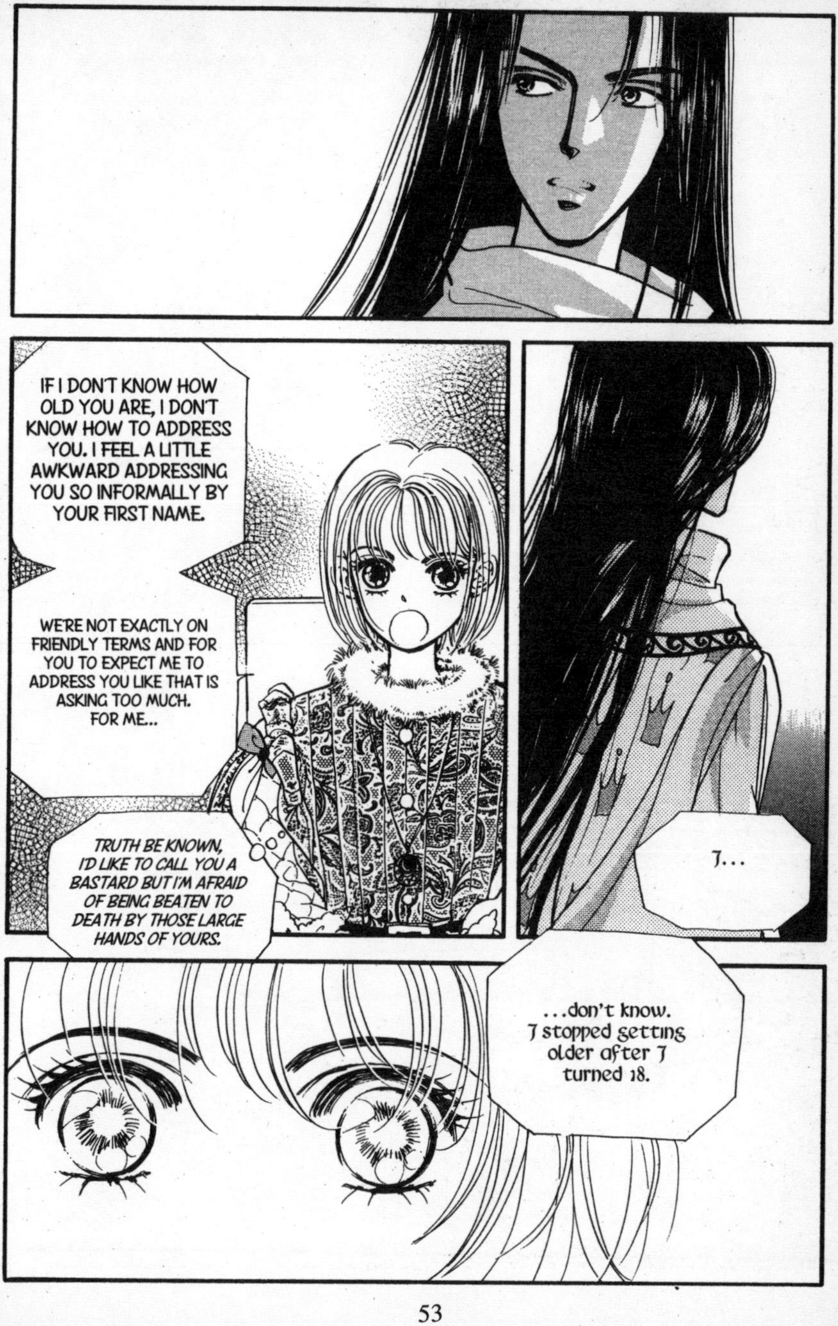
IF I DON'T KNOW HOW OLD YOU ARE, I DON'T KNOW HOW TO ADDRESS YOU. I FEEL A LITTLE AWKWARD ADDRESSING YOU SO INFORMALLY BY YOUR FIRST NAME.
WE'RE NOT EXACTLY ON FRIENDLY TERMS AND FOR YOU TO EXPECT ME TO ADDRESS YOU LIKE THAT IS ASKING TOO MUCH. FOR ME...
TRUTH BE KNOWN, I'D LIKE TO CALL YOU A BASTARD BUT I'M AFRAID OF BEING BEATEN TO DEATH BY THOSE LARGE HANDS OF YOURS.
I...
...don't know. I stopped getting older after I turned 18.

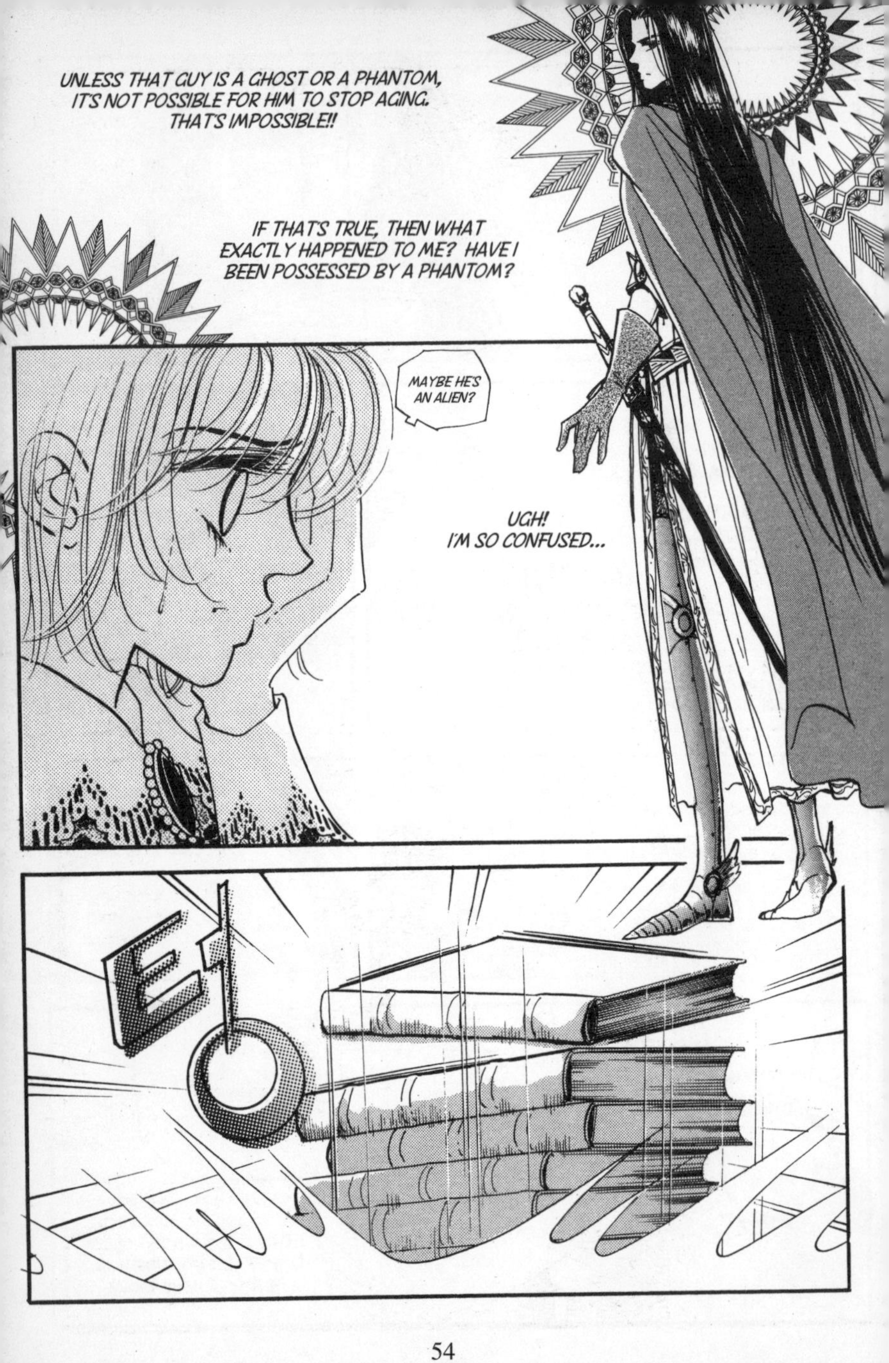
UNLESS THAT GUY IS A GHOST OR A PHANTOM, IT'S NOT POSSIBLE FOR HIM TO STOP AGING. THAT'S IMPOSSIBLE!!
IF THAT'S TRUE, THEN WHAT EXACTLY HAPPENED TO ME? HAVE I BEEN POSSESSED BY A PHANTOM?
MAYBE HE'S AN ALIEN?
UGH! I'M SO CONFUSED...

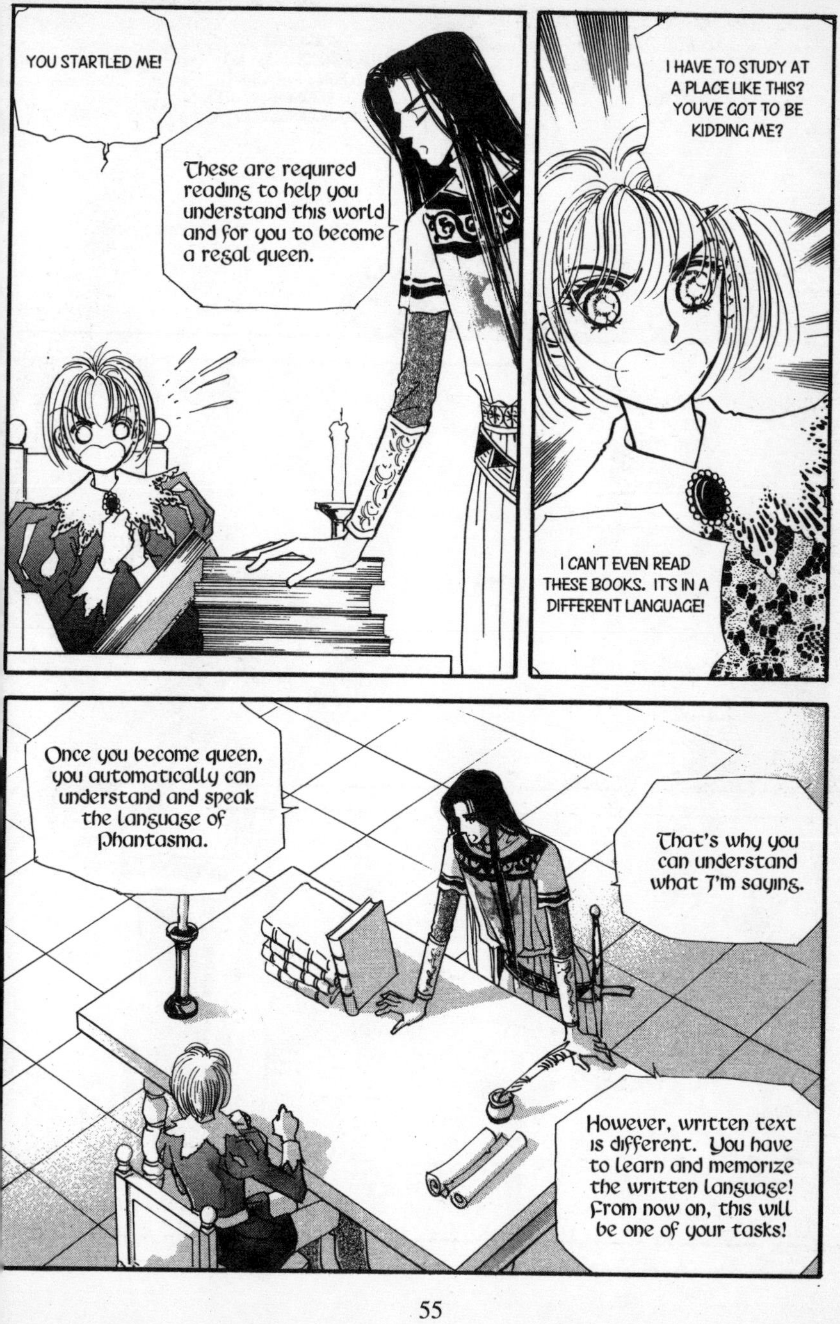
YOU STARTLED ME!
These are required reading to help you understand this world and for you to become a regal queen.
I HAVE TO STUDY AT A PLACE LIKE THIS? YOU'VE GOT TO BE KIDDING ME?
I CAN'T EVEN READ THESE BOOKS. IT'S IN A DIFFERENT LANGUAGE!
Once you become queen, you automatically can understand and speak the language of Phantasma.
That's why you can understand what I'm saying.
However, written text is different. You have to learn and memorize the written language! From now on, this will be one of your tasks!

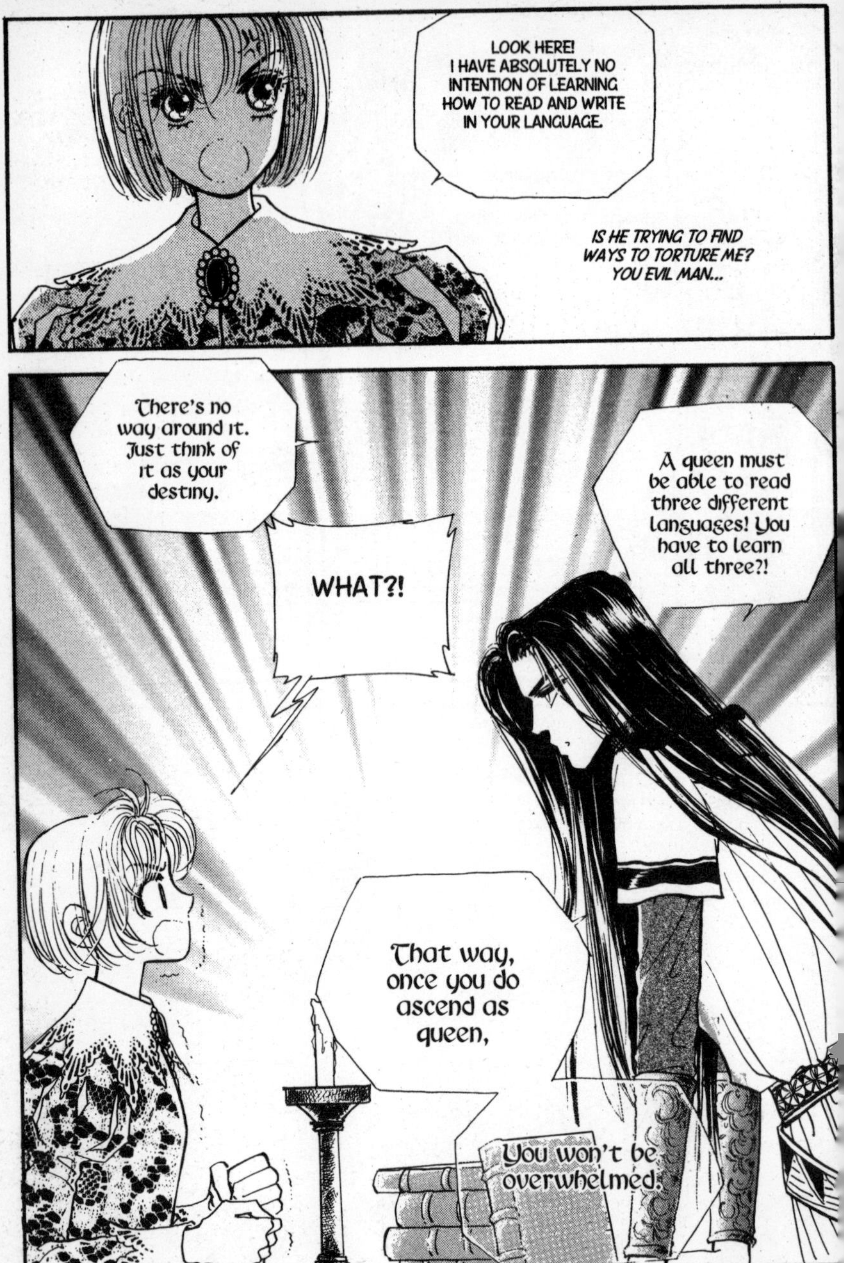

LOOK HERE! I HAVE ABSOLUTELY NO INTENTION OF LEARNING HOW TO READ AND WRITE IN YOUR LANGUAGE.
IS HE TRYING TO FIND WAYS TO TORTURE ME? YOU EVIL MAN...
There's no way around it. Just think of it as your destiny.
WHAT?!
A queen must be able to read three different languages! You have to learn all three?!
That way, once you do ascend as queen,
You won't be overwhelmed.

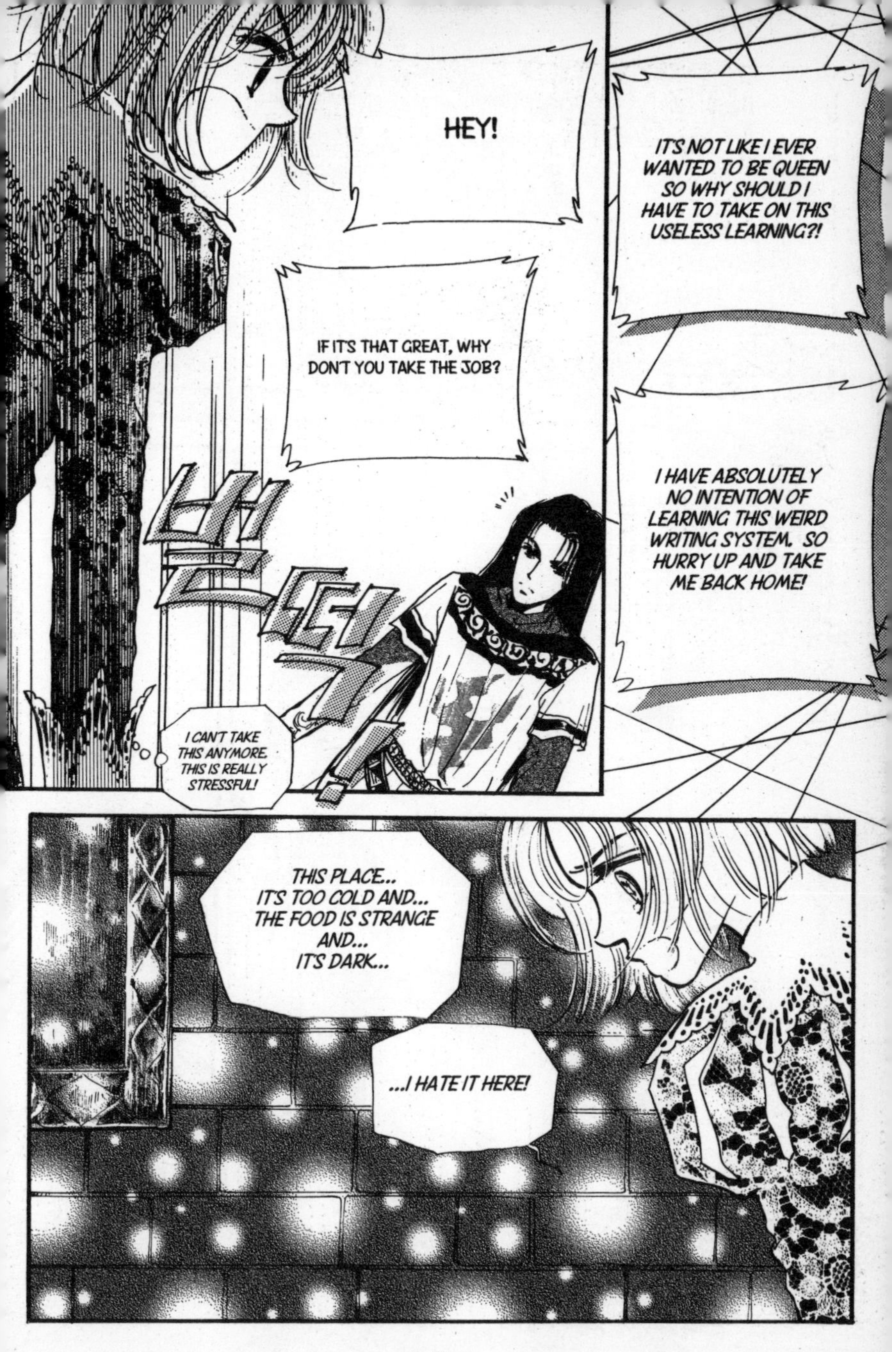
HEY!
IF IT'S THAT GREAT, WHY DON'T YOU TAKE THE JOB?
I CAN'T TAKE THIS ANYMORE. THIS IS REALLY STRESSFUL!
IT'S NOT LIKE I EVER WANTED TO BE QUEEN SO WHY SHOULD I HAVE TO TAKE ON THIS USELESS LEARNING?!
I HAVE ABSOLUTELY NO INTENTION OF LEARNING THIS WEIRD WRITING SYSTEM. SO HURRY UP AND TAKE ME BACK HOME!
THIS PLACE... IT'S TOO COLD AND... THE FOOD IS STRANGE AND... IT'S DARK...
...I HATE IT HERE!

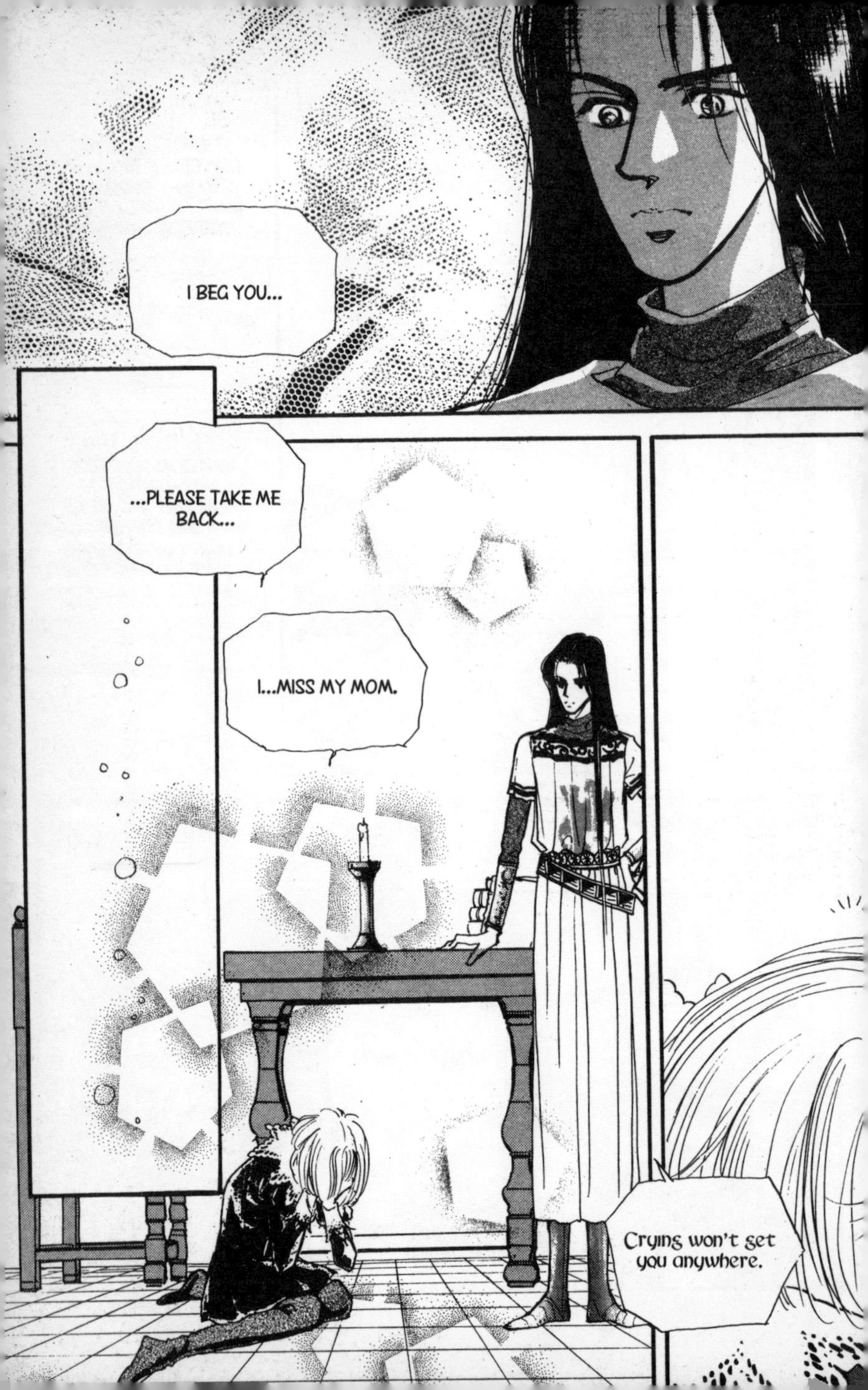
I BEG YOU...
...PLEASE TAKE ME BACK...
I...MISS MY MOM.
Crying won't get you anywhere.

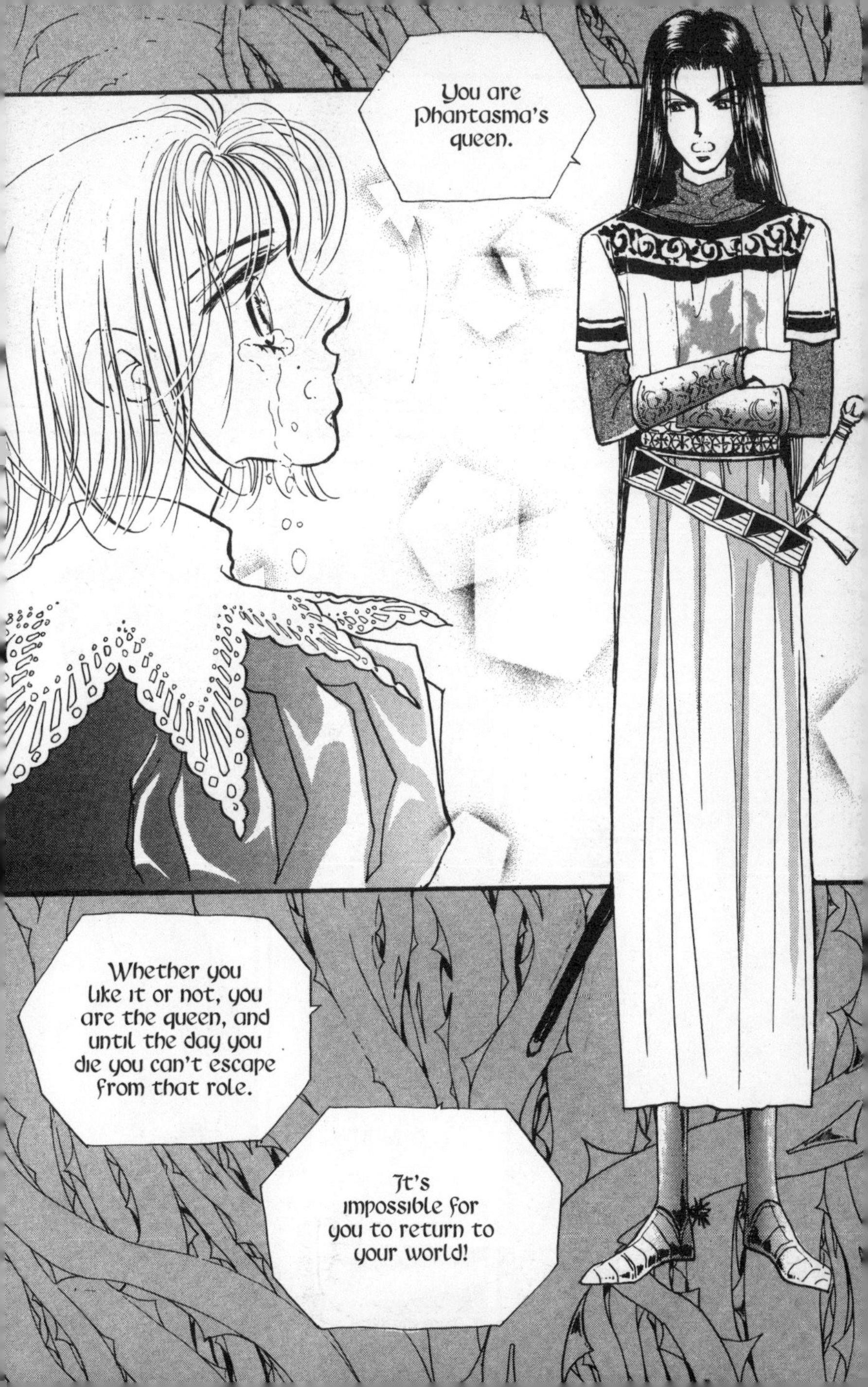
You are Phantasma's queen.
Whether you like it or not, you are the queen, and until the day you die you can't escape from that role.
It's impossible for you to return to your world!

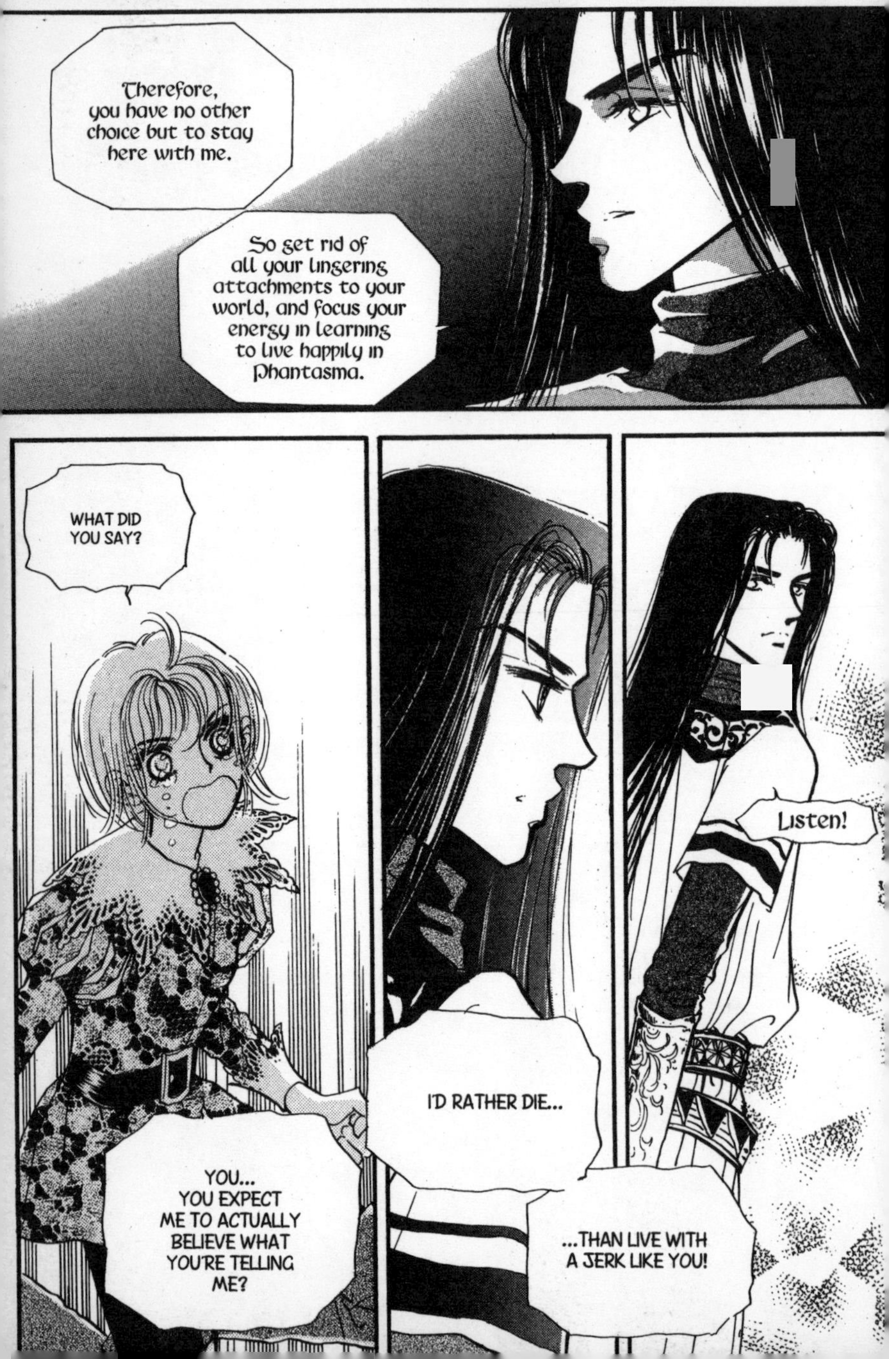
Therefore, you have no other choice but to stay here with me.
So get rid of all your lingering attachments to your world, and focus your energy in learning to live happily in Phantasma.
WHAT DID YOU SAY?
YOU... YOU EXPECT ME TO ACTUALLY BELIEVE WHAT YOU'RE TELLING ME?
I'D RATHER DIE...
...THAN LIVE WITH A JERK LIKE YOU!
Listen!

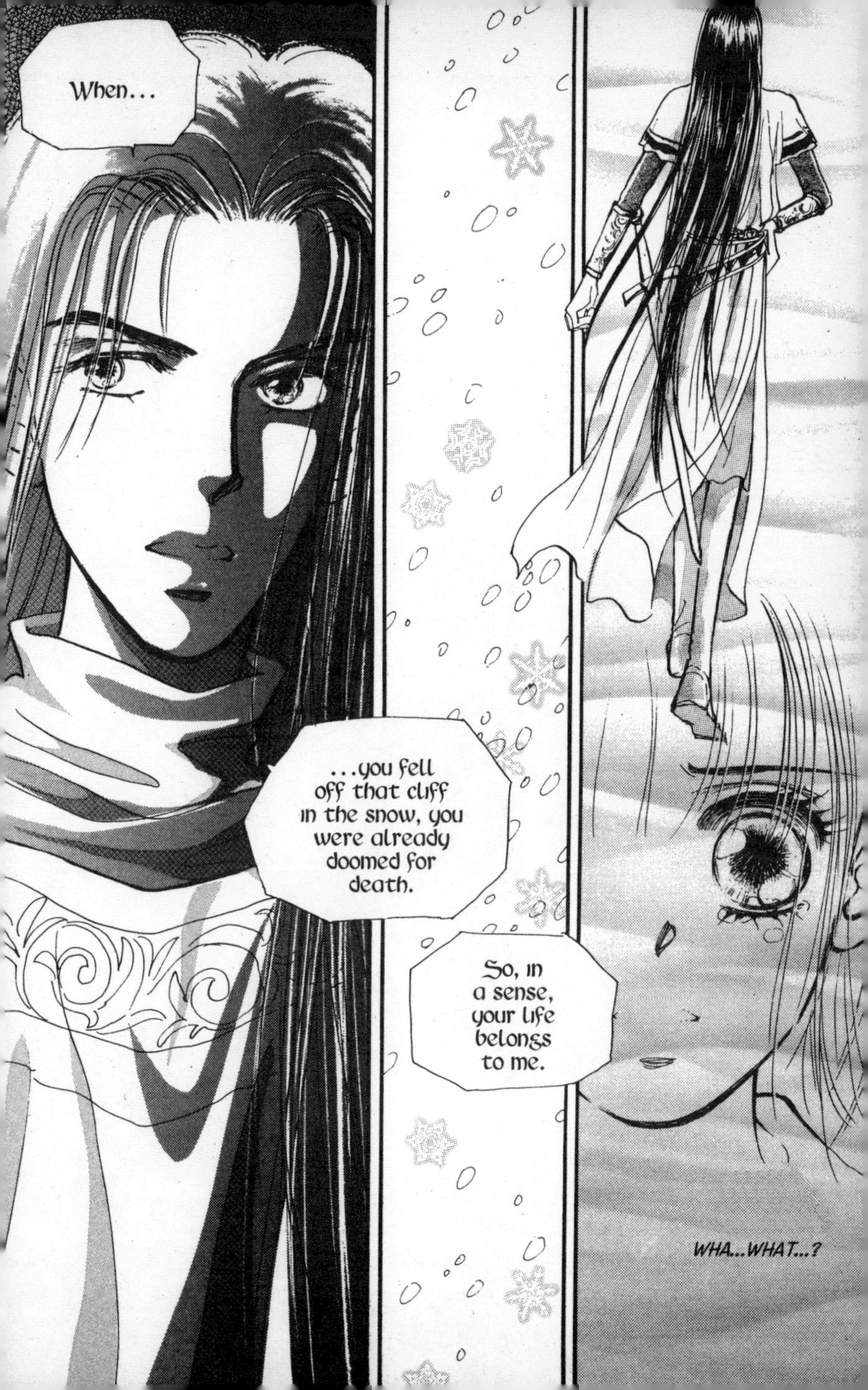
When...
...you fell off that cliff in the snow, you were already doomed for death.
So, in a sense, your life belongs to me.
WHA...WHAT...?

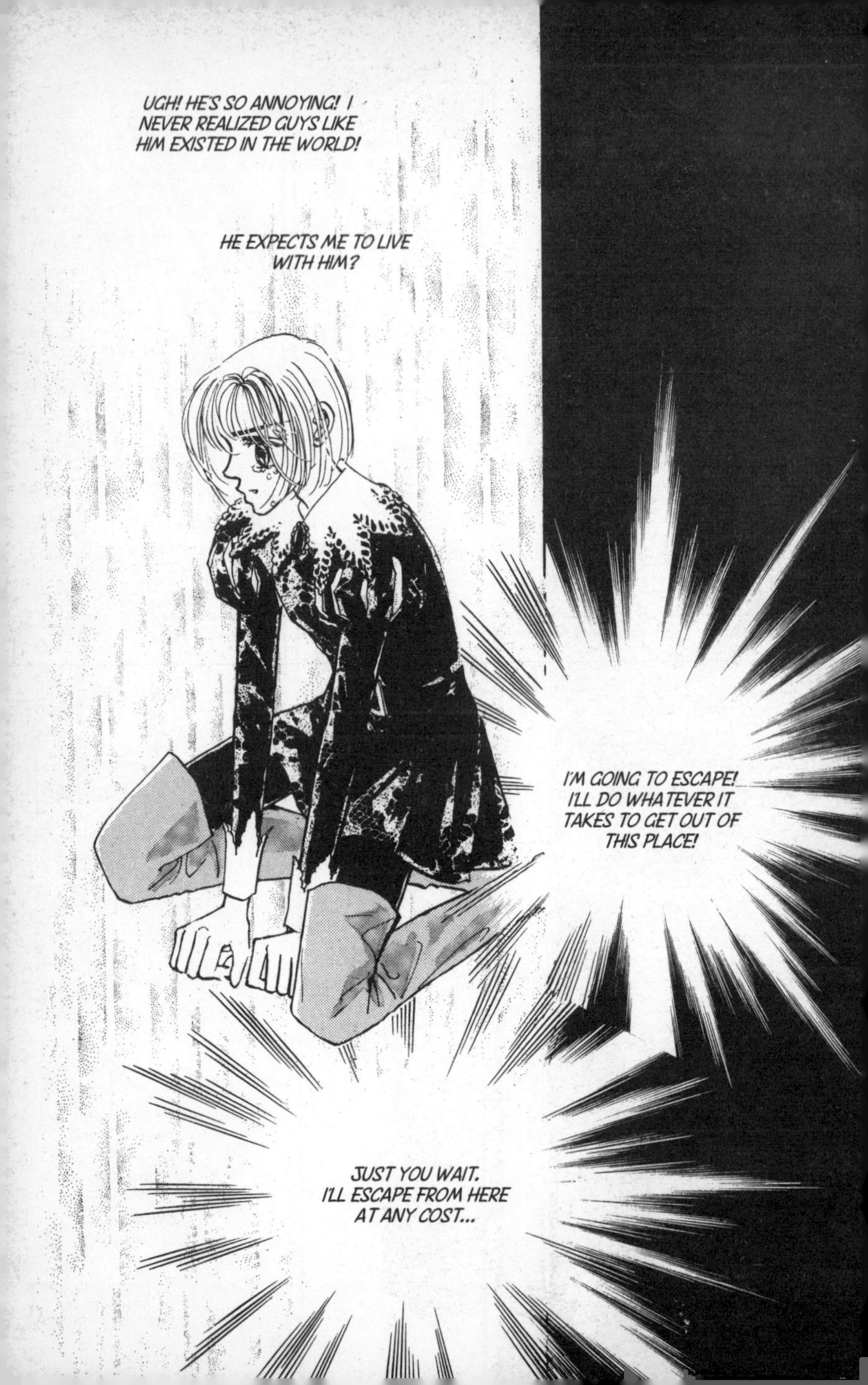
UGH! HE'S SO ANNOYING! I NEVER REALIZED GUYS LIKE HIM EXISTED IN THE WORLD!
HE EXPECTS ME TO LIVE WITH HIM?
I'M GOING TO ESCAPE! I'LL DO WHATEVER IT TAKES TO GET OUT OF THIS PLACE!
JUST YOU WAIT. I'LL ESCAPE FROM HERE AT ANY COST...

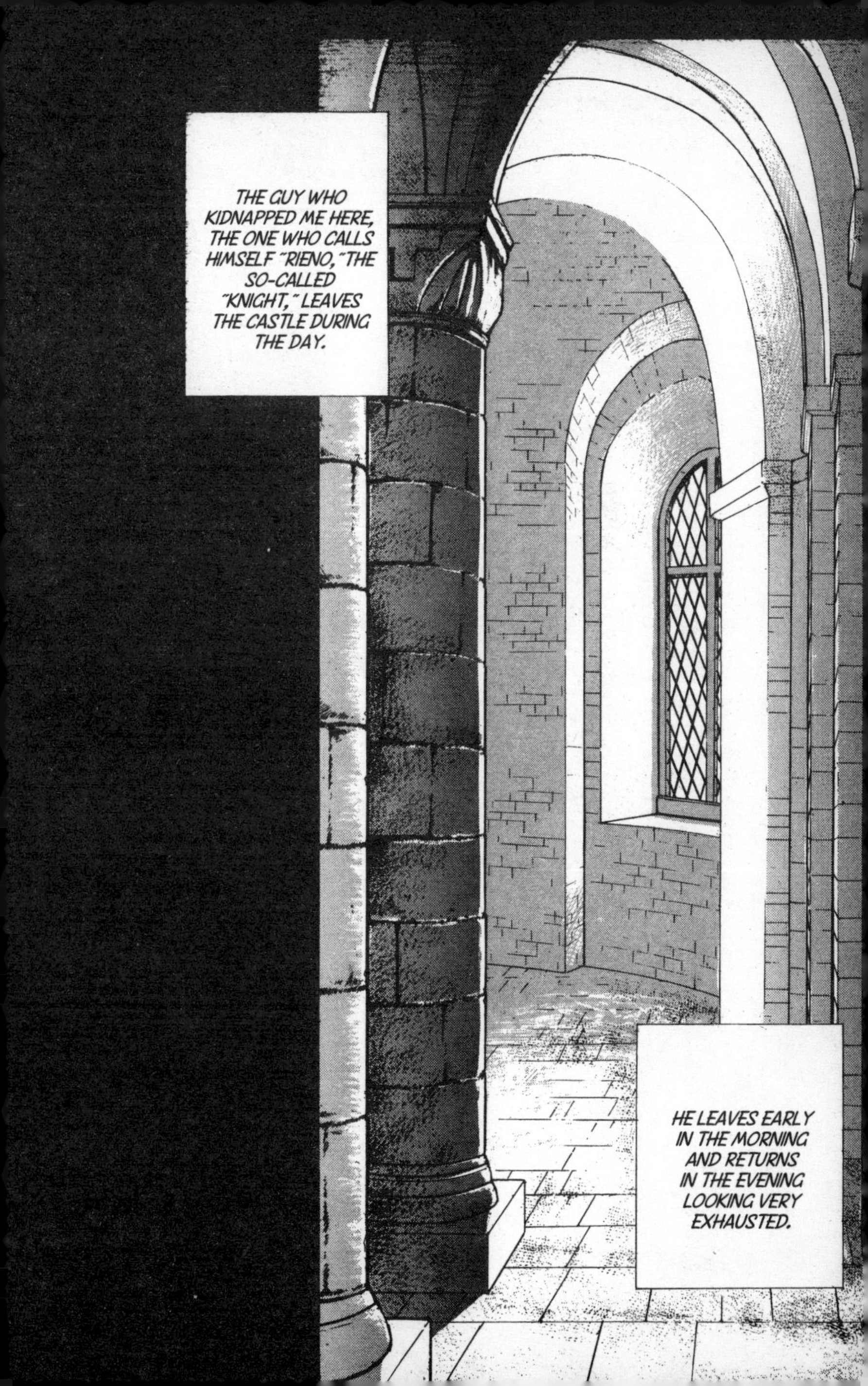
THE GUY WHO KIDNAPPED ME HERE, THE ONE WHO CALLS HIMSELF "RIENO," THE SO-CALLED "KNIGHT," LEAVES THE CASTLE DURING THE DAY.
HE LEAVES EARLY IN THE MORNING AND RETURNS IN THE EVENING LOOKING VERY EXHAUSTED.

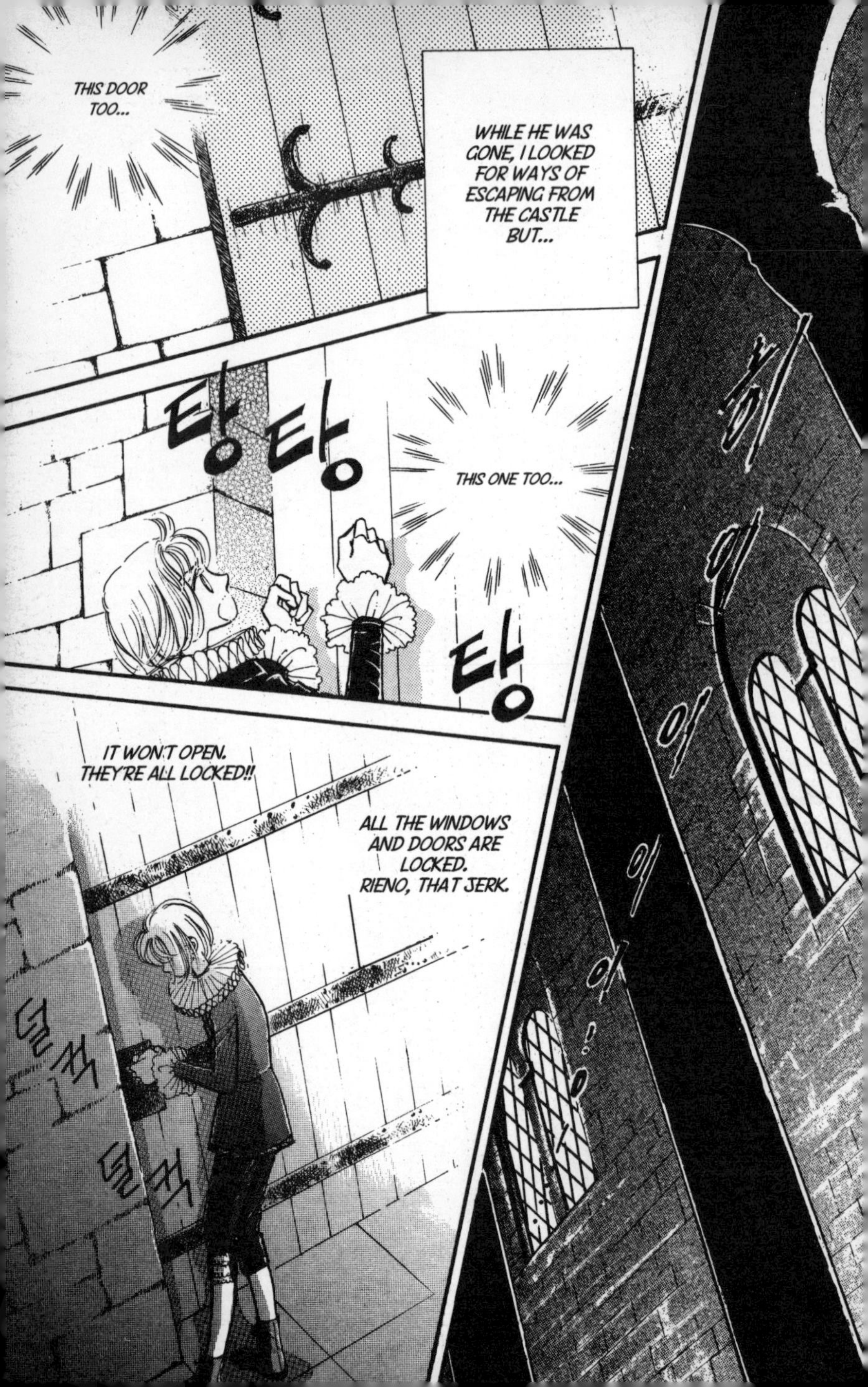
THIS DOOR TOO...
WHILE HE WAS GONE, I LOOKED FOR WAYS OF ESCAPING FROM THE CASTLE BUT...
탕 탕
THIS ONE TOO...
탕
IT WON'T OPEN. THEY'RE ALL LOCKED!!
ALL THE WINDOWS AND DOORS ARE LOCKED. RIENO, THAT JERK.
덜컥 덜컥

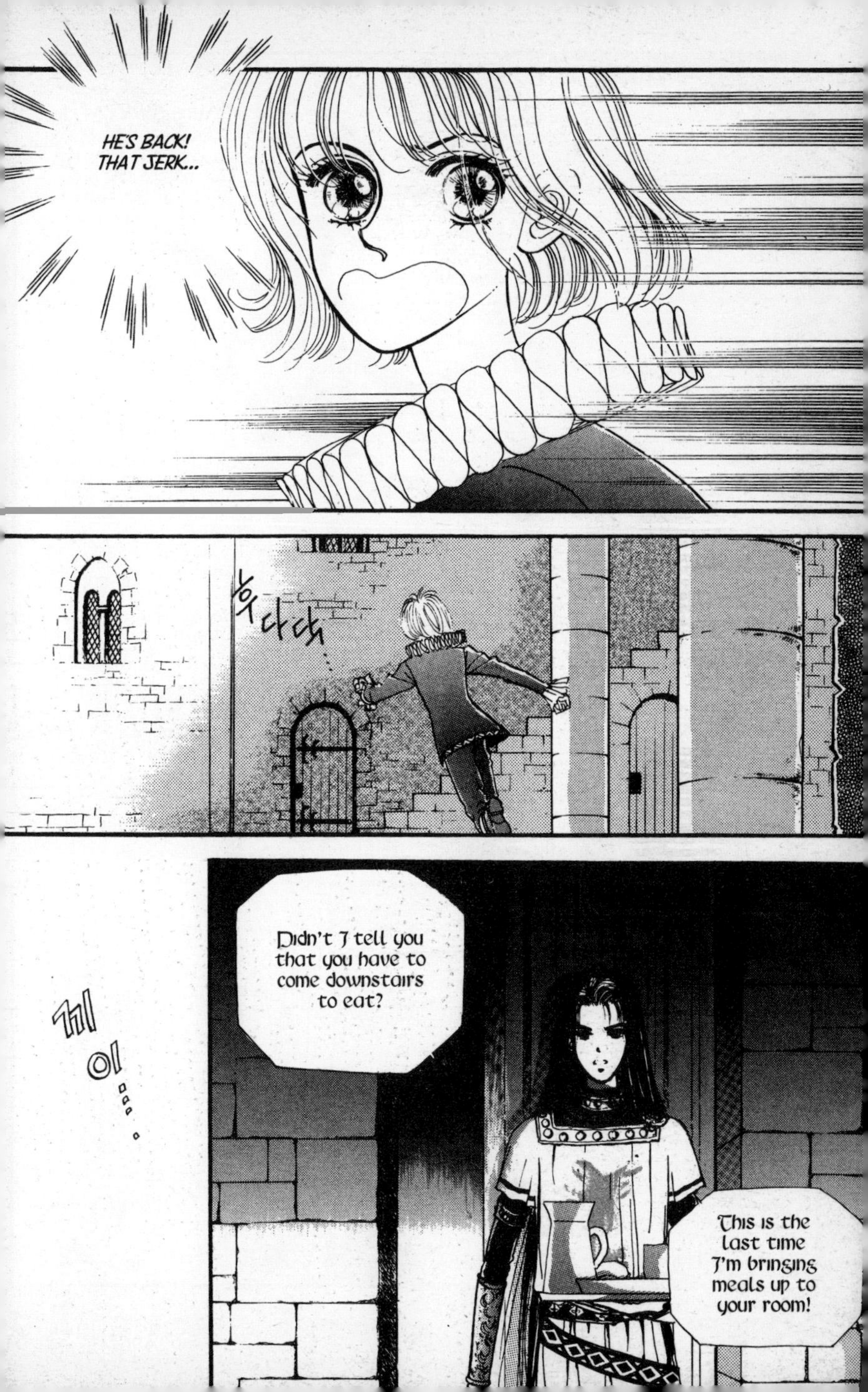
HE'S BACK! THAT JERK...
후다닥
끼이....
Didn't I tell you that you have to come downstairs to eat?
This is the last time I'm bringing meals up to your room!

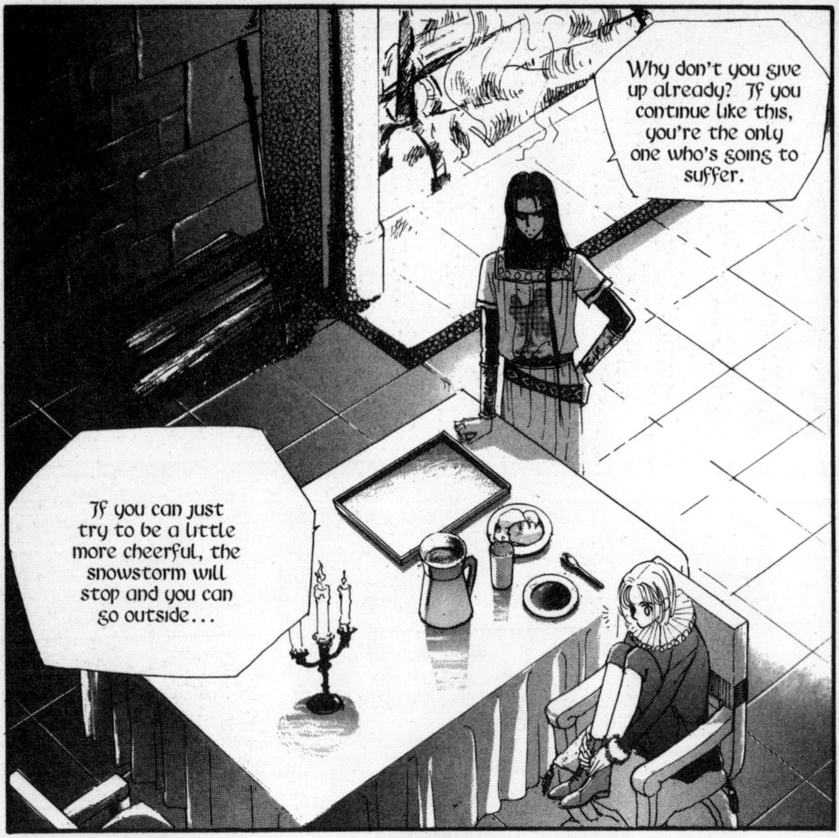
Why don't you give up already? If you continue like this, you're the only one who's going to suffer.
If you can just try to be a little more cheerful, the snowstorm will stop and you can go outside...
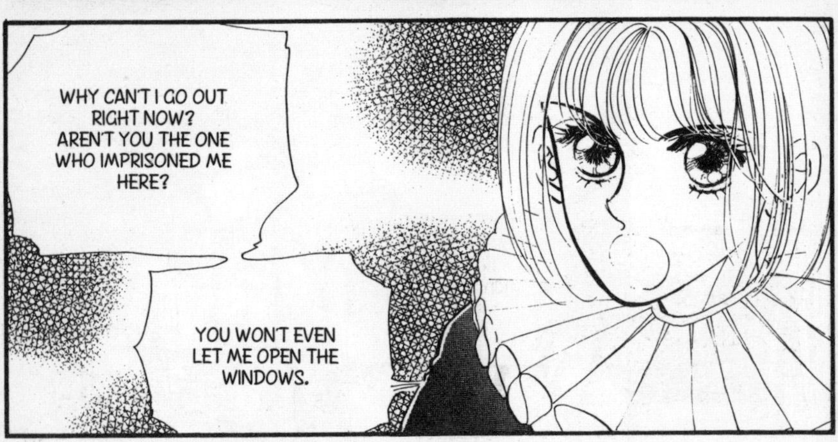
WHY CAN'T I GO OUT RIGHT NOW? AREN'T YOU THE ONE WHO IMPRISONED ME HERE?
YOU WON'T EVEN LET ME OPEN THE WINDOWS.

Now is not a good time to go out. If you were a little more obedient, sooner or later you'll be able to go out...

I PROMISE NOT TO RUN AWAY SO CAN'T YOU PLEASE LET ME GO OUTSIDE FOR JUST A MOMENT?

I'm not worried about you running away since it's virtually impossible.

It's rather pleasant having you here in person, rather than just seeing you in your dreams.

WHAT?! HOW DID YOU KNOW ABOUT THAT DREAM...?

Back then, I had to use whatever means possible to console you. I had to say things I didn't mean and I even had to kiss you!

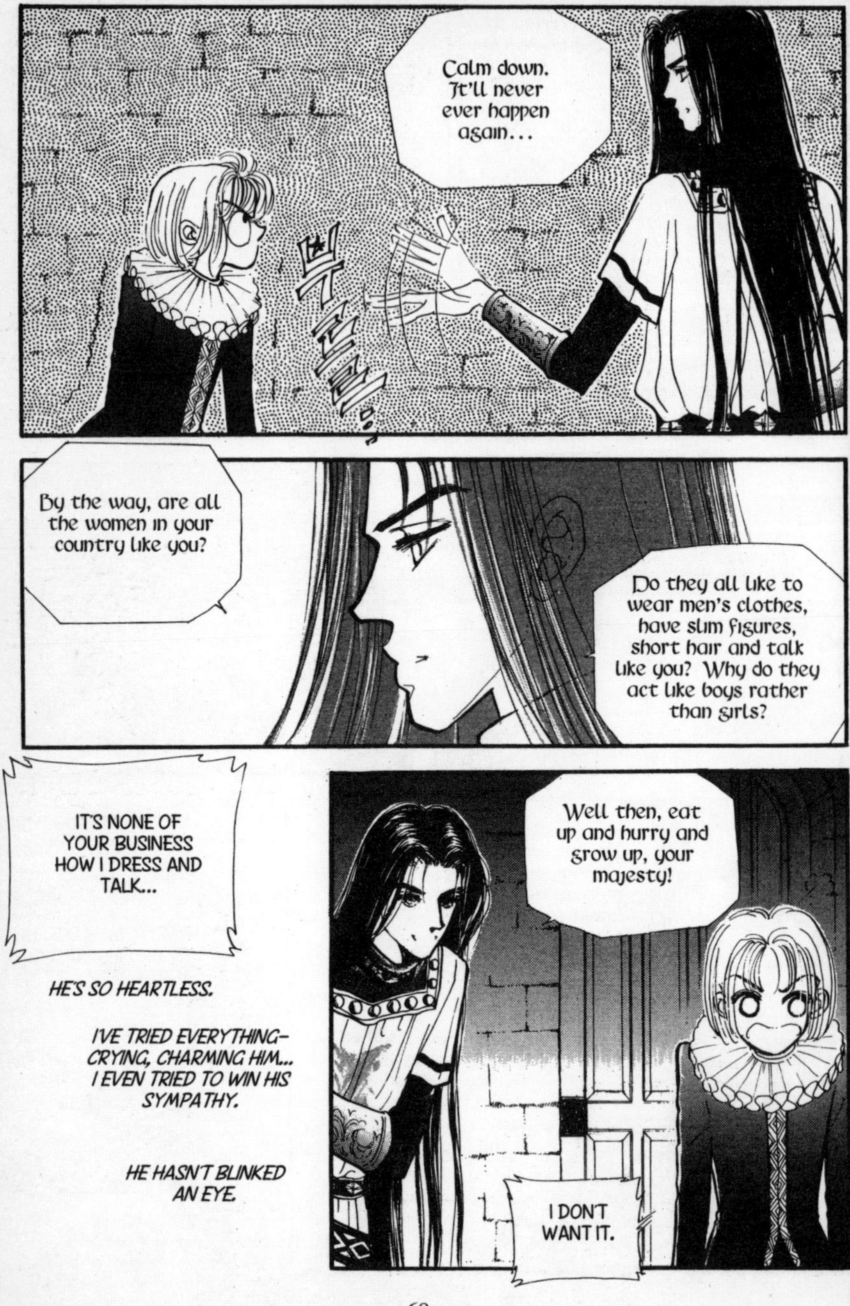
Calm down. It'll never ever happen again...
By the way, are all the women in your country like you?
Do they all like to wear men's clothes, have slim figures, short hair and talk like you? Why do they act like boys rather than girls?
IT'S NONE OF YOUR BUSINESS HOW I DRESS AND TALK...
HE'S SO HEARTLESS.
I'VE TRIED EVERYTHING-CRYING, CHARMING HIM... I EVEN TRIED TO WIN HIS SYMPATHY.
HE HASN'T BLINKED AN EYE.
Well then, eat up and hurry and grow up, your majesty!
I DON'T WANT IT.

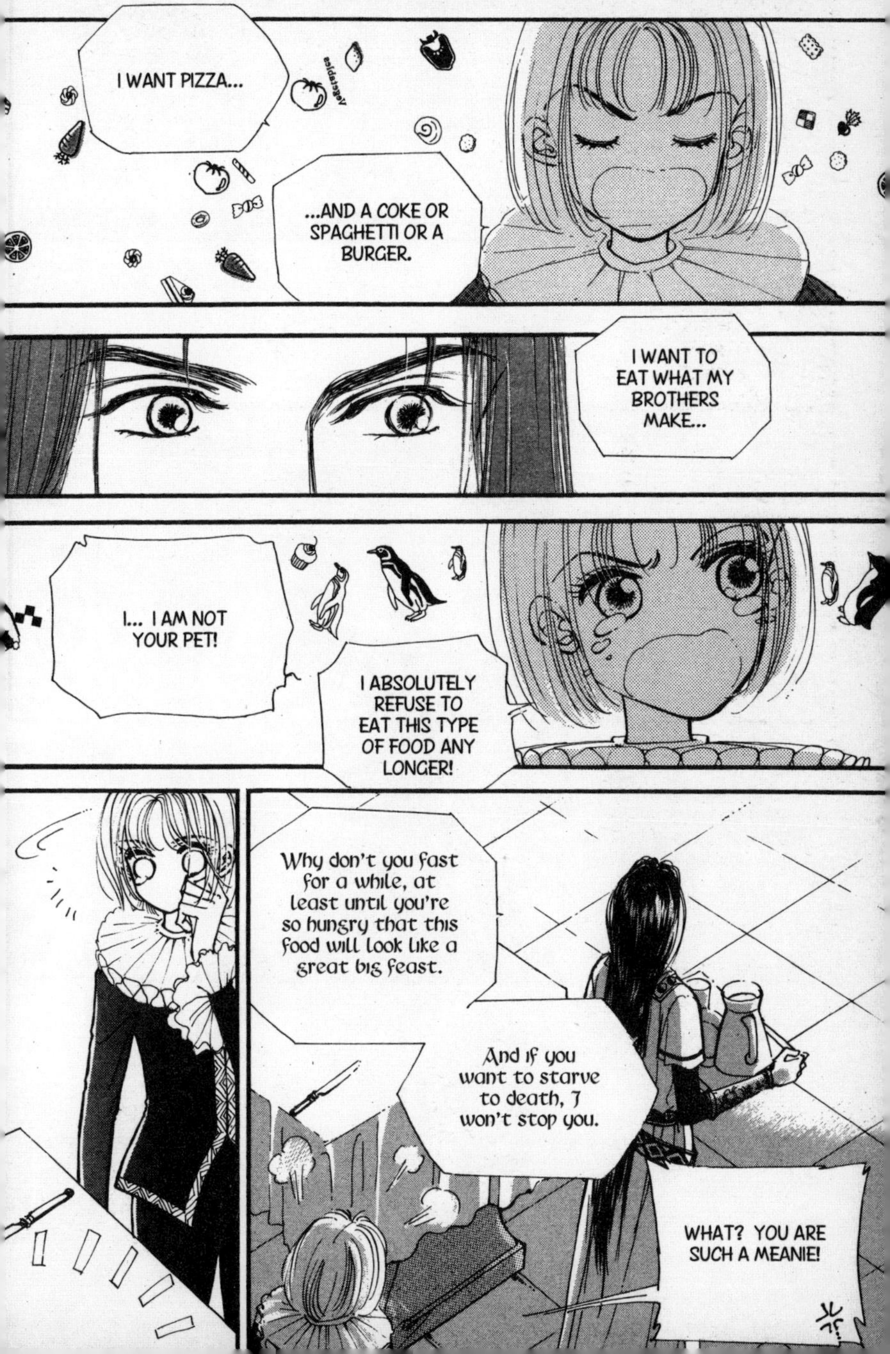
I WANT PIZZA...
...AND A COKE OR SPAGHETTI OR A BURGER.
I WANT TO EAT WHAT MY BROTHERS MAKE...
I... I AM NOT YOUR PET!
I ABSOLUTELY REFUSE TO EAT THIS TYPE OF FOOD ANY LONGER!
Why don't you fast for a while, at least until you're so hungry that this food will look like a great big feast.
And if you want to starve to death, I won't stop you.
WHAT? YOU ARE SUCH A MEANIE!

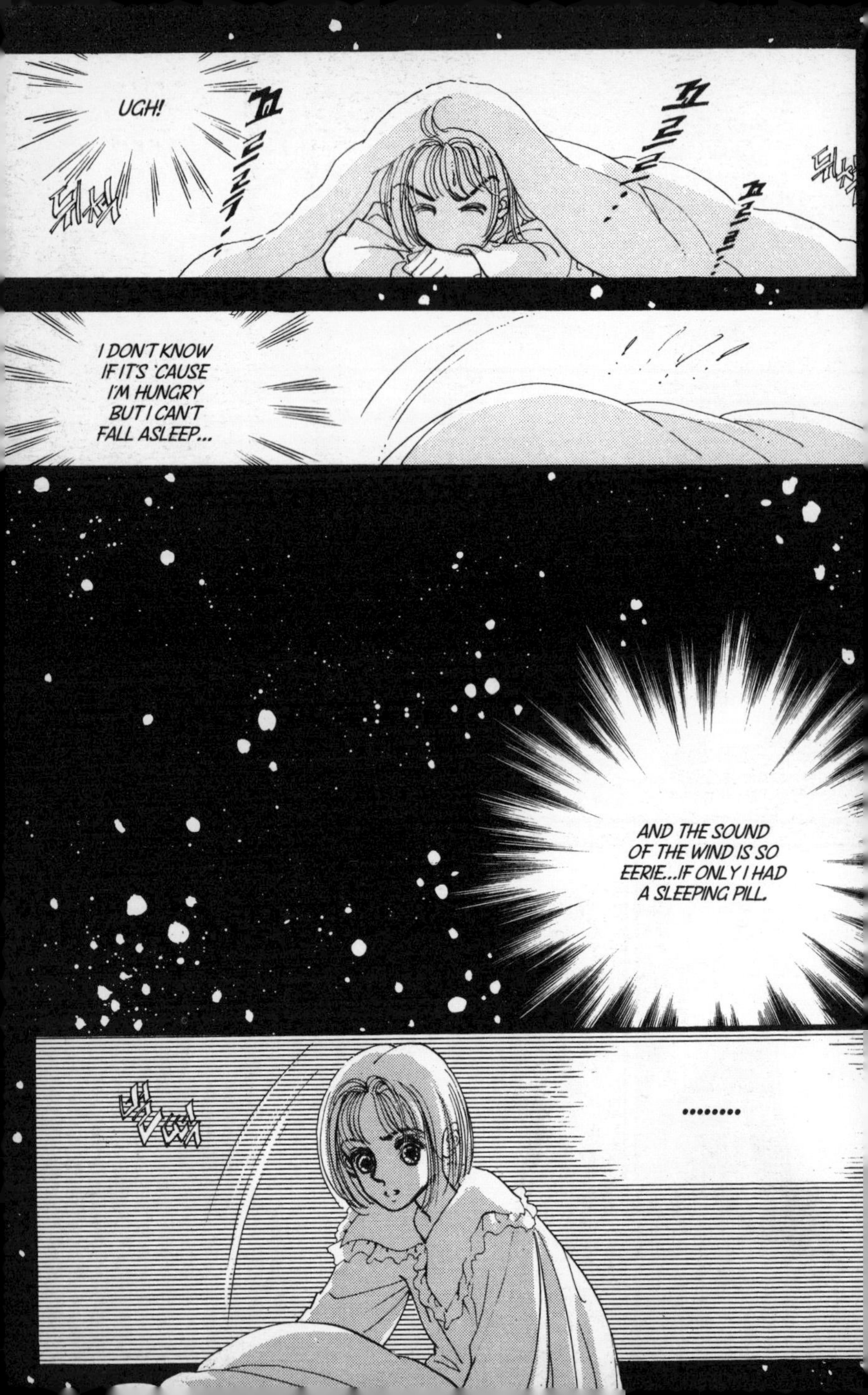
UGH!
I DON'T KNOW IF IT'S 'CAUSE I'M HUNGRY BUT I CAN'T FALL ASLEEP...
AND THE SOUND OF THE WIND IS SO EERIE...IF ONLY I HAD A SLEEPING PILL.
....

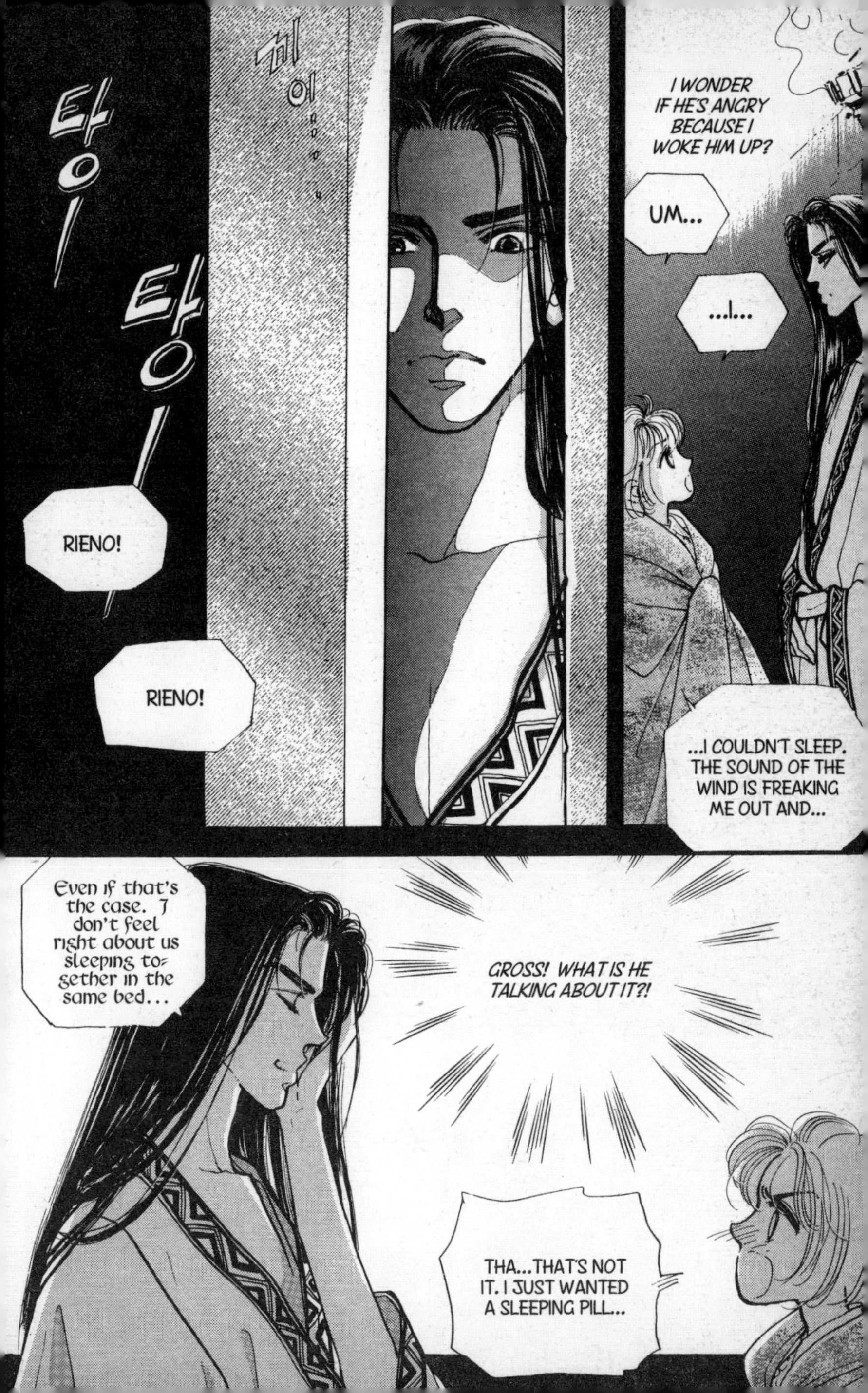
RIENO!
RIENO!
I WONDER IF HE'S ANGRY BECAUSE I WOKE HIM UP?
UM...
...I...
...I COULDN'T SLEEP. THE SOUND OF THE WIND IS FREAKING ME OUT AND...
Even if that's the case. I don't feel right about us sleeping to-gether in the same bed...
GROSS! WHAT IS HE TALKING ABOUT IT?!
THA...THAT'S NOT IT. I JUST WANTED A SLEEPING PILL...

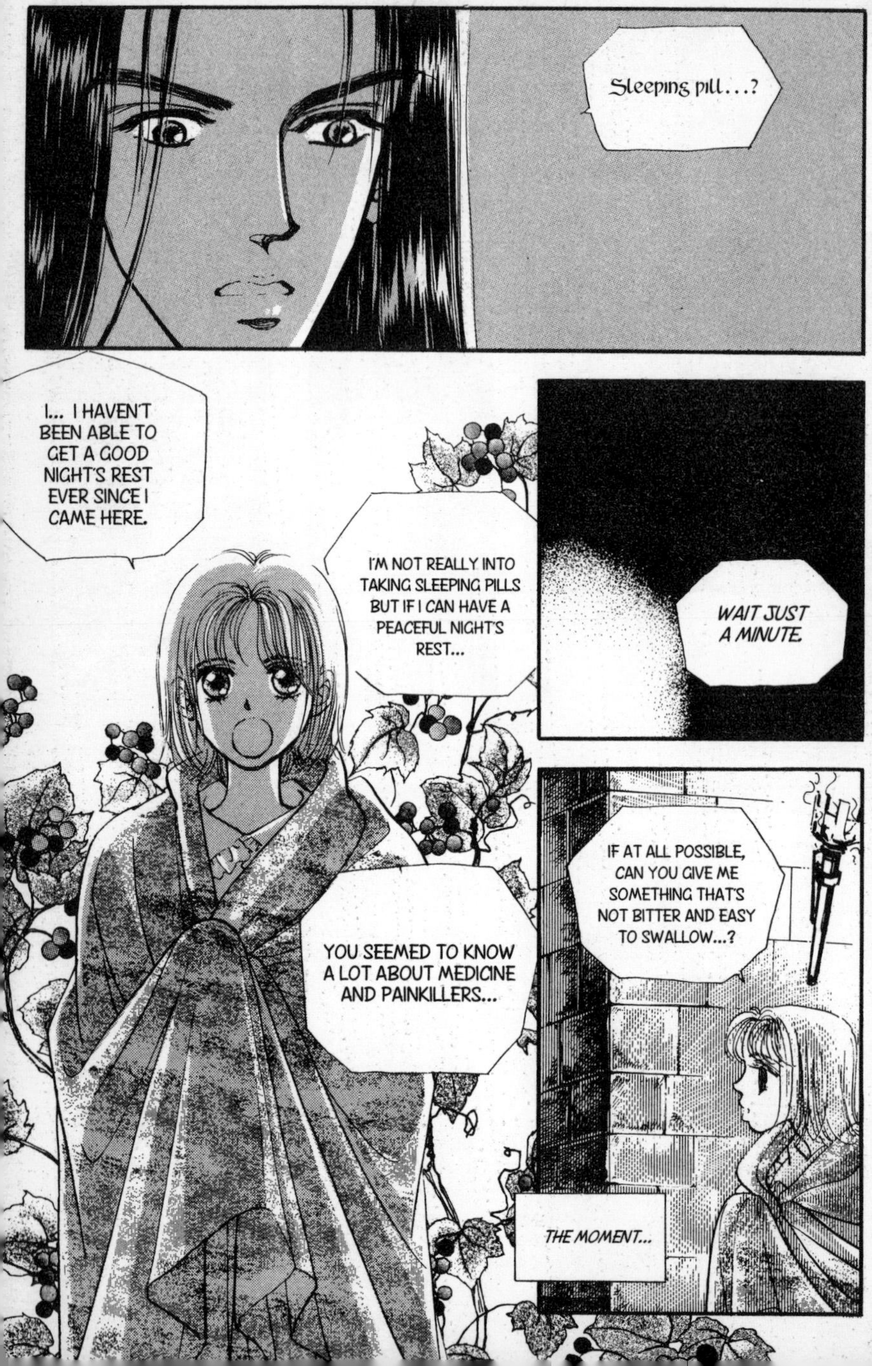

Sleeping pill...?
I... I HAVEN'T BEEN ABLE TO GET A GOOD NIGHT'S REST EVER SINCE I CAME HERE.
I'M NOT REALLY INTO TAKING SLEEPING PILLS BUT IF I CAN HAVE A PEACEFUL NIGHT'S REST...
YOU SEEMED TO KNOW A LOT ABOUT MEDICINE AND PAINKILLERS...
WAIT JUST A MINUTE.
IF AT ALL POSSIBLE, CAN YOU GIVE ME SOMETHING THAT'S NOT BITTER AND EASY TO SWALLOW...?
THE MOMENT...

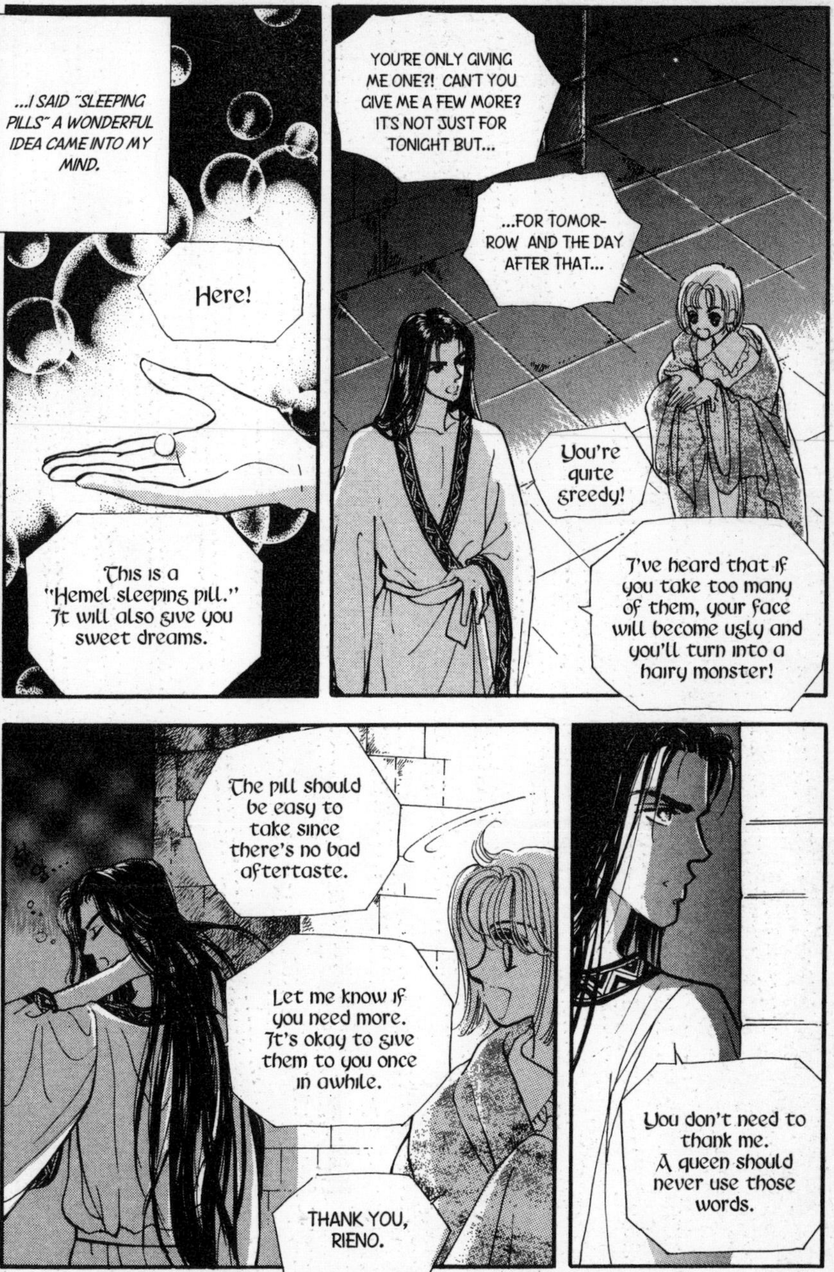
...I SAID "SLEEPING PILLS" A WONDERFUL IDEA CAME INTO MY MIND.
Here!
This is a "Hemel sleeping pill." It will also give you sweet dreams.
YOU'RE ONLY GIVING ME ONE?! CAN'T YOU GIVE ME A FEW MORE? IT'S NOT JUST FOR TONIGHT BUT...
...FOR TOMOR-ROW AND THE DAY AFTER THAT...
You're quite greedy!
I've heard that if you take too many of them, your face will become ugly and you'll turn into a hairy monster!
The pill should be easy to take since there's no bad aftertaste.
Let me know if you need more. It's okay to give them to you once in awhile.
THANK YOU, RIENO.
You don't need to thank me. A queen should never use those words.

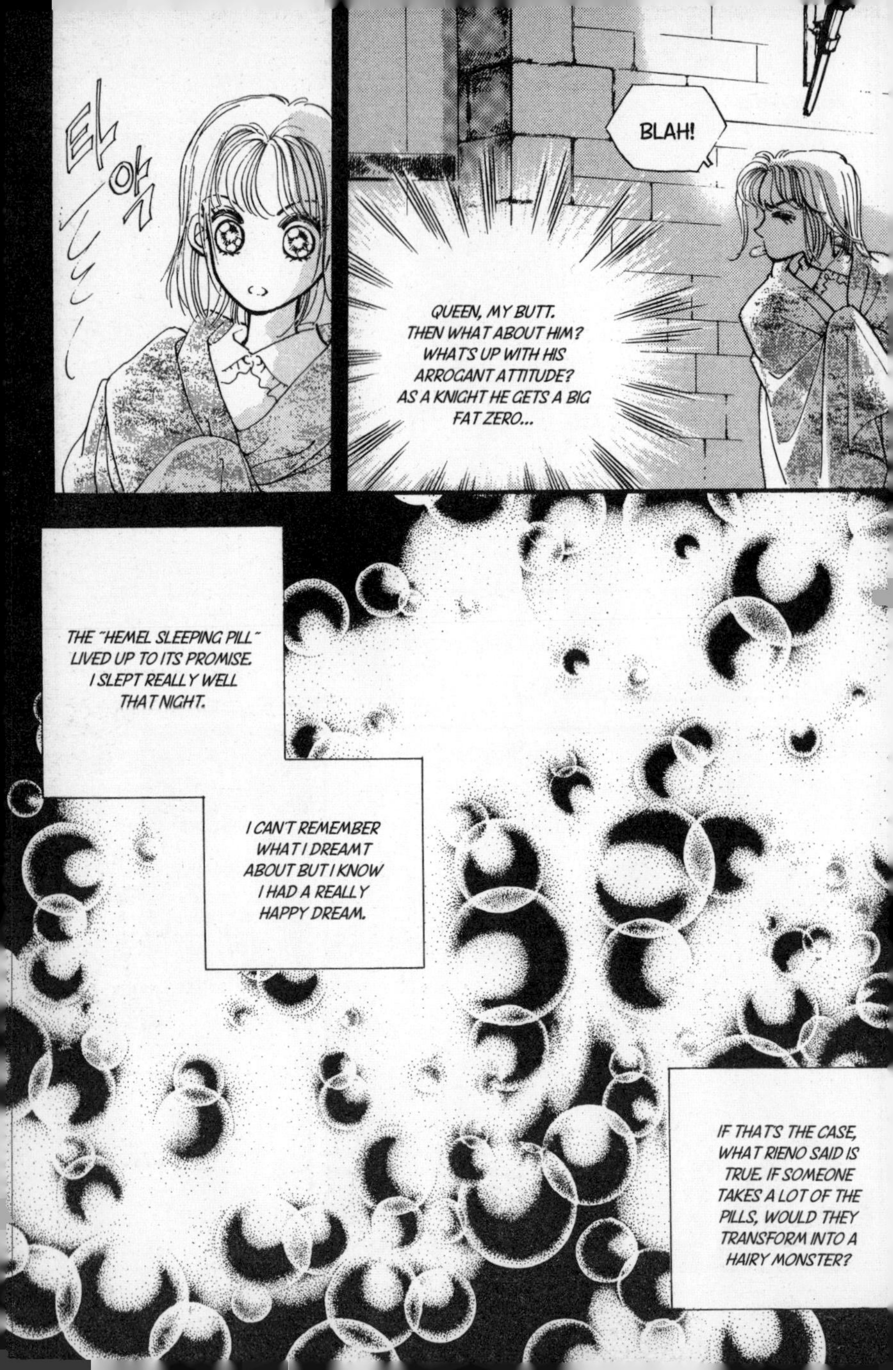
BLAH!
QUEEN, MY BUTT. THEN WHAT ABOUT HIM? WHAT'S UP WITH HIS ARROGANT ATTITUDE? AS A KNIGHT HE GETS A BIG FAT ZERO...
THE "HEMEL SLEEPING PILL" LIVED UP TO ITS PROMISE. I SLEPT REALLY WELL THAT NIGHT.
I CAN'T REMEMBER WHAT I DREAMT ABOUT BUT I KNOW I HAD A REALLY HAPPY DREAM.
IF THAT'S THE CASE, WHAT RIENO SAID IS TRUE. IF SOMEONE TAKES A LOT OF THE PILLS, WOULD THEY TRANSFORM INTO A HAIRY MONSTER?

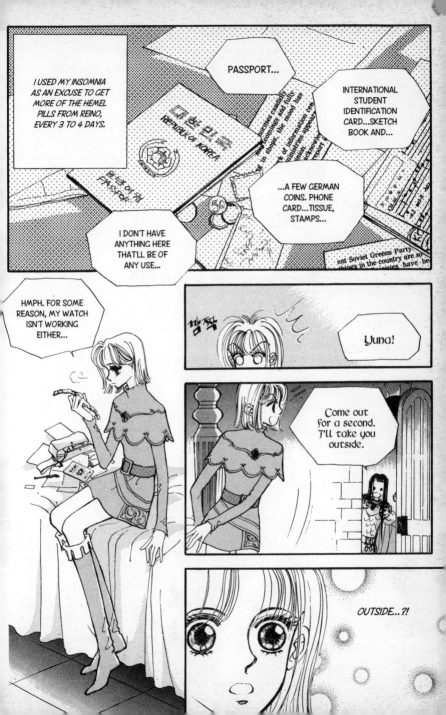

I USED MY INSOMNIA AS AN EXCUSE TO GET MORE OF THE HEMEL PILLS FROM REINO, EVERY 3 TO 4 DAYS.

PASSPORT...

INTERNATIONAL STUDENT IDENTIFICATION CARD...SKETCH BOOK AND...

...A FEW GERMAN COINS. PHONE CARD...TISSUE, STAMPS...

I DON'T HAVE ANYTHING HERE THAT'LL BE OF ANY USE...

HMPH. FOR SOME REASON, MY WATCH ISN'T WORKING EITHER...

Yuna!

Come out for a second. I'll take you outside.

OUTSIDE...?!

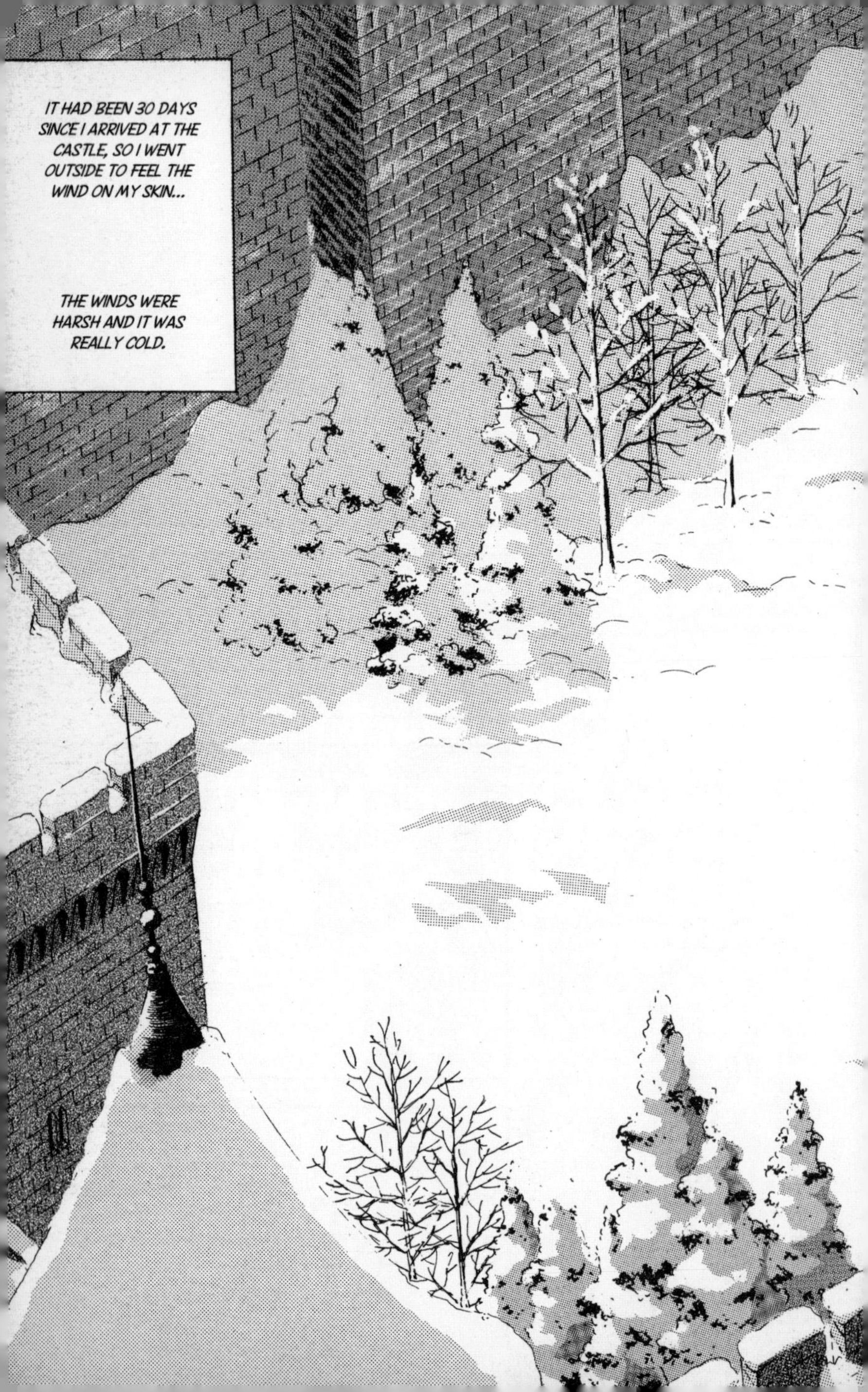
IT HAD BEEN 30 DAYS SINCE I ARRIVED AT THE CASTLE, SO I WENT OUTSIDE TO FEEL THE WIND ON MY SKIN...
THE WINDS WERE HARSH AND IT WAS REALLY COLD.

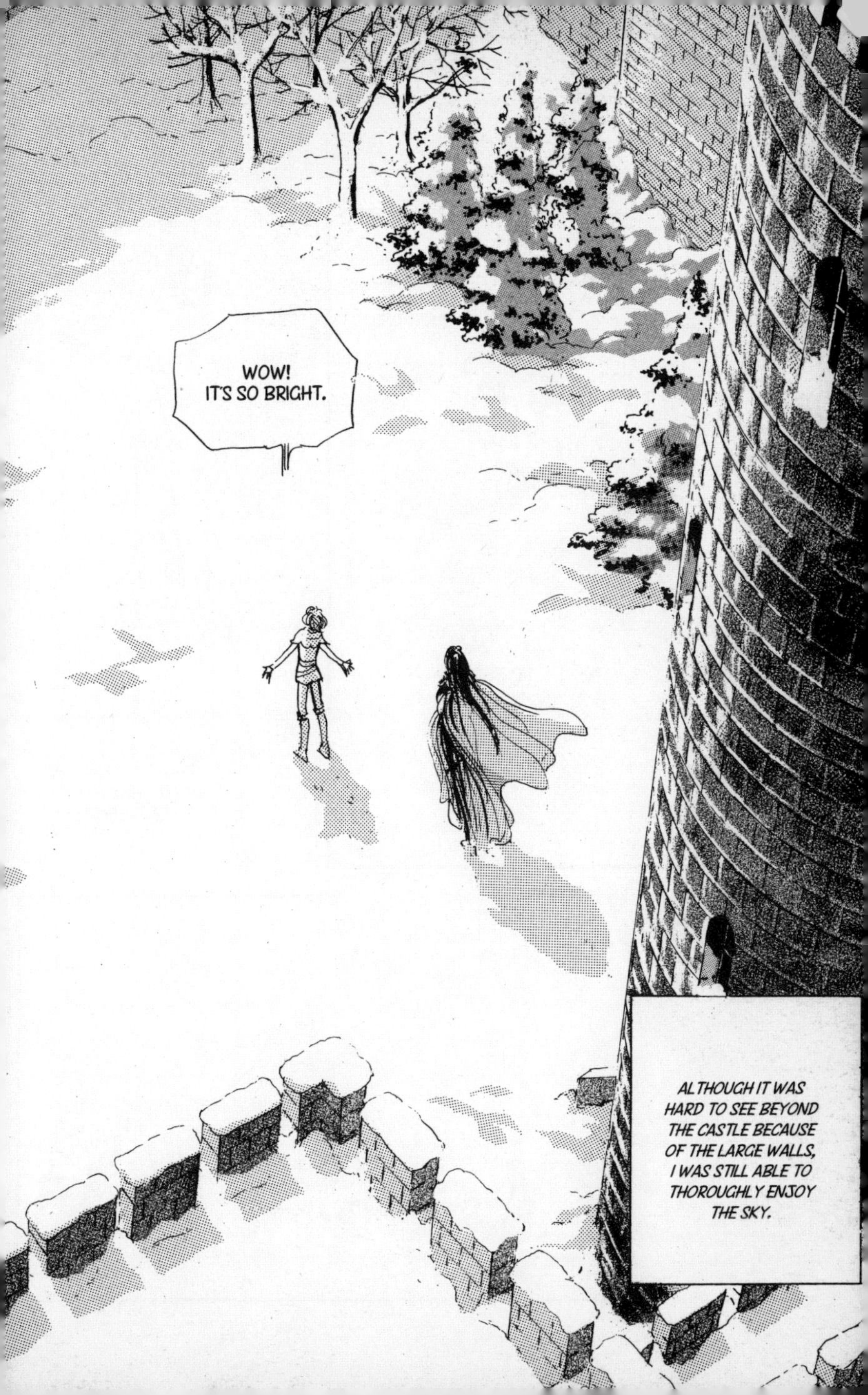
WOW!
IT'S SO BRIGHT.
ALTHOUGH IT WAS HARD TO SEE BEYOND THE CASTLE BECAUSE OF THE LARGE WALLS, I WAS STILL ABLE TO THOROUGHLY ENJOY THE SKY.

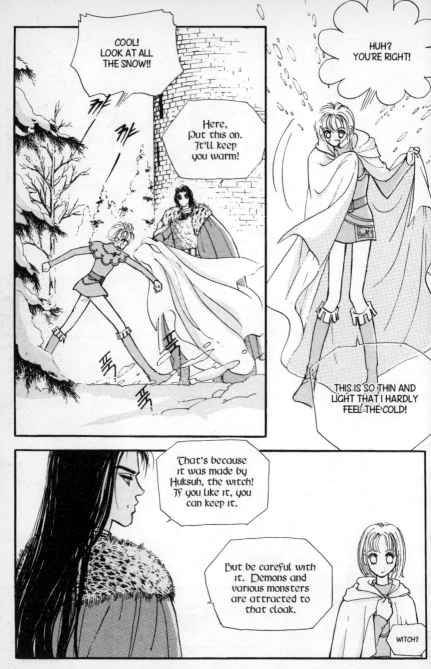

COOL! LOOK AT ALL THE SNOW!!

Here, put this on. It'll keep you warm!

HUH? YOU'RE RIGHT!

THIS IS SO THIN AND LIGHT THAT I HARDLY FEEL THE COLD!

That's because it was made by Huksuh, the witch! If you like it, you can keep it.

But be careful with it. Demons and various monsters are attracted to that cloak.

WITCH?

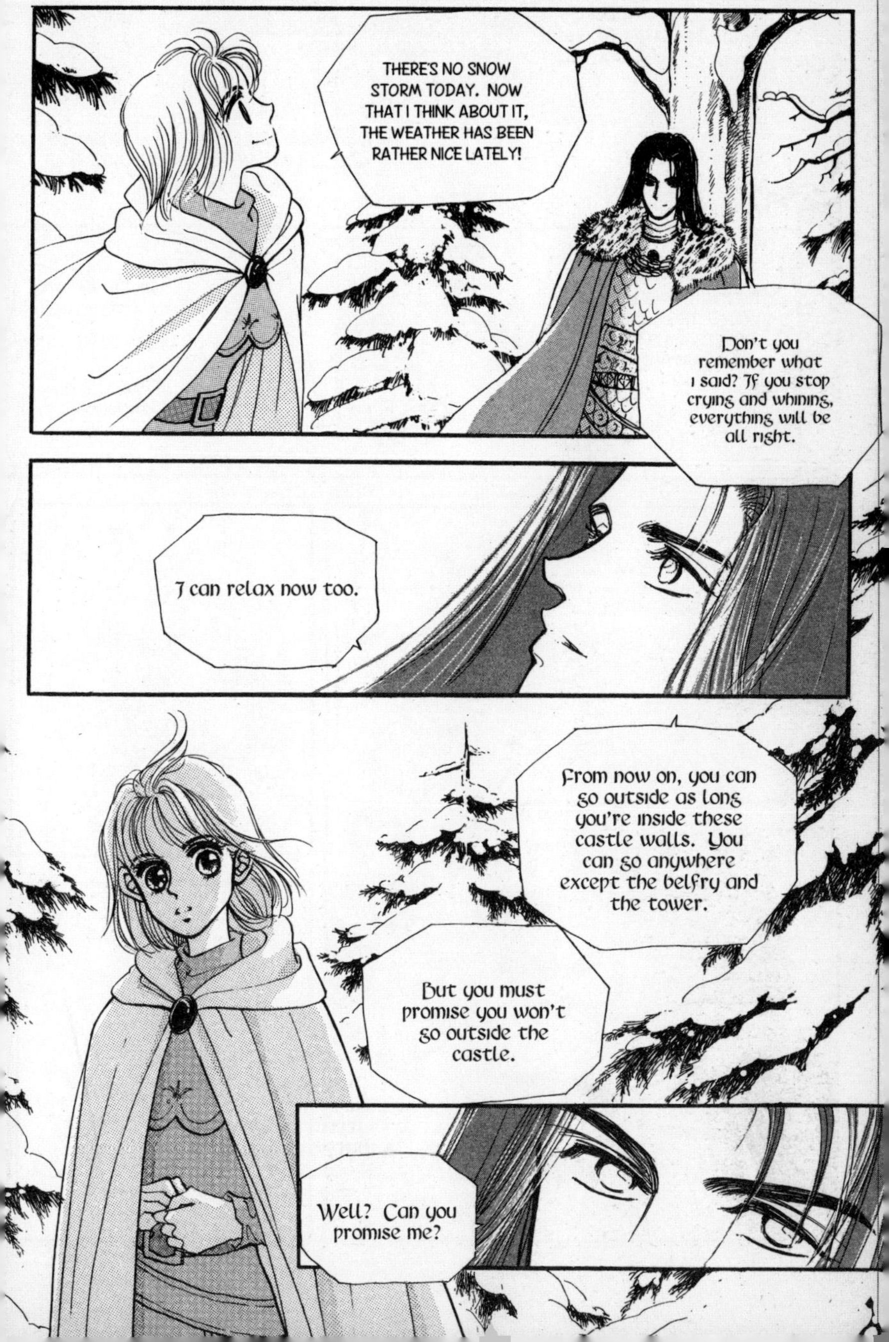
THERE'S NO SNOW STORM TODAY. NOW THAT I THINK ABOUT IT, THE WEATHER HAS BEEN RATHER NICE LATELY!
Don't you remember what I said? If you stop crying and whining, everything will be all right.
I can relax now too.
From now on, you can go outside as long you're inside these castle walls. You can go anywhere except the belfry and the tower.
But you must promise you won't go outside the castle.
Well? Can you promise me?

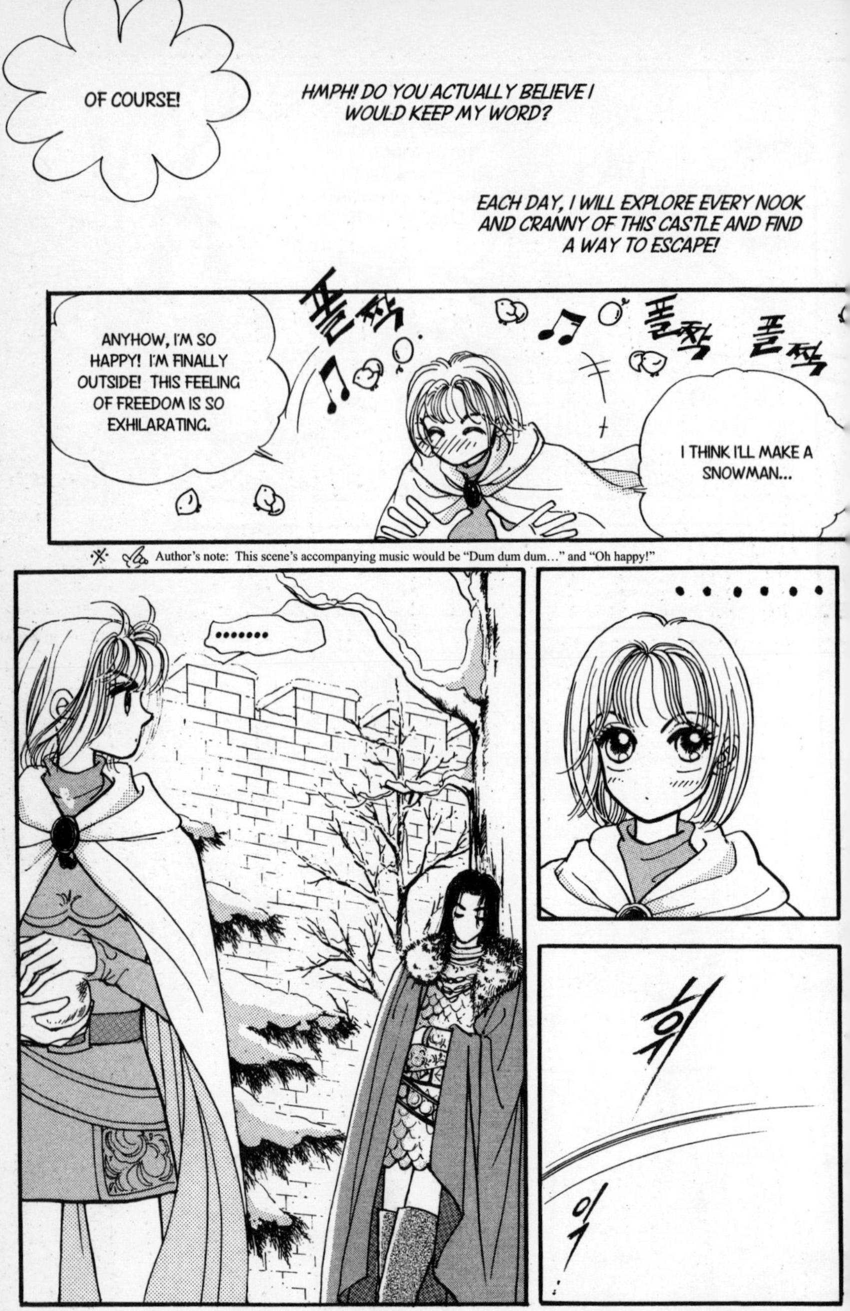
OF COURSE!
HMPH! DO YOU ACTUALLY BELIEVE I WOULD KEEP MY WORD?
EACH DAY, I WILL EXPLORE EVERY NOOK AND CRANNY OF THIS CASTLE AND FIND A WAY TO ESCAPE!
폴짝
ANYHOW, I'M SO HAPPY! I'M FINALLY OUTSIDE! THIS FEELING OF FREEDOM IS SO EXHILARATING.
폴짝 폴짝
I THINK I'LL MAKE A SNOWMAN...
※ Author's note: This scene's accompanying music would be "Dum dum dum…" and "Oh happy!"
....
• • • • • •
휘익

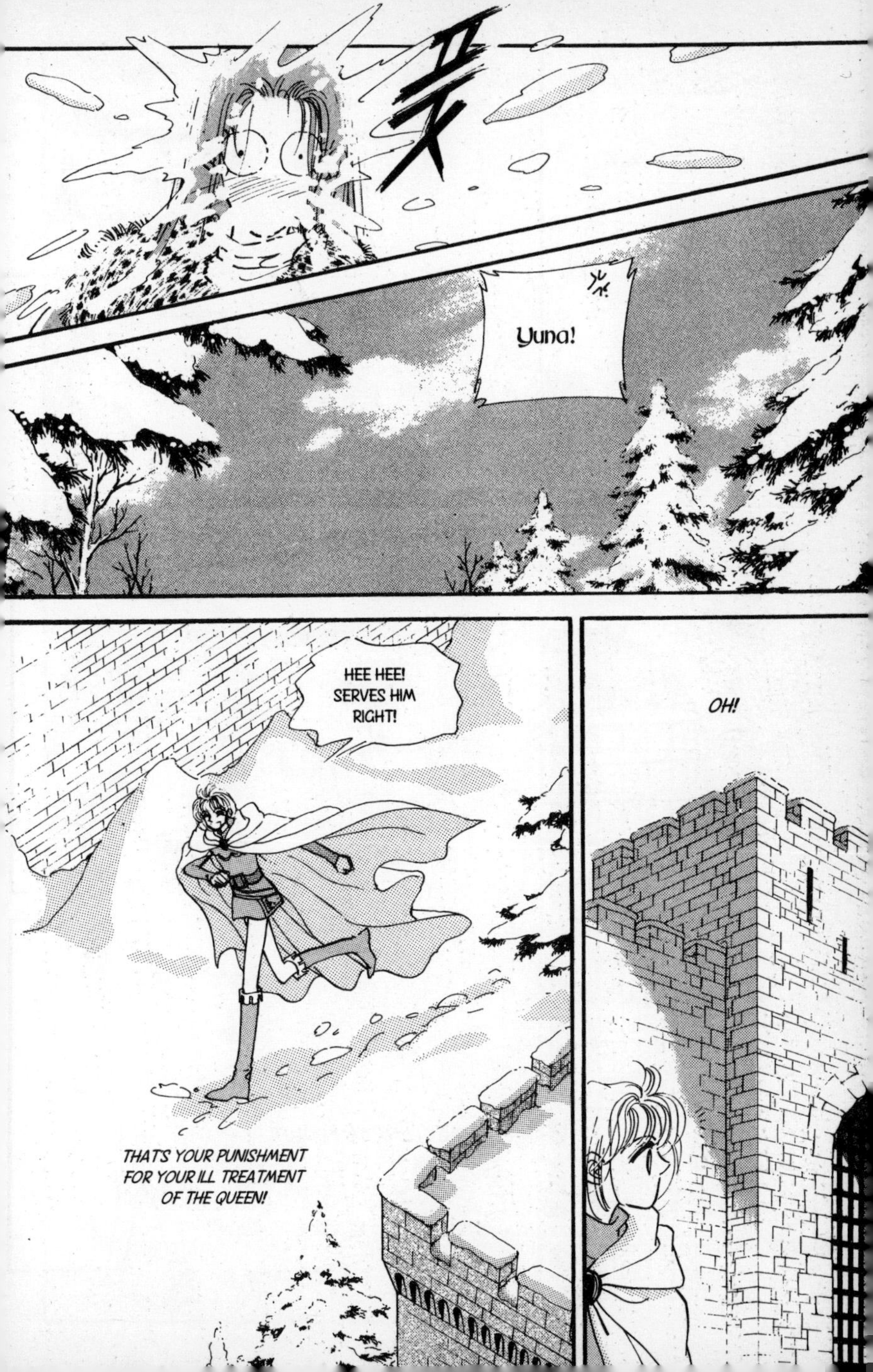
Yuna!
HEE HEE! SERVES HIM RIGHT!
THATS YOUR PUNISHMENT FOR YOUR ILL TREATMENT OF THE QUEEN!
OH!

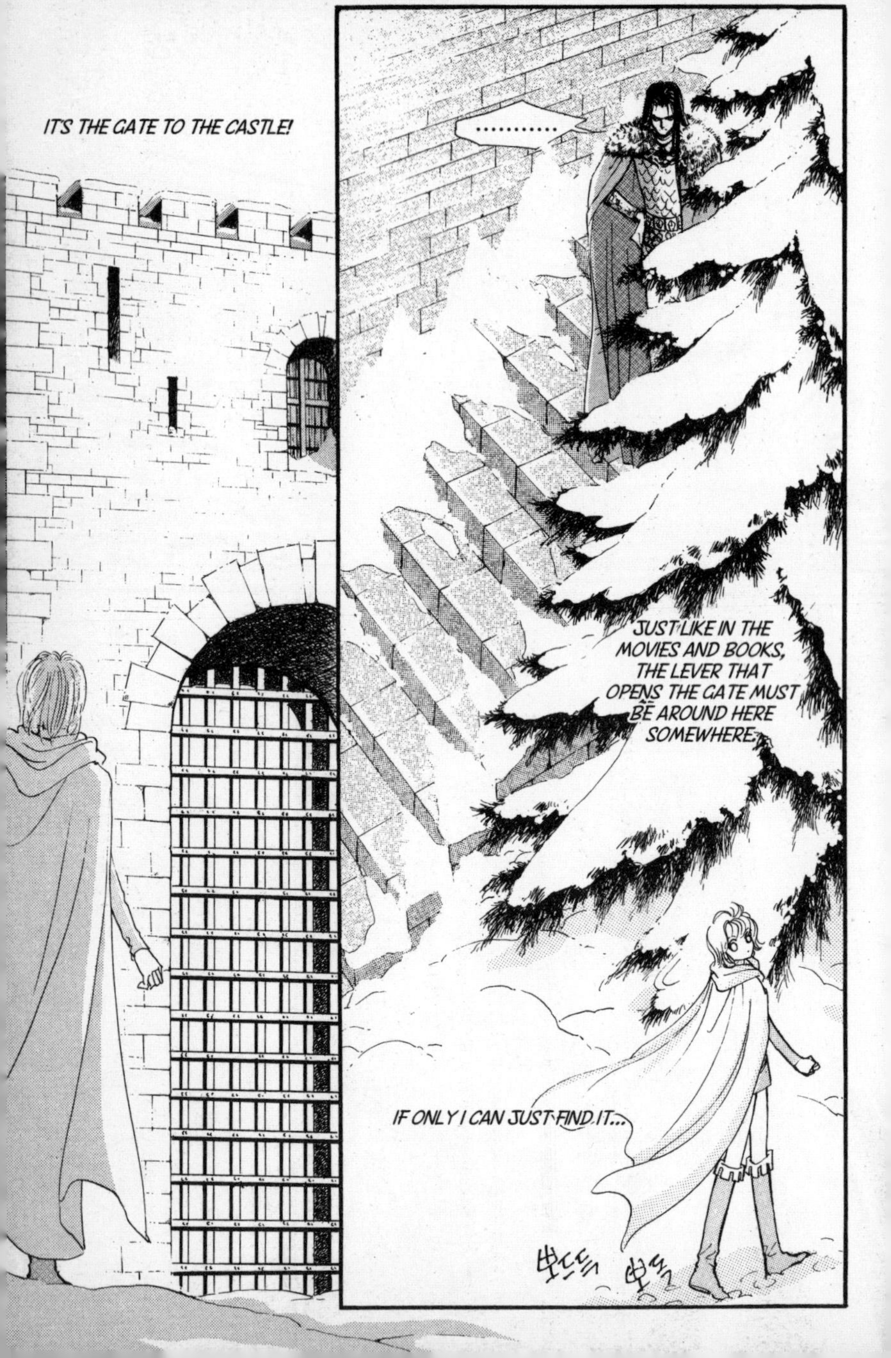
IT'S THE GATE TO THE CASTLE!
....
JUST LIKE IN THE MOVIES AND BOOKS, THE LEVER THAT OPENS THE GATE MUST BE AROUND HERE SOMEWHERE.
IF ONLY I CAN JUST FIND IT...
뽀드득 뽀득

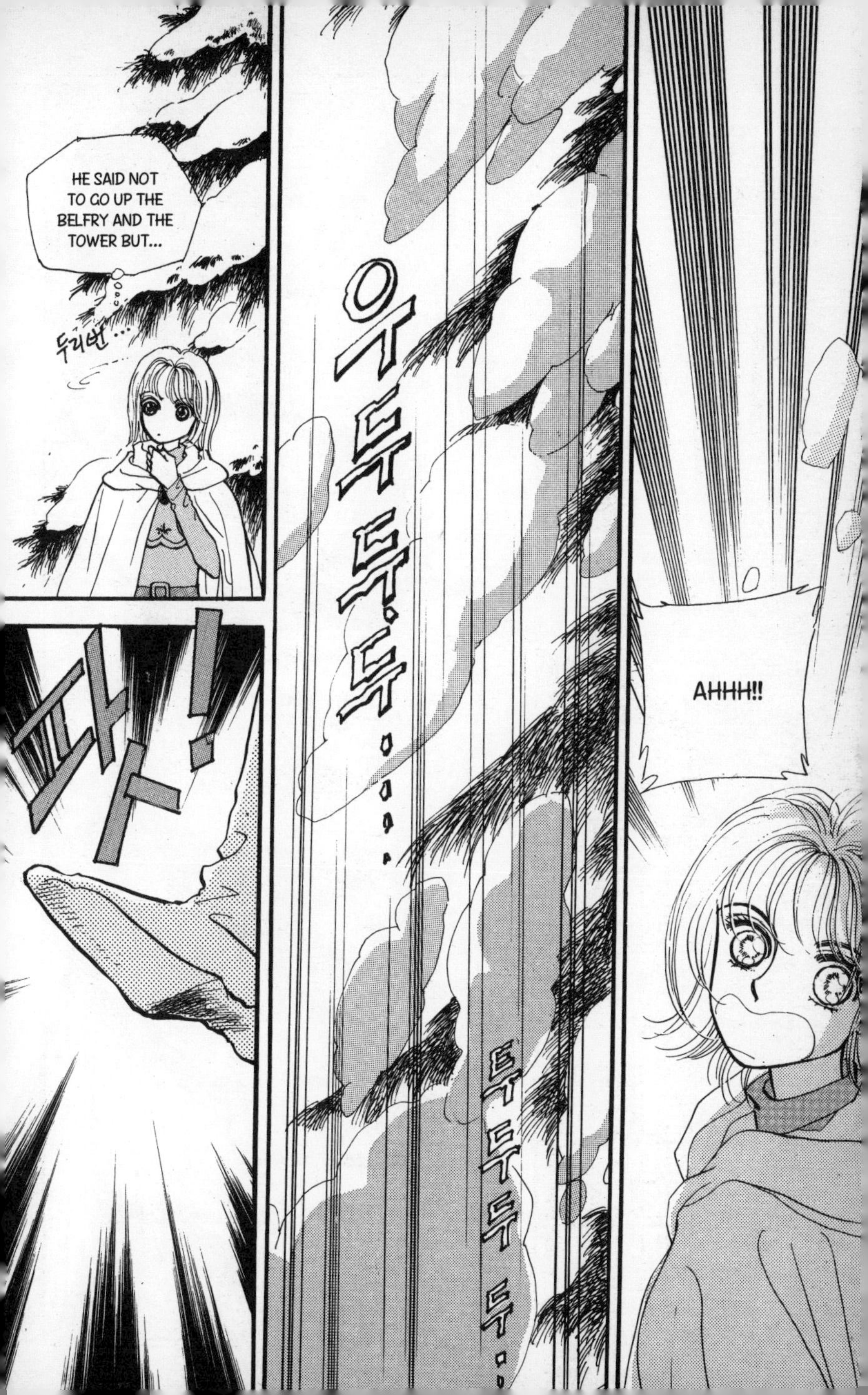
HE SAID NOT TO GO UP THE BELFRY AND THE TOWER BUT...
두리번...
AHHH!!

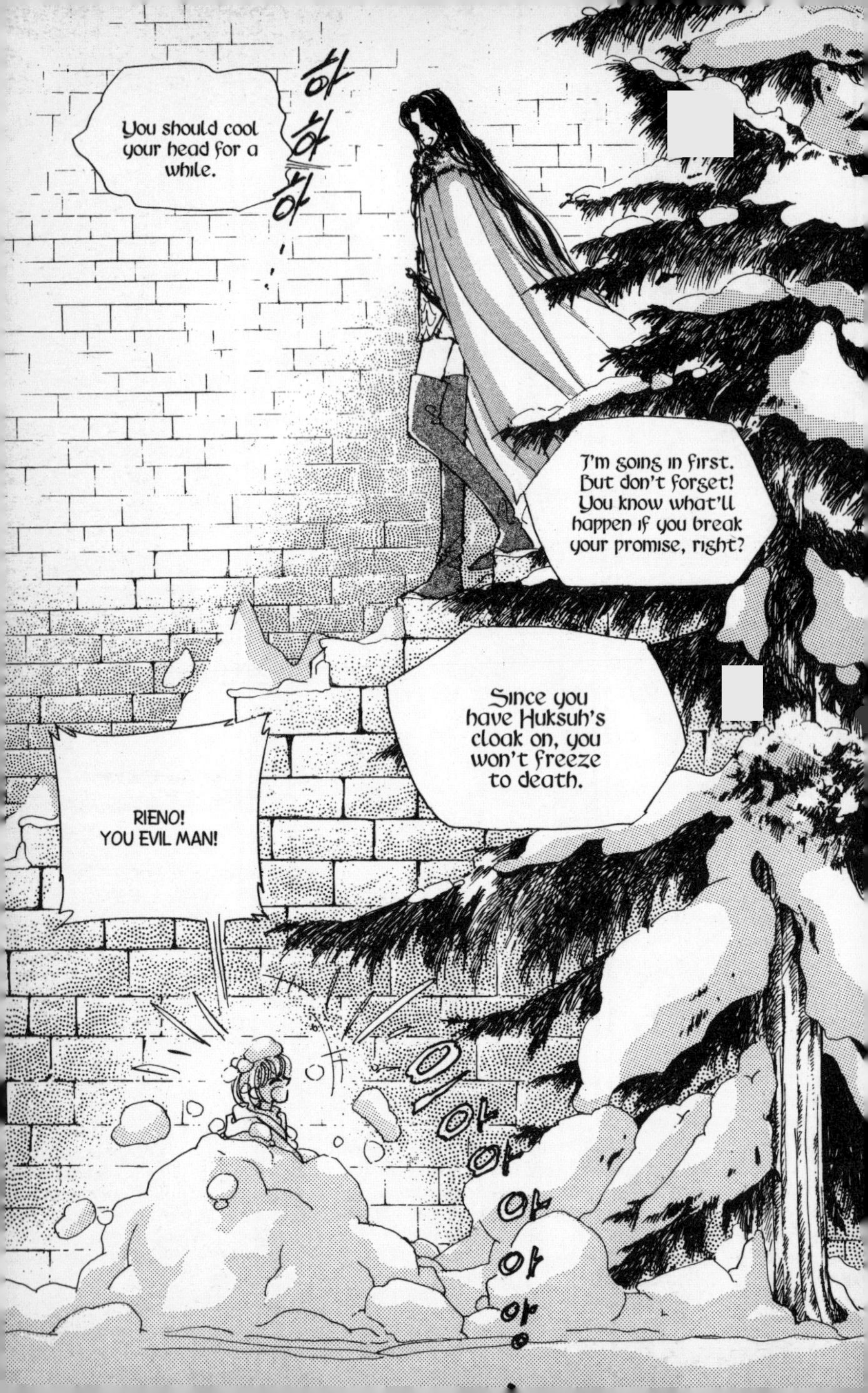
You should cool your head for a while.
하하하...
I'm going in first. But don't forget! You know what'll happen if you break your promise, right?
Since you have Huksuh's cloak on, you won't freeze to death.
RIENO! YOU EVIL MAN!

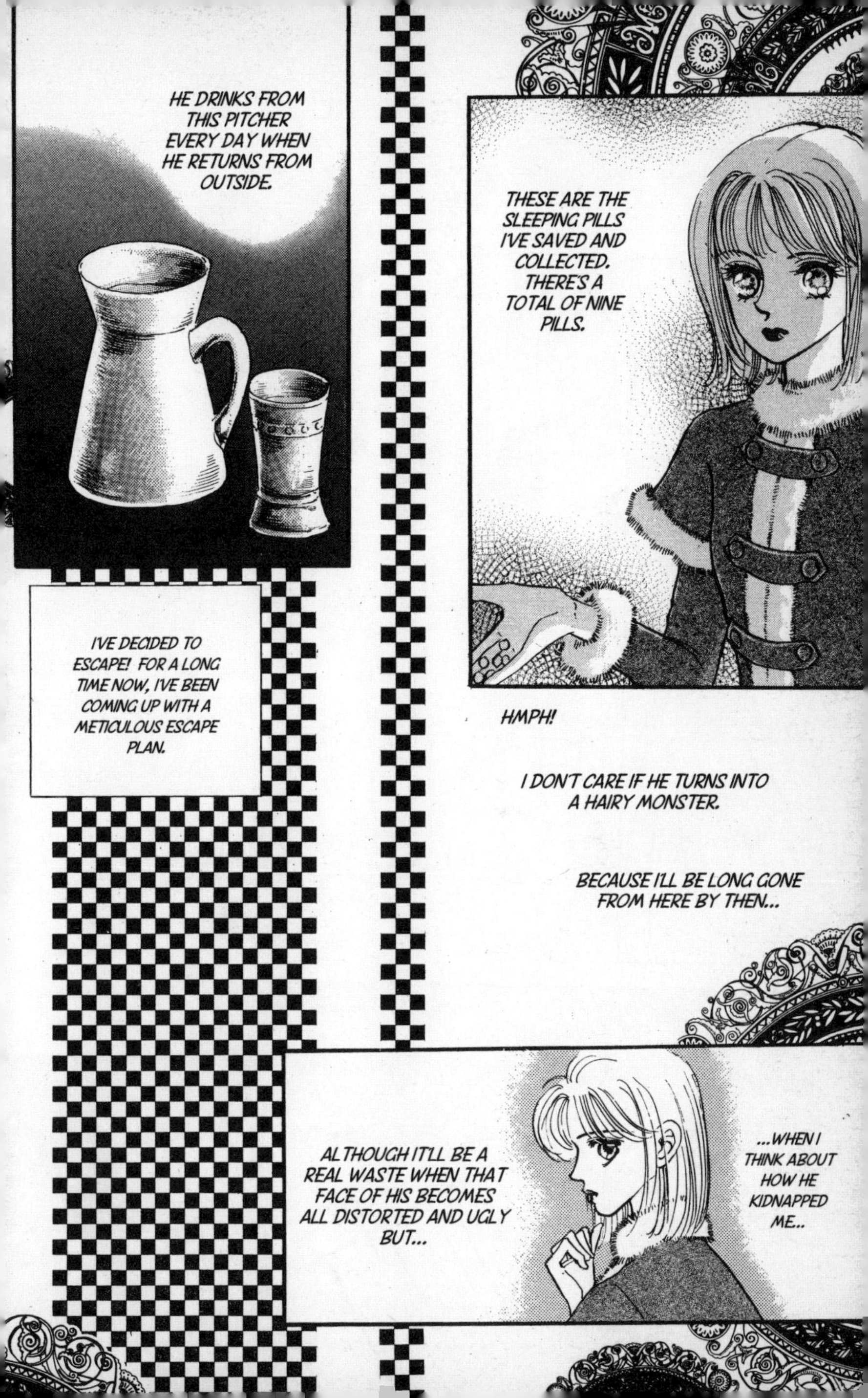
HE DRINKS FROM THIS PITCHER EVERY DAY WHEN HE RETURNS FROM OUTSIDE.
I'VE DECIDED TO ESCAPE! FOR A LONG TIME NOW, I'VE BEEN COMING UP WITH A METICULOUS ESCAPE PLAN.
THESE ARE THE SLEEPING PILLS I'VE SAVED AND COLLECTED. THERE'S A TOTAL OF NINE PILLS.
HMPH!
I DON'T CARE IF HE TURNS INTO A HAIRY MONSTER.
BECAUSE I'LL BE LONG GONE FROM HERE BY THEN...
ALTHOUGH IT'LL BE A REAL WASTE WHEN THAT FACE OF HIS BECOMES ALL DISTORTED AND UGLY BUT...
...WHEN I THINK ABOUT HOW HE KIDNAPPED ME...

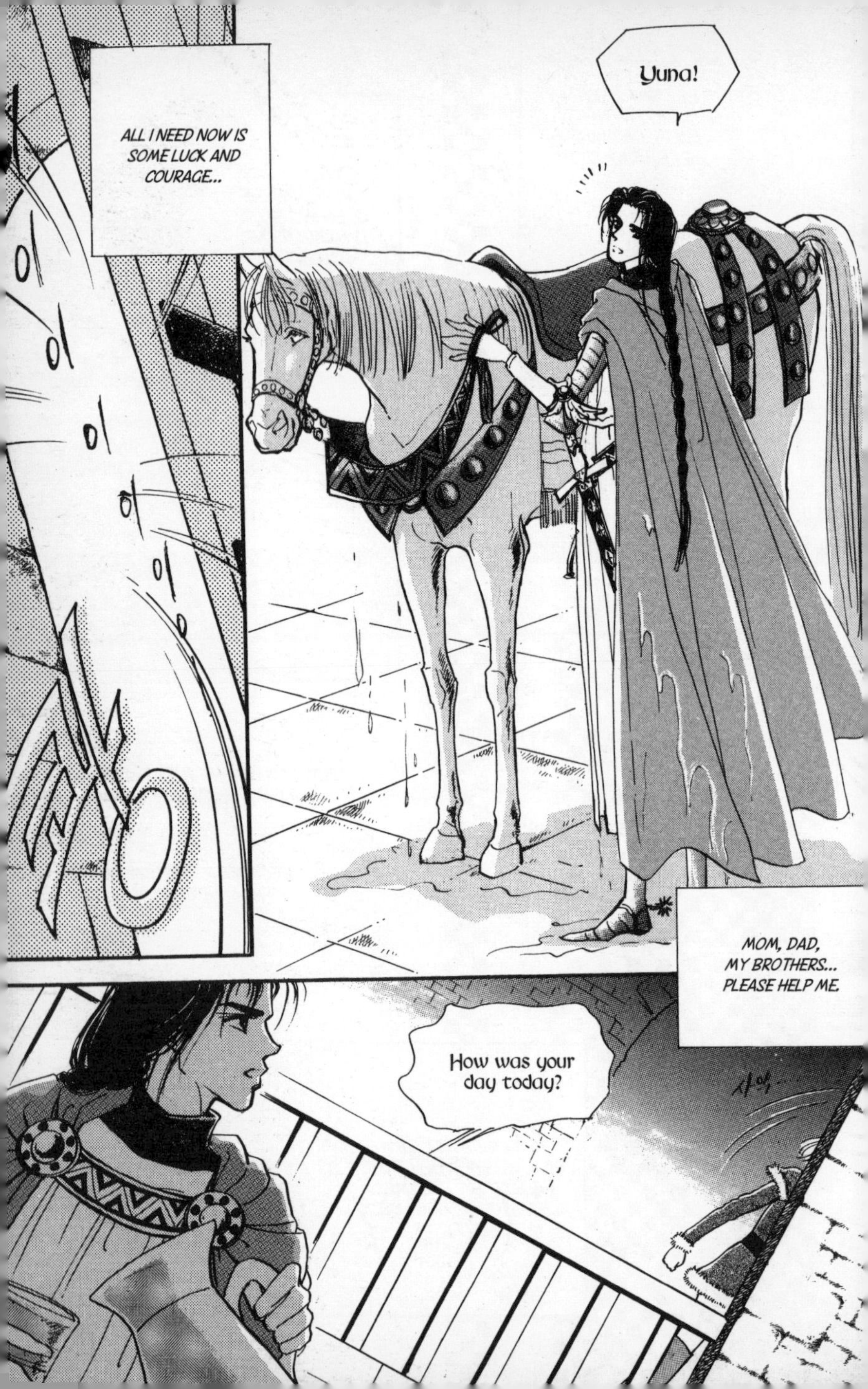
ALL I NEED NOW IS SOME LUCK AND COURAGE...
Yuna!
MOM, DAD, MY BROTHERS... PLEASE HELP ME.
How was your day today?

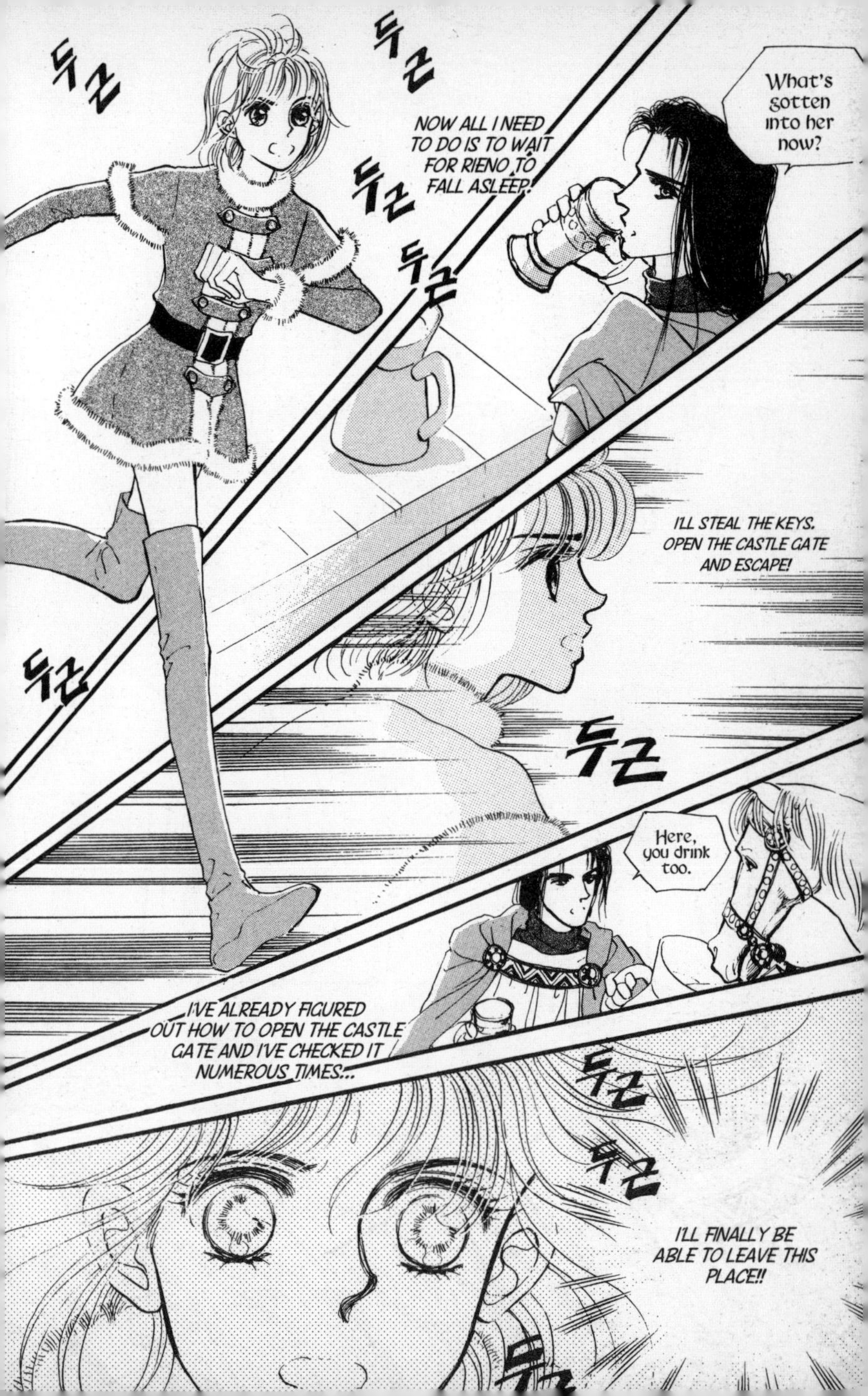
두근
두근
두근
두근
두근
NOW ALL I NEED TO DO IS TO WAIT FOR RIENO TO FALL ASLEEP!
What's gotten into her now?
I'LL STEAL THE KEYS. OPEN THE CASTLE GATE AND ESCAPE!
두근
Here, you drink too.
I'VE ALREADY FIGURED OUT HOW TO OPEN THE CASTLE GATE AND I'VE CHECKED IT NUMEROUS TIMES...
두근
두근
I'LL FINALLY BE ABLE TO LEAVE THIS PLACE!!

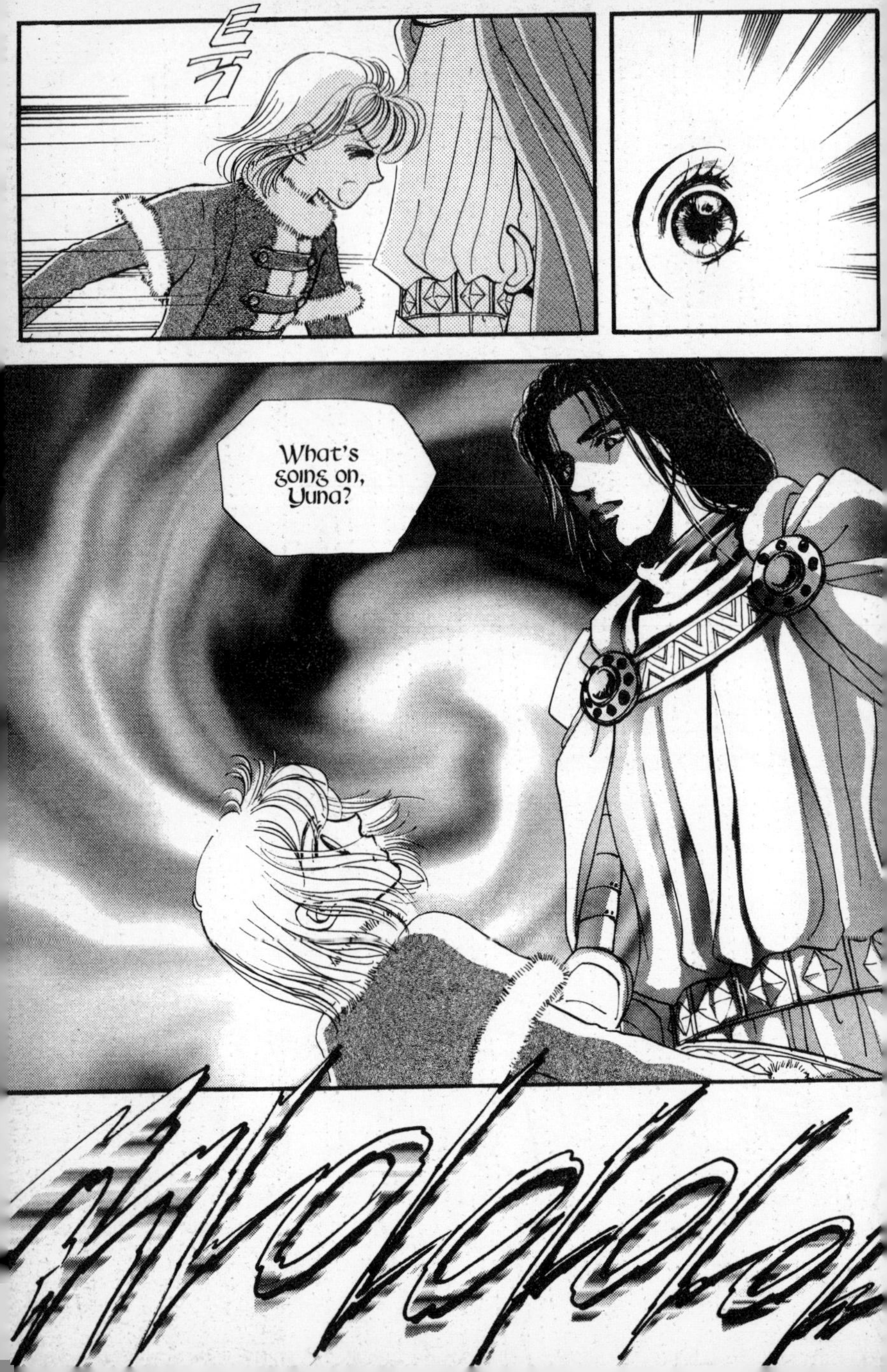
What's going on, Yuna?

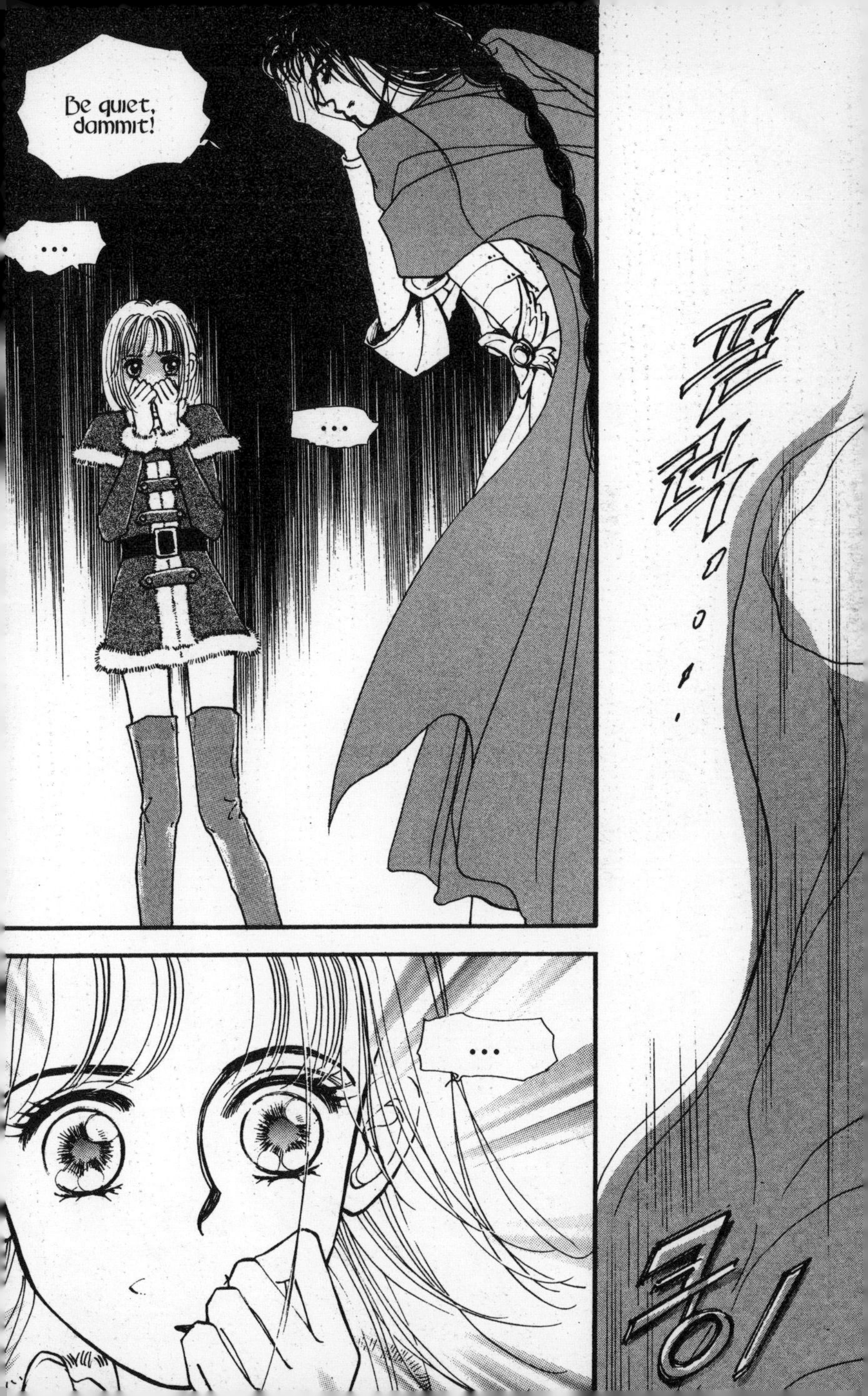

Be quiet, dammit!
...
...
...
펄럭
쿵!

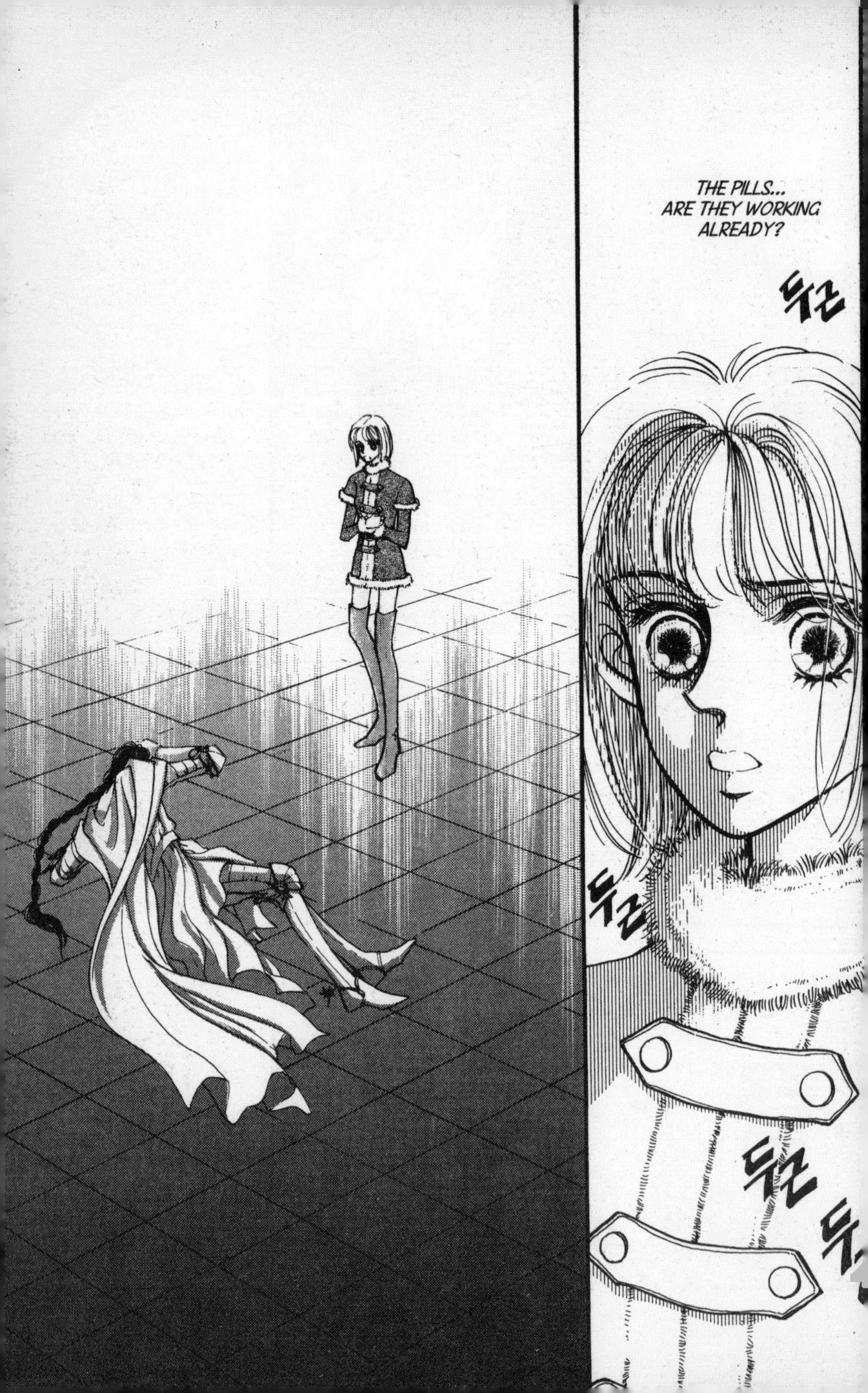
THE PILLS... ARE THEY WORKING ALREADY?
두근
두근
두근

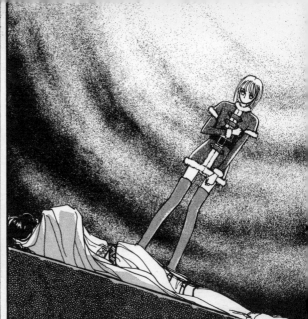

MAYBE IT'S BECAUSE I GAVE HIM NINE OF THEM...?

I NEED THE KEYS...

RIENO...

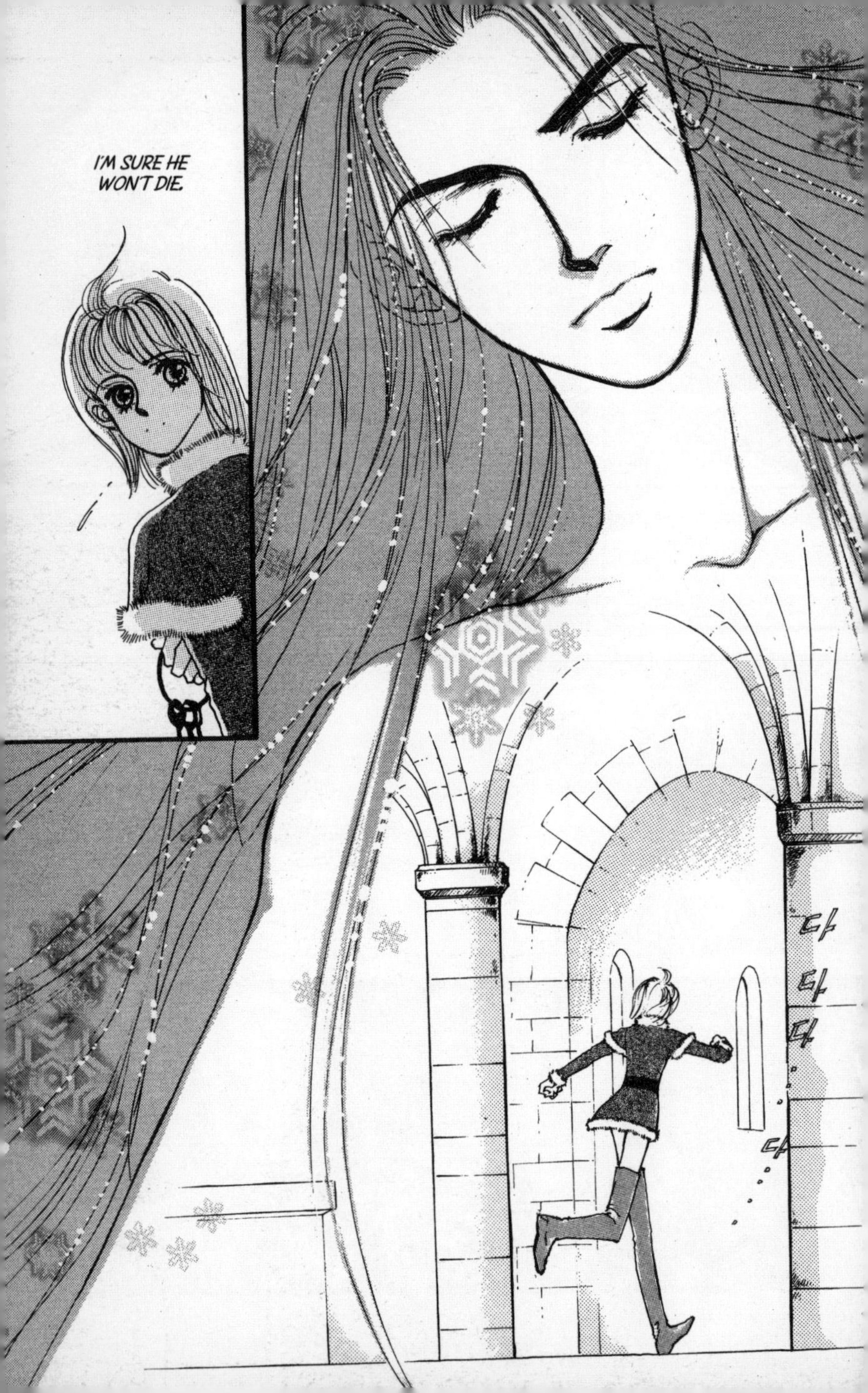
I'M SURE HE WON'T DIE.

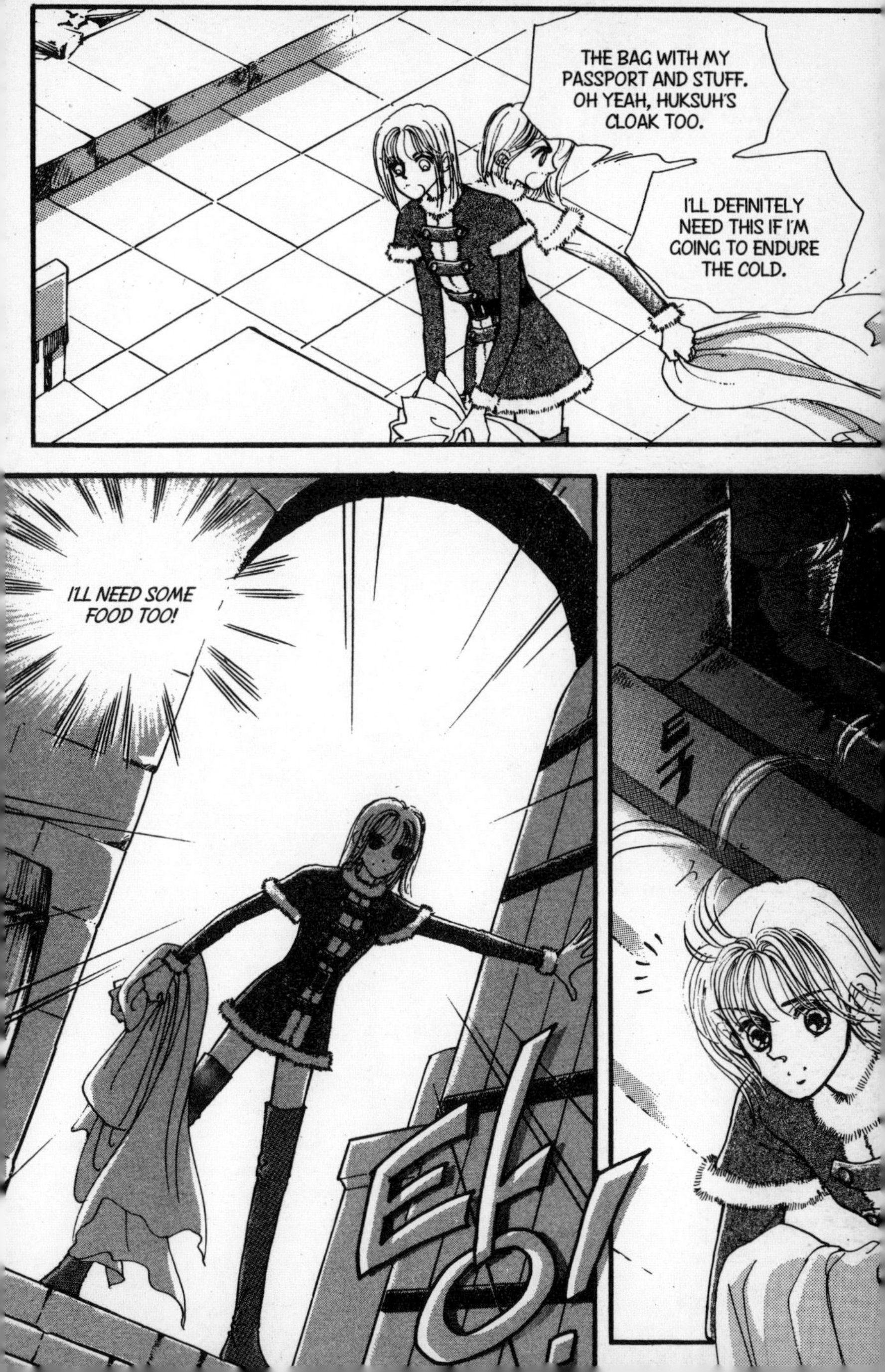
THE BAG WITH MY PASSPORT AND STUFF. OH YEAH, HUKSUH'S CLOAK TOO.
I'LL DEFINITELY NEED THIS IF I'M GOING TO ENDURE THE COLD.
I'LL NEED SOME FOOD TOO!

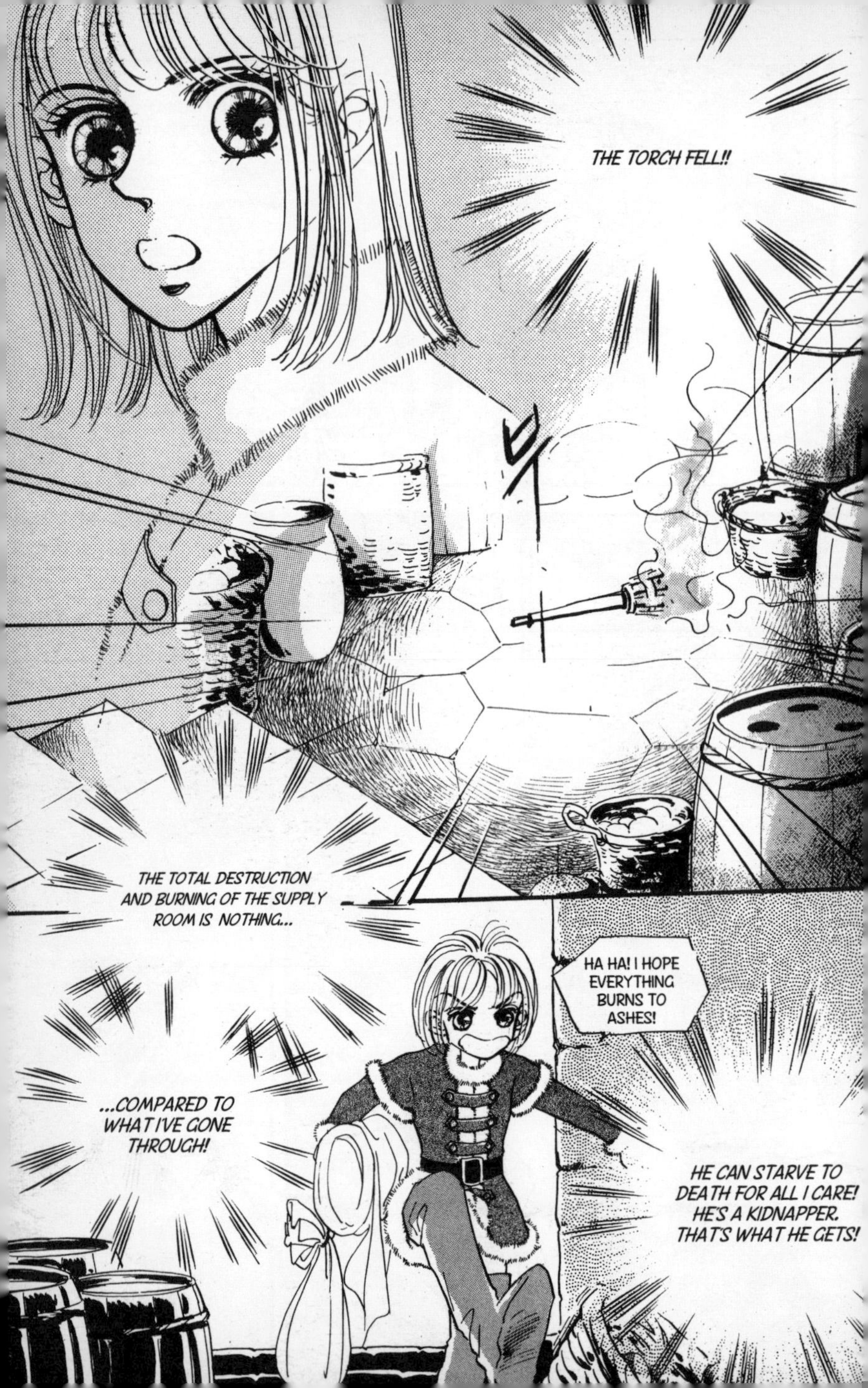
THE TORCH FELL!!
THE TOTAL DESTRUCTION AND BURNING OF THE SUPPLY ROOM IS NOTHING...
...COMPARED TO WHAT I'VE GONE THROUGH!
HA HA! I HOPE EVERYTHING BURNS TO ASHES!
HE CAN STARVE TO DEATH FOR ALL I CARE! HE'S A KIDNAPPER. THAT'S WHAT HE GETS!

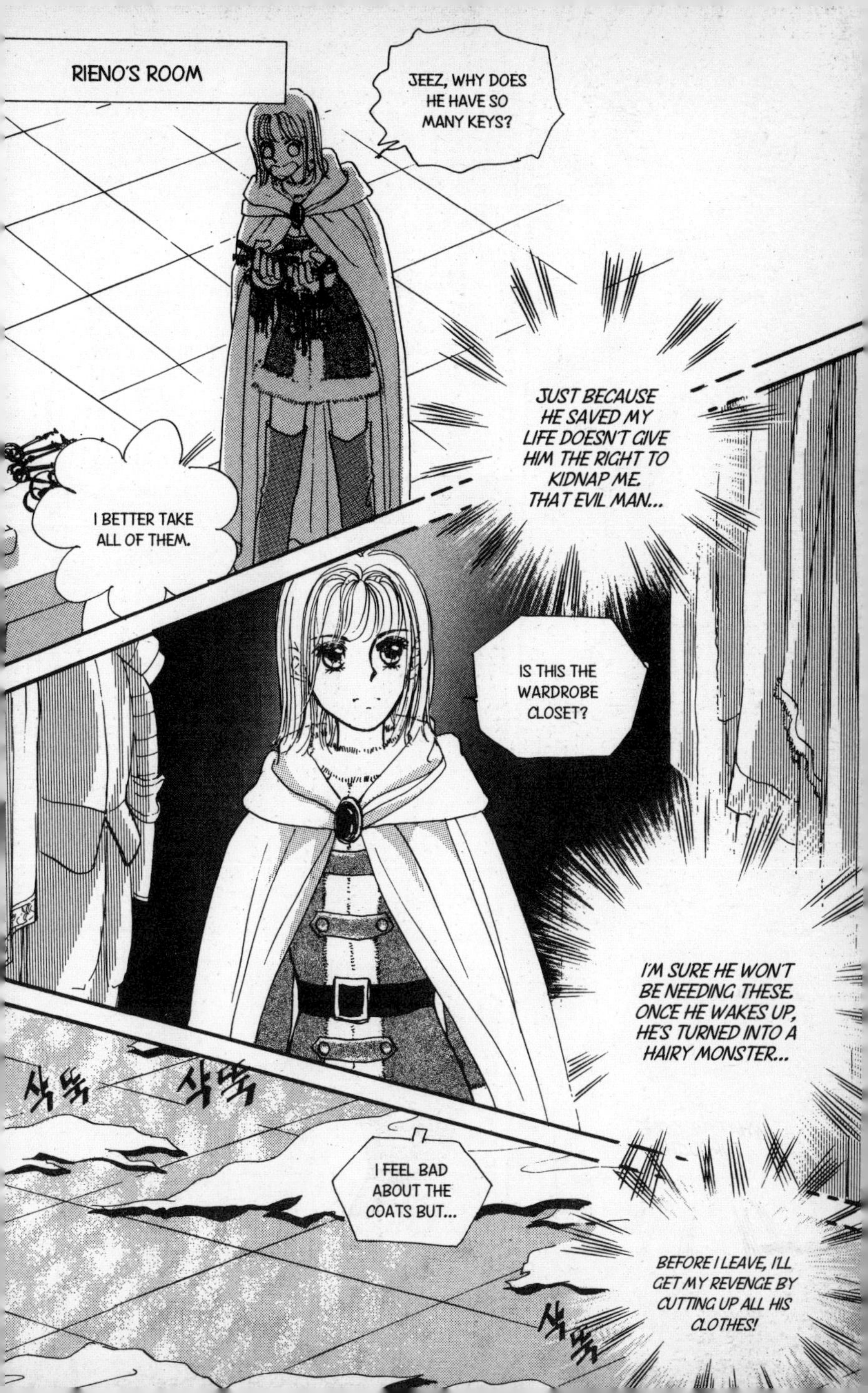
RIENO'S ROOM
JEEZ, WHY DOES HE HAVE SO MANY KEYS?
I BETTER TAKE ALL OF THEM.
JUST BECAUSE HE SAVED MY LIFE DOESN'T GIVE HIM THE RIGHT TO KIDNAP ME. THAT EVIL MAN...
IS THIS THE WARDROBE CLOSET?
I'M SURE HE WON'T BE NEEDING THESE. ONCE HE WAKES UP, HE'S TURNED INTO A HAIRY MONSTER...
I FEEL BAD ABOUT THE COATS BUT...
BEFORE I LEAVE, I'LL GET MY REVENGE BY CUTTING UP ALL HIS CLOTHES!

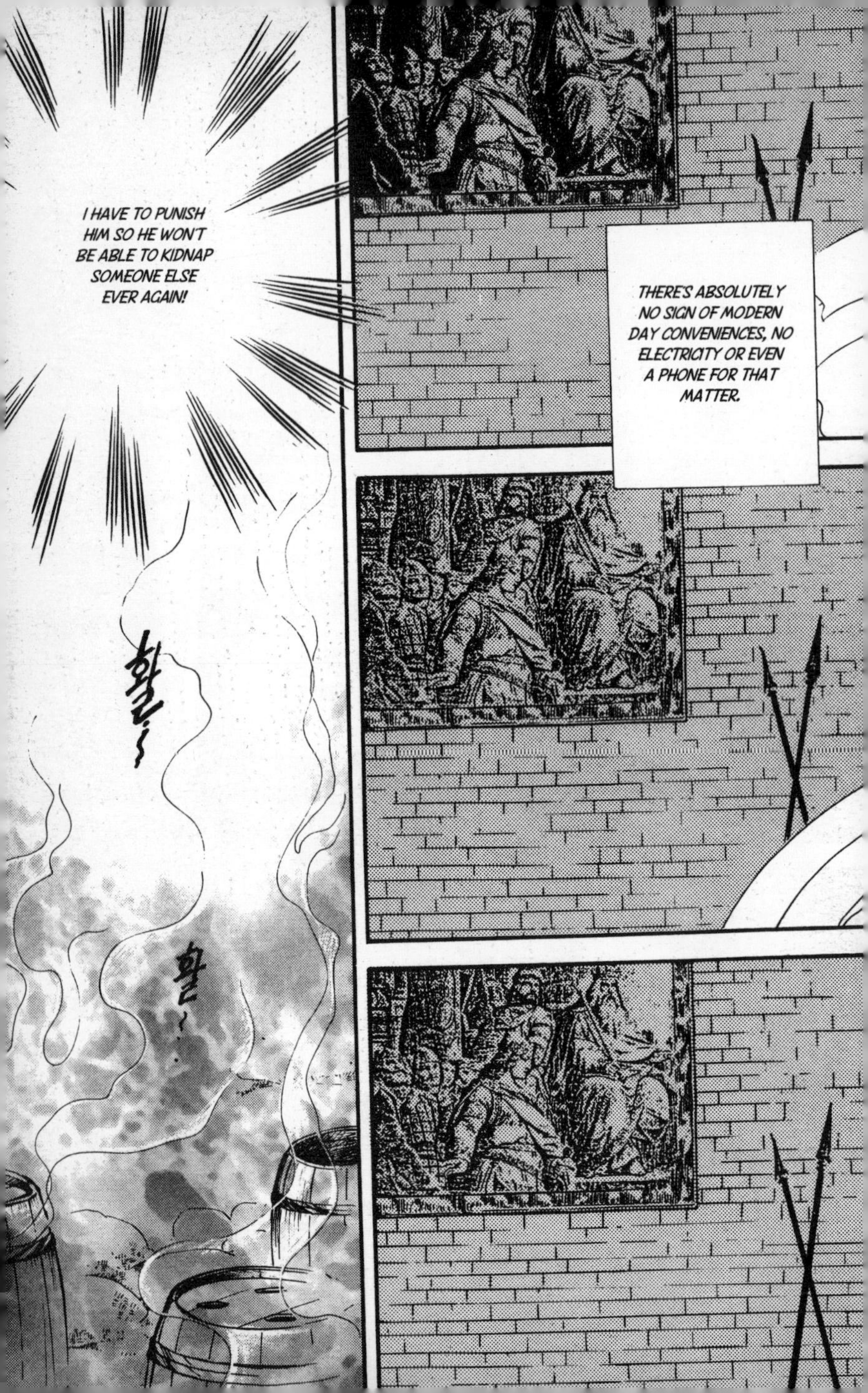
I HAVE TO PUNISH HIM SO HE WON'T BE ABLE TO KIDNAP SOMEONE ELSE EVER AGAIN!
활~
활~...
THERE'S ABSOLUTELY NO SIGN OF MODERN DAY CONVENIENCES, NO ELECTRICITY OR EVEN A PHONE FOR THAT MATTER.

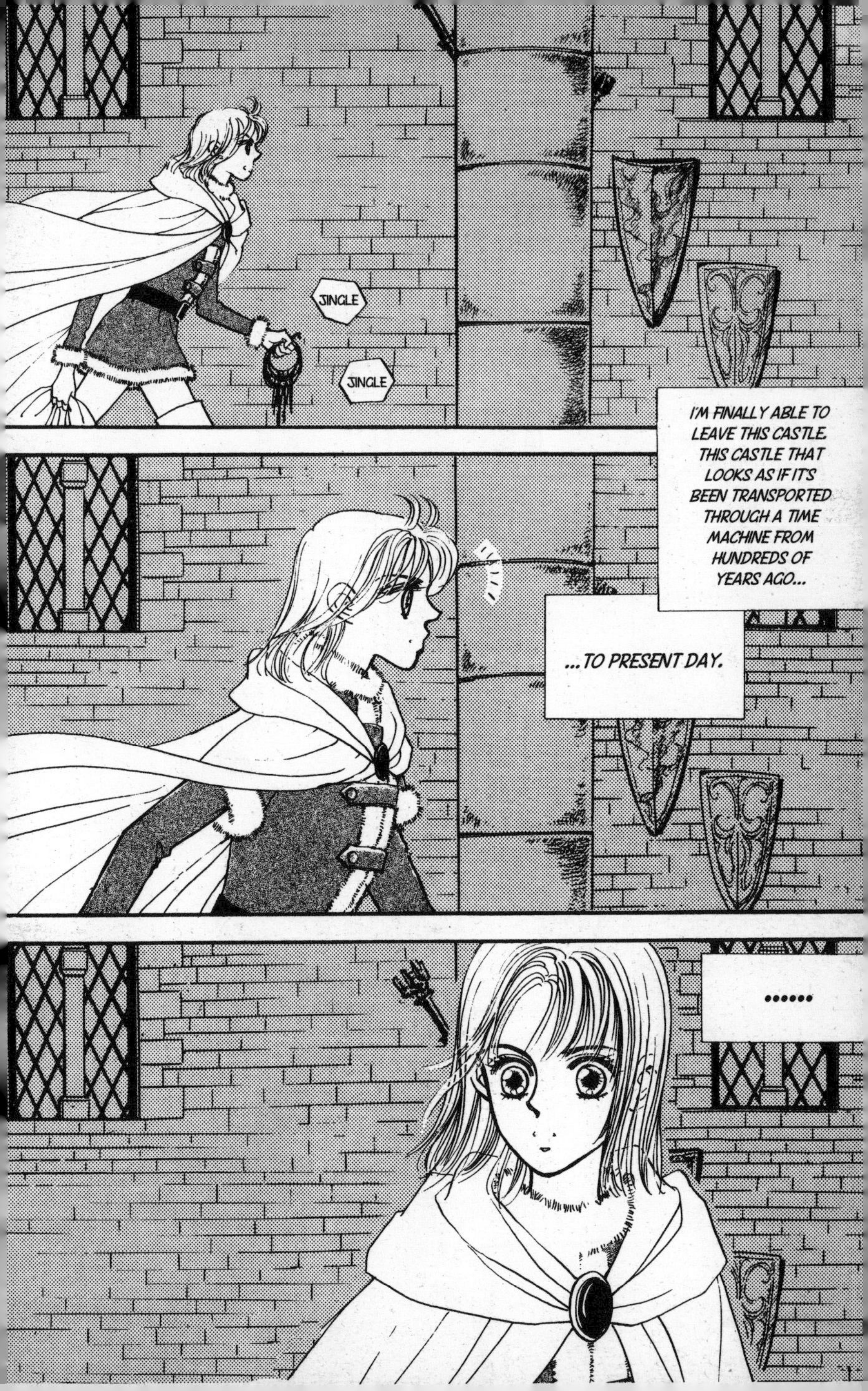
JINGLE
JINGLE
I'M FINALLY ABLE TO LEAVE THIS CASTLE. THIS CASTLE THAT LOOKS AS IF ITS BEEN TRANSPORTED THROUGH A TIME MACHINE FROM HUNDREDS OF YEARS AGO...
...TO PRESENT DAY.
......

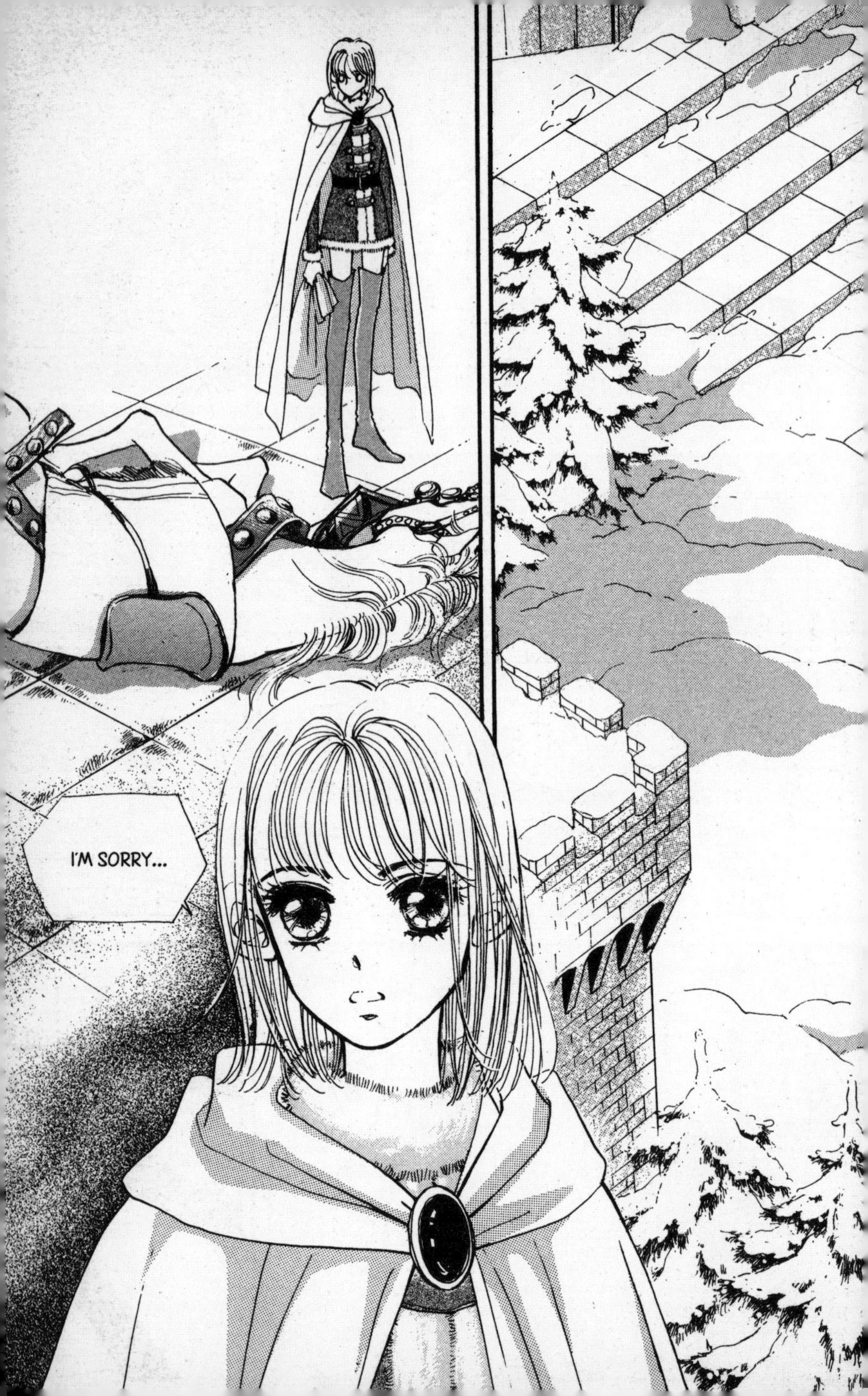
I'M SORRY...

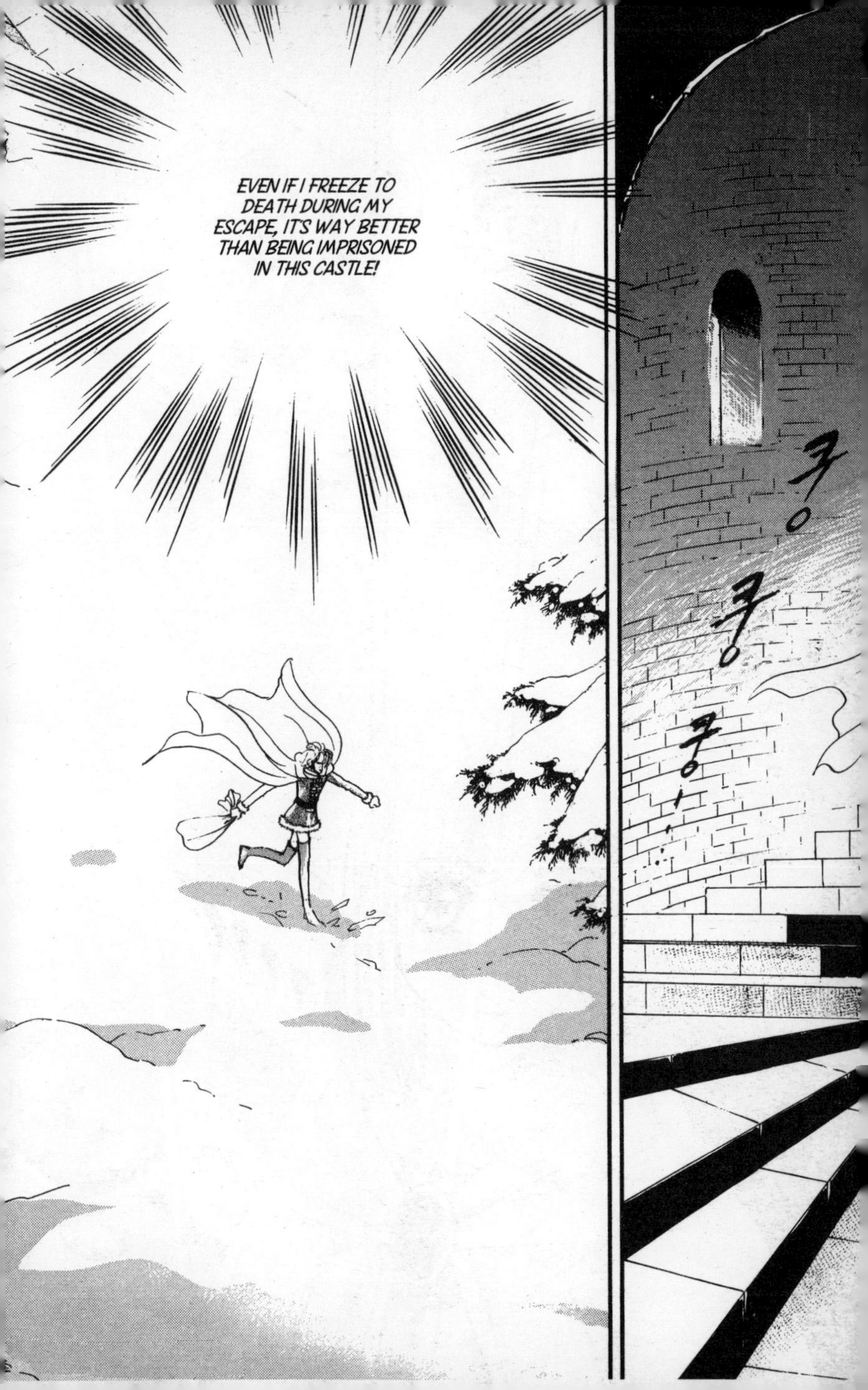
EVEN IF I FREEZE TO DEATH DURING MY ESCAPE, IT'S WAY BETTER THAN BEING IMPRISONED IN THIS CASTLE!
쿵
쿵
쿵!

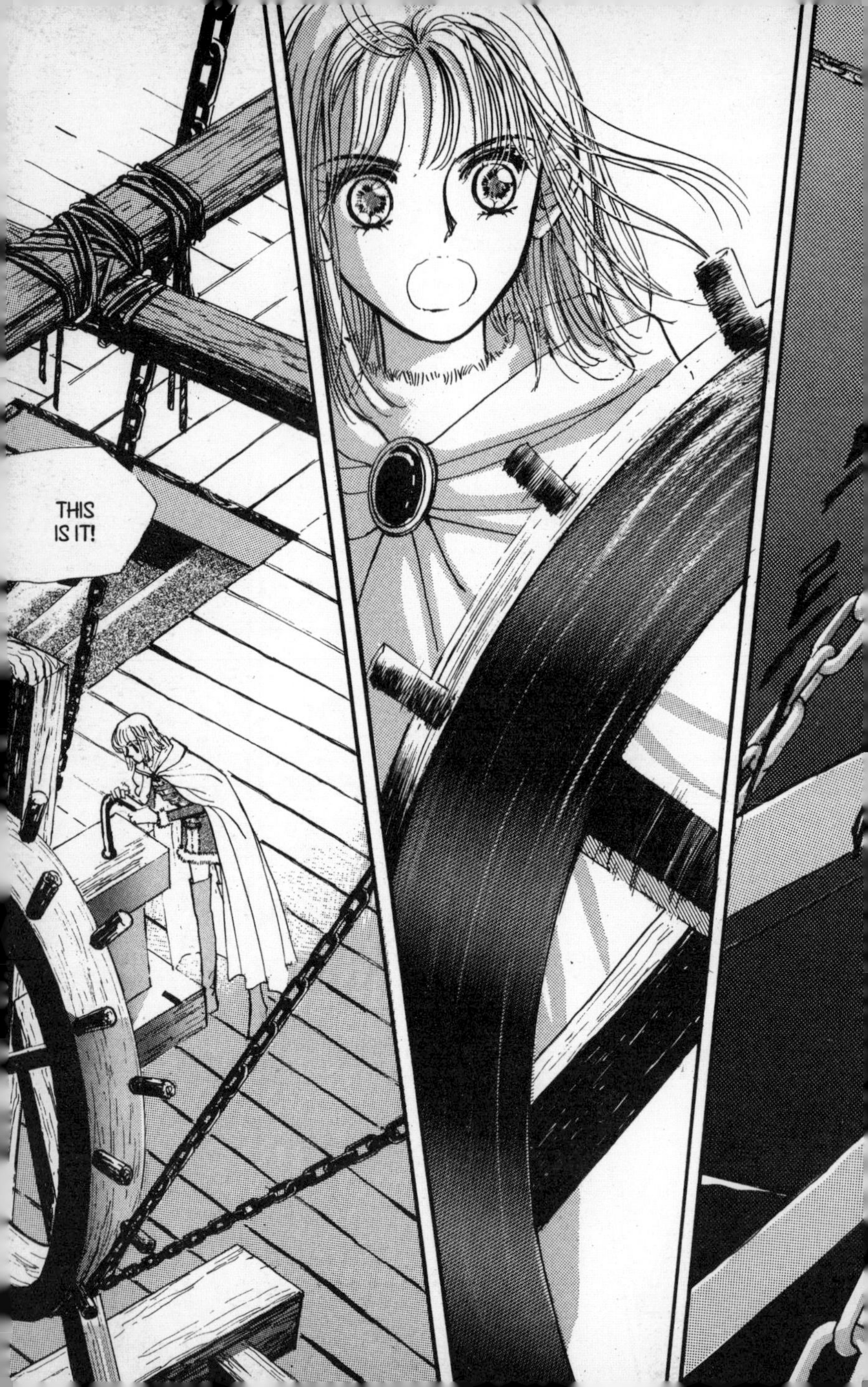
THIS IS IT!

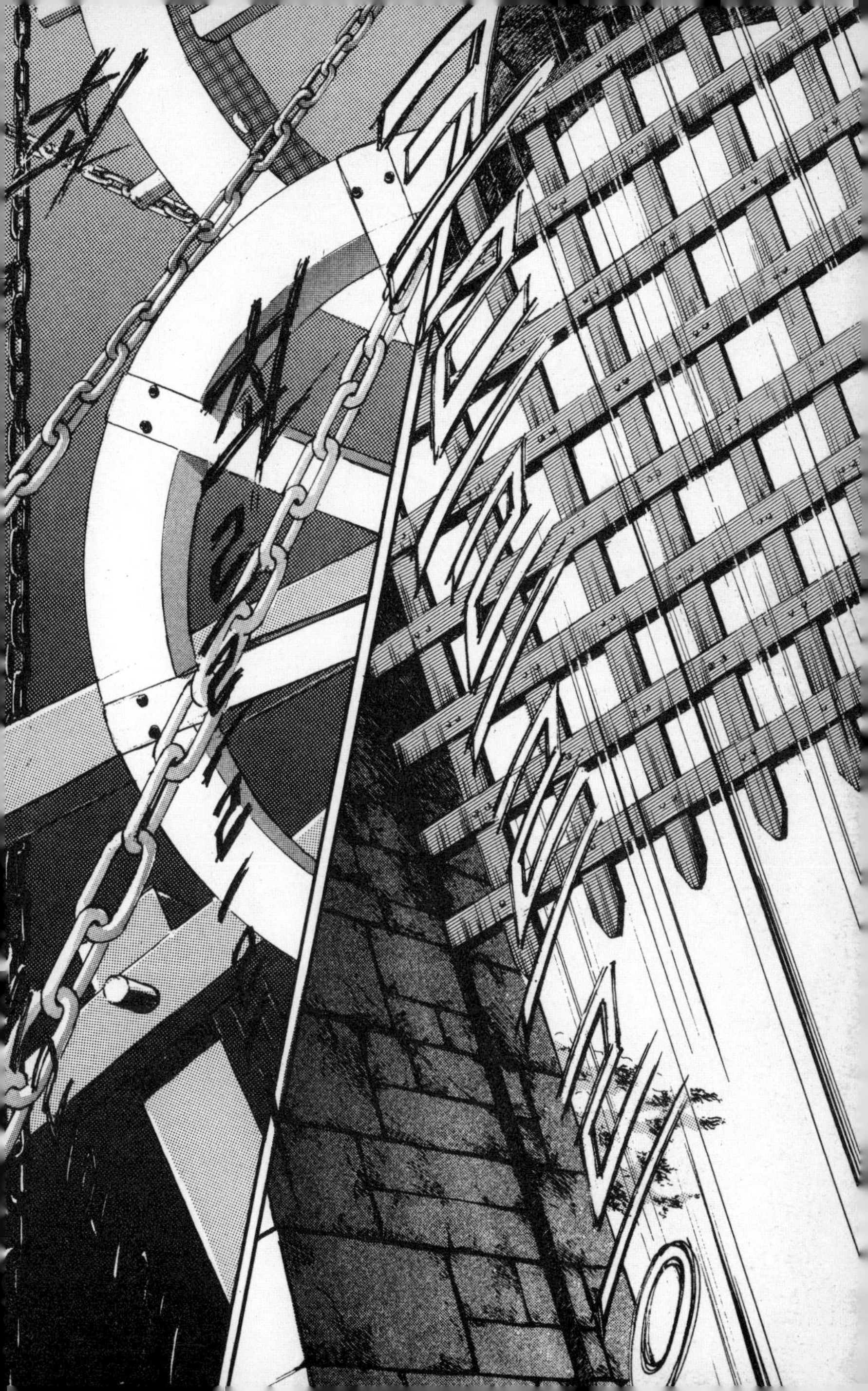

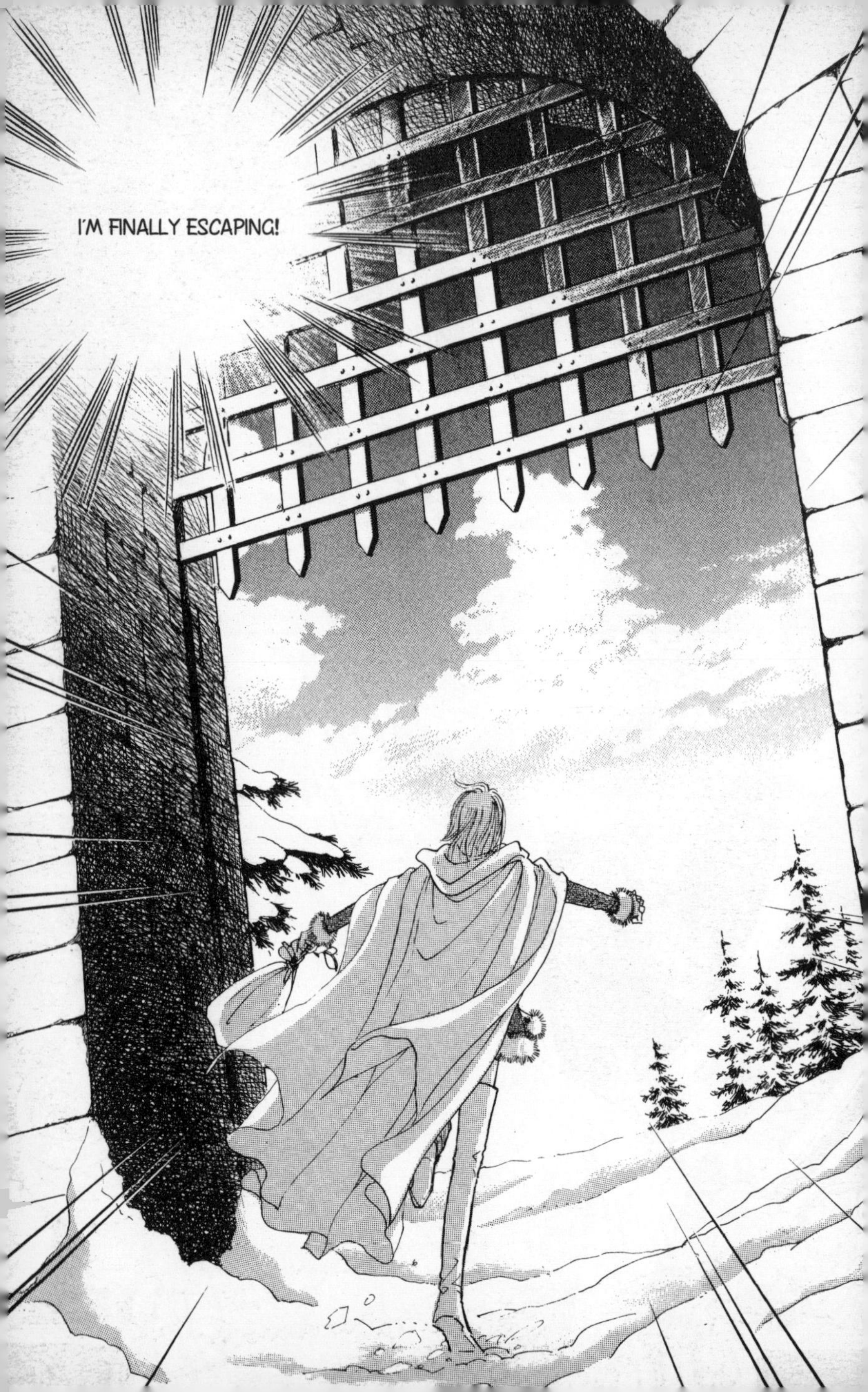
I'M FINALLY ESCAPING!

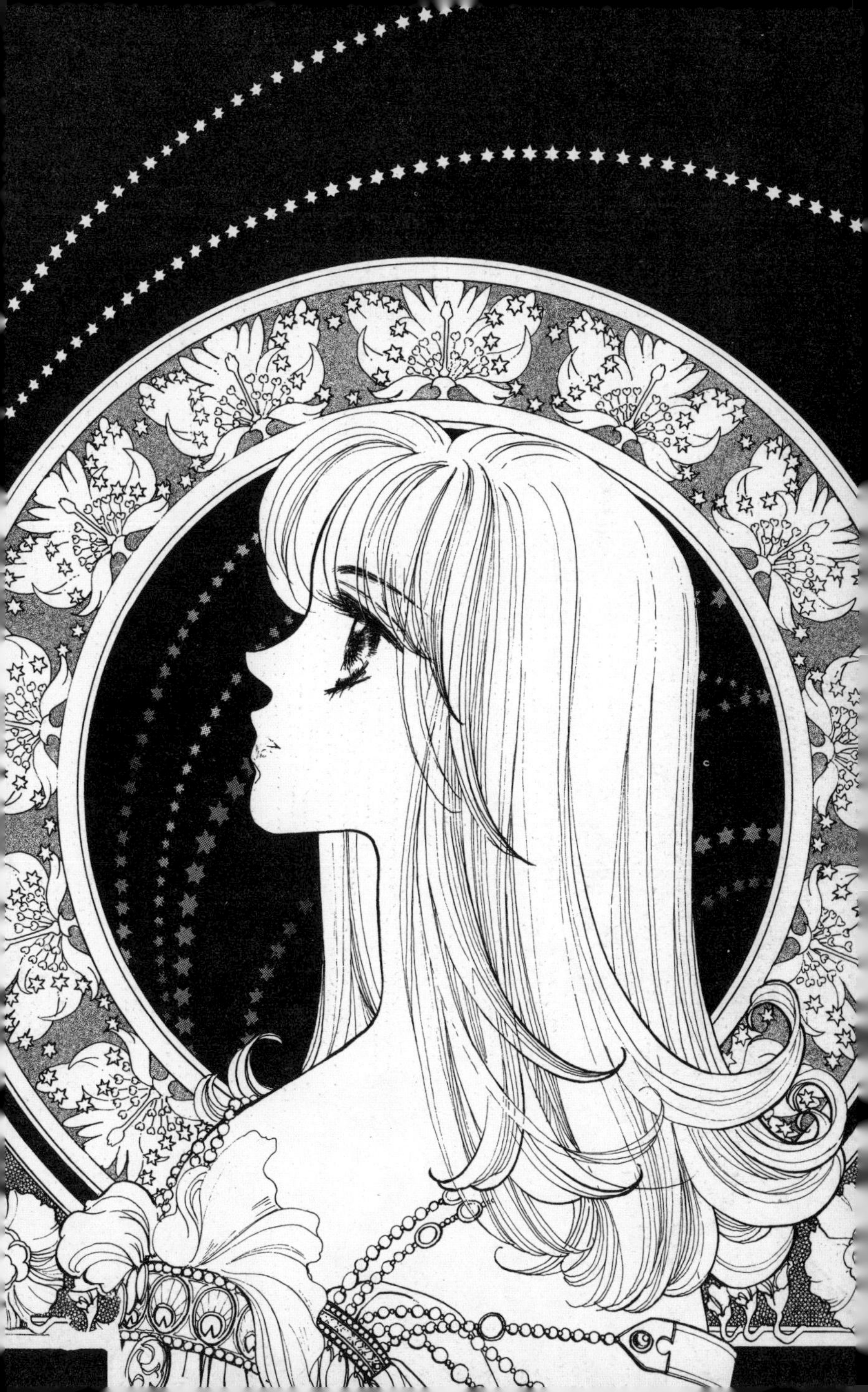

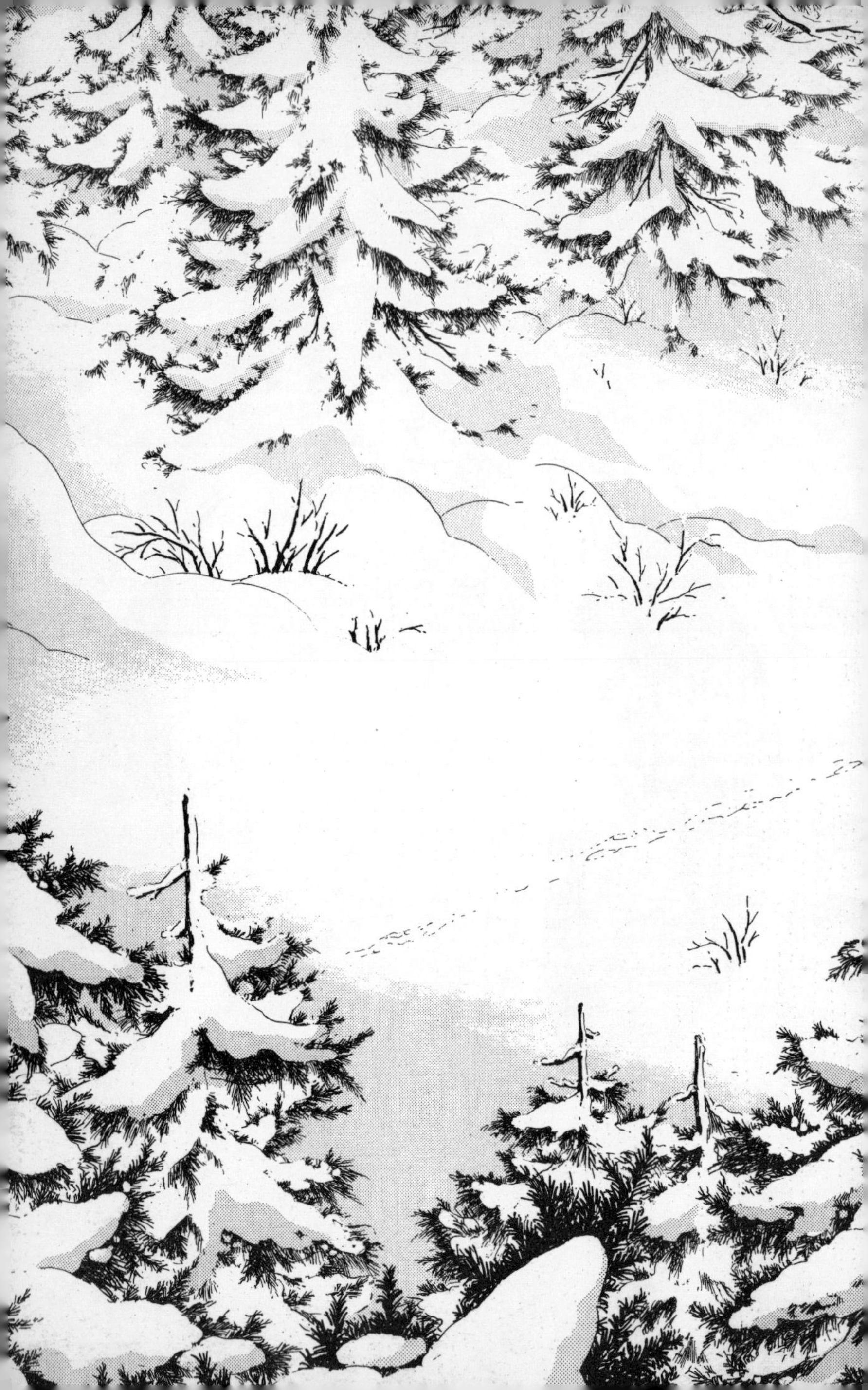

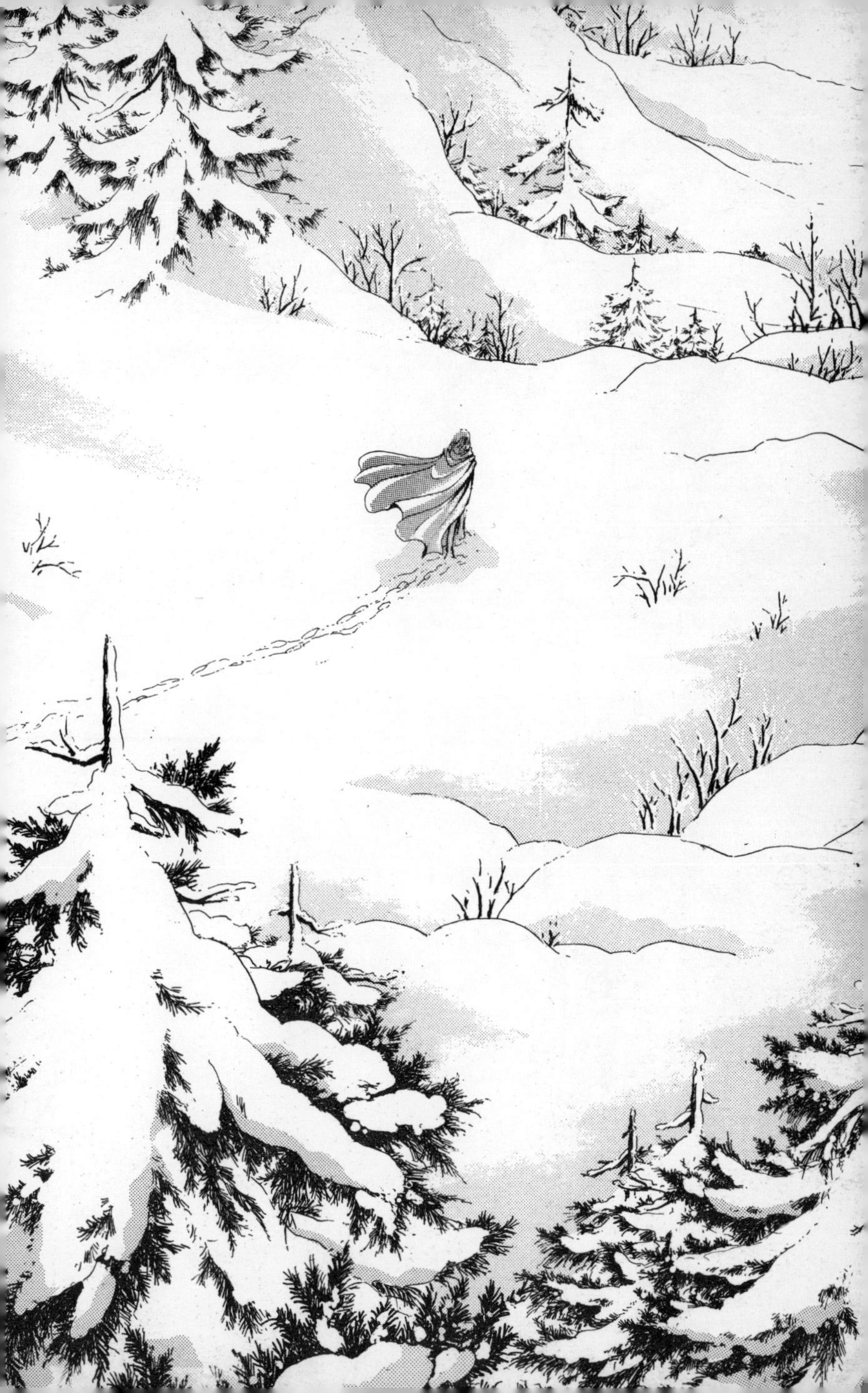

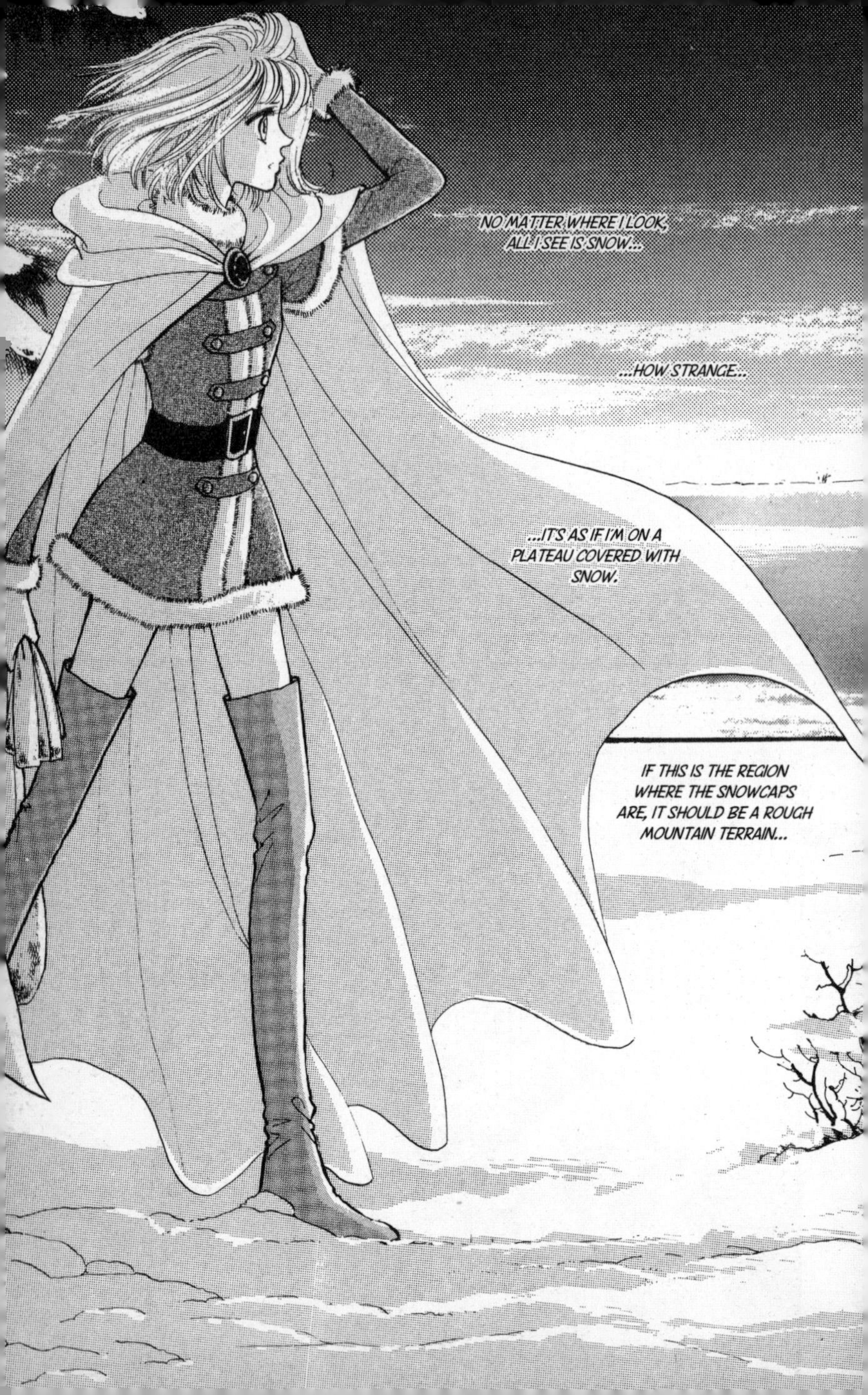
NO MATTER WHERE I LOOK, ALL I SEE IS SNOW...
...HOW STRANGE...
...IT'S AS IF I'M ON A PLATEAU COVERED WITH SNOW.
IF THIS IS THE REGION WHERE THE SNOWCAPS ARE, IT SHOULD BE A ROUGH MOUNTAIN TERRAIN...

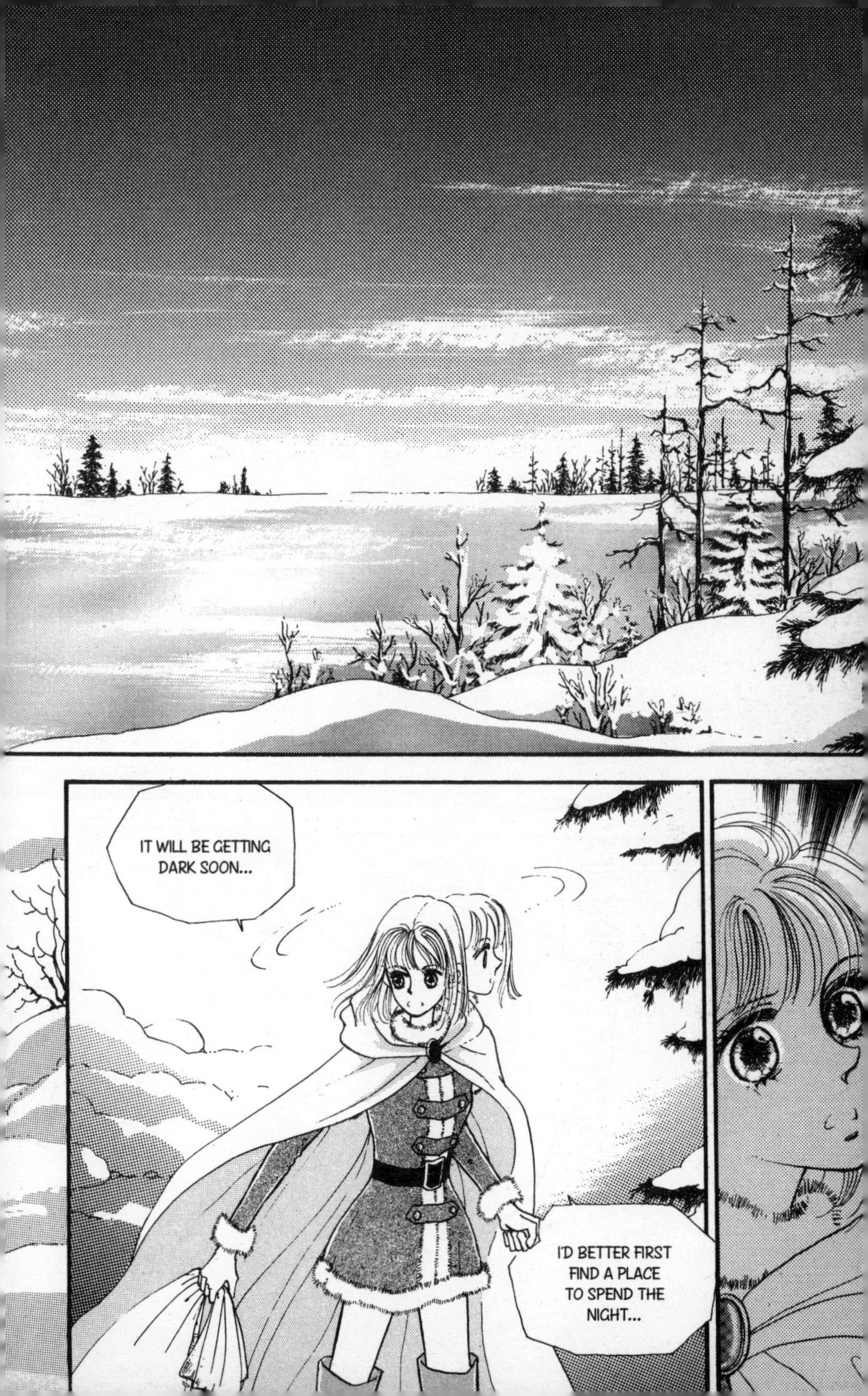
IT WILL BE GETTING DARK SOON...
I'D BETTER FIRST FIND A PLACE TO SPEND THE NIGHT...

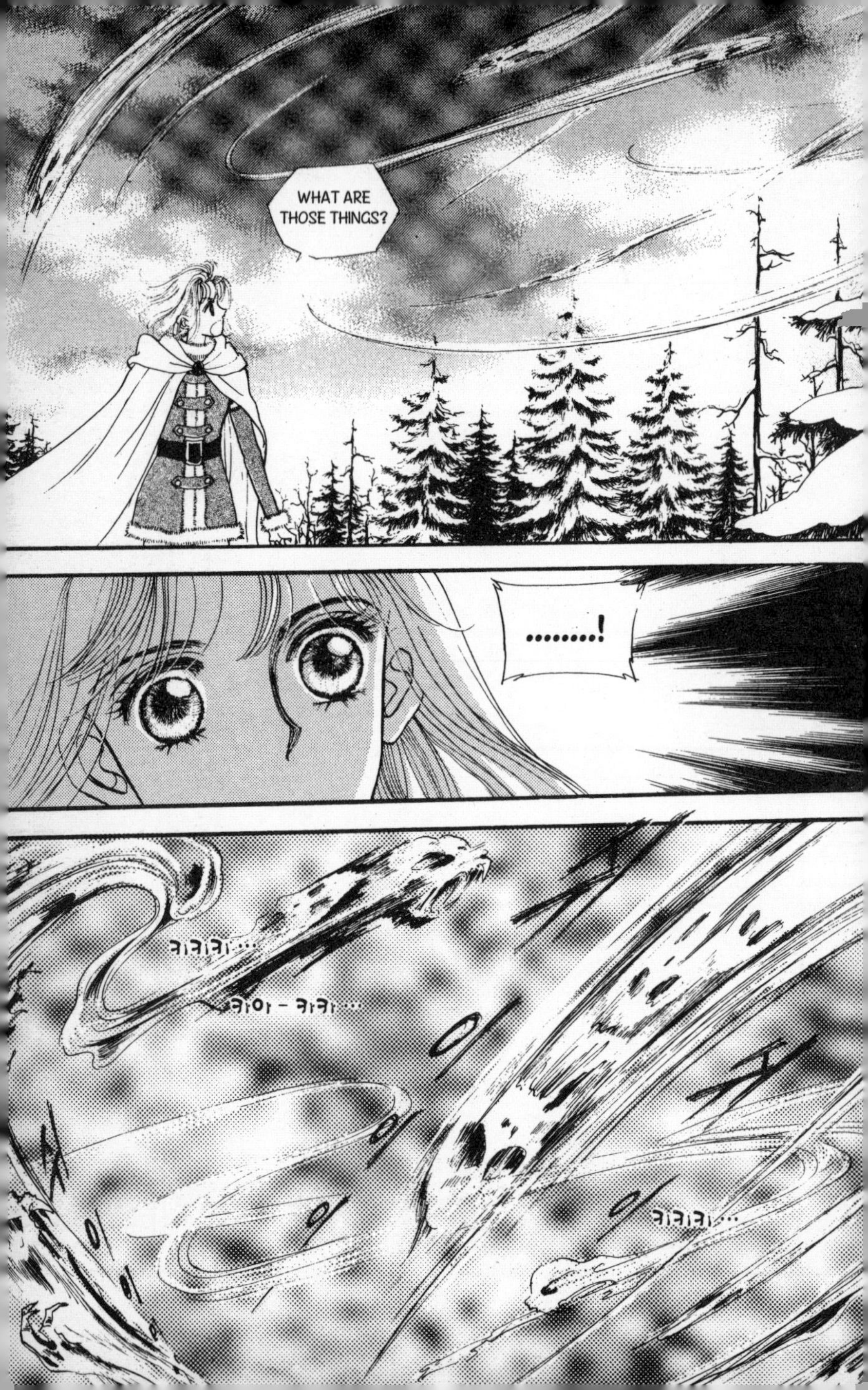
WHAT ARE THOSE THINGS?
........!
키키키…
카아 - 카카…
키키키…

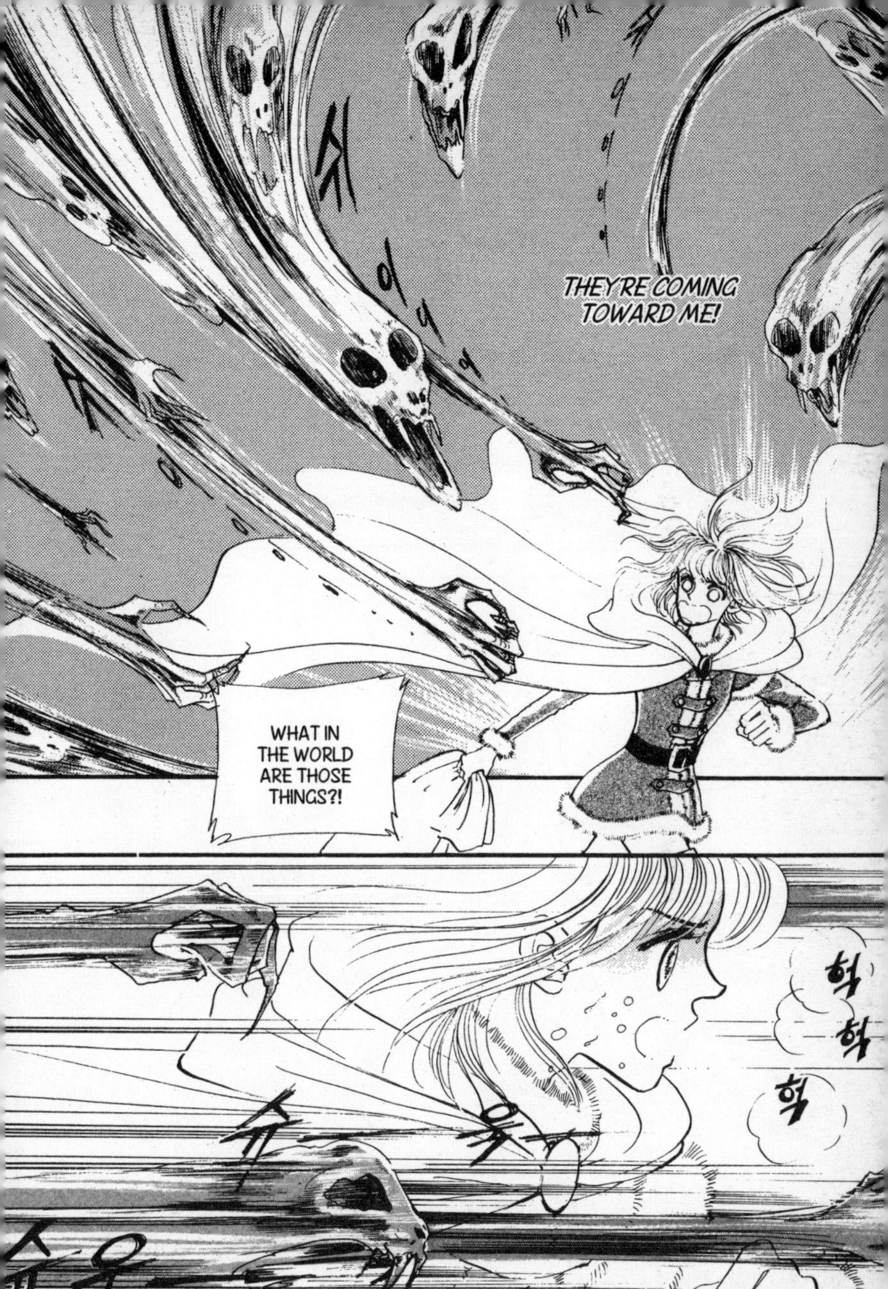
THEY'RE COMING TOWARD ME!
WHAT IN THE WORLD ARE THOSE THINGS?!
헉
헉
헉
슈우
슈우

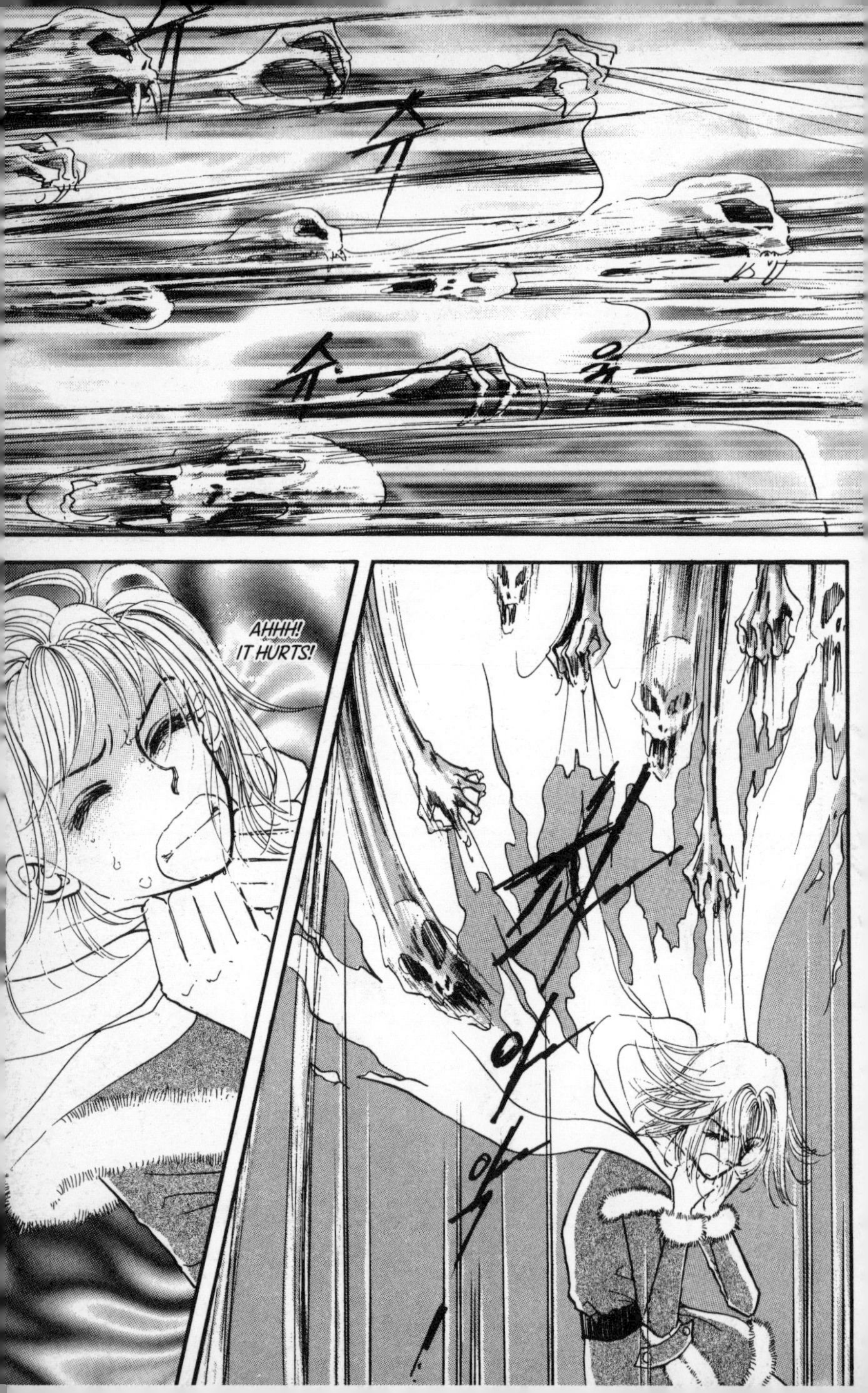
AHHH!
IT HURTS!

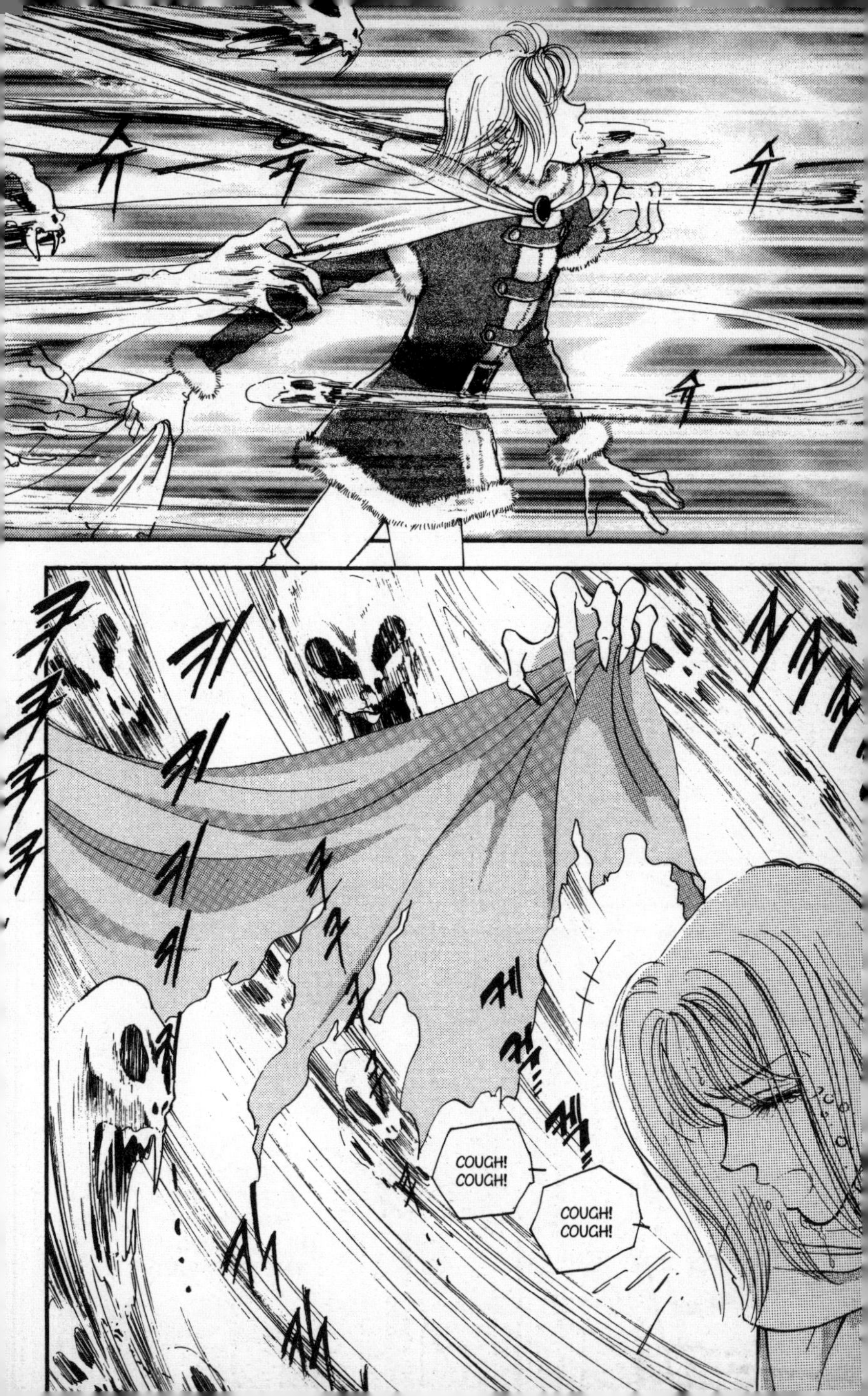
COUGH! COUGH!
COUGH! COUGH!

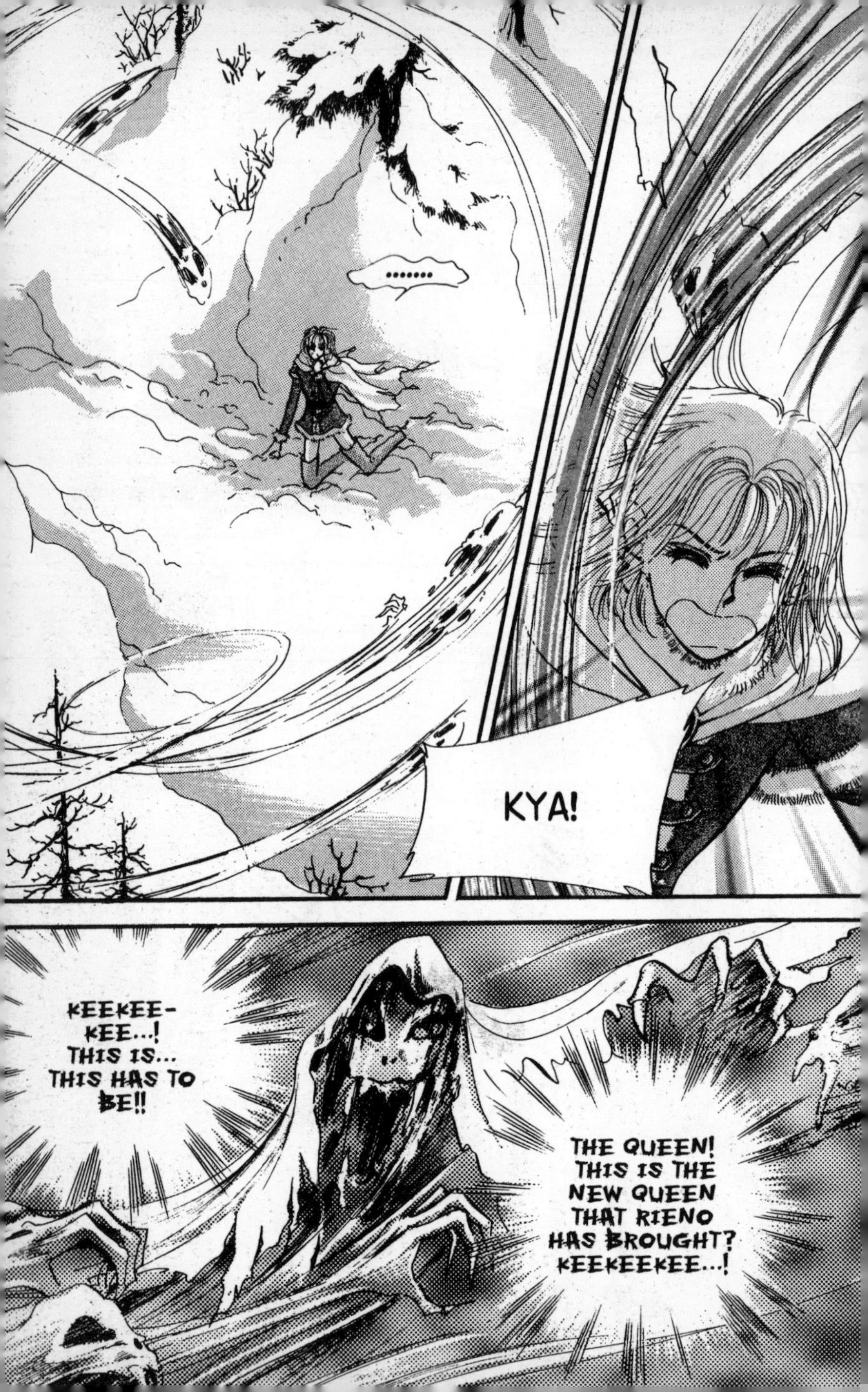
....
KYA!
KEEKEE-KEE...! THIS IS... THIS HAS TO BE!!
THE QUEEN! THIS IS THE NEW QUEEN THAT RIENO HAS BROUGHT? KEEKEEKEE...!

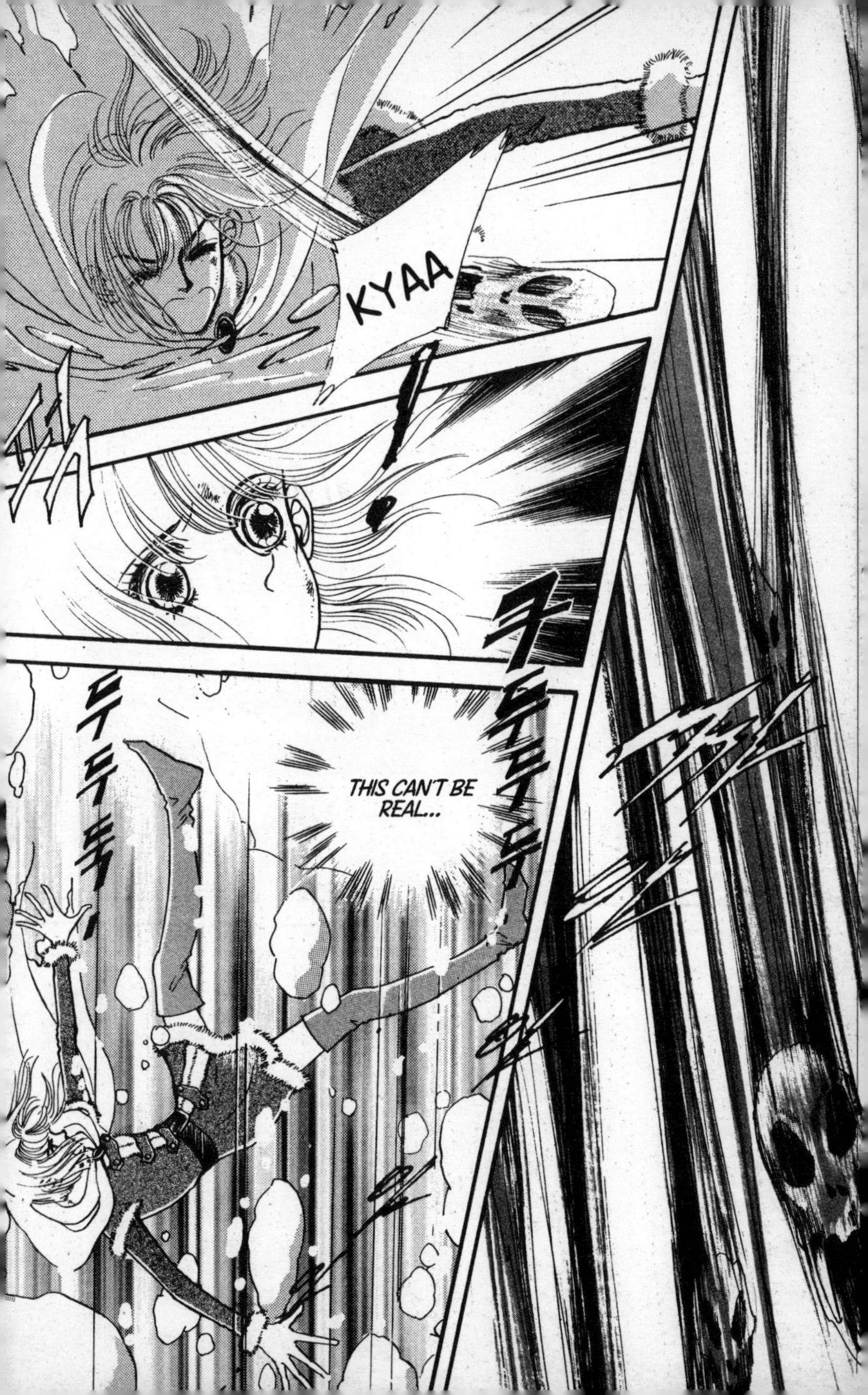
KYAA
THIS CAN'T BE REAL...

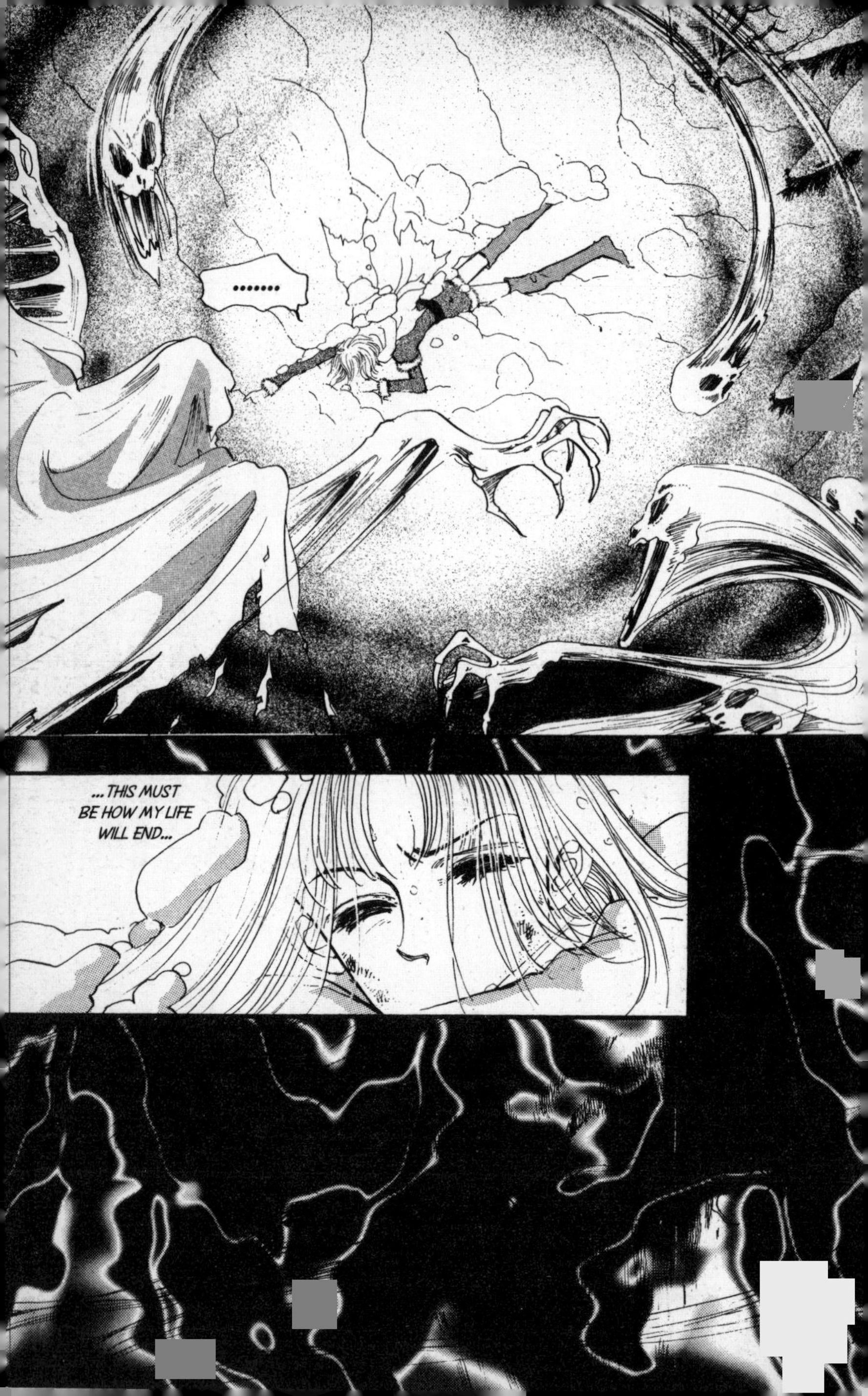
....
...THIS MUST BE HOW MY LIFE WILL END...

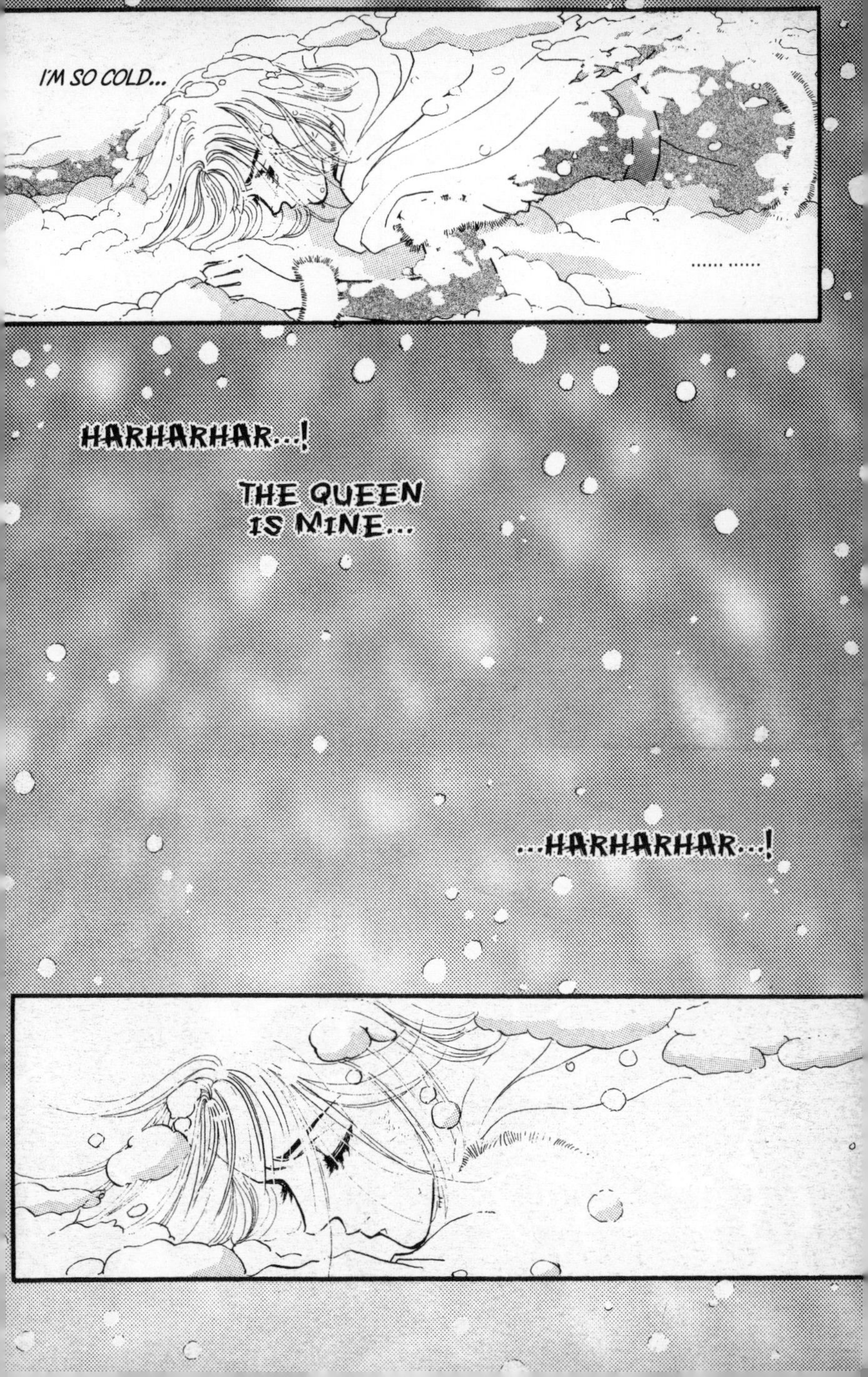
I'M SO COLD...
....
HARHARHAR...!
THE QUEEN IS MINE...
...HARHARHAR...!

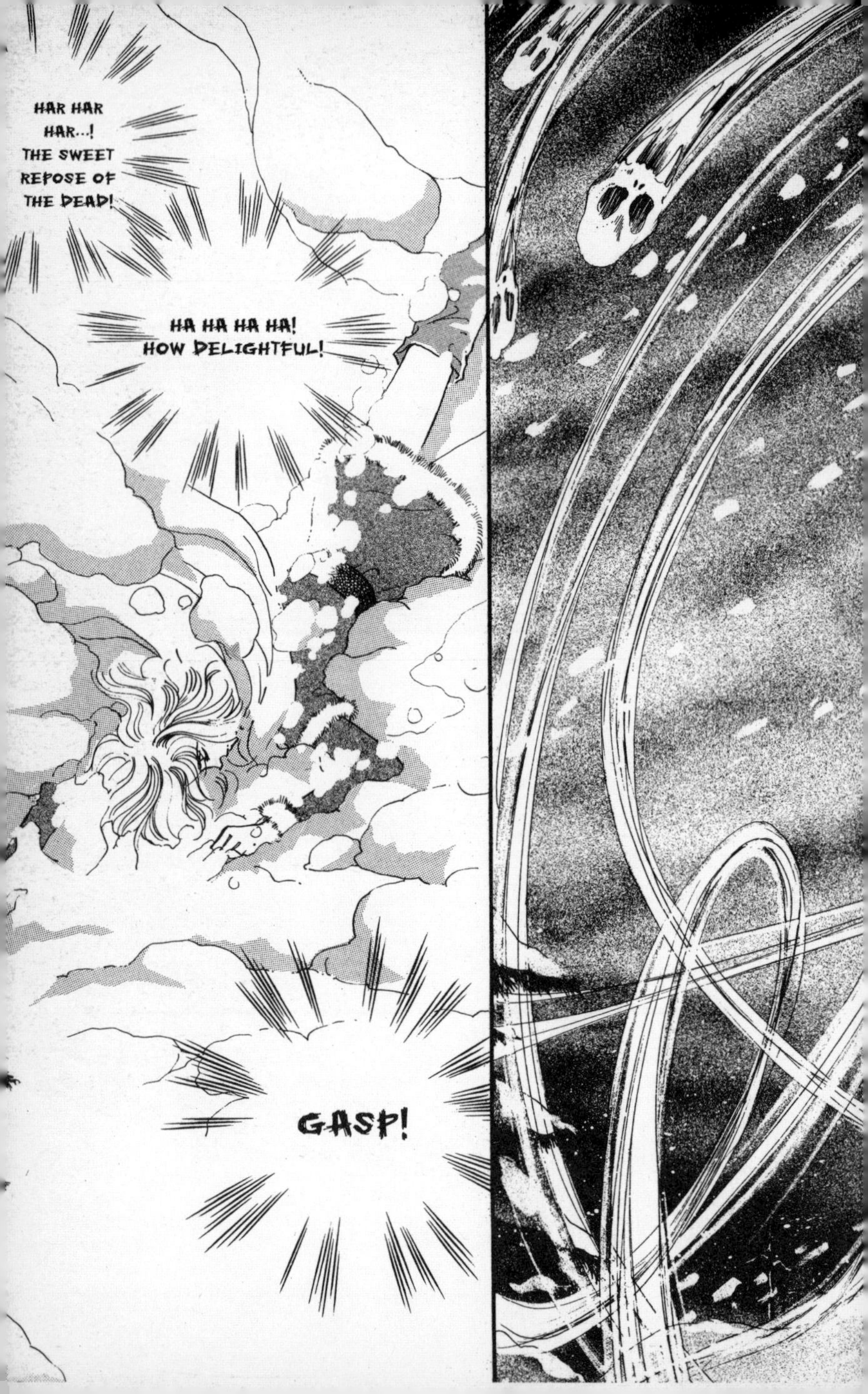
HAR HAR HAR...! THE SWEET REPOSE OF THE DEAD!
HA HA HA HA! HOW DELIGHTFUL!
GASP!

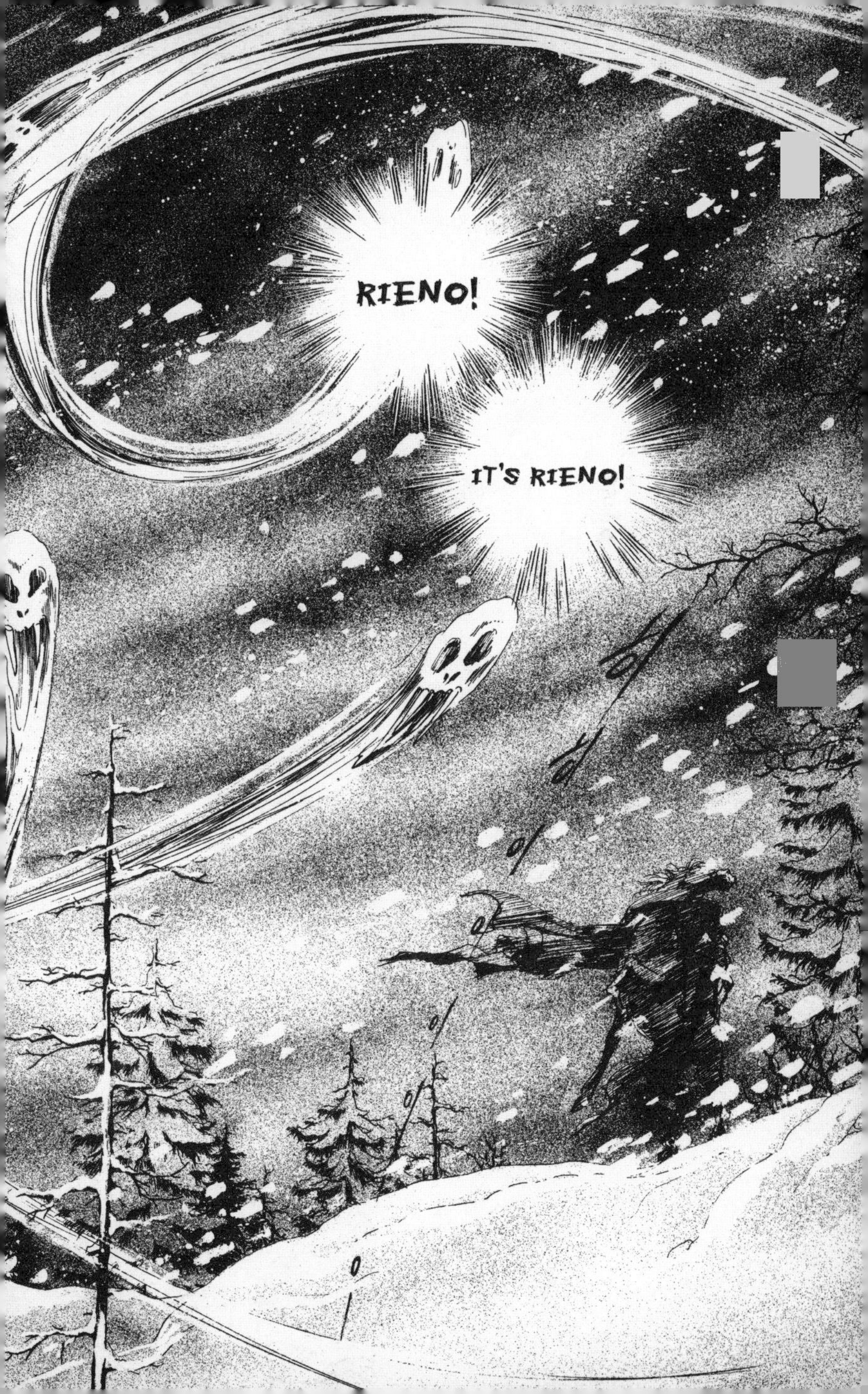
RIENO!
IT'S RIENO!

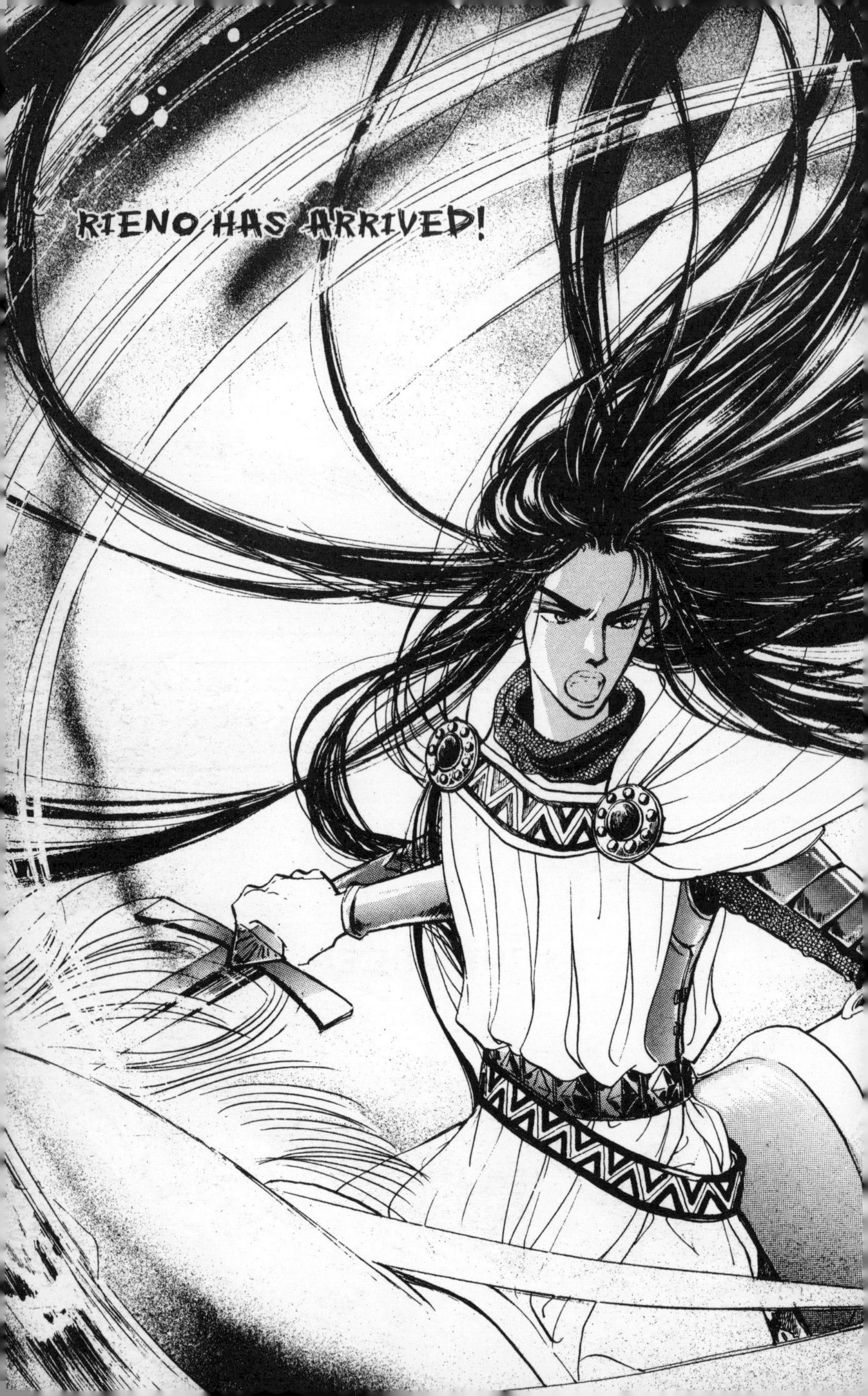
RIENO HAS ARRIVED!

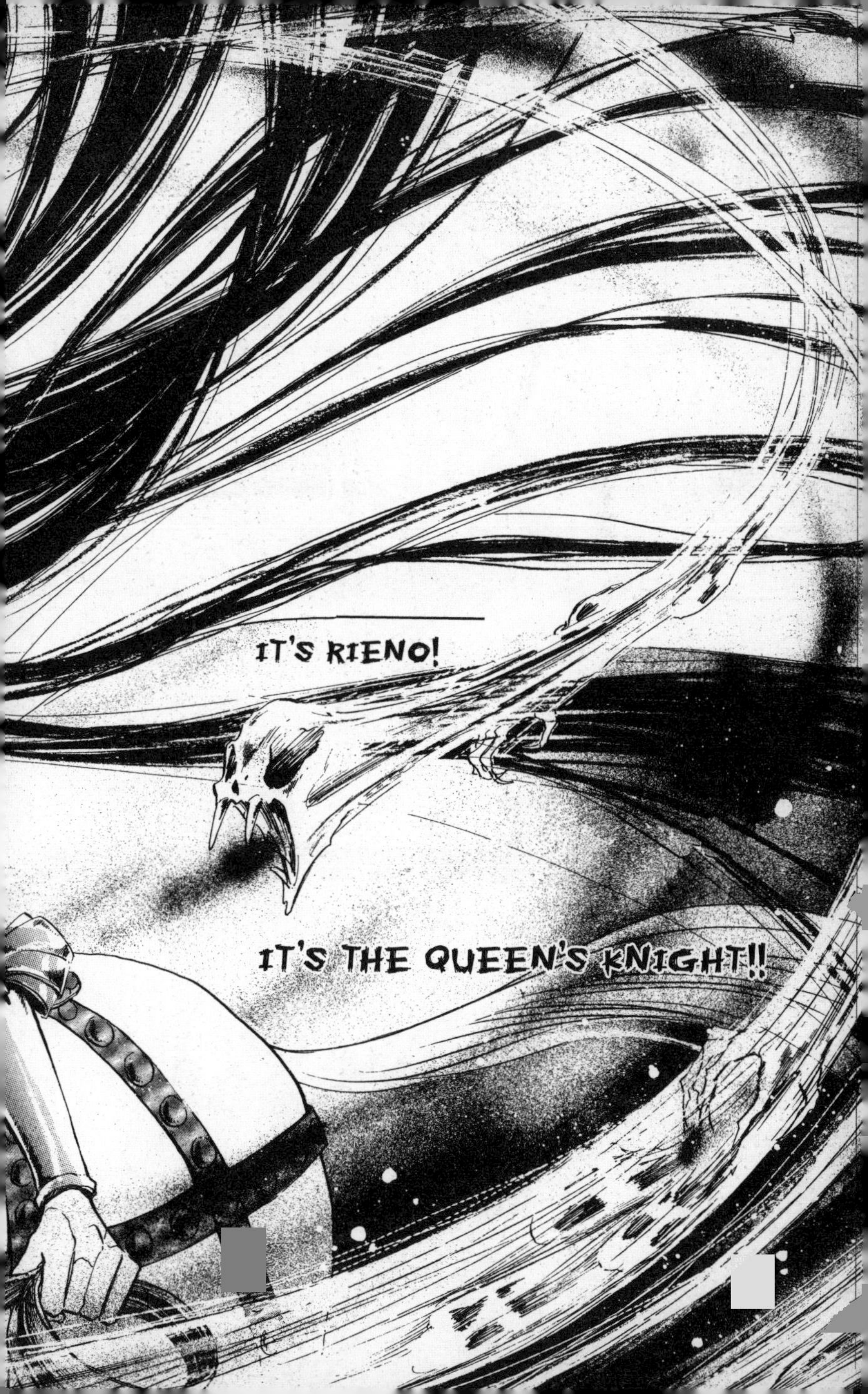
IT'S RIENO!
IT'S THE QUEEN'S KNIGHT!!

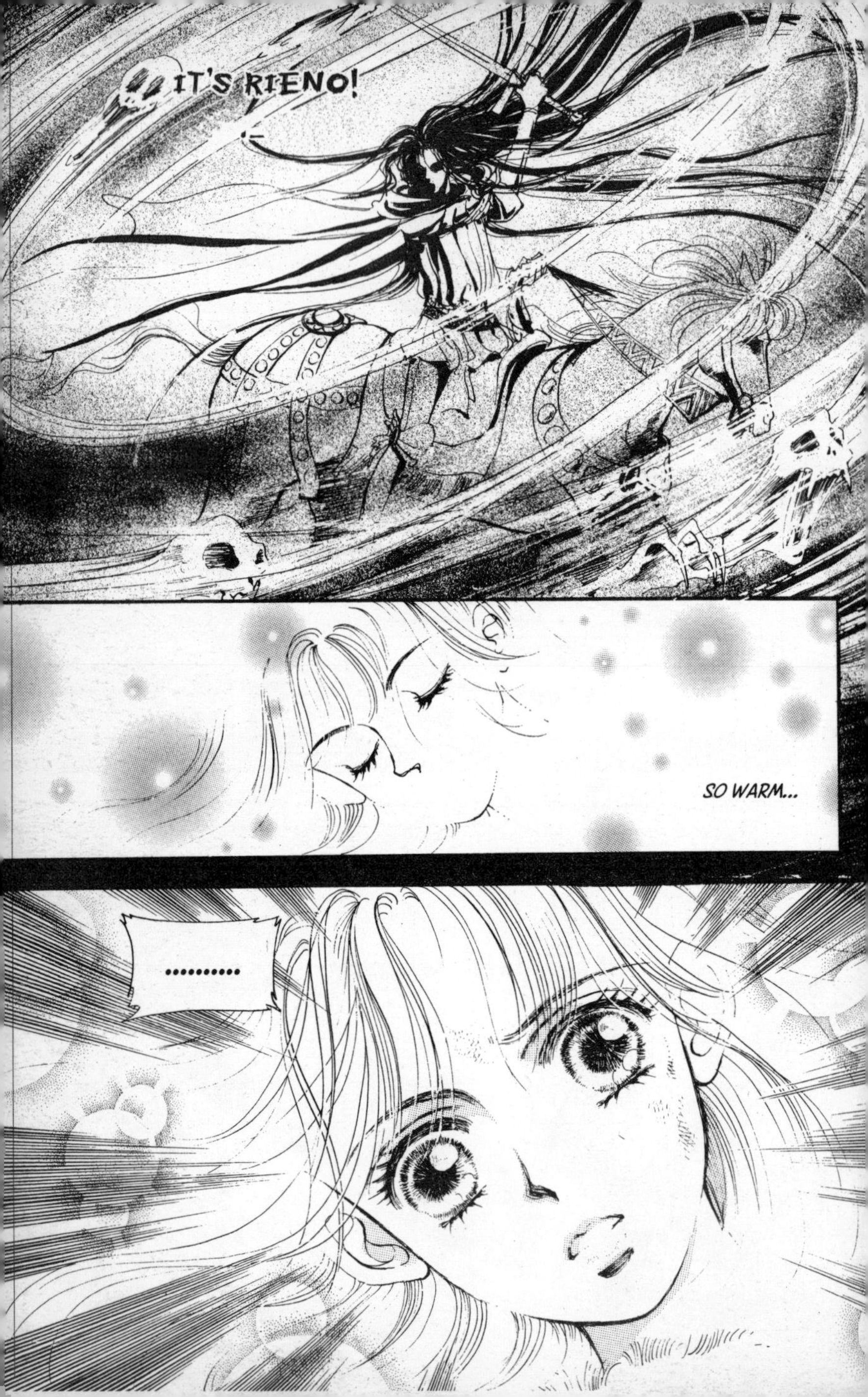
IT'S RIENO!
SO WARM...
....

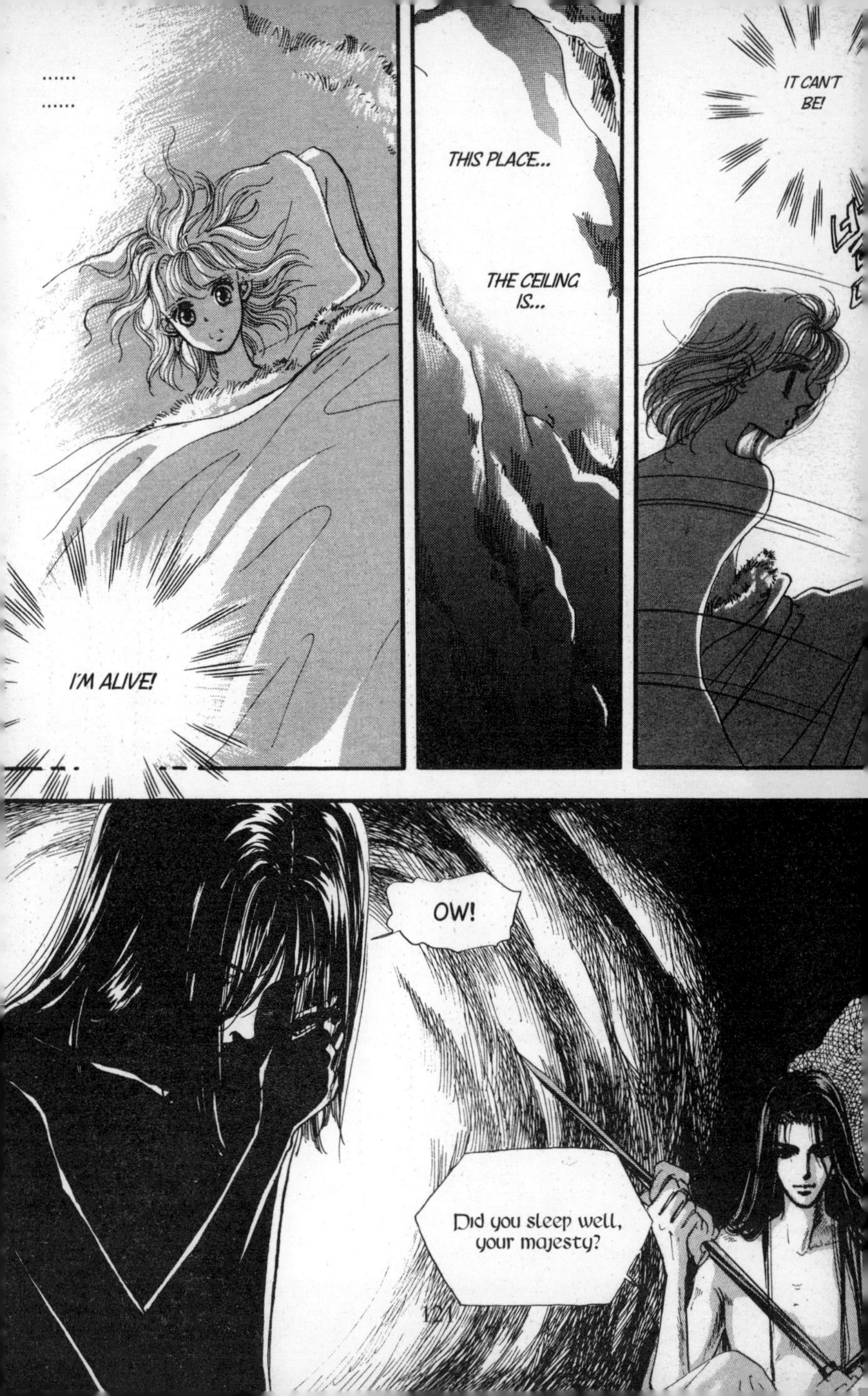
......
......
I'M ALIVE!
THIS PLACE...
THE CEILING IS...
IT CAN'T BE!
OW!
Did you sleep well, your majesty?

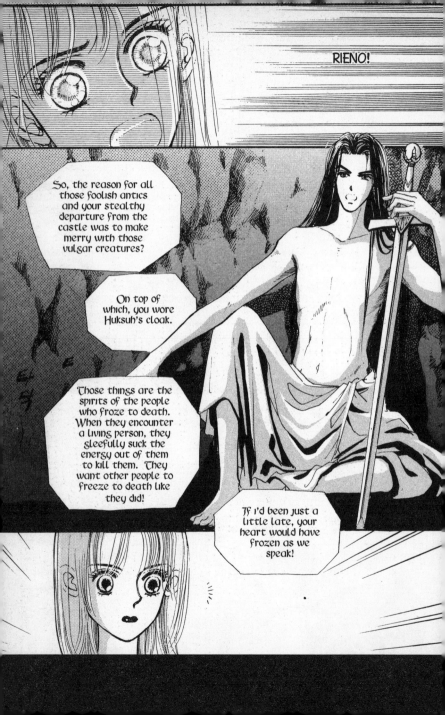

RIENO!

So, the reason for all those foolish antics and your stealthy departure from the castle was to make merry with those vulgar creatures?

On top of which, you wore Huksuh's cloak.

Those things are the spirits of the people who froze to death. When they encounter a living person, they gleefully suck the energy out of them to kill them. They want other people to freeze to death like they did!

If I'd been just a little late, your heart would have frozen as we speak!

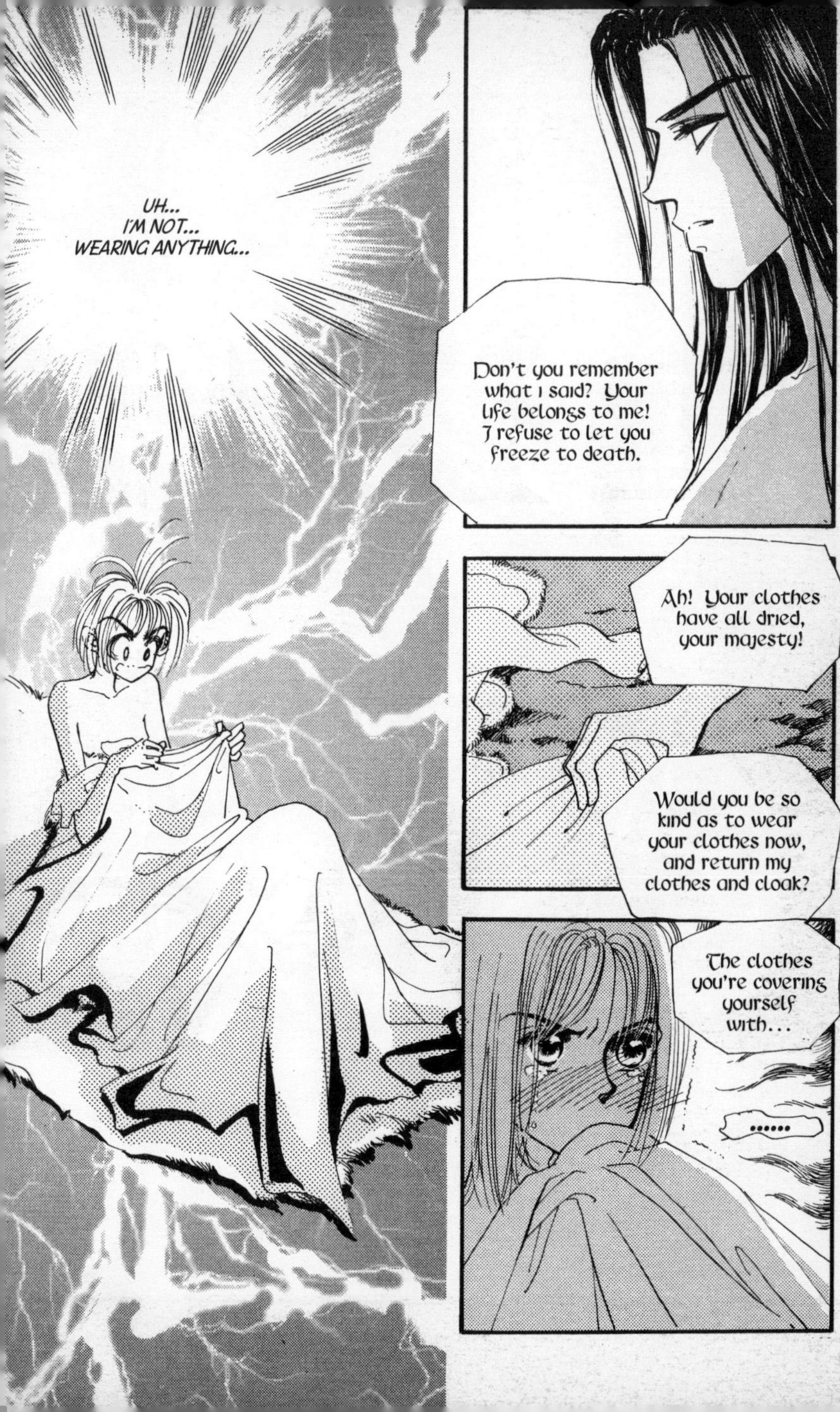
UH... I'M NOT... WEARING ANYTHING...
Don't you remember what I said? Your life belongs to me! I refuse to let you freeze to death.
Ah! Your clothes have all dried, your majesty!
Would you be so kind as to wear your clothes now, and return my clothes and cloak?
The clothes you're covering yourself with...
......

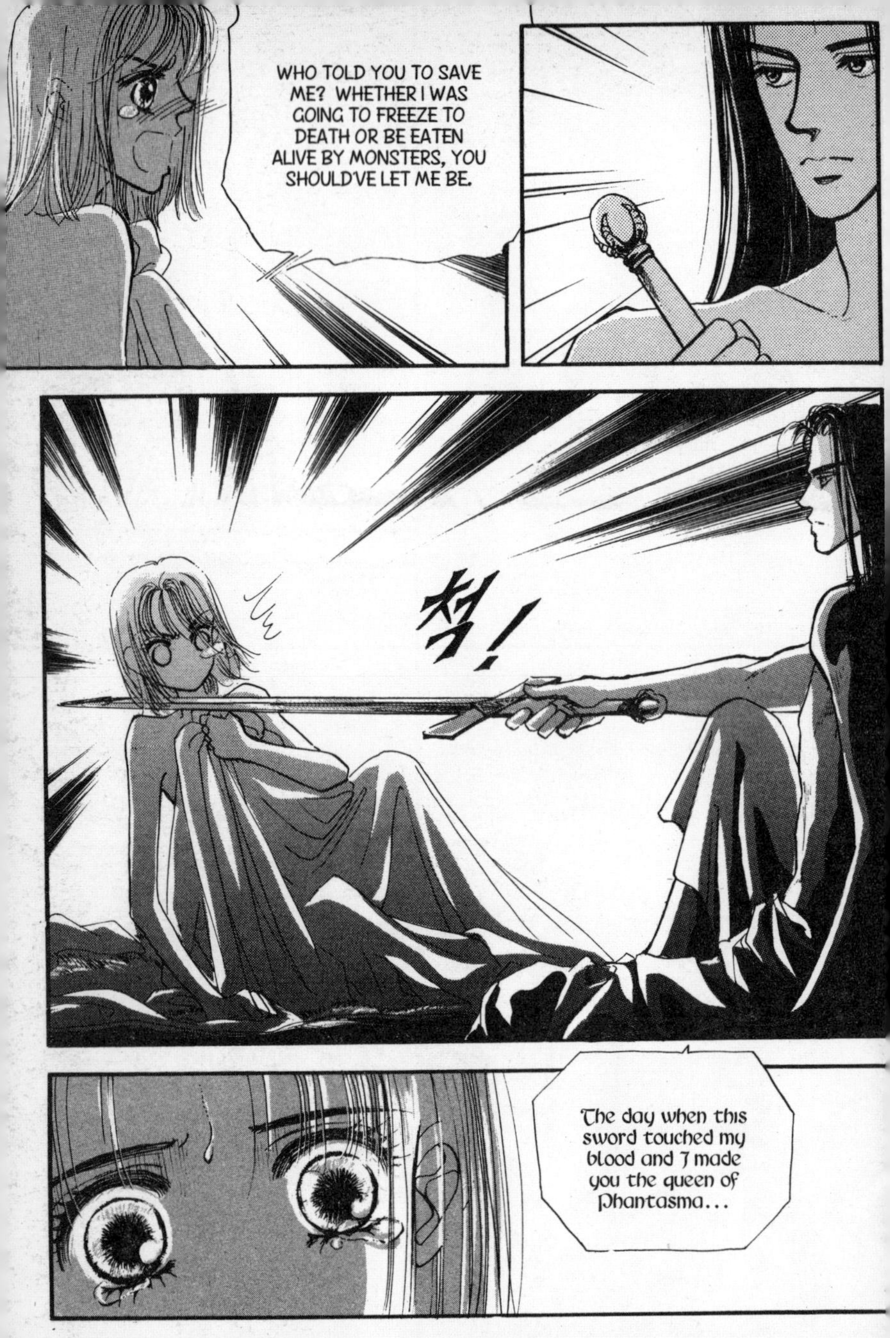
WHO TOLD YOU TO SAVE ME? WHETHER I WAS GOING TO FREEZE TO DEATH OR BE EATEN ALIVE BY MONSTERS, YOU SHOULD'VE LET ME BE.
척!
The day when this sword touched my blood and I made you the queen of Phantasma...

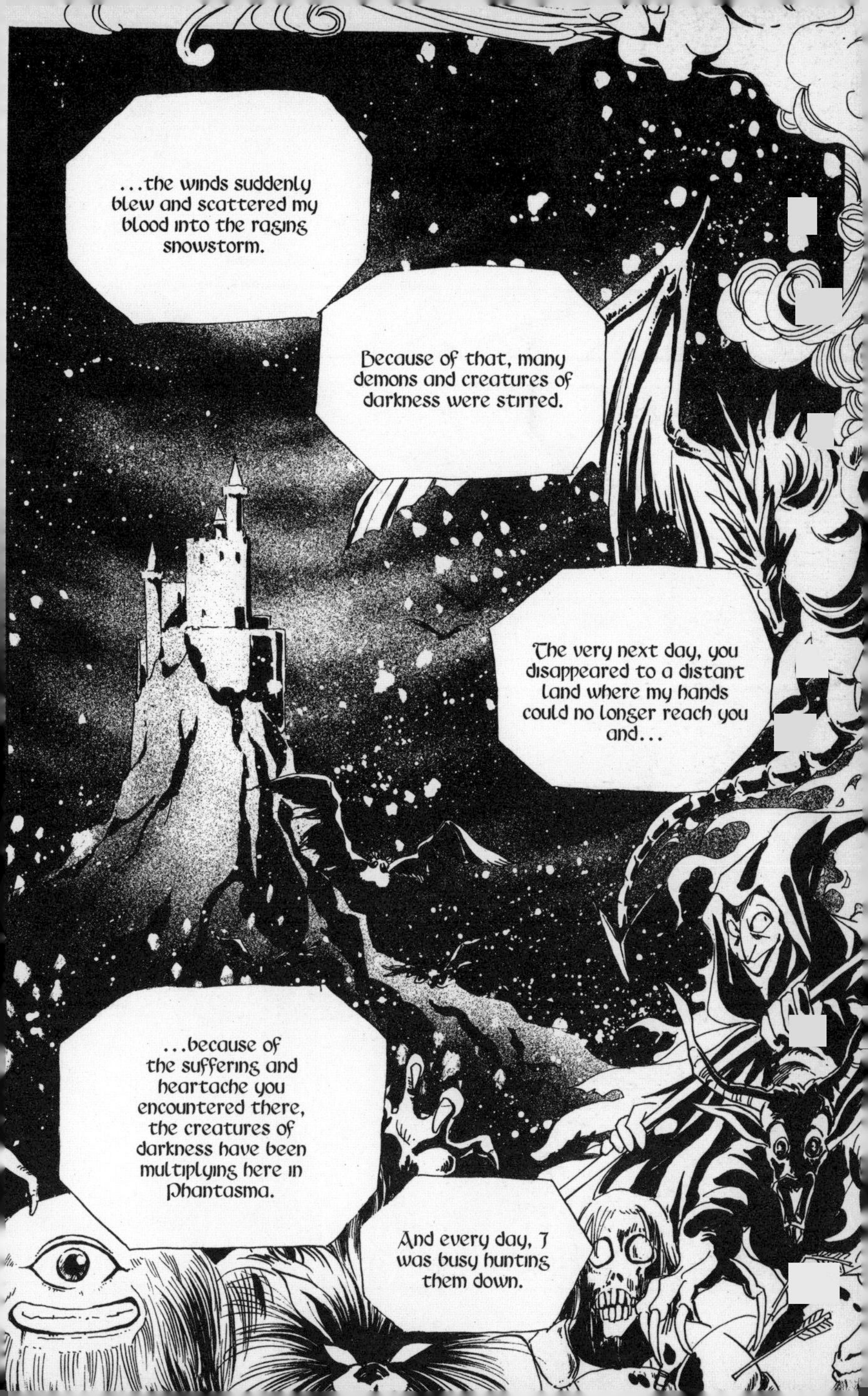
...the winds suddenly blew and scattered my blood into the raging snowstorm.
Because of that, many demons and creatures of darkness were stirred.
The very next day, you disappeared to a distant land where my hands could no longer reach you and...
...because of the suffering and heartache you encountered there, the creatures of darkness have been multiplying here in Phantasma.
And every day, I was busy hunting them down.

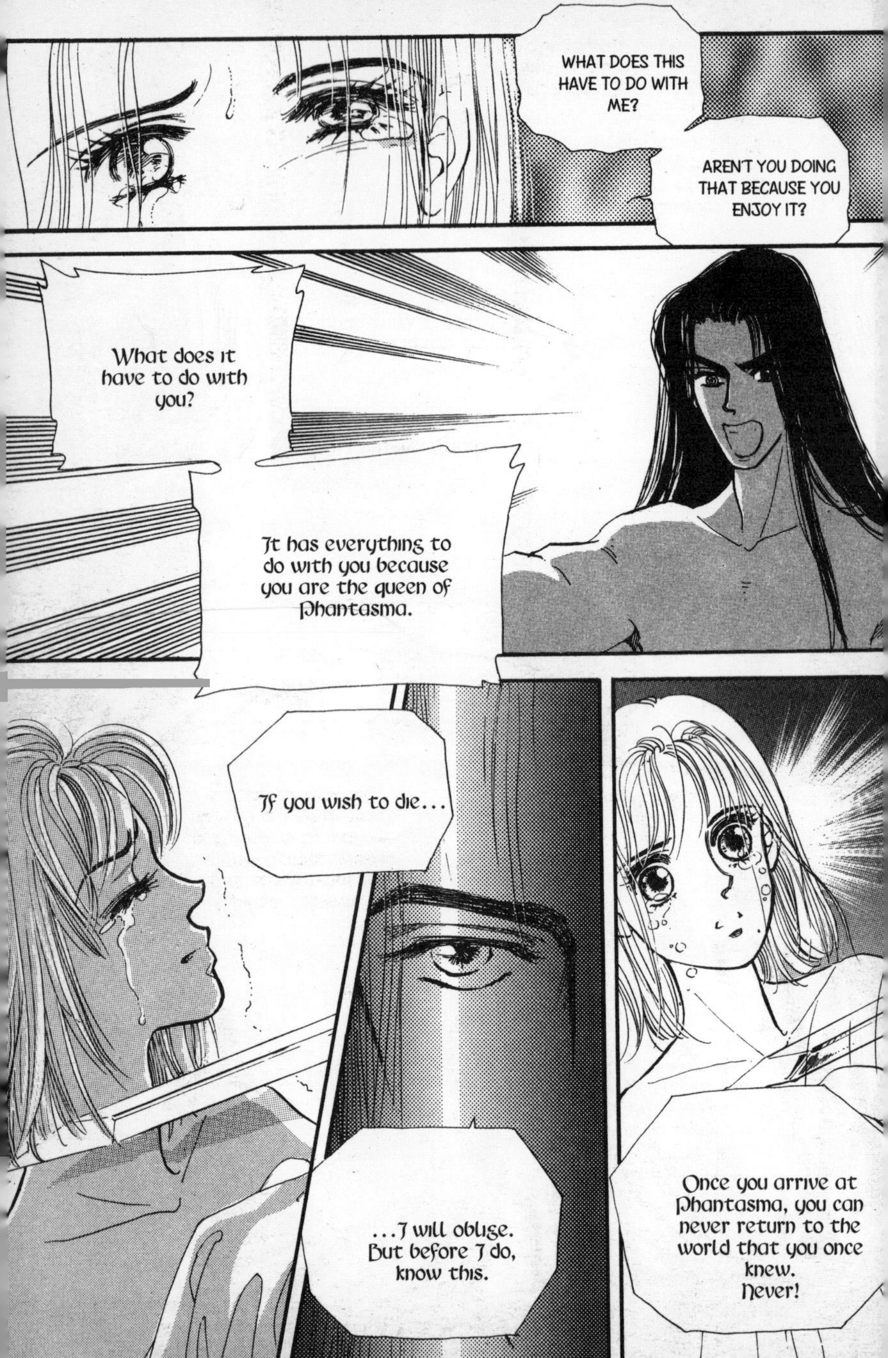
WHAT DOES THIS HAVE TO DO WITH ME?
AREN'T YOU DOING THAT BECAUSE YOU ENJOY IT?
What does it have to do with you?
It has everything to do with you because you are the queen of Phantasma.
If you wish to die...
...I will oblige. But before I do, know this.
Once you arrive at Phantasma, you can never return to the world that you once knew. Never!

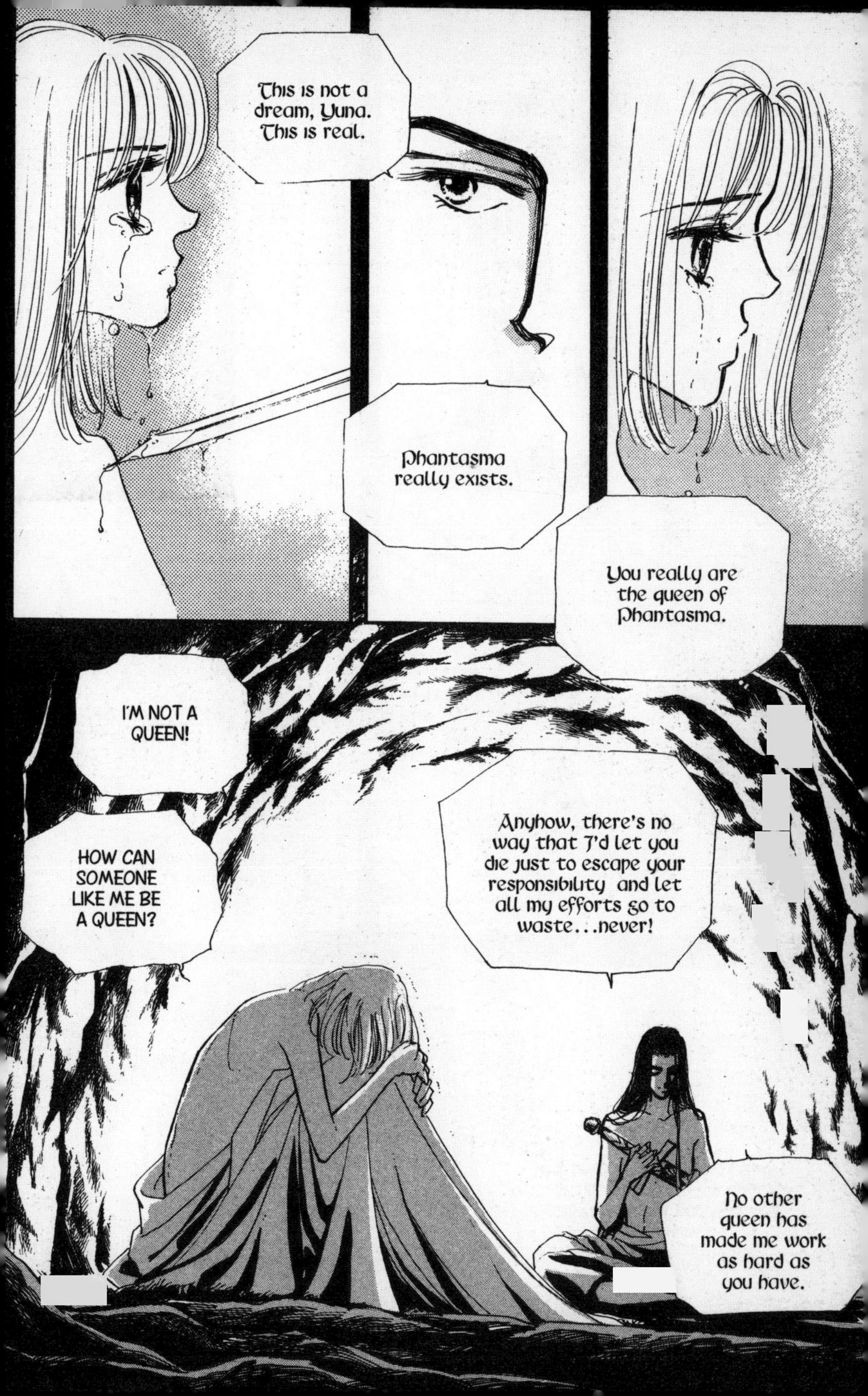
This is not a dream, Yuna. This is real.
Phantasma really exists.
You really are the queen of Phantasma.
I'M NOT A QUEEN!
HOW CAN SOMEONE LIKE ME BE A QUEEN?
Anyhow, there's no way that I'd let you die just to escape your responsibility and let all my efforts go to waste...never!
No other queen has made me work as hard as you have.

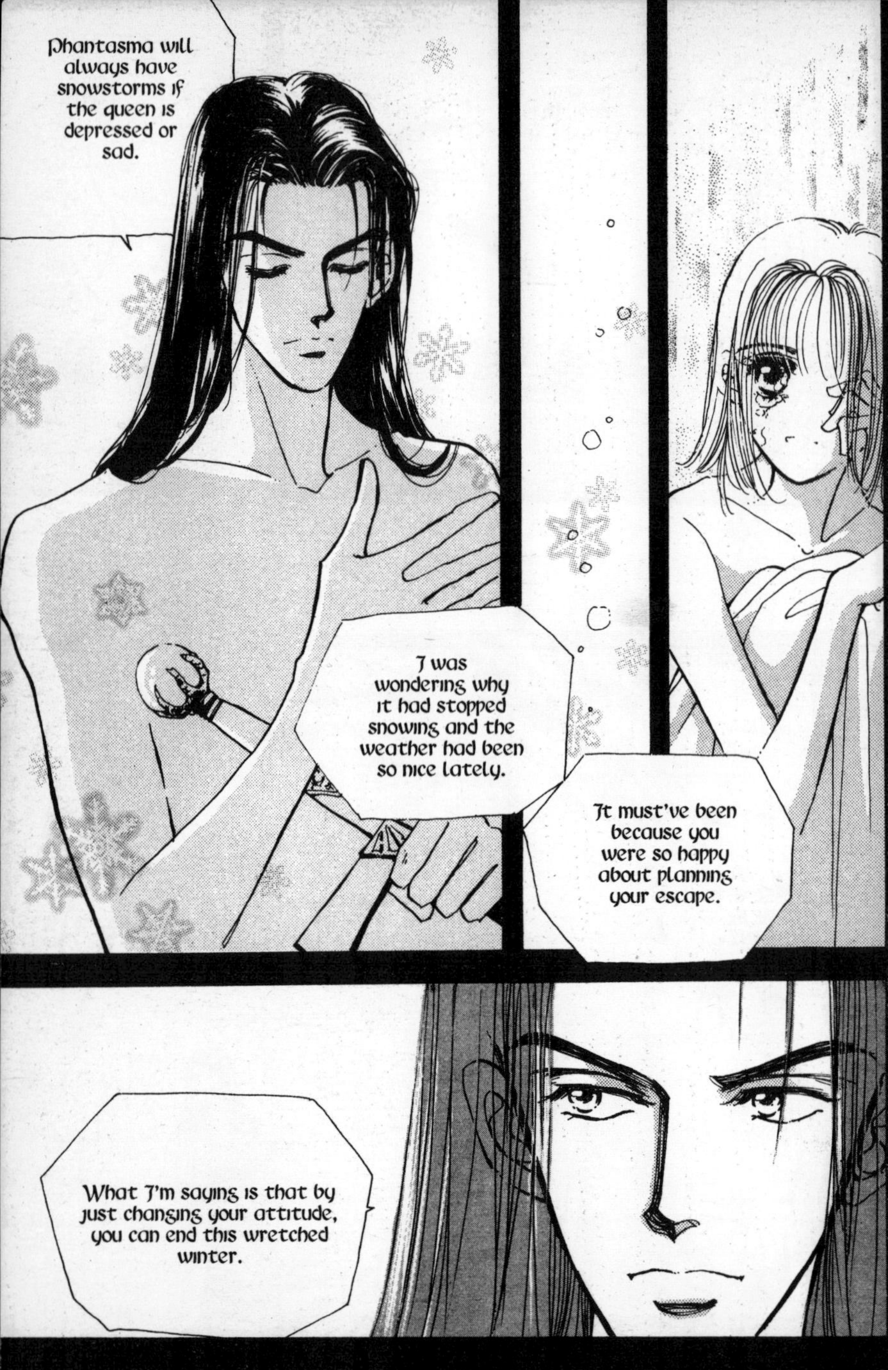

Phantasma will always have snowstorms if the queen is depressed or sad.
I was wondering why it had stopped snowing and the weather had been so nice lately.
It must've been because you were so happy about planning your escape.
What I'm saying is that by just changing your attitude, you can end this wretched winter.

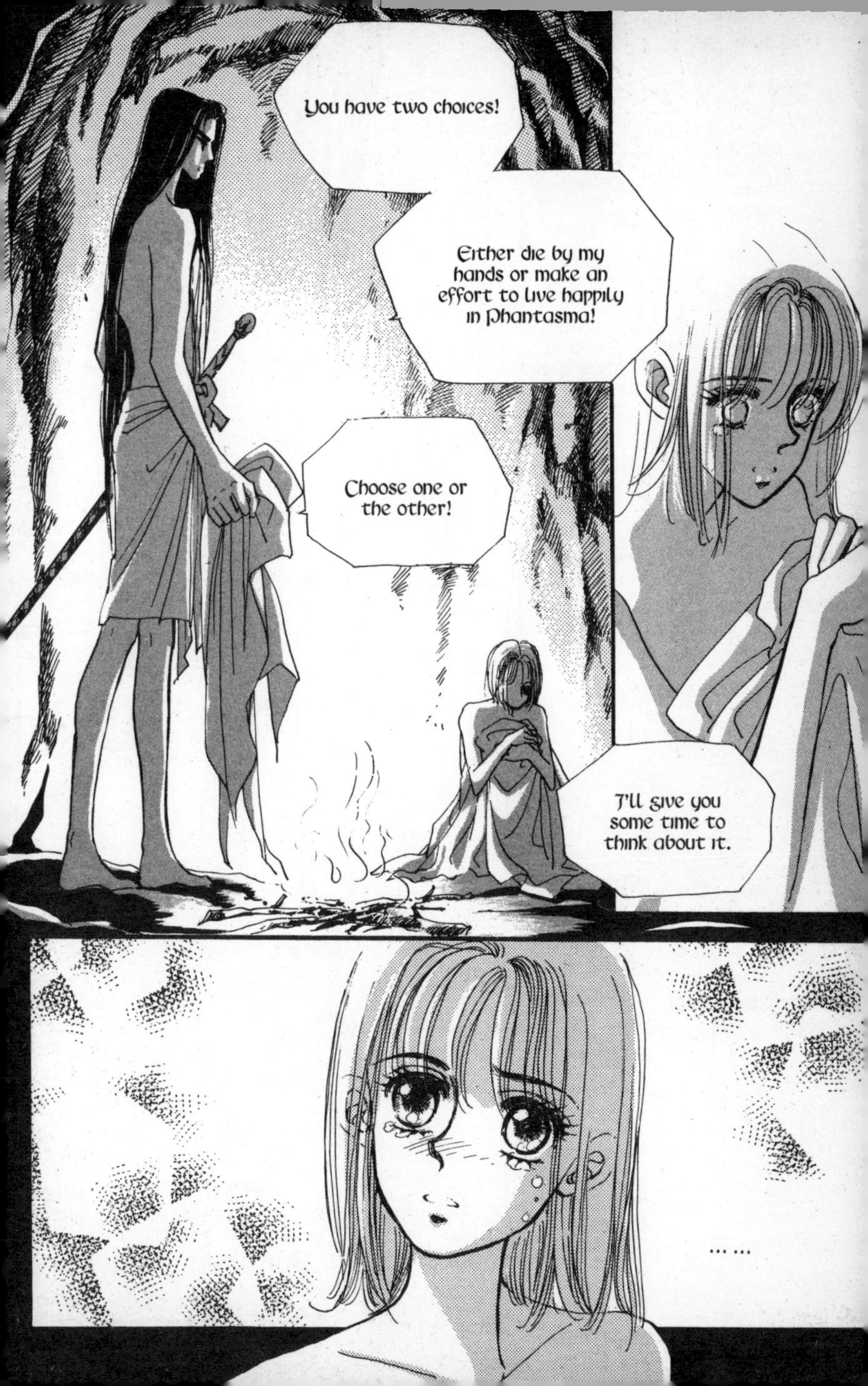
You have two choices!
Either die by my hands or make an effort to live happily in Phantasma!
Choose one or the other!
...
I'll give you some time to think about it.
... ...

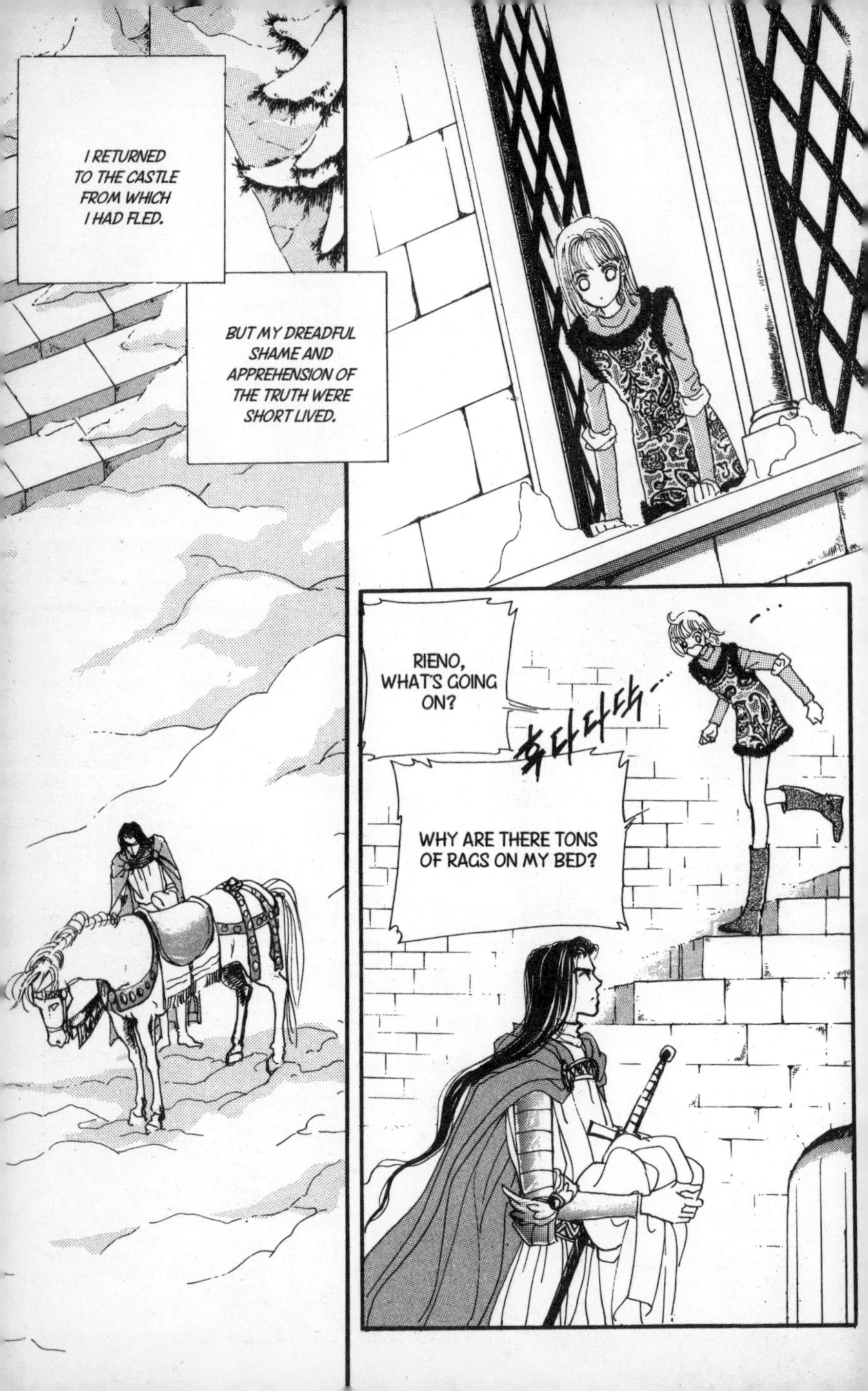
I RETURNED TO THE CASTLE FROM WHICH I HAD FLED.
BUT MY DREADFUL SHAME AND APPREHENSION OF THE TRUTH WERE SHORT LIVED.
RIENO, WHAT'S GOING ON?
후다다닥...
WHY ARE THERE TONS OF RAGS ON MY BED?

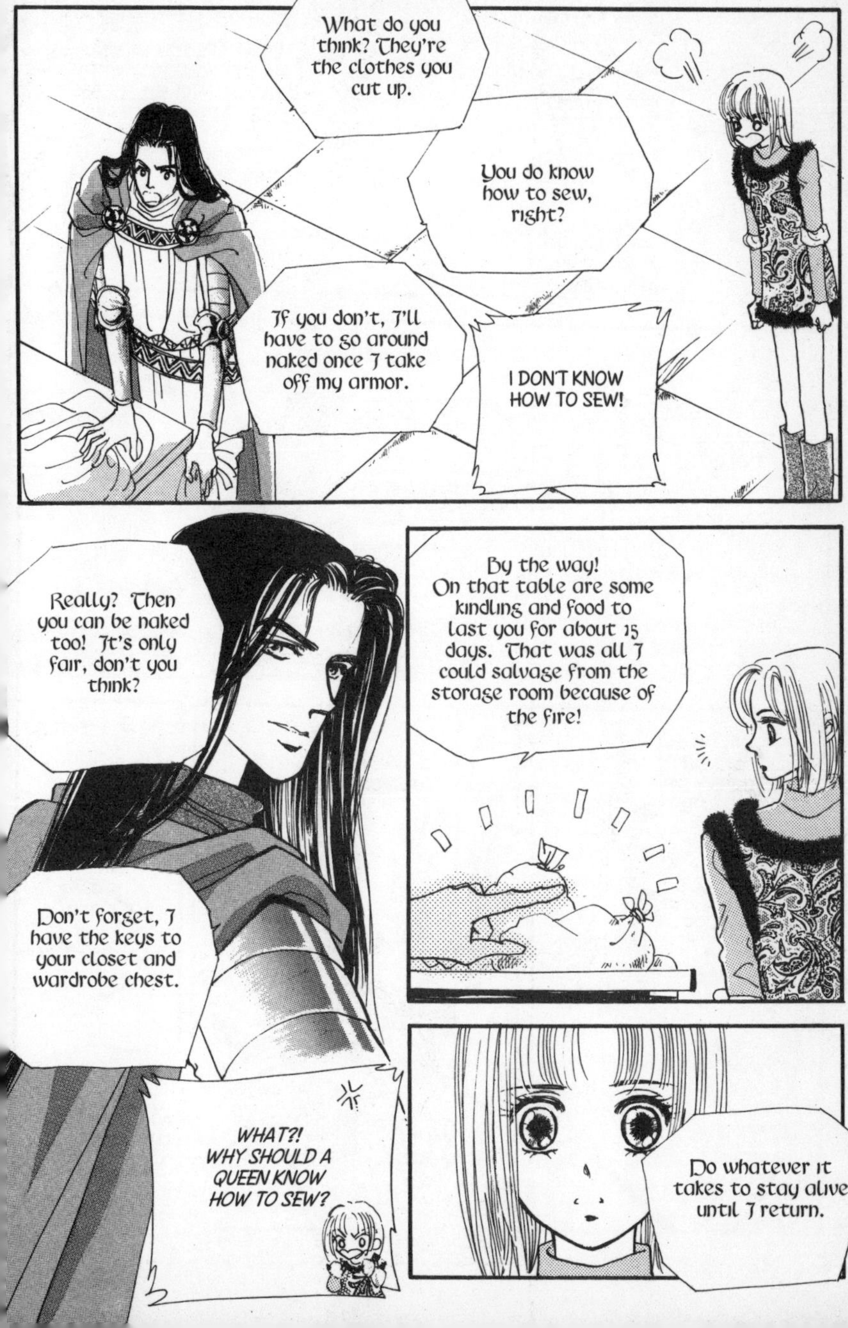
What do you think? They're the clothes you cut up.
You do know how to sew, right?
If you don't, I'll have to go around naked once I take off my armor.
I DON'T KNOW HOW TO SEW!
Really? Then you can be naked too! It's only fair, don't you think?
Don't forget, I have the keys to your closet and wardrobe chest.
By the way! On that table are some kindling and food to last you for about 15 days. That was all I could salvage from the storage room because of the fire!
WHAT?! WHY SHOULD A QUEEN KNOW HOW TO SEW?
Do whatever it takes to stay alive until I return.

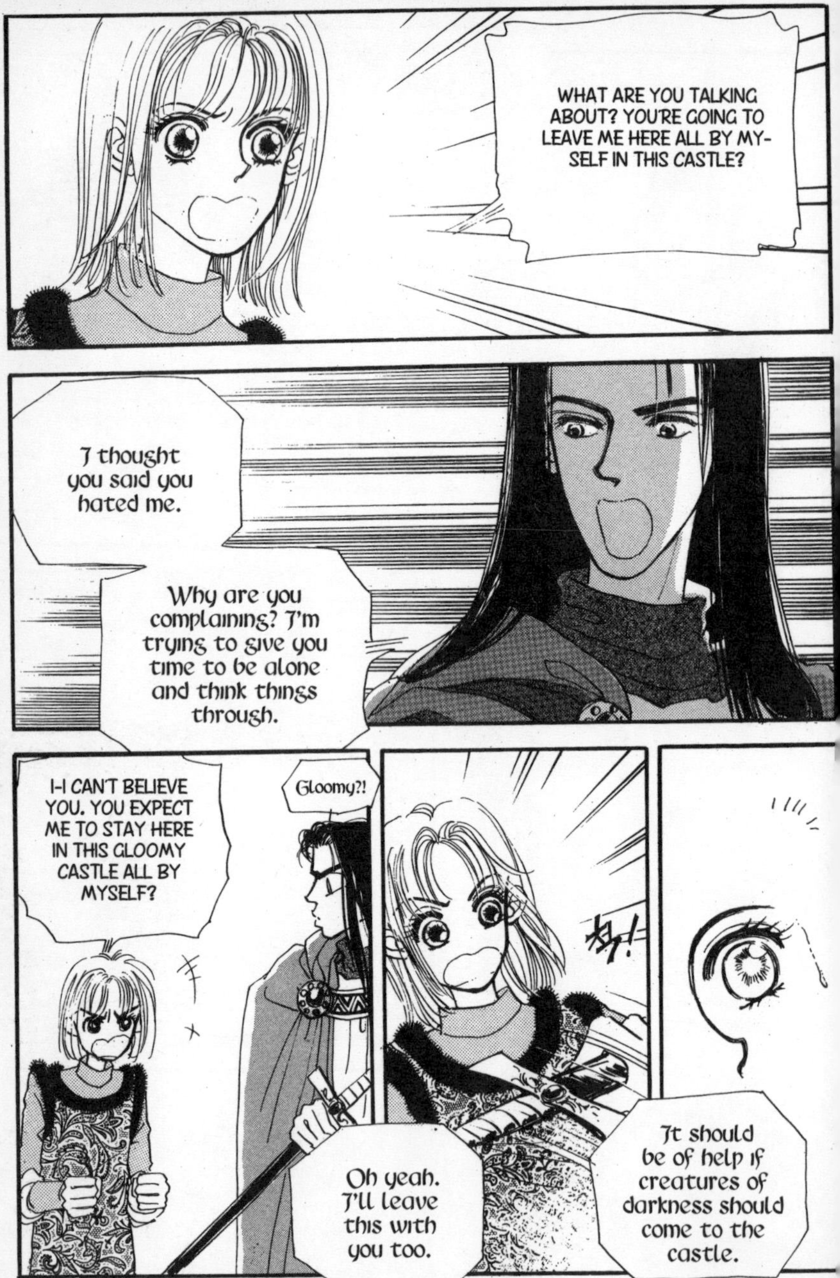
WHAT ARE YOU TALKING ABOUT? YOU'RE GOING TO LEAVE ME HERE ALL BY MY-SELF IN THIS CASTLE?
I thought you said you hated me.
Why are you complaining? I'm trying to give you time to be alone and think things through.
I-I CAN'T BELIEVE YOU. YOU EXPECT ME TO STAY HERE IN THIS GLOOMY CASTLE ALL BY MYSELF?
Gloomy?!
Oh yeah. I'll leave this with you too.
It should be of help if creatures of darkness should come to the castle.

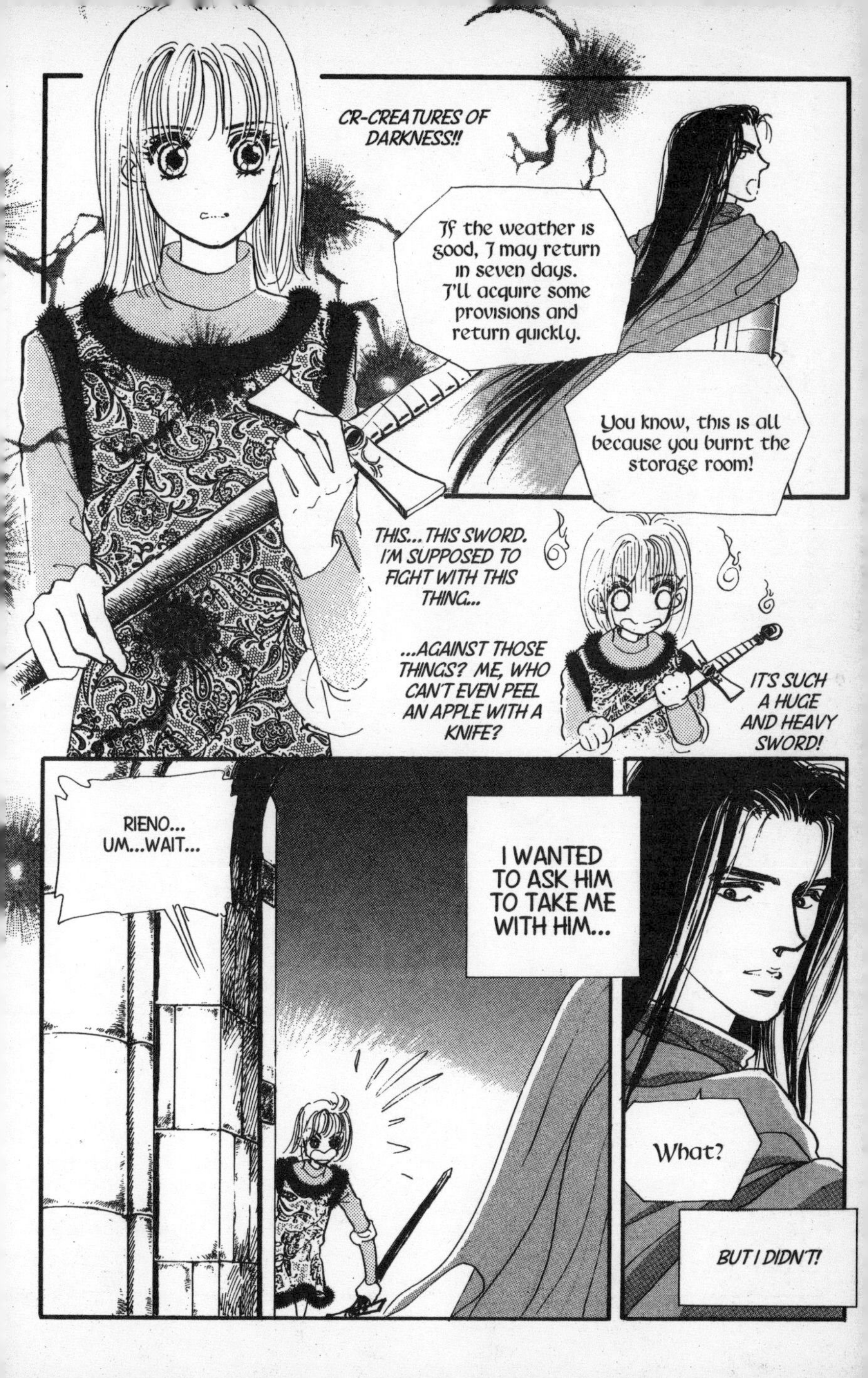
CR-CREATURES OF DARKNESS!!
If the weather is good, I may return in seven days. I'll acquire some provisions and return quickly.
You know, this is all because you burnt the storage room!
THIS...THIS SWORD. I'M SUPPOSED TO FIGHT WITH THIS THING...
...AGAINST THOSE THINGS? ME, WHO CAN'T EVEN PEEL AN APPLE WITH A KNIFE?
IT'S SUCH A HUGE AND HEAVY SWORD!
RIENO... UM...WAIT...
I WANTED TO ASK HIM TO TAKE ME WITH HIM...
What?
BUT I DIDN'T!

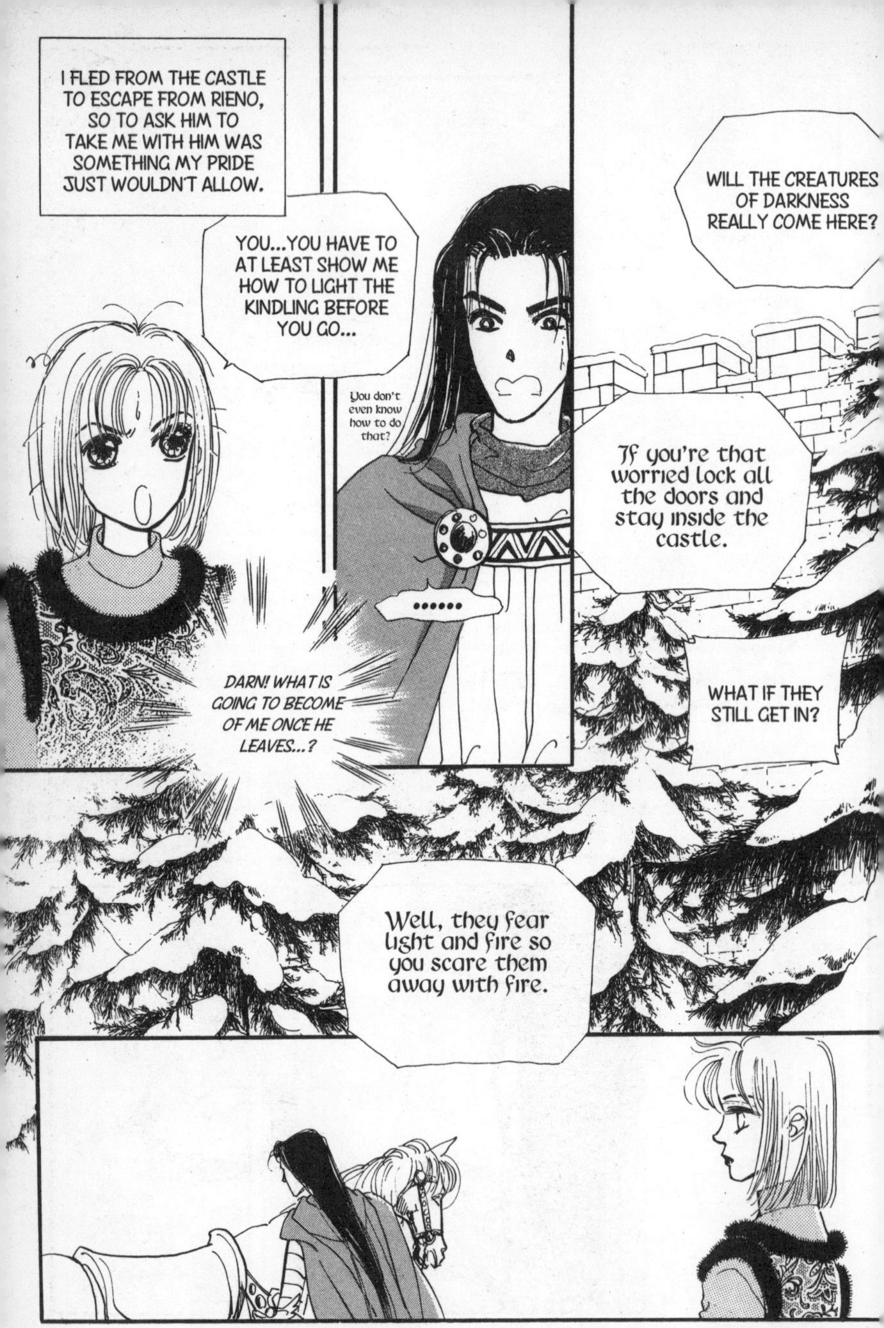
I FLED FROM THE CASTLE TO ESCAPE FROM RIENO, SO TO ASK HIM TO TAKE ME WITH HIM WAS SOMETHING MY PRIDE JUST WOULDN'T ALLOW.
YOU...YOU HAVE TO AT LEAST SHOW ME HOW TO LIGHT THE KINDLING BEFORE YOU GO...
You don't even know how to do that?
......
DARN! WHAT IS GOING TO BECOME OF ME ONCE HE LEAVES...?
WILL THE CREATURES OF DARKNESS REALLY COME HERE?
If you're that worried lock all the doors and stay inside the castle.
WHAT IF THEY STILL GET IN?
Well, they fear light and fire so you scare them away with fire.

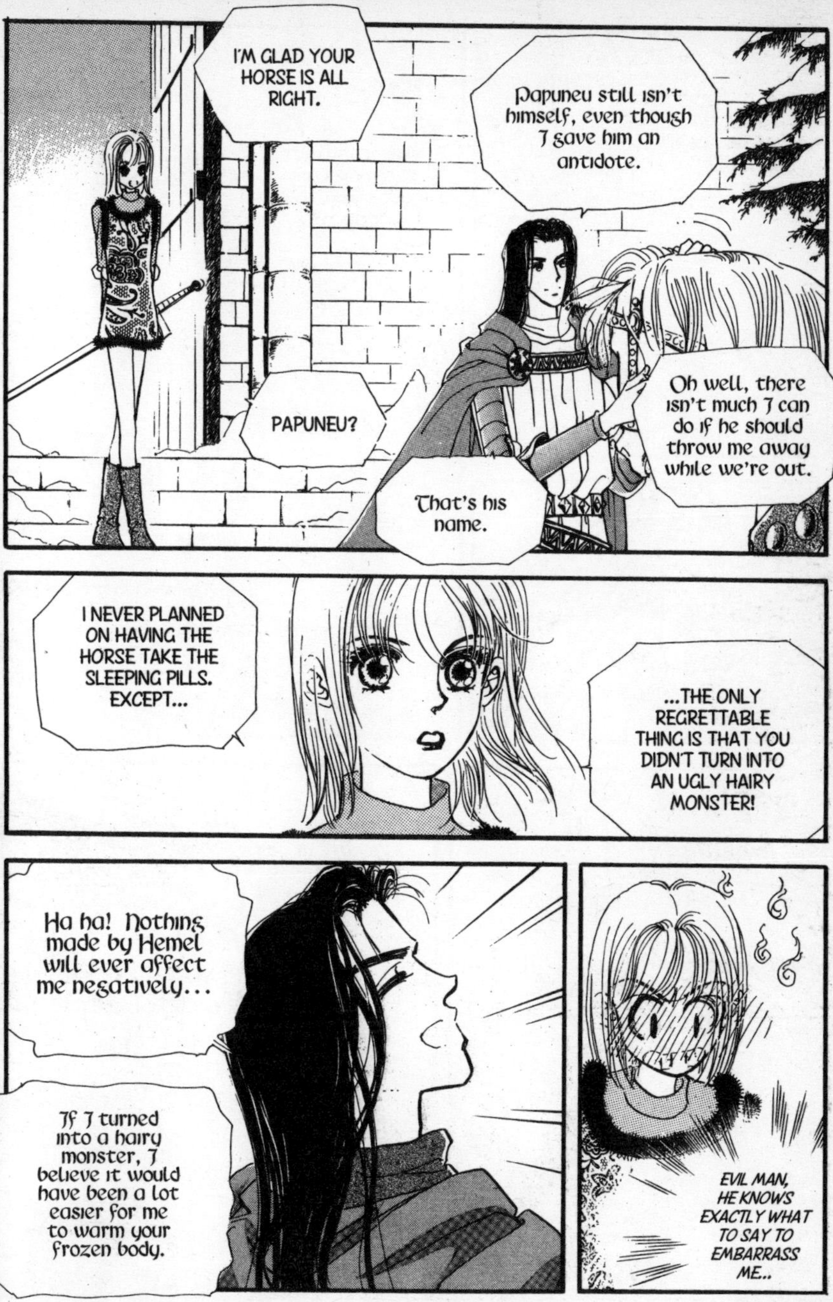
I'M GLAD YOUR HORSE IS ALL RIGHT.
Papuneu still isn't himself, even though I gave him an antidote.
PAPUNEU?
That's his name.
Oh well, there isn't much I can do if he should throw me away while we're out.
I NEVER PLANNED ON HAVING THE HORSE TAKE THE SLEEPING PILLS. EXCEPT...
...THE ONLY REGRETTABLE THING IS THAT YOU DIDN'T TURN INTO AN UGLY HAIRY MONSTER!
Ha ha! Nothing made by Hemel will ever affect me negatively...
If I turned into a hairy monster, I believe it would have been a lot easier for me to warm your frozen body.
EVIL MAN, HE KNOWS EXACTLY WHAT TO SAY TO EMBARRASS ME...

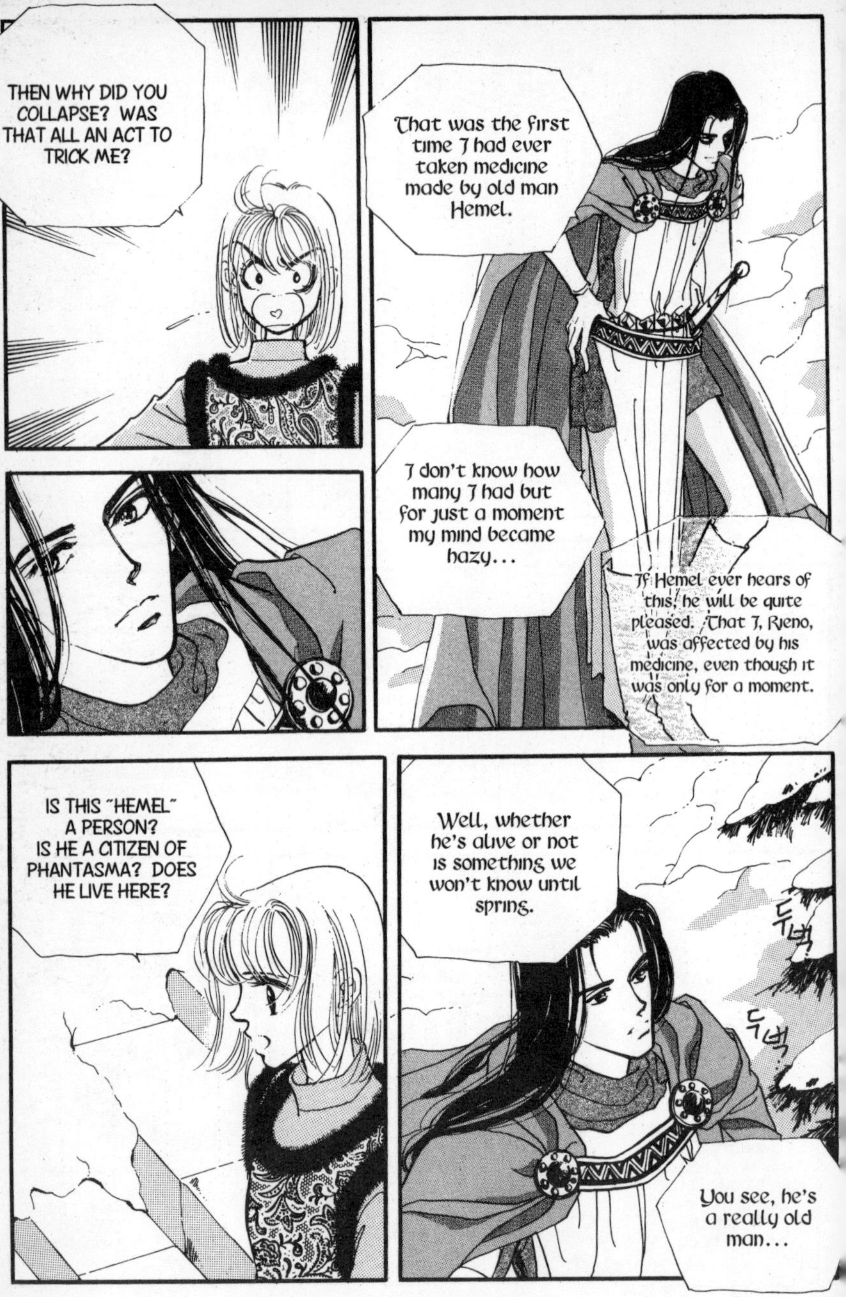
THEN WHY DID YOU COLLAPSE? WAS THAT ALL AN ACT TO TRICK ME?
That was the first time I had ever taken medicine made by old man Hemel.
I don't know how many I had but for just a moment my mind became hazy...
If Hemel ever hears of this, he will be quite pleased. That I, Rieno, was affected by his medicine, even though it was only for a moment.
IS THIS "HEMEL" A PERSON? IS HE A CITIZEN OF PHANTASMA? DOES HE LIVE HERE?
Well, whether he's alive or not is something we won't know until spring.
You see, he's a really old man...

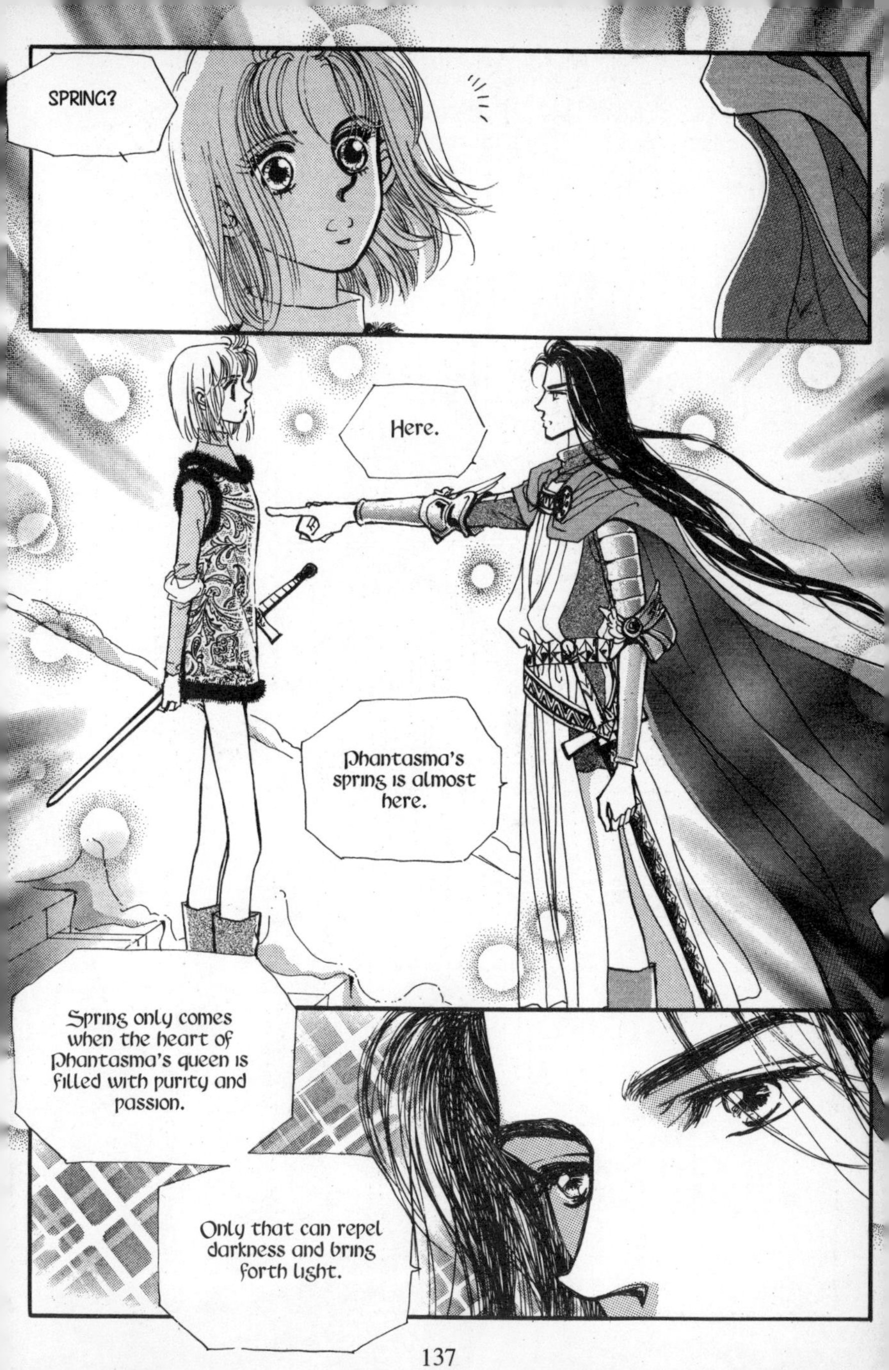
SPRING?
Here.
Phantasma's spring is almost here.
Spring only comes when the heart of Phantasma's queen is filled with purity and passion.
Only that can repel darkness and bring forth light.

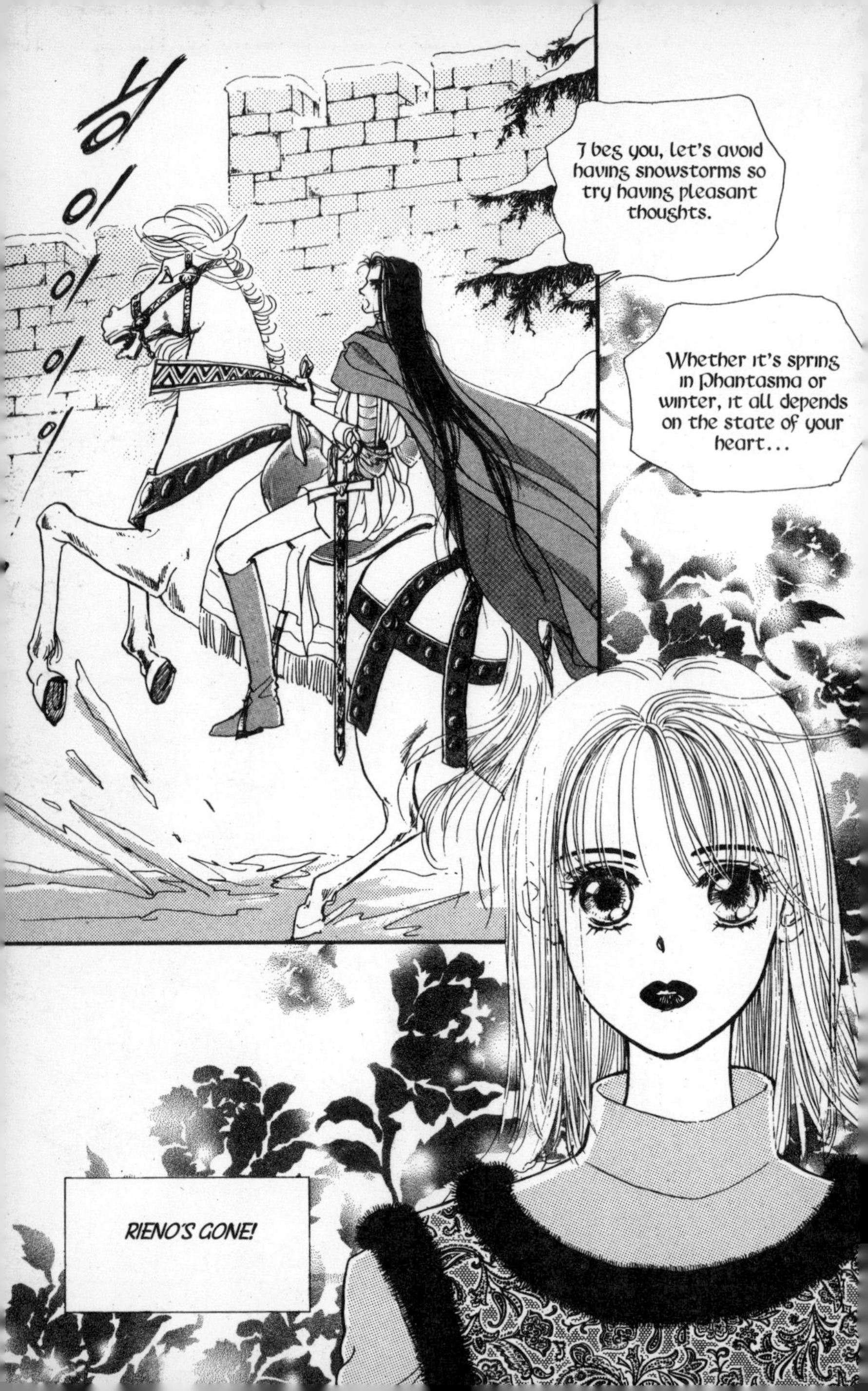
I beg you, let's avoid having snowstorms so try having pleasant thoughts.
Whether it's spring in Phantasma or winter, it all depends on the state of your heart...
RIENO'S GONE!

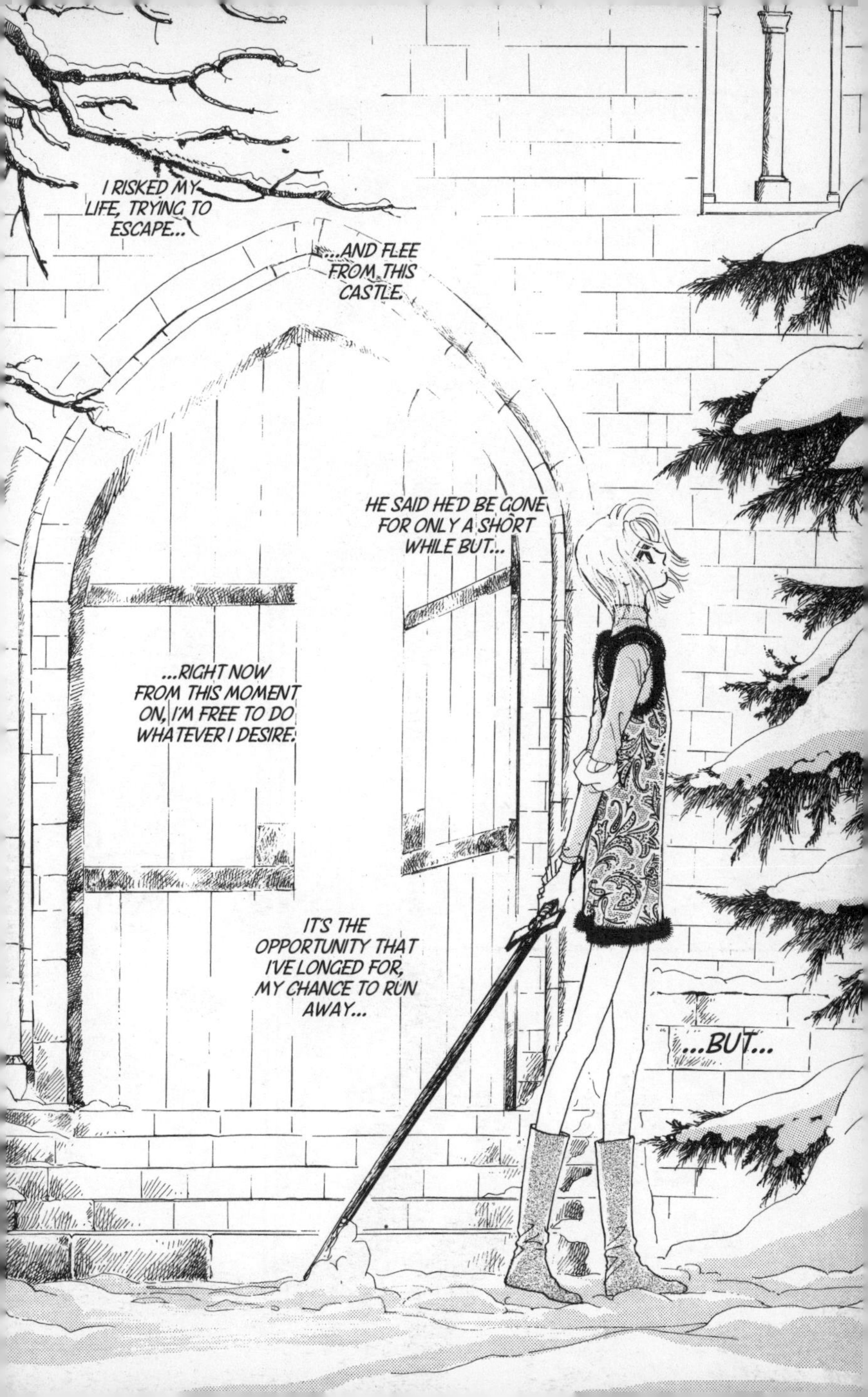
I RISKED MY LIFE, TRYING TO ESCAPE...
...AND FLEE FROM THIS CASTLE.
HE SAID HE'D BE GONE FOR ONLY A SHORT WHILE BUT...
...RIGHT NOW FROM THIS MOMENT ON, I'M FREE TO DO WHATEVER I DESIRE.
IT'S THE OPPORTUNITY THAT I'VE LONGED FOR, MY CHANCE TO RUN AWAY...
...BUT...

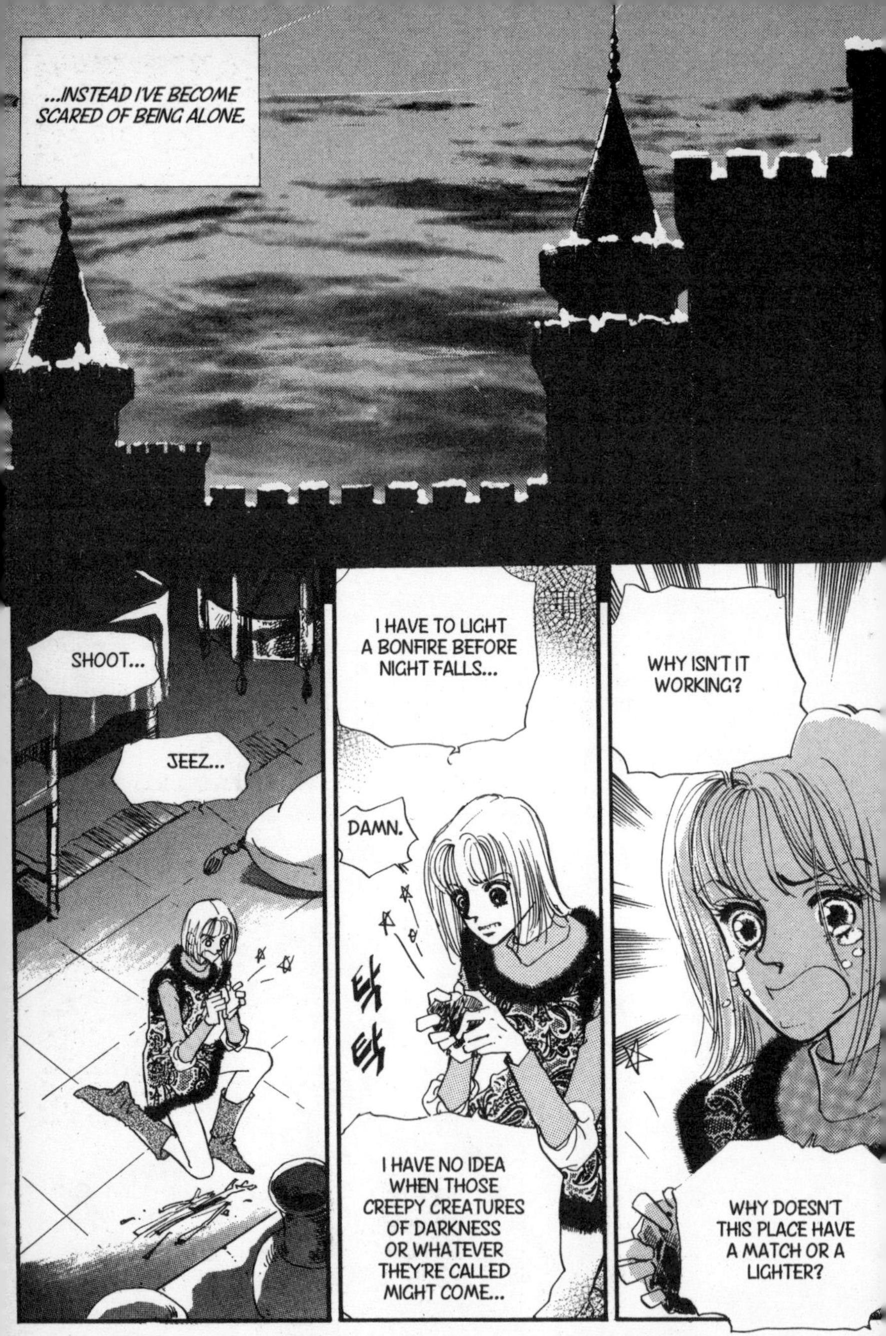
...INSTEAD I'VE BECOME SCARED OF BEING ALONE.
SHOOT...
JEEZ...
I HAVE TO LIGHT A BONFIRE BEFORE NIGHT FALLS...
DAMN.
탁
탁
I HAVE NO IDEA WHEN THOSE CREEPY CREATURES OF DARKNESS OR WHATEVER THEY'RE CALLED MIGHT COME...
WHY ISN'T IT WORKING?
WHY DOESN'T THIS PLACE HAVE A MATCH OR A LIGHTER?

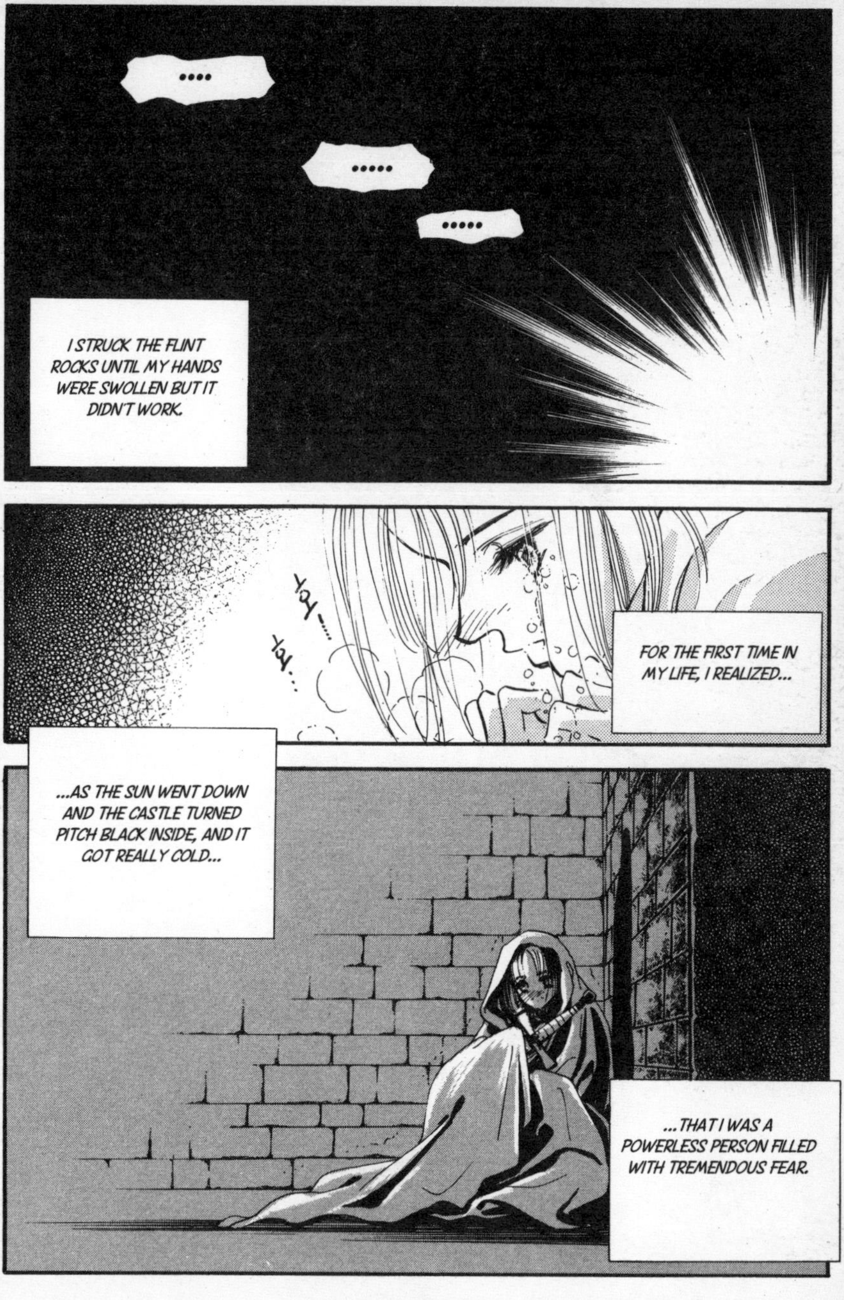
....
.....
.....
I STRUCK THE FLINT ROCKS UNTIL MY HANDS WERE SWOLLEN BUT IT DIDN'T WORK.
FOR THE FIRST TIME IN MY LIFE, I REALIZED...
...AS THE SUN WENT DOWN AND THE CASTLE TURNED PITCH BLACK INSIDE, AND IT GOT REALLY COLD...
...THAT I WAS A POWERLESS PERSON FILLED WITH TREMENDOUS FEAR.

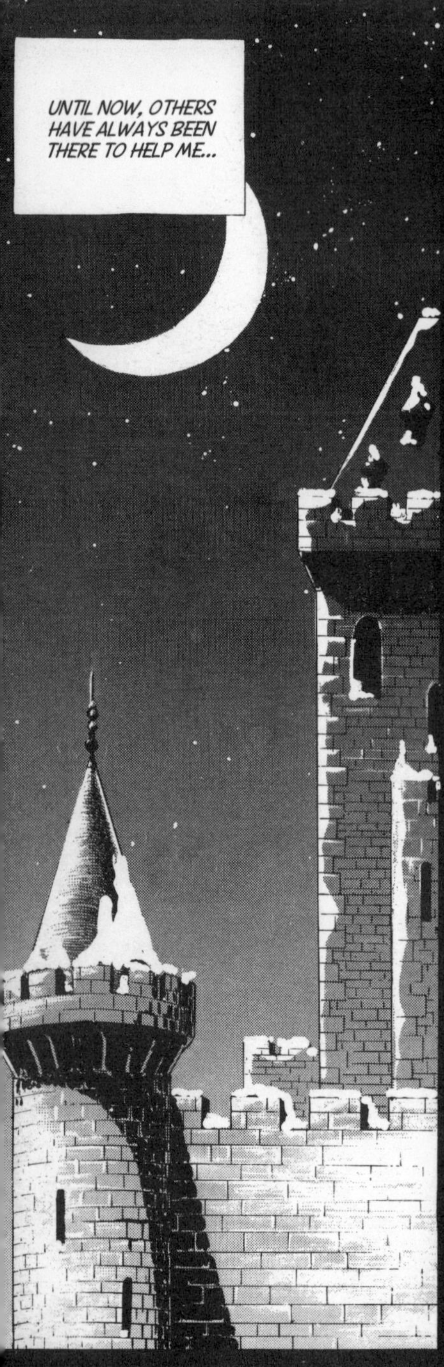
UNTIL NOW, OTHERS HAVE ALWAYS BEEN THERE TO HELP ME...

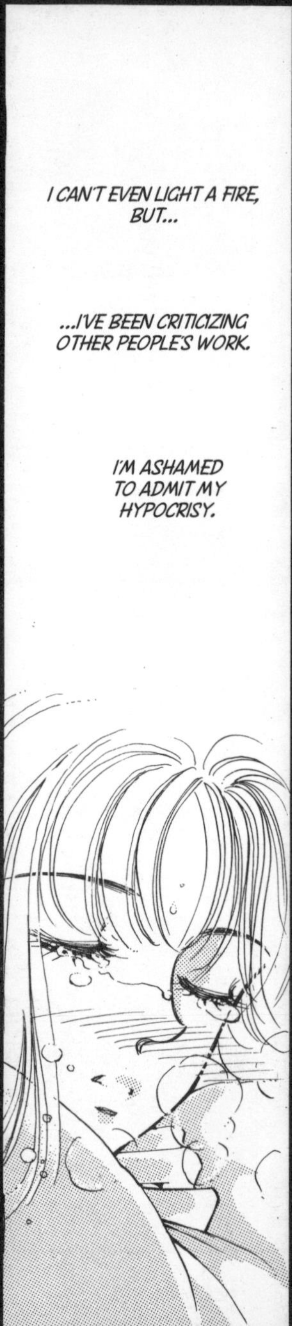
I CAN'T EVEN LIGHT A FIRE, BUT...
...I'VE BEEN CRITICIZING OTHER PEOPLE'S WORK.
I'M ASHAMED TO ADMIT MY HYPOCRISY.

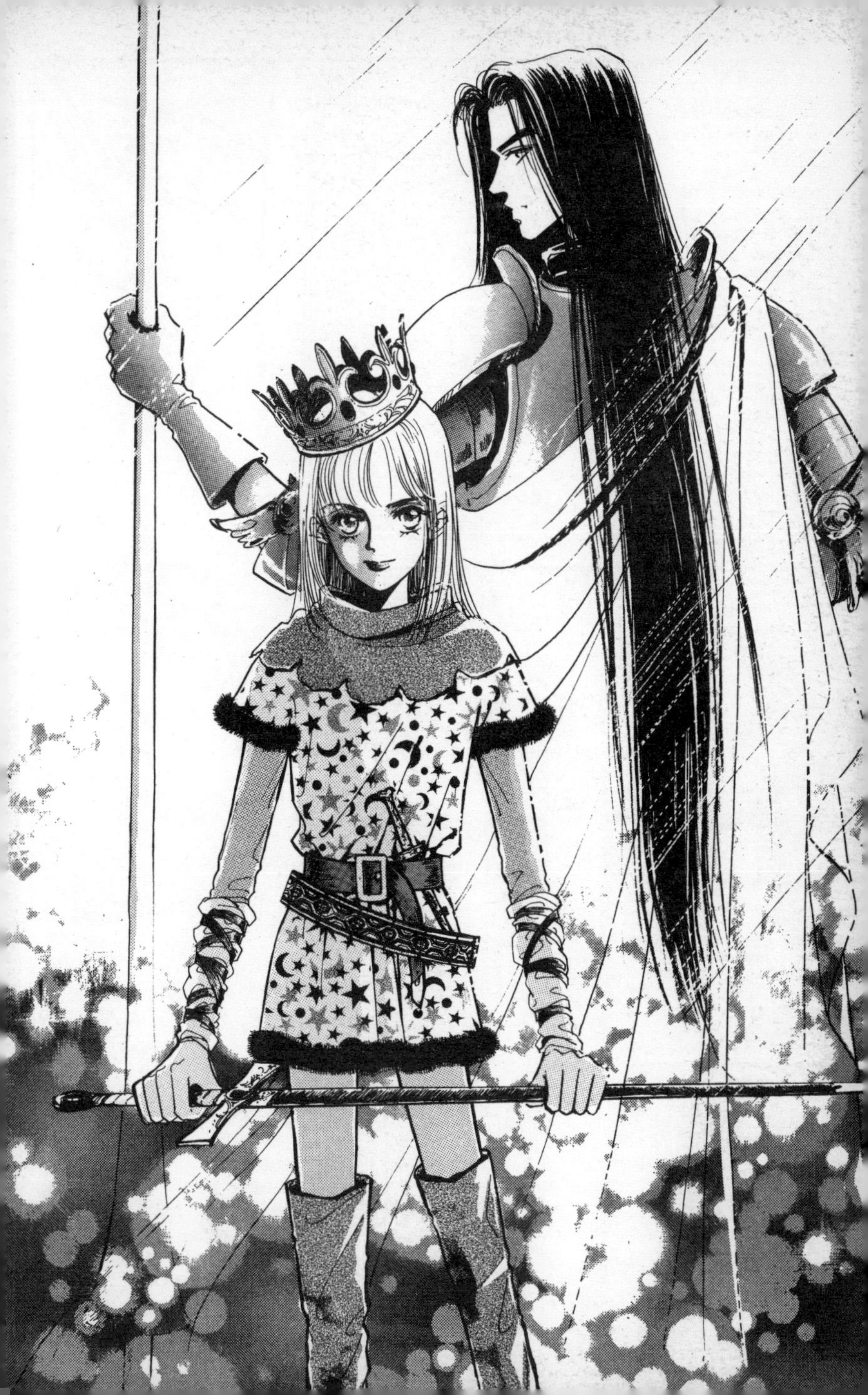

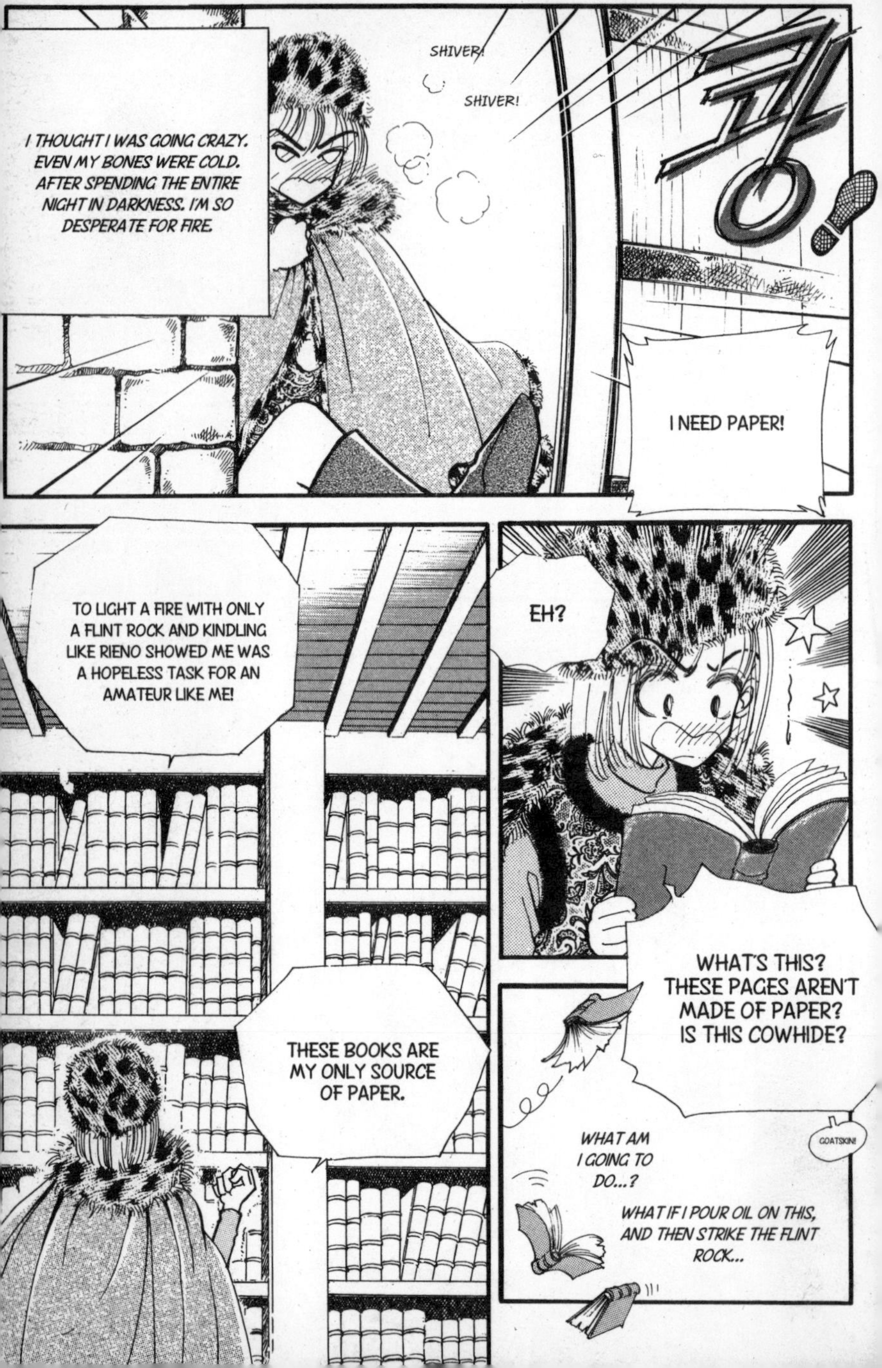
I THOUGHT I WAS GOING CRAZY. EVEN MY BONES WERE COLD. AFTER SPENDING THE ENTIRE NIGHT IN DARKNESS. I'M SO DESPERATE FOR FIRE.
SHIVER!
SHIVER!
I NEED PAPER!
TO LIGHT A FIRE WITH ONLY A FLINT ROCK AND KINDLING LIKE RIENO SHOWED ME WAS A HOPELESS TASK FOR AN AMATEUR LIKE ME!
THESE BOOKS ARE MY ONLY SOURCE OF PAPER.
EH?
WHAT'S THIS? THESE PAGES AREN'T MADE OF PAPER? IS THIS COWHIDE?
GOATSKIN!
WHAT AM I GOING TO DO...?
WHAT IF I POUR OIL ON THIS, AND THEN STRIKE THE FLINT ROCK...

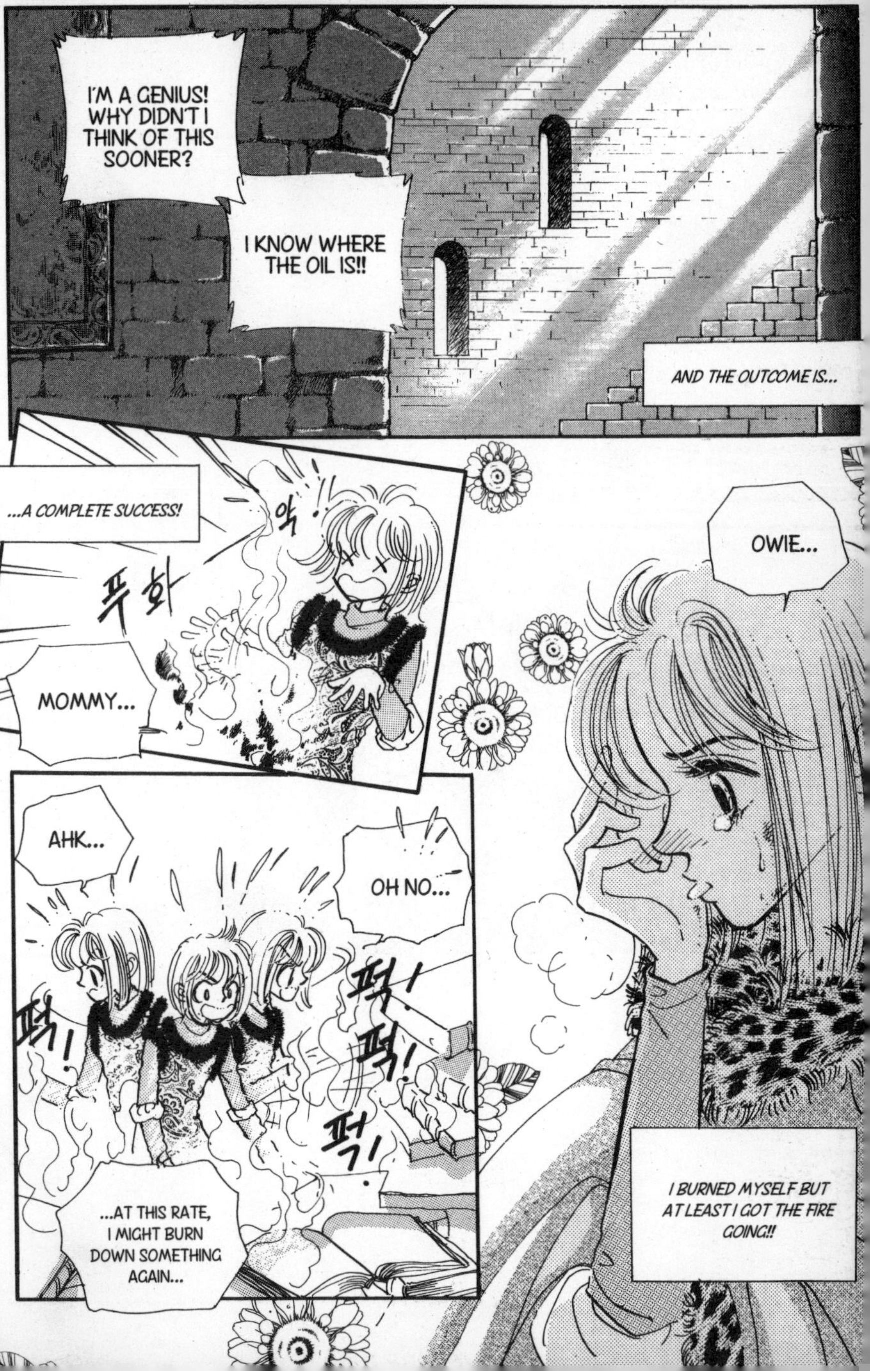
I'M A GENIUS! WHY DIDN'T I THINK OF THIS SOONER?
I KNOW WHERE THE OIL IS!!
AND THE OUTCOME IS...
...A COMPLETE SUCCESS!
악
푸화
MOMMY...
AHK...
OH NO...
퍽!
퍽!
퍽!
퍽!
...AT THIS RATE, I MIGHT BURN DOWN SOMETHING AGAIN...
OWIE...
I BURNED MYSELF BUT AT LEAST I GOT THE FIRE GOING!!

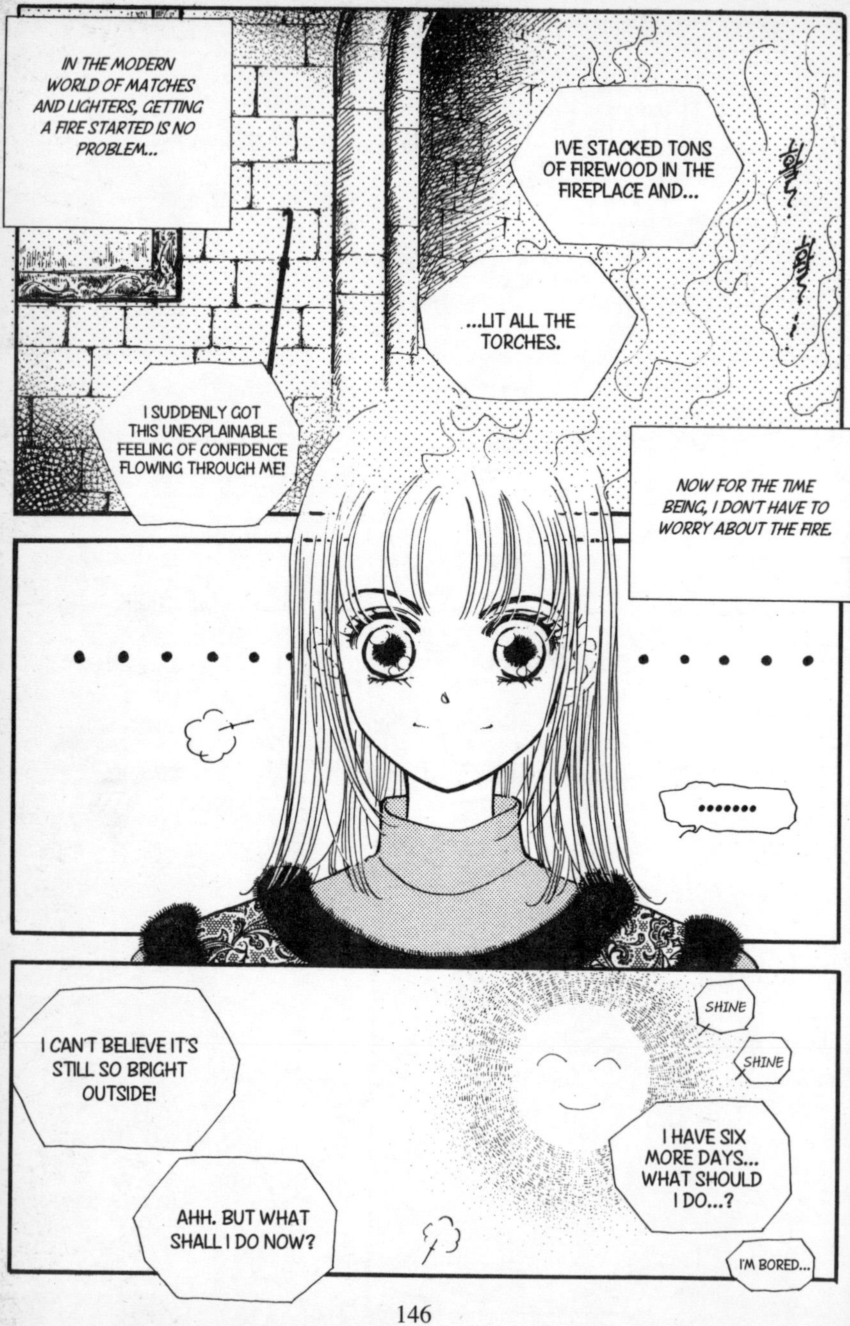
IN THE MODERN WORLD OF MATCHES AND LIGHTERS, GETTING A FIRE STARTED IS NO PROBLEM...
I'VE STACKED TONS OF FIREWOOD IN THE FIREPLACE AND...
...LIT ALL THE TORCHES.
I SUDDENLY GOT THIS UNEXPLAINABLE FEELING OF CONFIDENCE FLOWING THROUGH ME!
NOW FOR THE TIME BEING, I DON'T HAVE TO WORRY ABOUT THE FIRE.
• • • • •
• • • • •
....
SHINE
SHINE
I CAN'T BELIEVE IT'S STILL SO BRIGHT OUTSIDE!
I HAVE SIX MORE DAYS... WHAT SHOULD I DO...?
AHH. BUT WHAT SHALL I DO NOW?
I'M BORED...

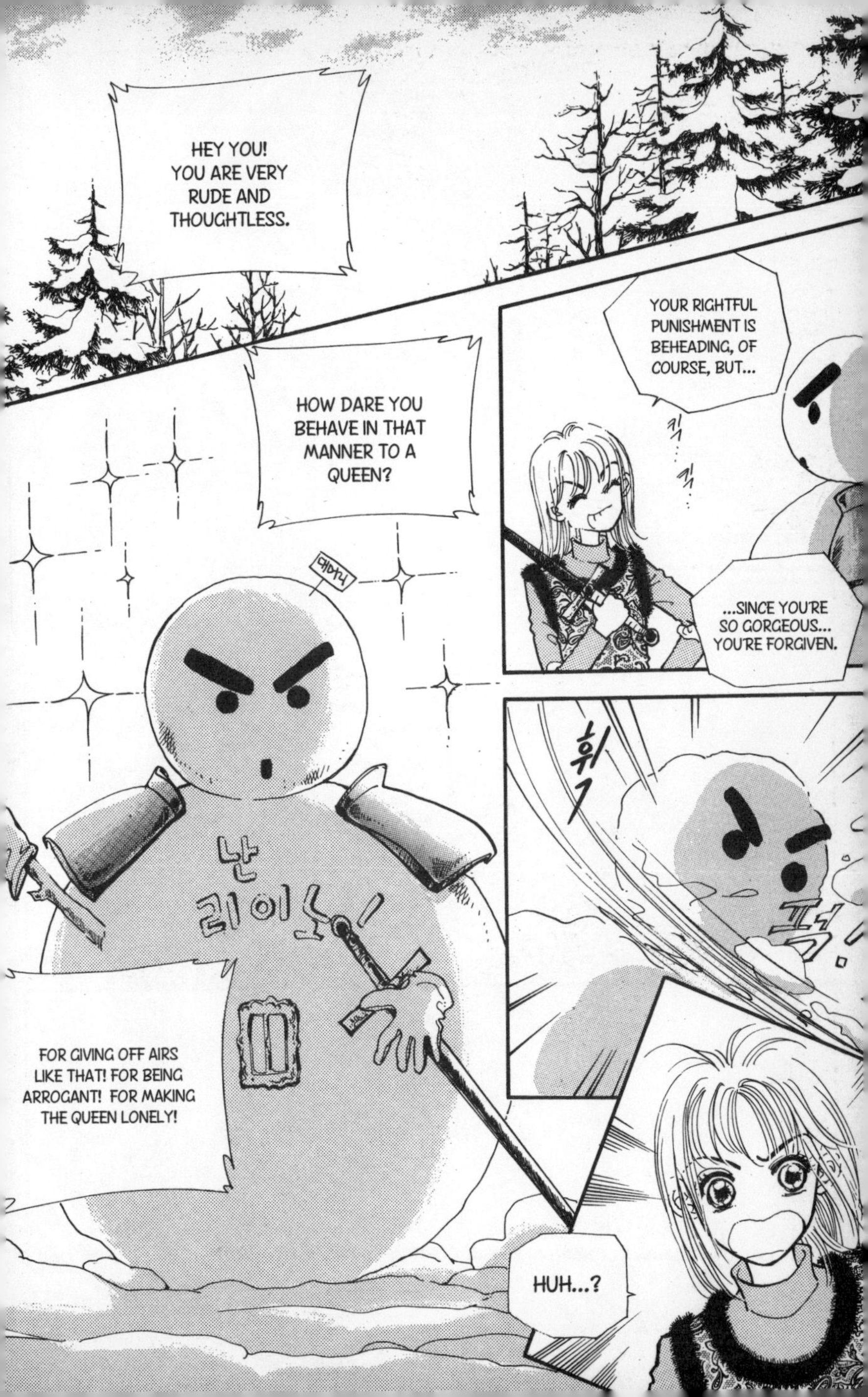
HEY YOU! YOU ARE VERY RUDE AND THOUGHTLESS.
HOW DARE YOU BEHAVE IN THAT MANNER TO A QUEEN?
FOR GIVING OFF AIRS LIKE THAT! FOR BEING ARROGANT! FOR MAKING THE QUEEN LONELY!
YOUR RIGHTFUL PUNISHMENT IS BEHEADING, OF COURSE, BUT...
...SINCE YOU'RE SO GORGEOUS... YOU'RE FORGIVEN.
HUH...?

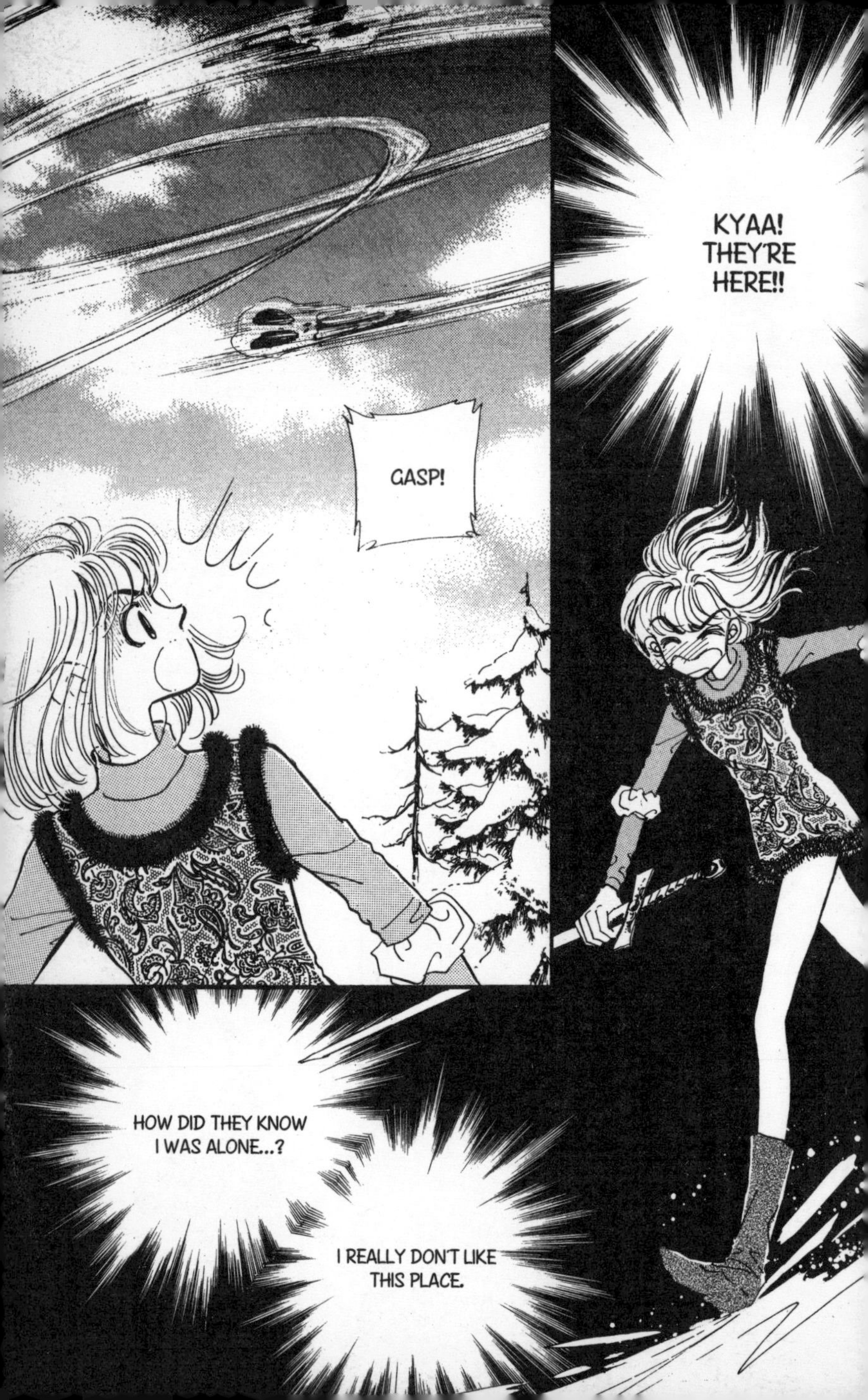
GASP!
HOW DID THEY KNOW I WAS ALONE...?
I REALLY DON'T LIKE THIS PLACE.
KYAA! THEY'RE HERE!!

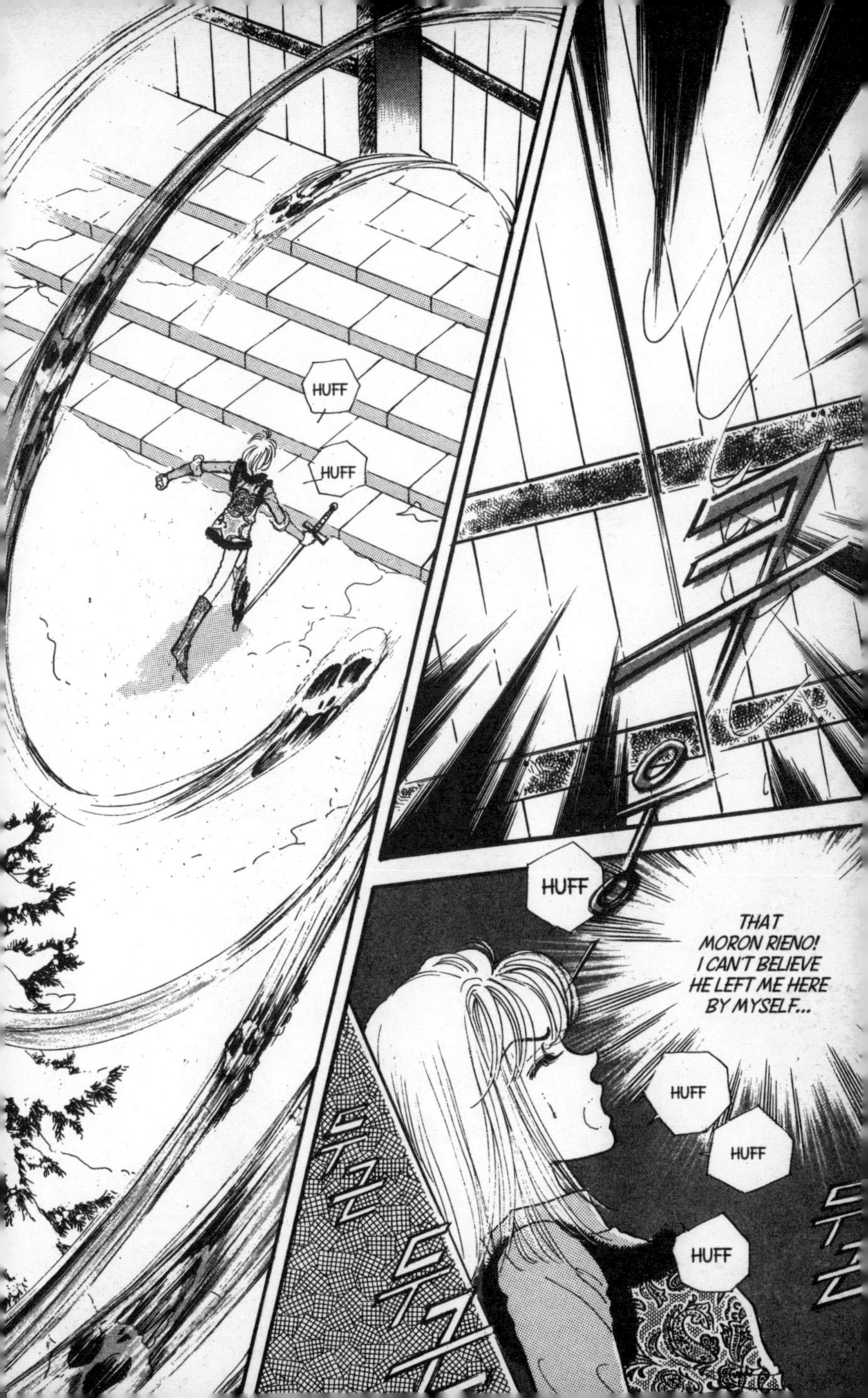
HUFF
HUFF
HUFF
THAT MORON RIENO! I CAN'T BELIEVE HE LEFT ME HERE BY MYSELF...
HUFF
HUFF
HUFF

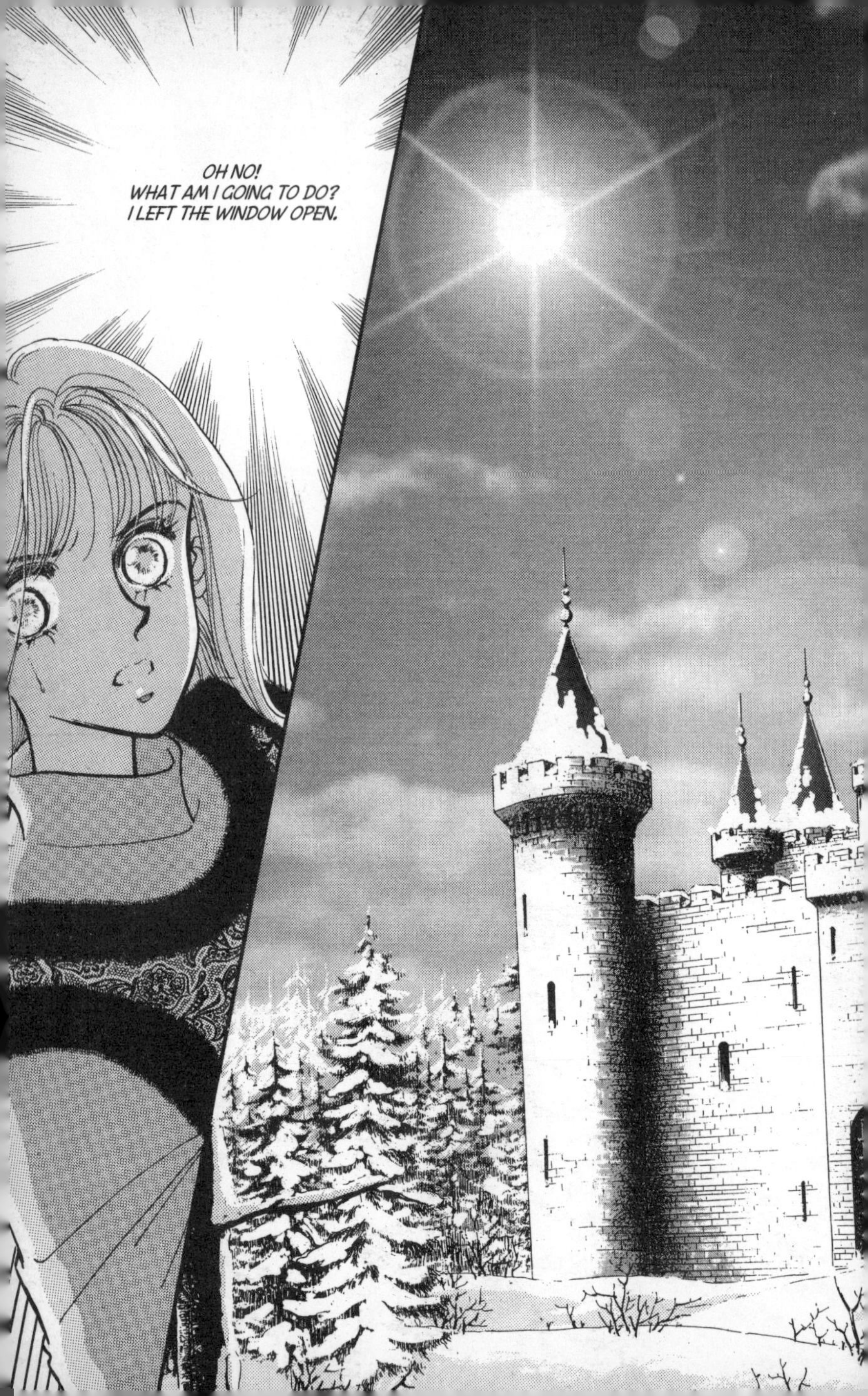
OH NO!
WHAT AM I GOING TO DO?
I LEFT THE WINDOW OPEN.

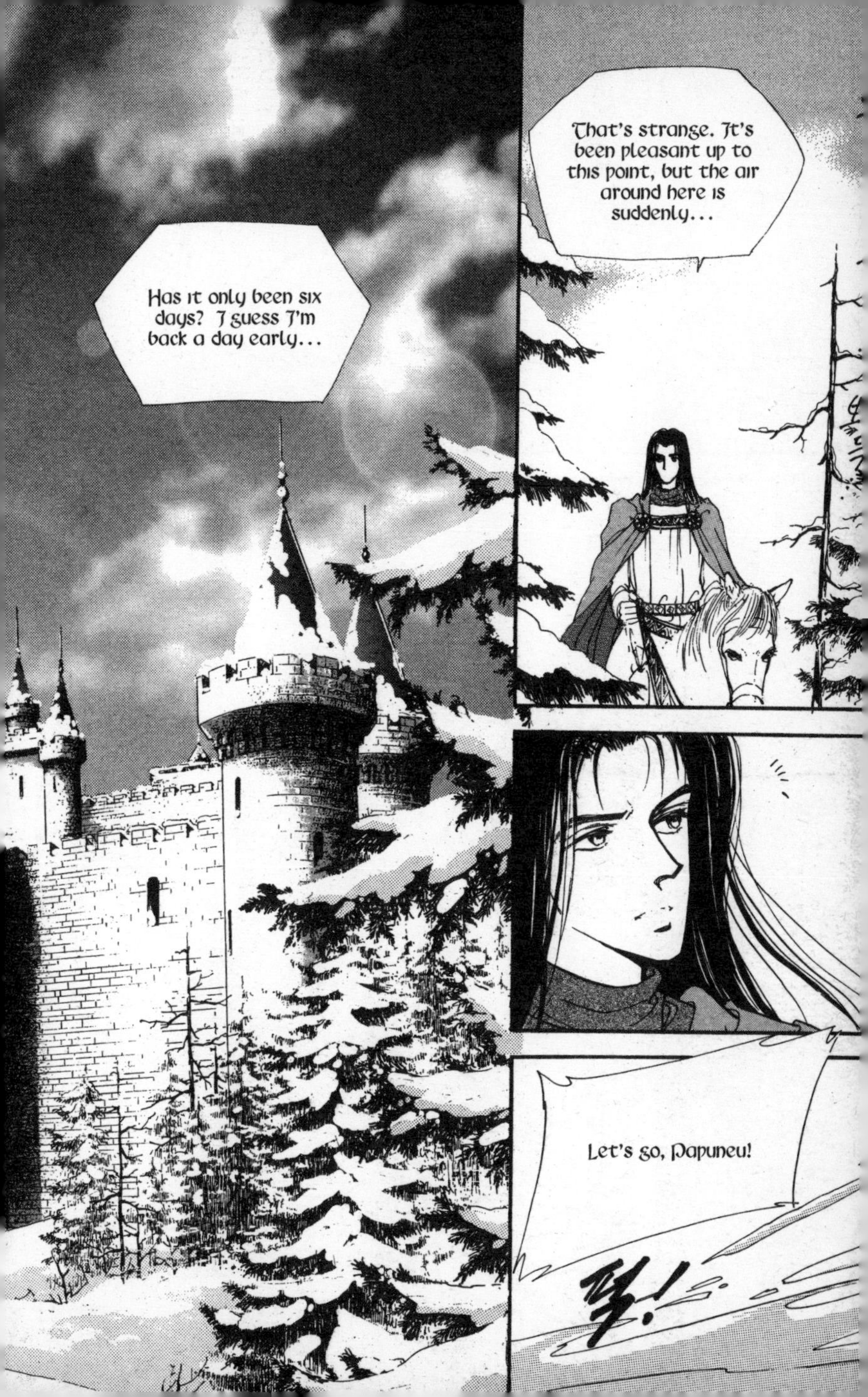
Has it only been six days? I guess I'm back a day early...
That's strange. It's been pleasant up to this point, but the air around here is suddenly...
Let's go, Papuneu!

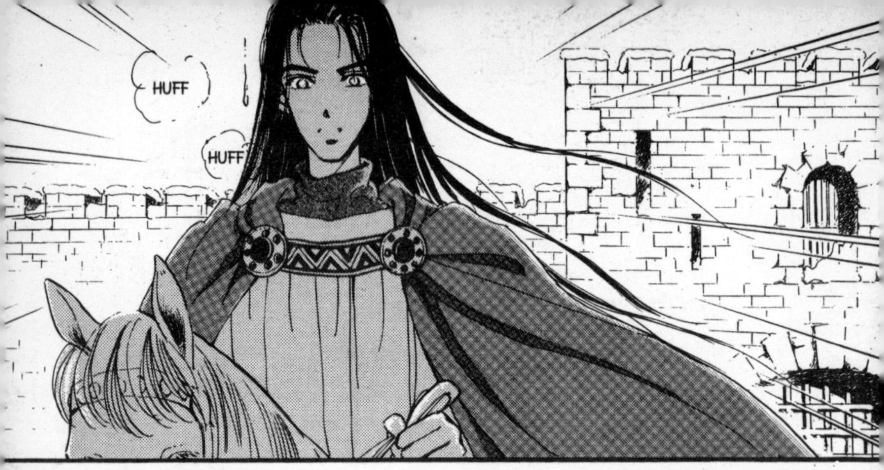
HUFF
HUFF

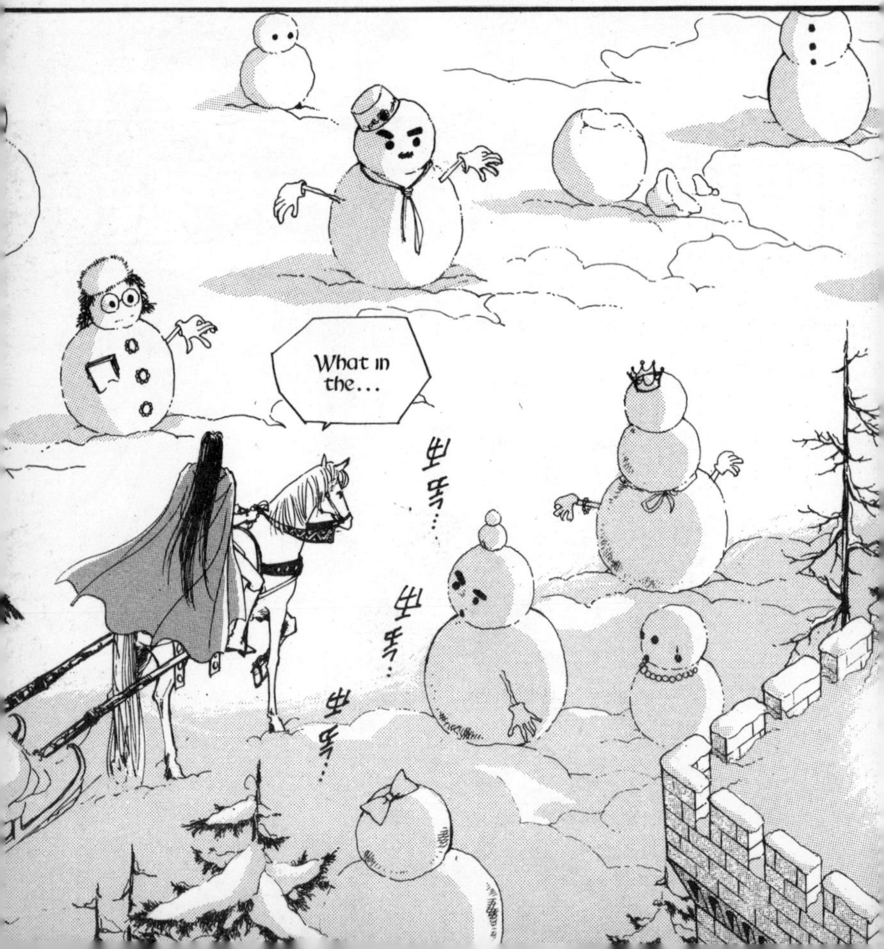
What in the…

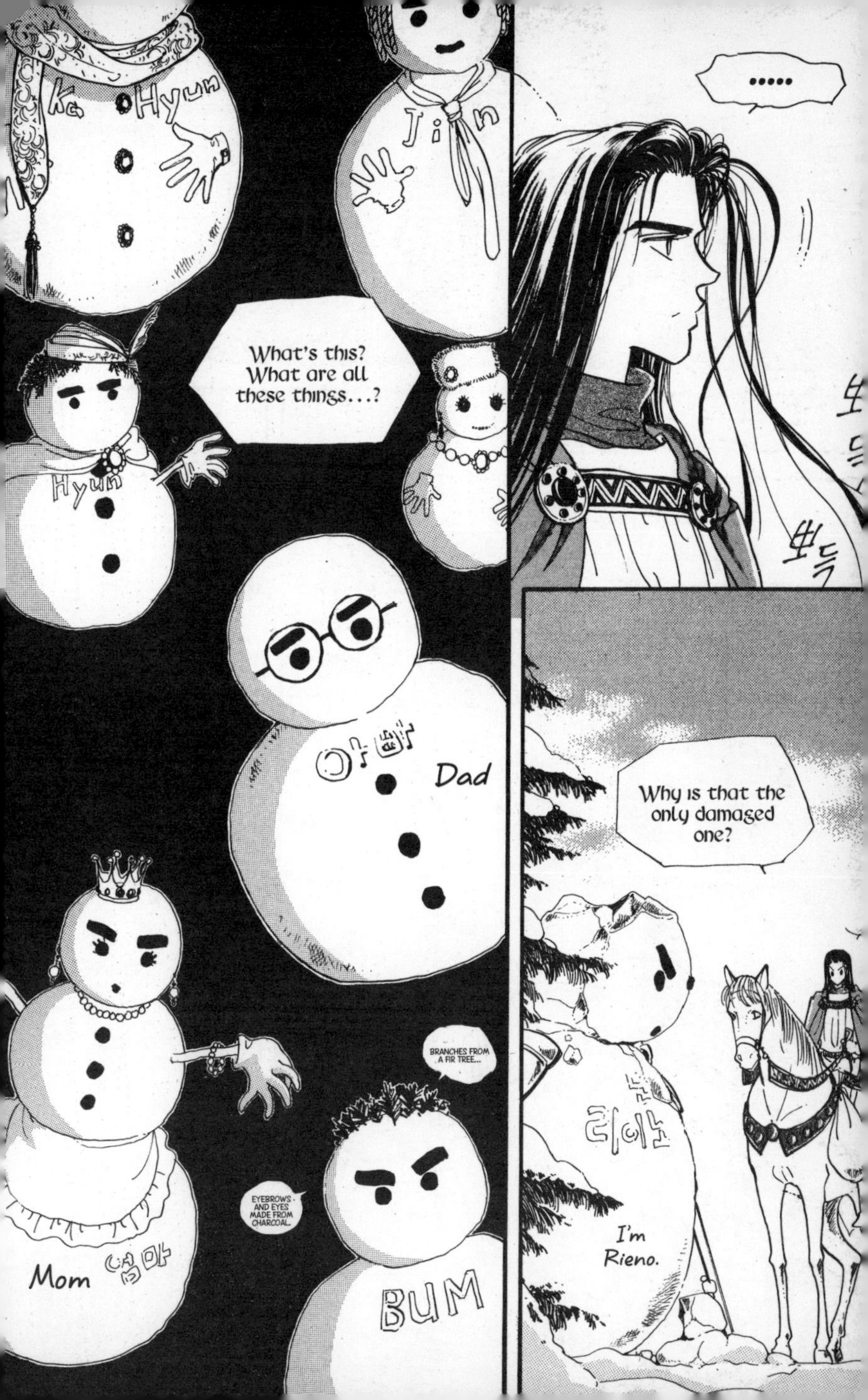
Ka Hyun
Jin
What's this? What are all these things...?
Hyun
아빠
Dad
BRANCHES FROM A FIR TREE...
EYEBROWS AND EYES MADE FROM CHARCOAL.
Mom
엄마
BUM
......
Why is that the only damaged one?
리에노
I'm Rieno.

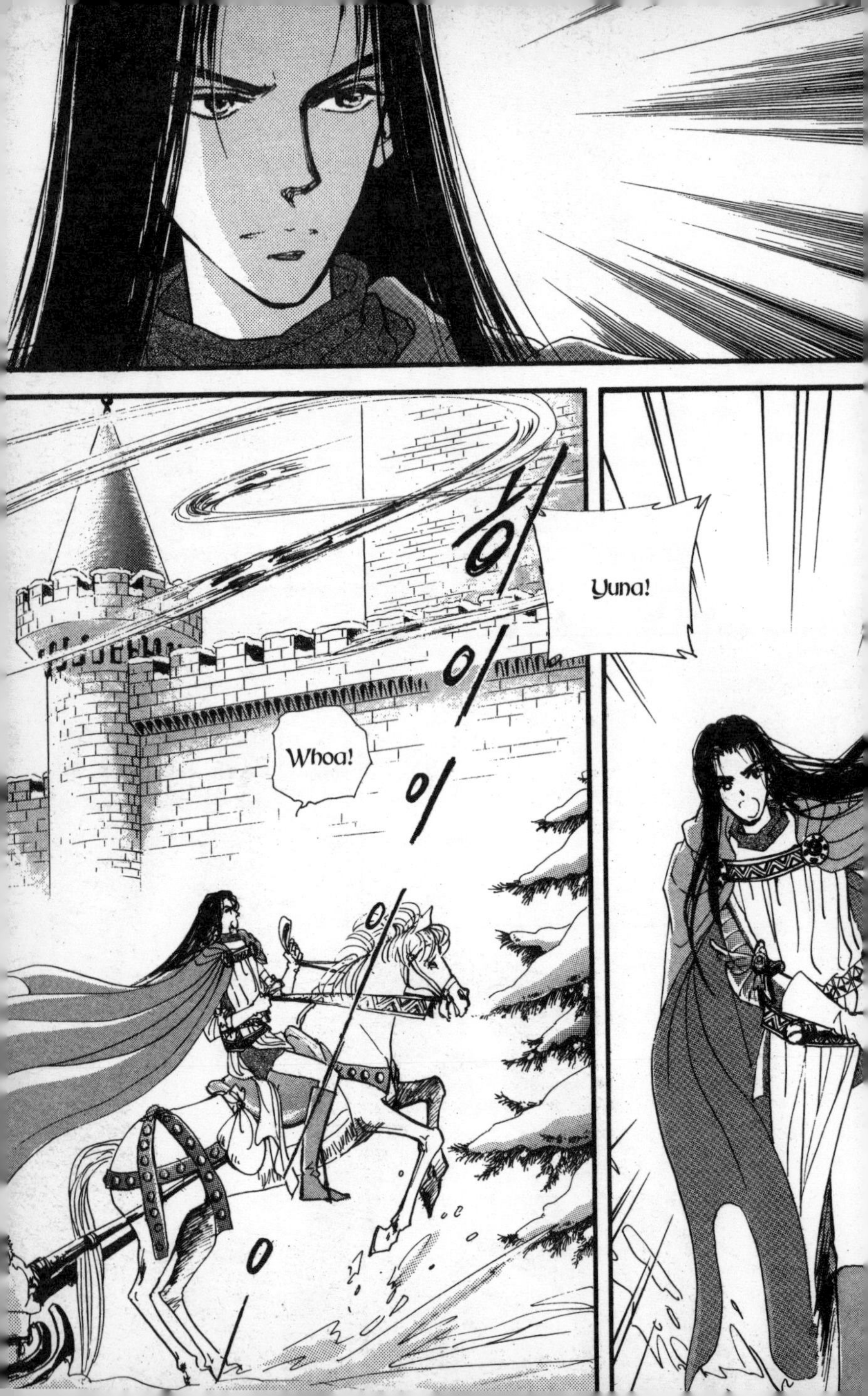
Whoa!
Yuna!

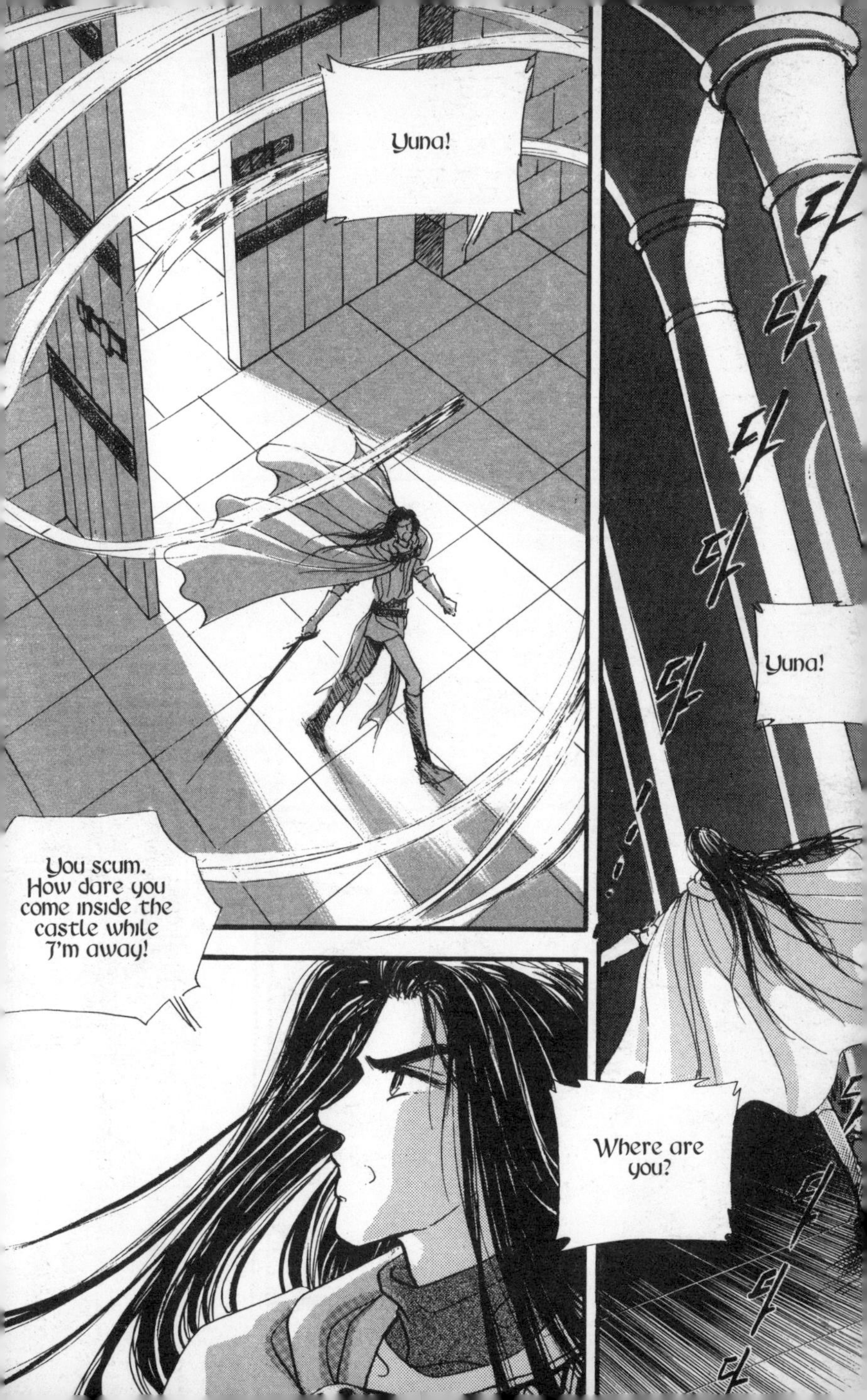
Yuna!
You scum. How dare you come inside the castle while I'm away!
Where are you?
Yuna!

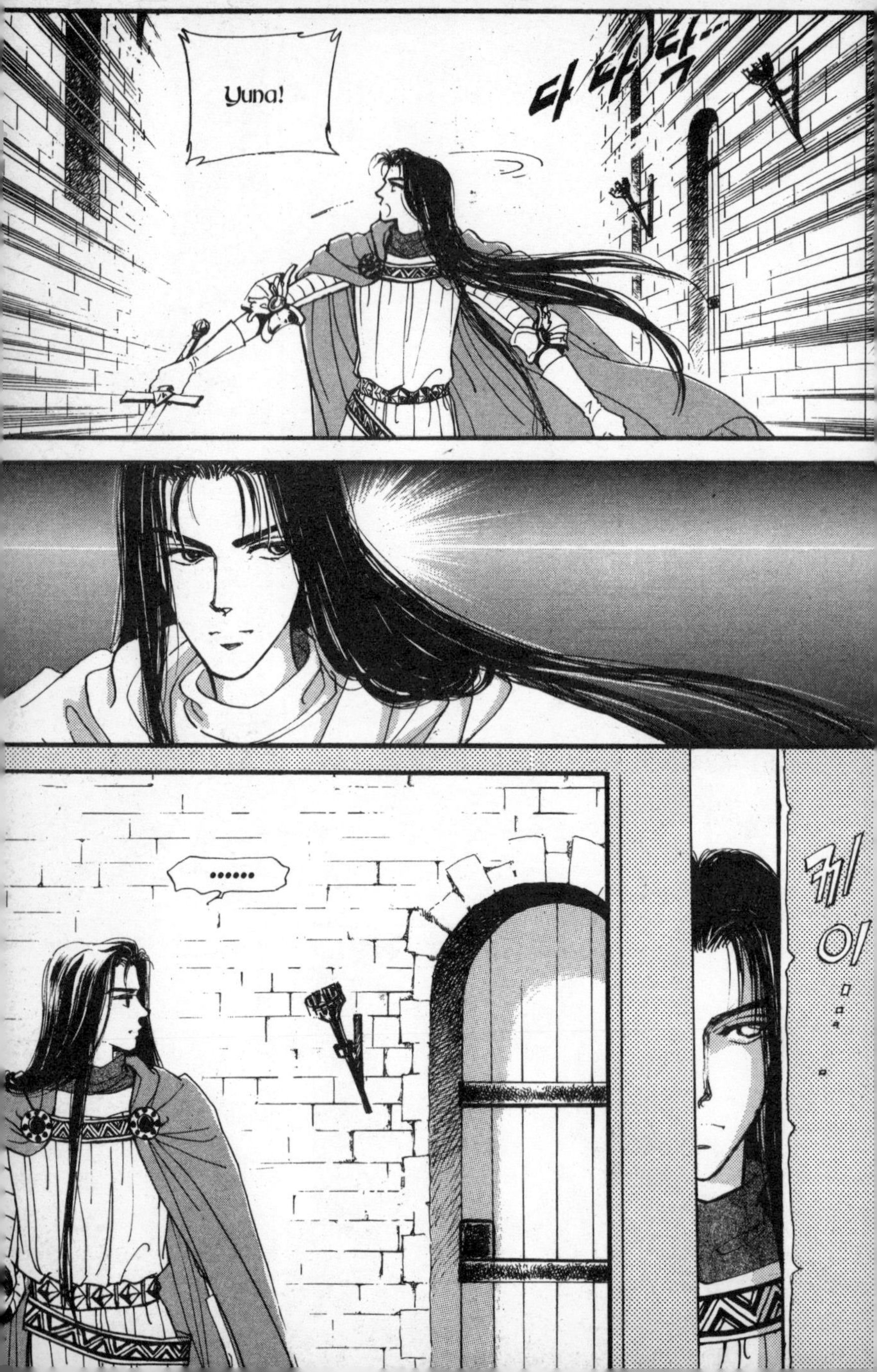
Yuna!
다다닥…
……
끼이

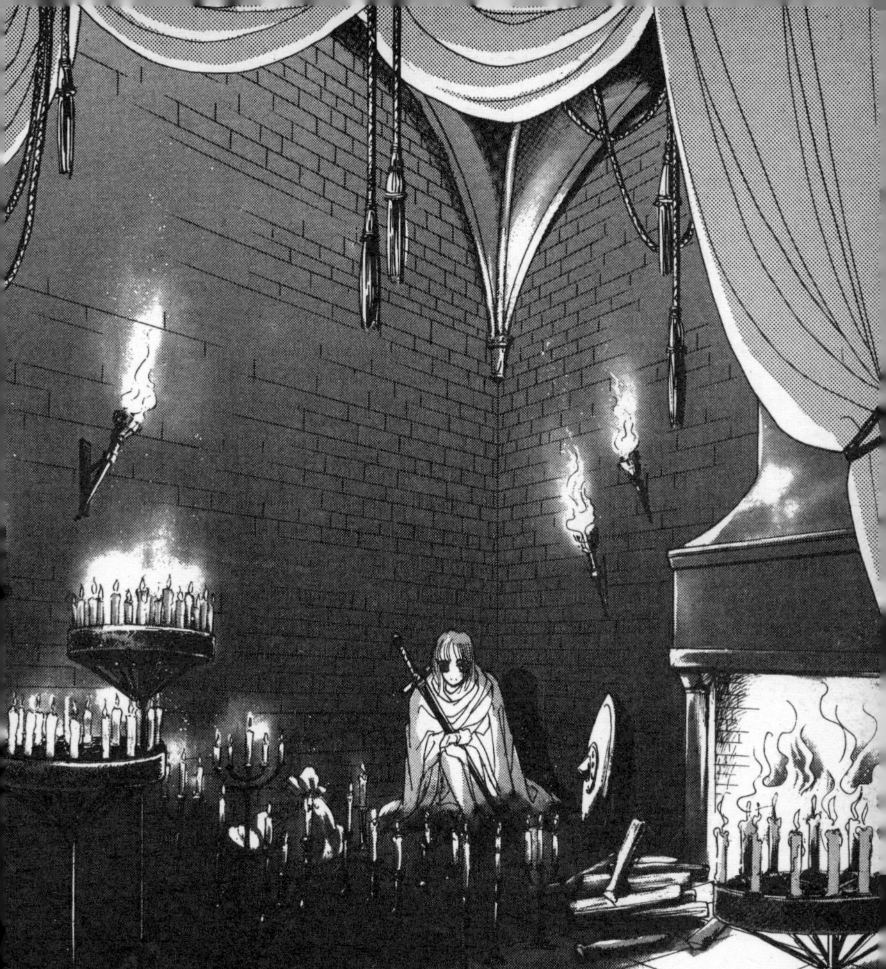
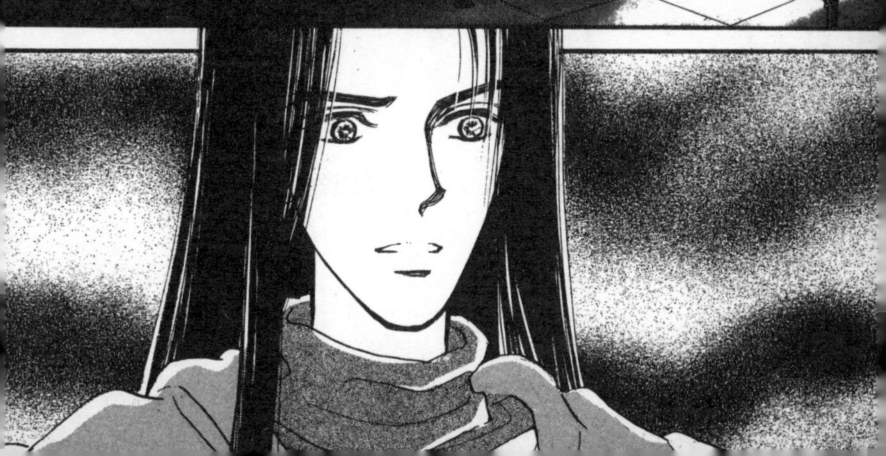

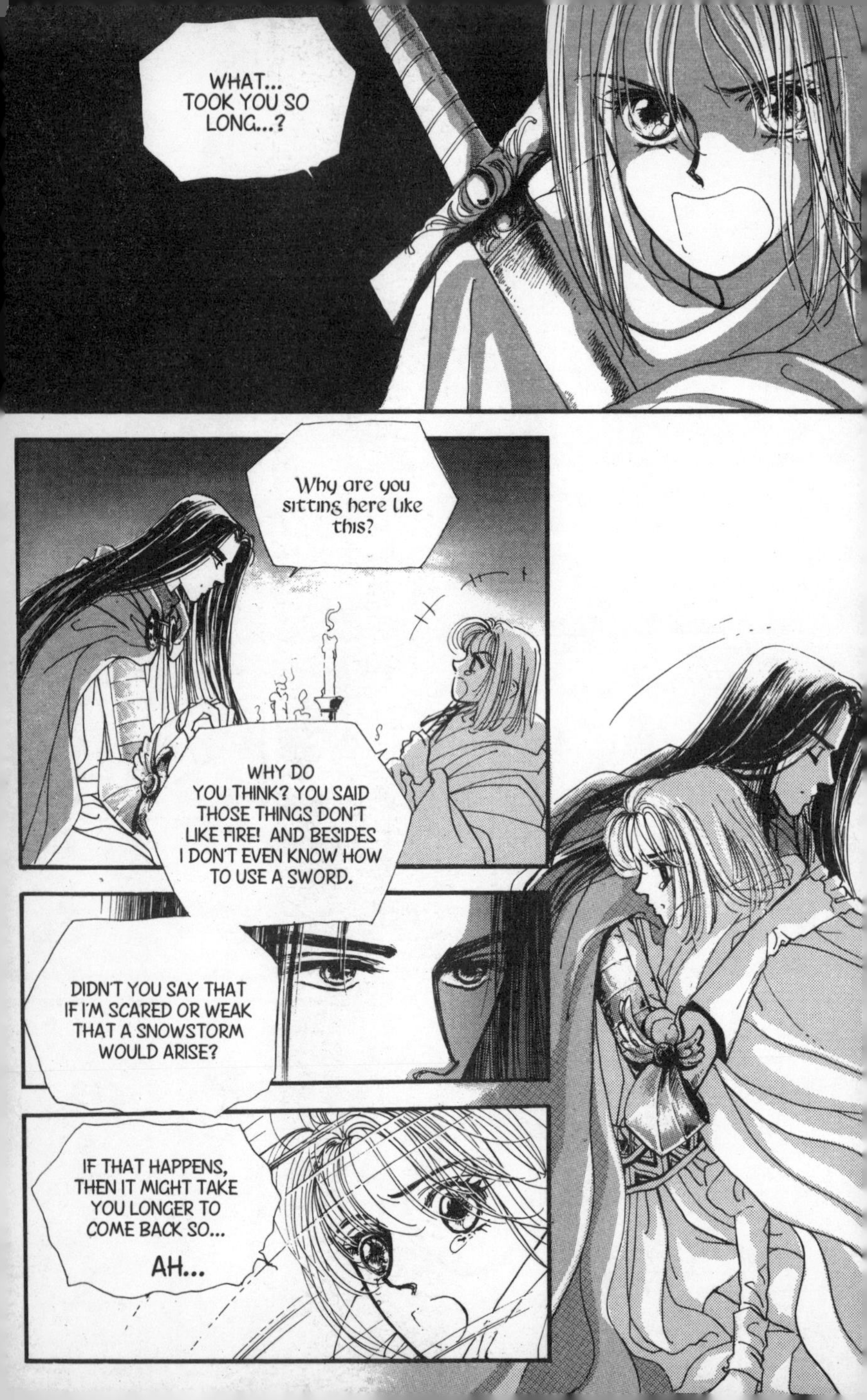
WHAT... TOOK YOU SO LONG...?
Why are you sitting here like this?
WHY DO YOU THINK? YOU SAID THOSE THINGS DON'T LIKE FIRE! AND BESIDES I DON'T EVEN KNOW HOW TO USE A SWORD.
DIDN'T YOU SAY THAT IF I'M SCARED OR WEAK THAT A SNOWSTORM WOULD ARISE?
IF THAT HAPPENS, THEN IT MIGHT TAKE YOU LONGER TO COME BACK SO...
AH...

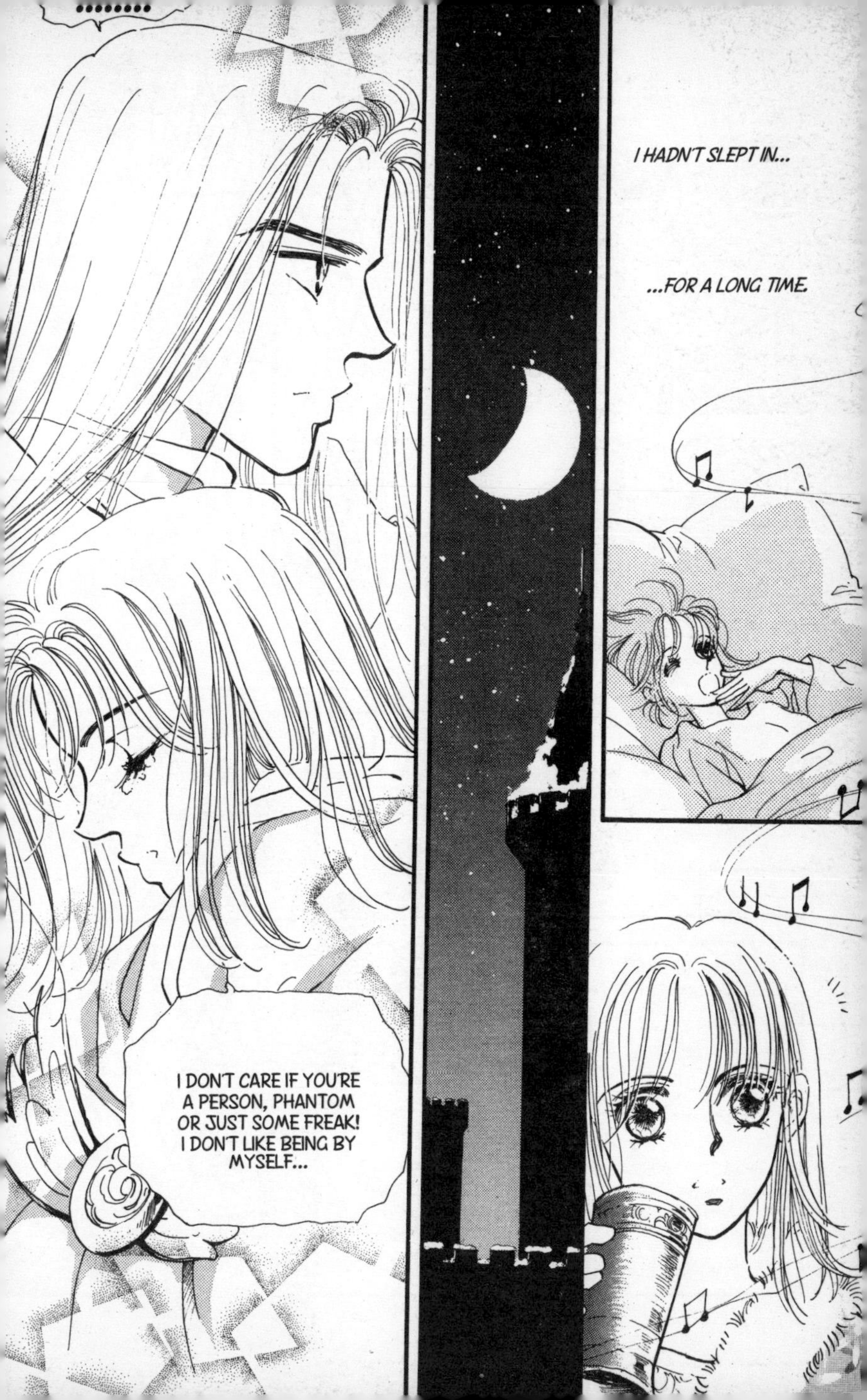
I DON'T CARE IF YOU'RE A PERSON, PHANTOM OR JUST SOME FREAK! I DON'T LIKE BEING BY MYSELF...
I HADN'T SLEPT IN...
...FOR A LONG TIME.

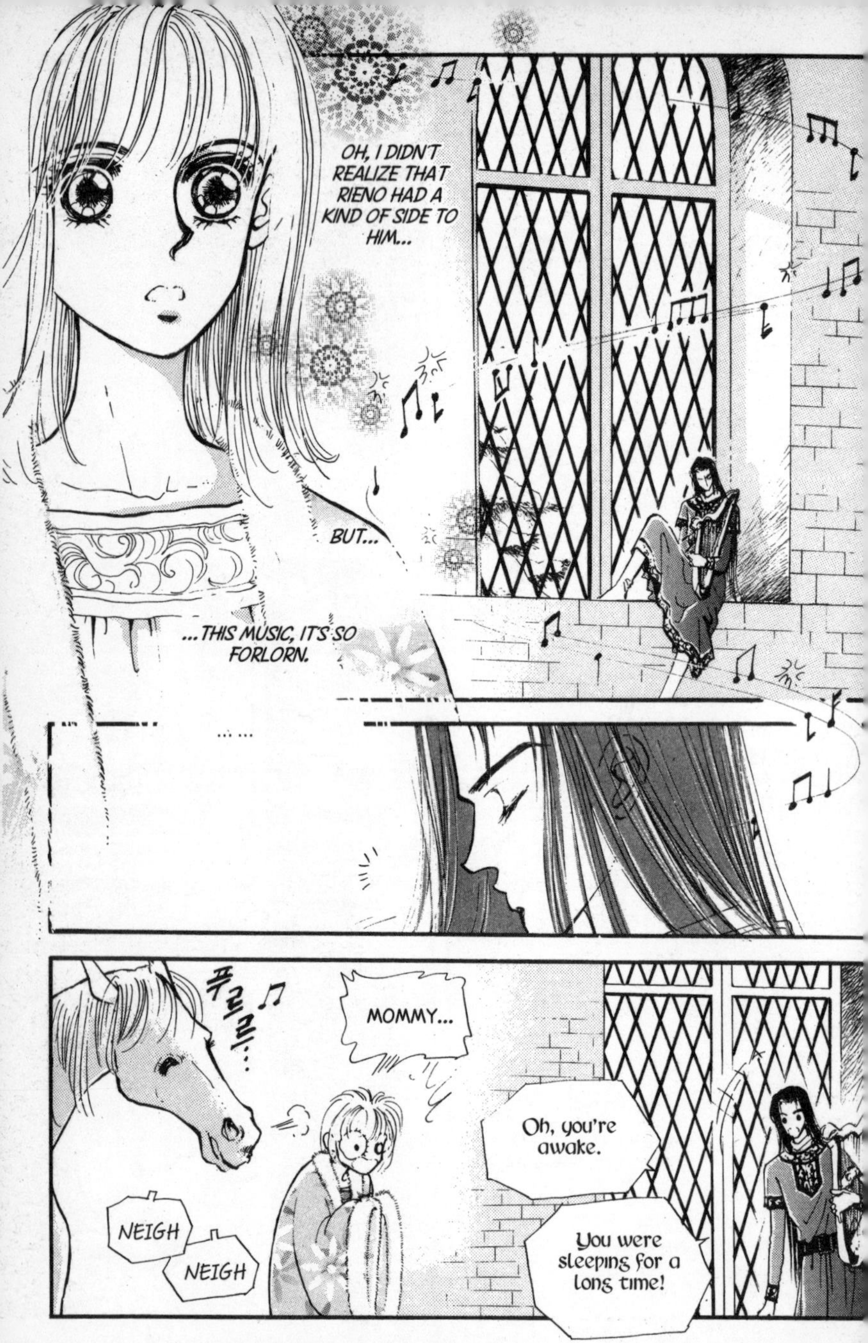
OH, I DIDN'T REALIZE THAT RIENO HAD A KIND OF SIDE TO HIM...
BUT...
...THIS MUSIC, IT'S SO FORLORN.
......
푸르르...
MOMMY...
NEIGH
NEIGH
Oh, you're awake.
You were sleeping for a long time!

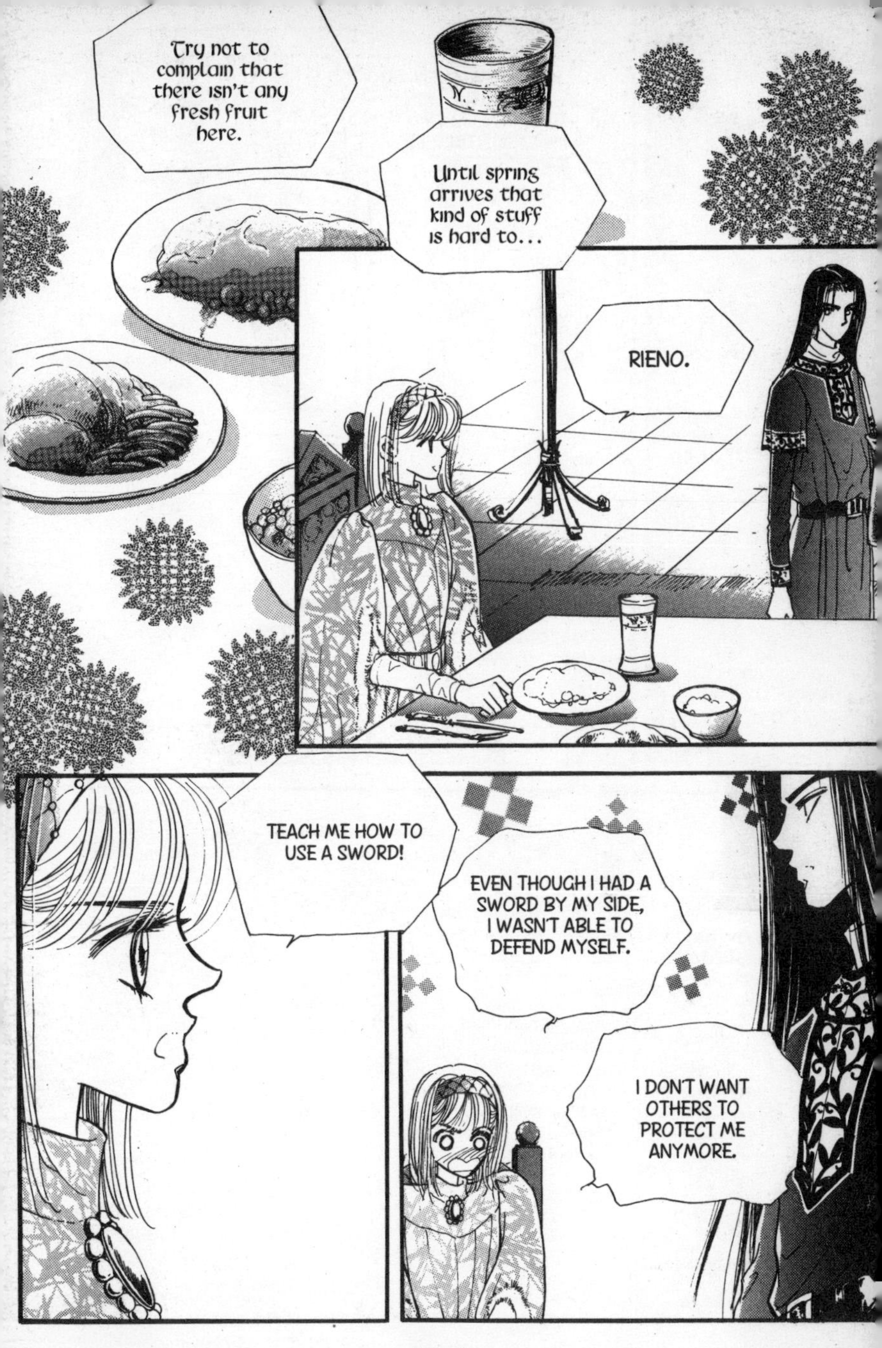

Try not to complain that there isn't any fresh fruit here.
Until spring arrives that kind of stuff is hard to...
RIENO.
TEACH ME HOW TO USE A SWORD!
EVEN THOUGH I HAD A SWORD BY MY SIDE, I WASN'T ABLE TO DEFEND MYSELF.
I DON'T WANT OTHERS TO PROTECT ME ANYMORE.

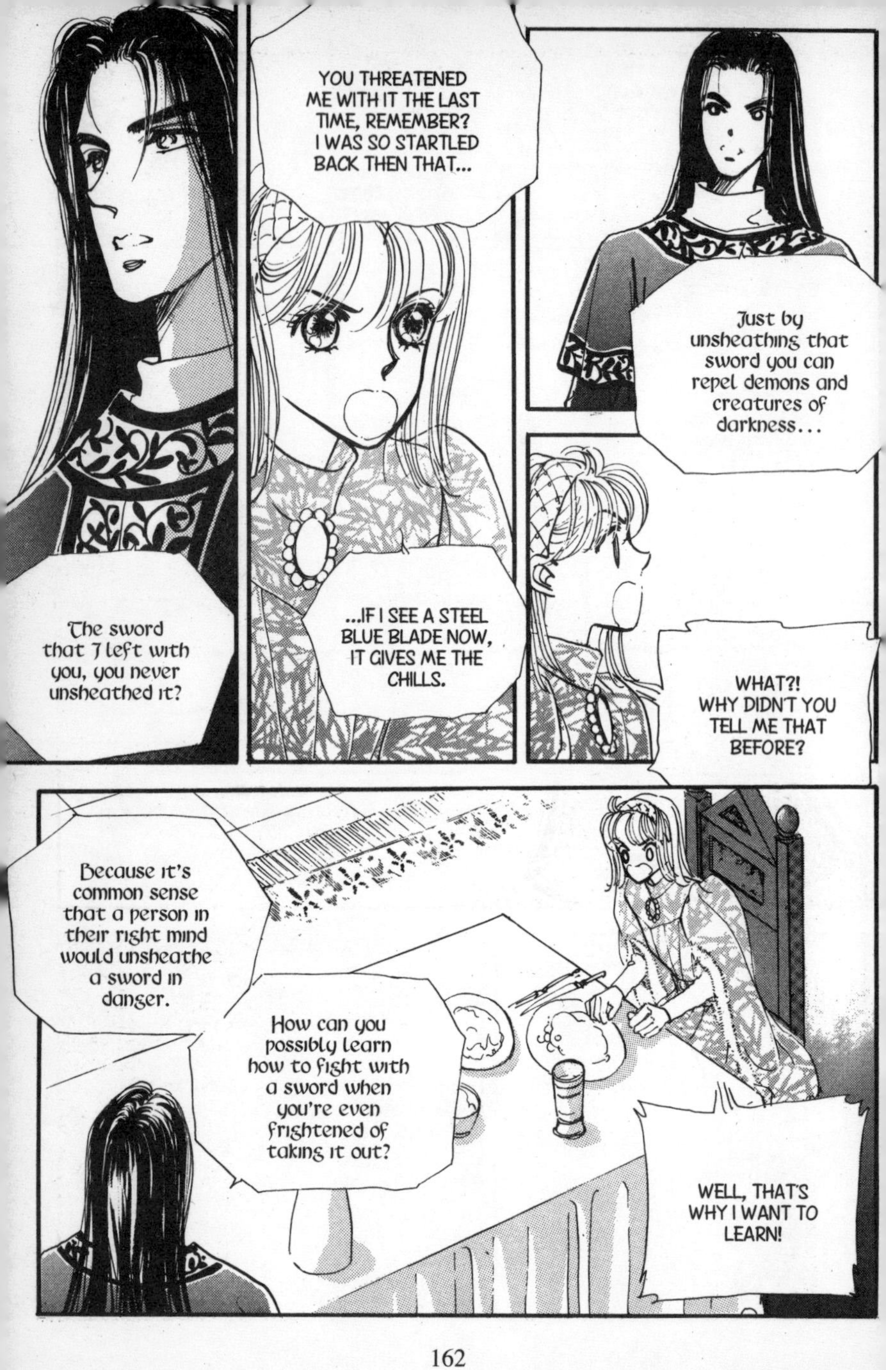
The sword that I left with you, you never unsheathed it?
YOU THREATENED ME WITH IT THE LAST TIME, REMEMBER? I WAS SO STARTLED BACK THEN THAT...
...IF I SEE A STEEL BLUE BLADE NOW, IT GIVES ME THE CHILLS.
Just by unsheathing that sword you can repel demons and creatures of darkness...
WHAT?! WHY DIDN'T YOU TELL ME THAT BEFORE?
Because it's common sense that a person in their right mind would unsheathe a sword in danger.
How can you possibly learn how to fight with a sword when you're even frightened of taking it out?
WELL, THAT'S WHY I WANT TO LEARN!

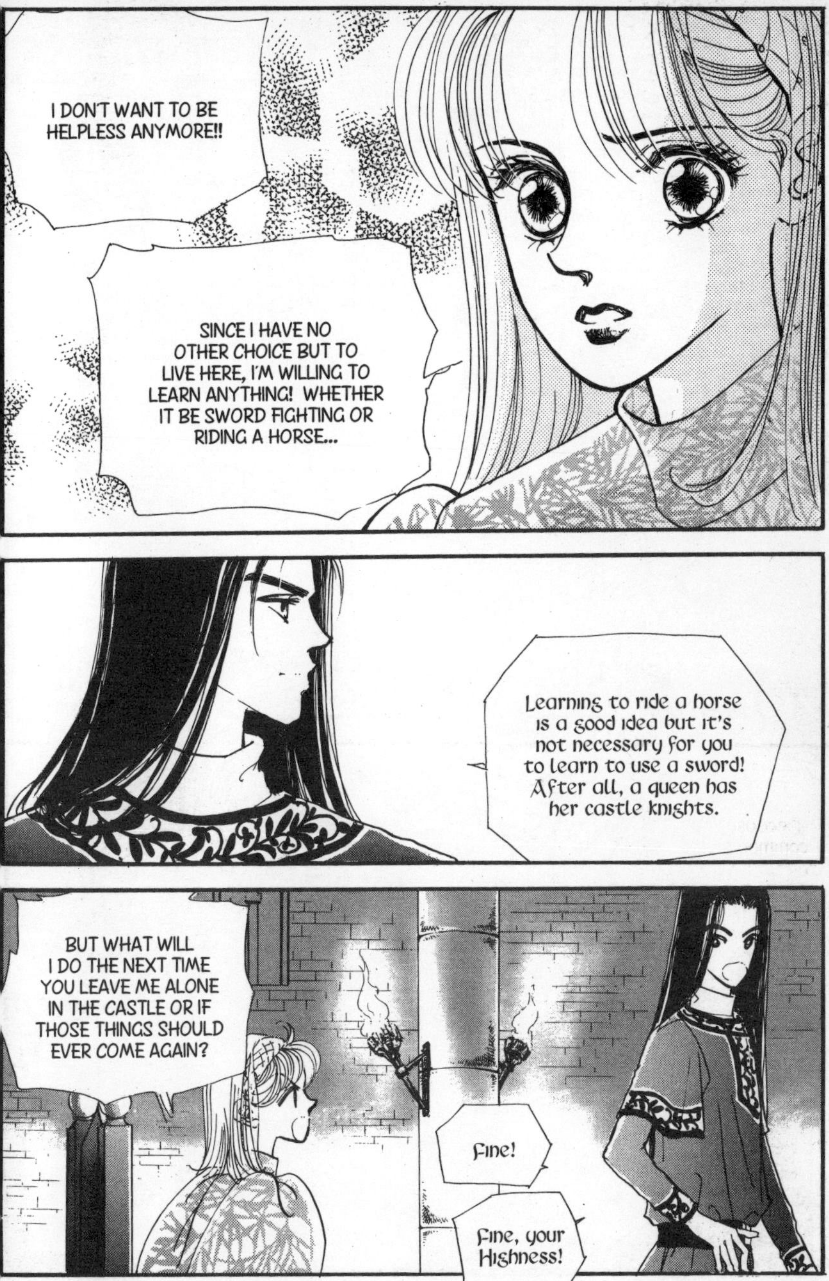
I DON'T WANT TO BE HELPLESS ANYMORE!!
SINCE I HAVE NO OTHER CHOICE BUT TO LIVE HERE, I'M WILLING TO LEARN ANYTHING! WHETHER IT BE SWORD FIGHTING OR RIDING A HORSE...
Learning to ride a horse is a good idea but it's not necessary for you to learn to use a sword! After all, a queen has her castle knights.
BUT WHAT WILL I DO THE NEXT TIME YOU LEAVE ME ALONE IN THE CASTLE OR IF THOSE THINGS SHOULD EVER COME AGAIN?
Fine!
Fine, your Highness!

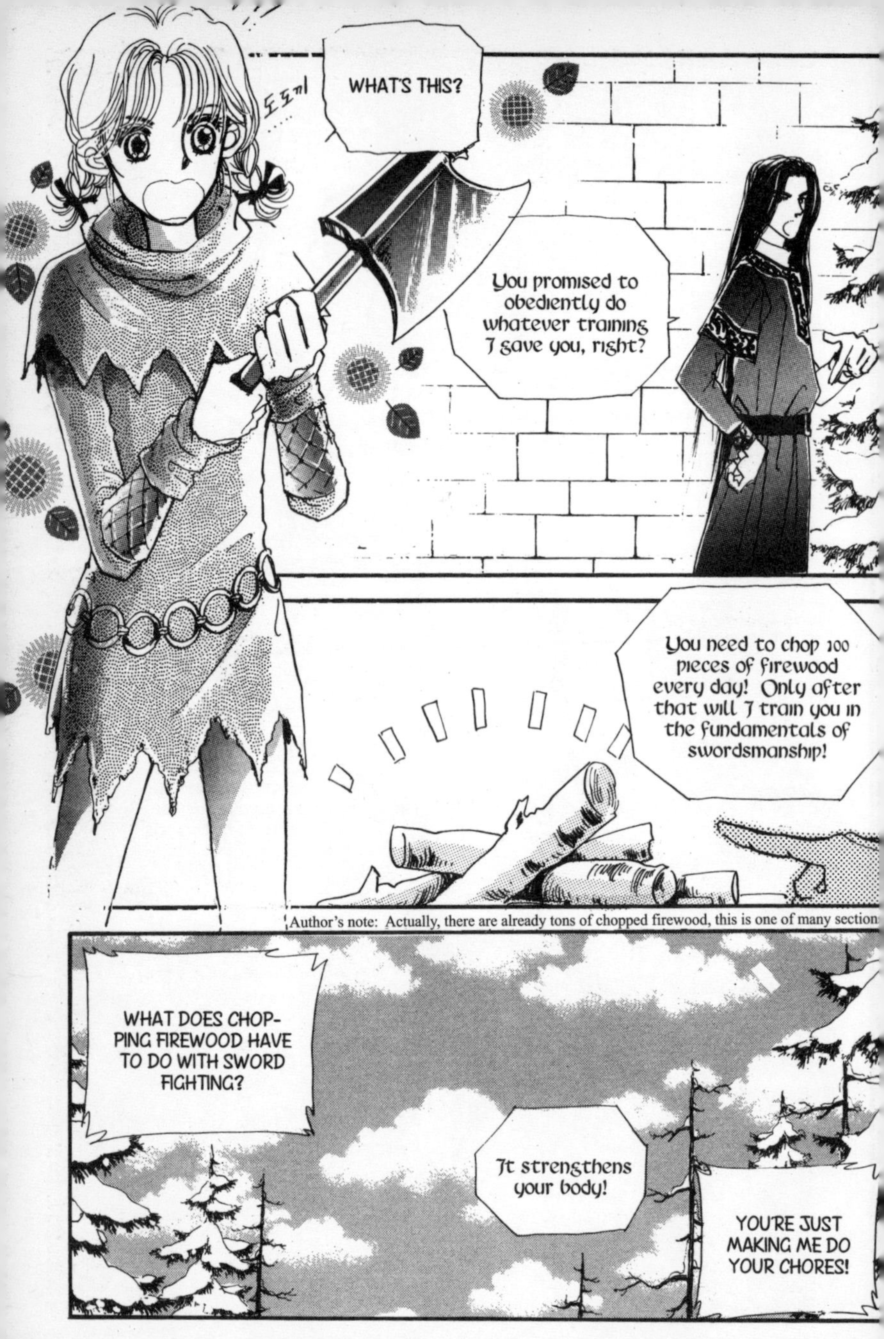

도도끼...
WHAT'S THIS?
You promised to obediently do whatever training I gave you, right?
You need to chop 100 pieces of firewood every day! Only after that will I train you in the fundamentals of swordsmanship!
Author's note: Actually, there are already tons of chopped firewood, this is one of many section
WHAT DOES CHOPPING FIREWOOD HAVE TO DO WITH SWORD FIGHTING?
It strengthens your body!
YOU'RE JUST MAKING ME DO YOUR CHORES!

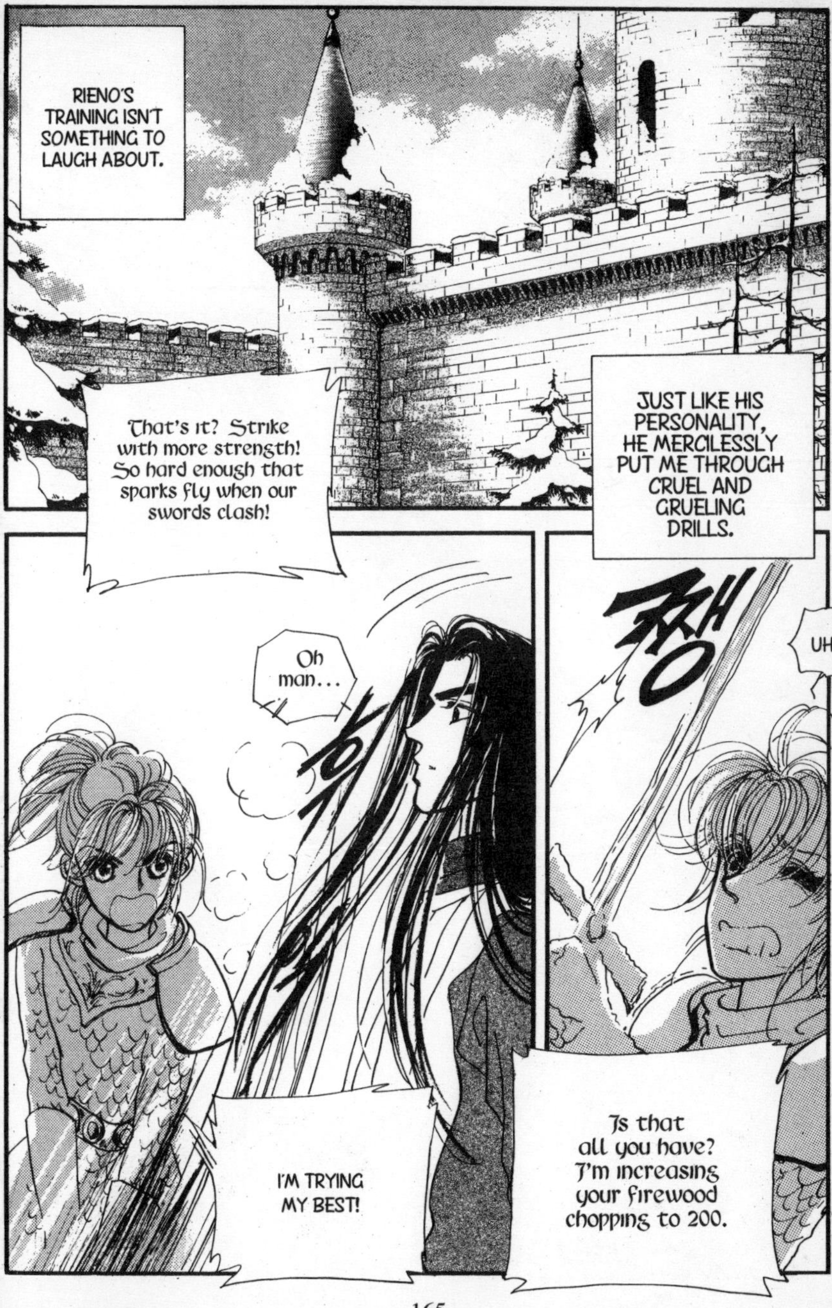
RIENO'S TRAINING ISN'T SOMETHING TO LAUGH ABOUT.
That's it? Strike with more strength! So hard enough that sparks fly when our swords clash!
JUST LIKE HIS PERSONALITY, HE MERCILESSLY PUT ME THROUGH CRUEL AND GRUELING DRILLS.
Oh man...
I'M TRYING MY BEST!
UHK!
Is that all you have? I'm increasing your firewood chopping to 200.

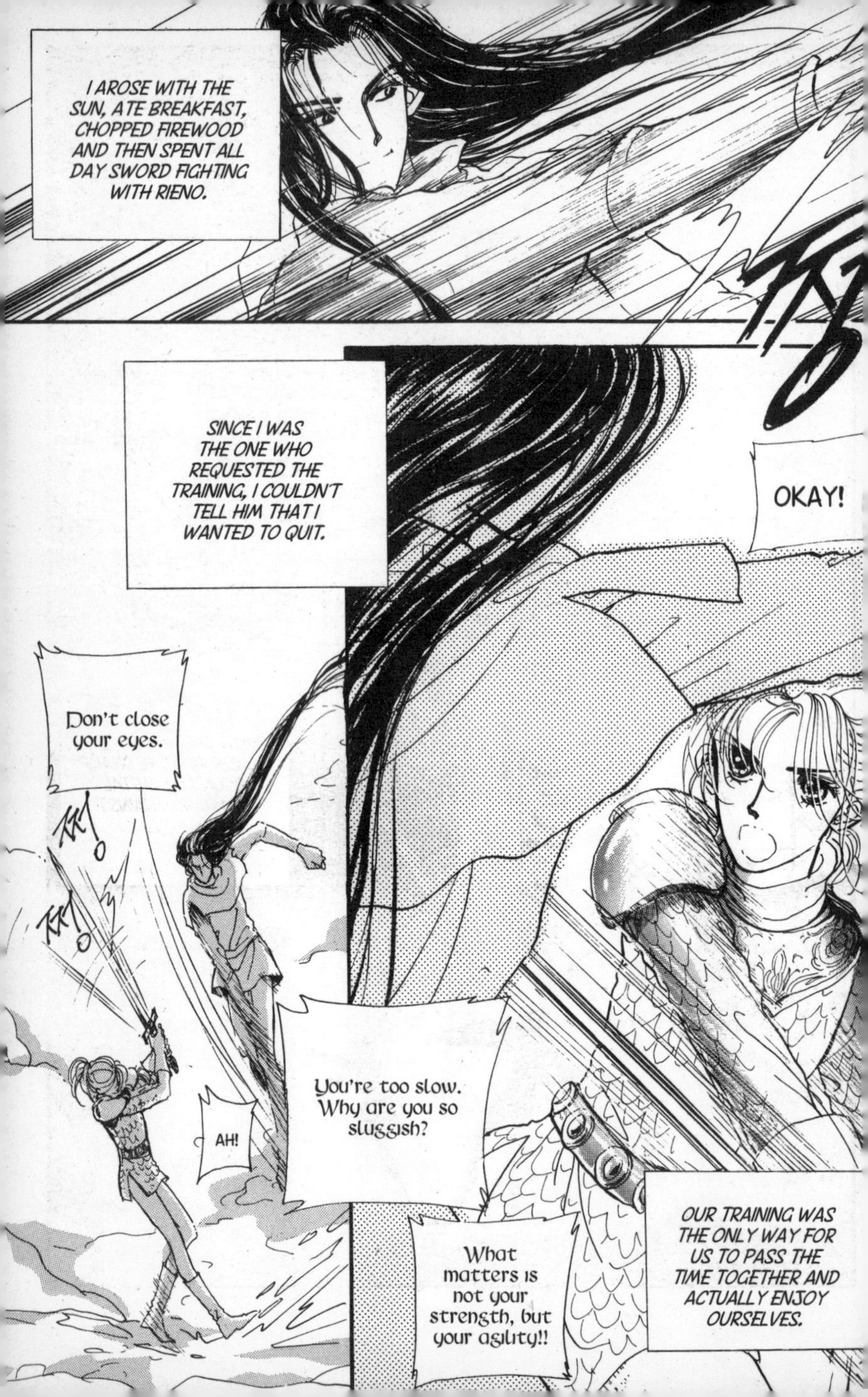
I AROSE WITH THE SUN, ATE BREAKFAST, CHOPPED FIREWOOD AND THEN SPENT ALL DAY SWORD FIGHTING WITH RIENO.
SINCE I WAS THE ONE WHO REQUESTED THE TRAINING, I COULDN'T TELL HIM THAT I WANTED TO QUIT.
OKAY!
Don't close your eyes.
AH!
You're too slow. Why are you so sluggish?
What matters is not your strength, but your agility!!
OUR TRAINING WAS THE ONLY WAY FOR US TO PASS THE TIME TOGETHER AND ACTUALLY ENJOY OURSELVES.

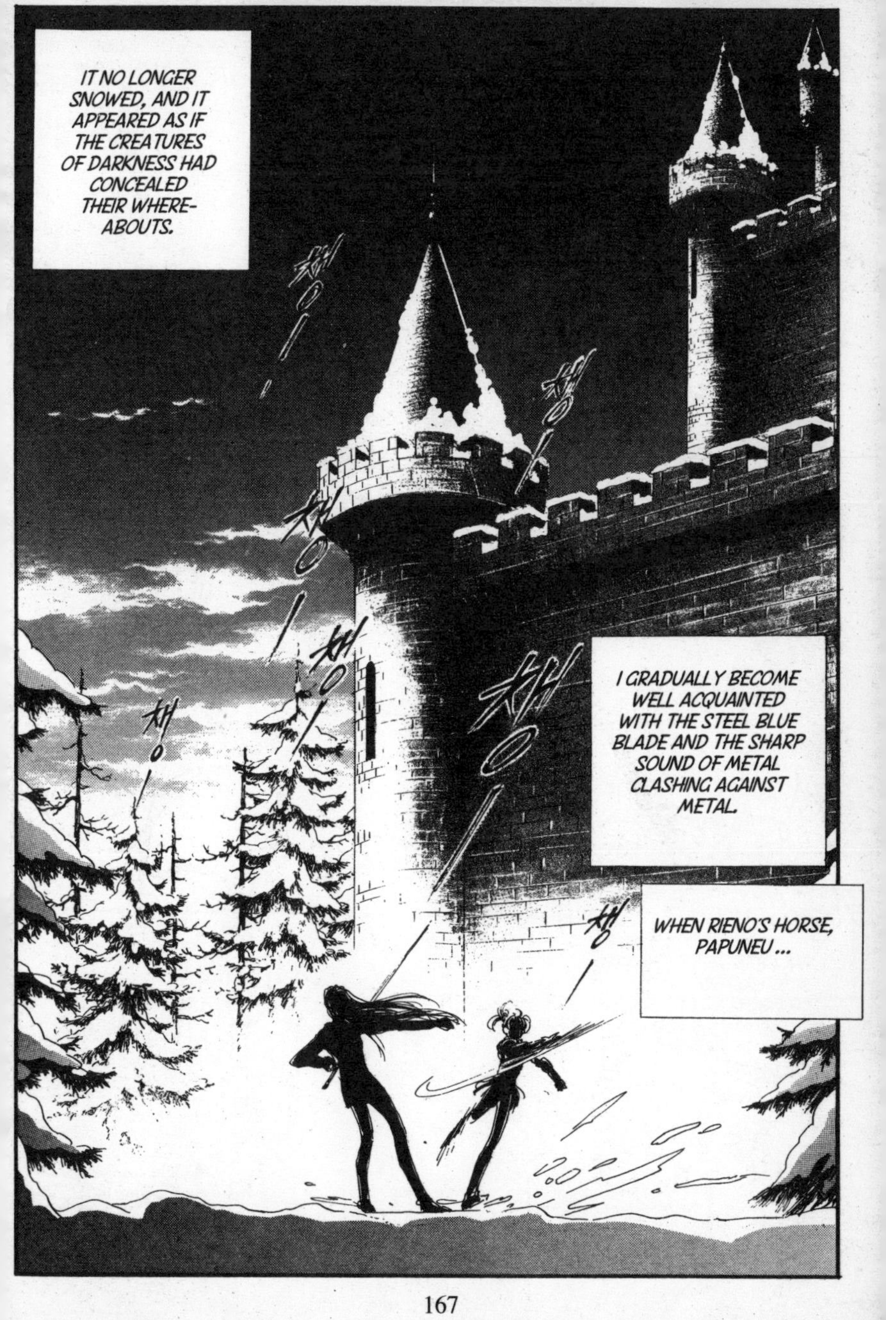
IT NO LONGER SNOWED, AND IT APPEARED AS IF THE CREATURES OF DARKNESS HAD CONCEALED THEIR WHERE-ABOUTS.
챙
챙
챙
챙
챙
챙
I GRADUALLY BECOME WELL ACQUAINTED WITH THE STEEL BLUE BLADE AND THE SHARP SOUND OF METAL CLASHING AGAINST METAL.
챙
WHEN RIENO'S HORSE, PAPUNEU ...

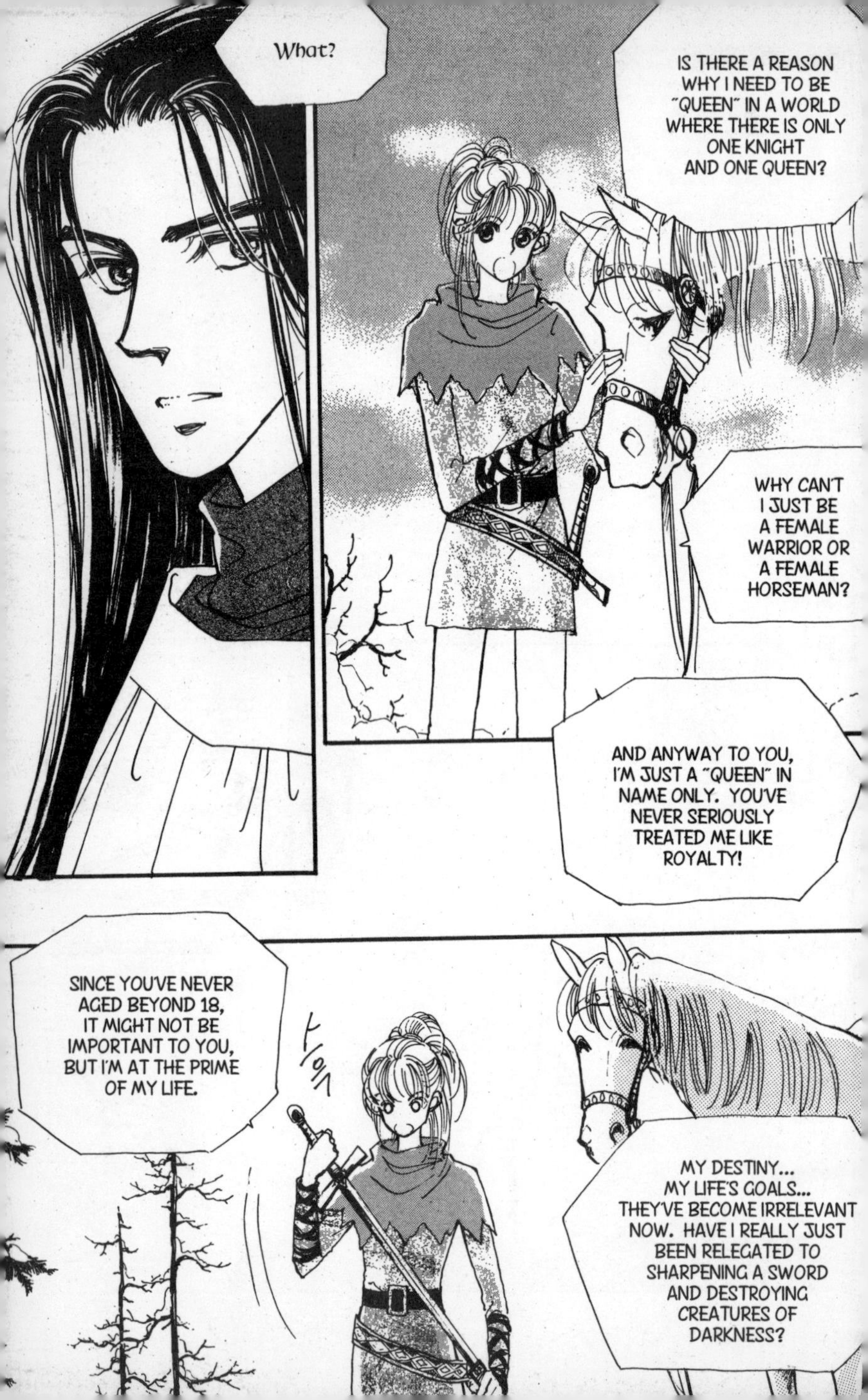
What?
IS THERE A REASON WHY I NEED TO BE "QUEEN" IN A WORLD WHERE THERE IS ONLY ONE KNIGHT AND ONE QUEEN?
WHY CAN'T I JUST BE A FEMALE WARRIOR OR A FEMALE HORSEMAN?
AND ANYWAY TO YOU, I'M JUST A "QUEEN" IN NAME ONLY. YOU'VE NEVER SERIOUSLY TREATED ME LIKE ROYALTY!
SINCE YOU'VE NEVER AGED BEYOND 18, IT MIGHT NOT BE IMPORTANT TO YOU, BUT I'M AT THE PRIME OF MY LIFE.
MY DESTINY... MY LIFE'S GOALS... THEY'VE BECOME IRRELEVANT NOW. HAVE I REALLY JUST BEEN RELEGATED TO SHARPENING A SWORD AND DESTROYING CREATURES OF DARKNESS?

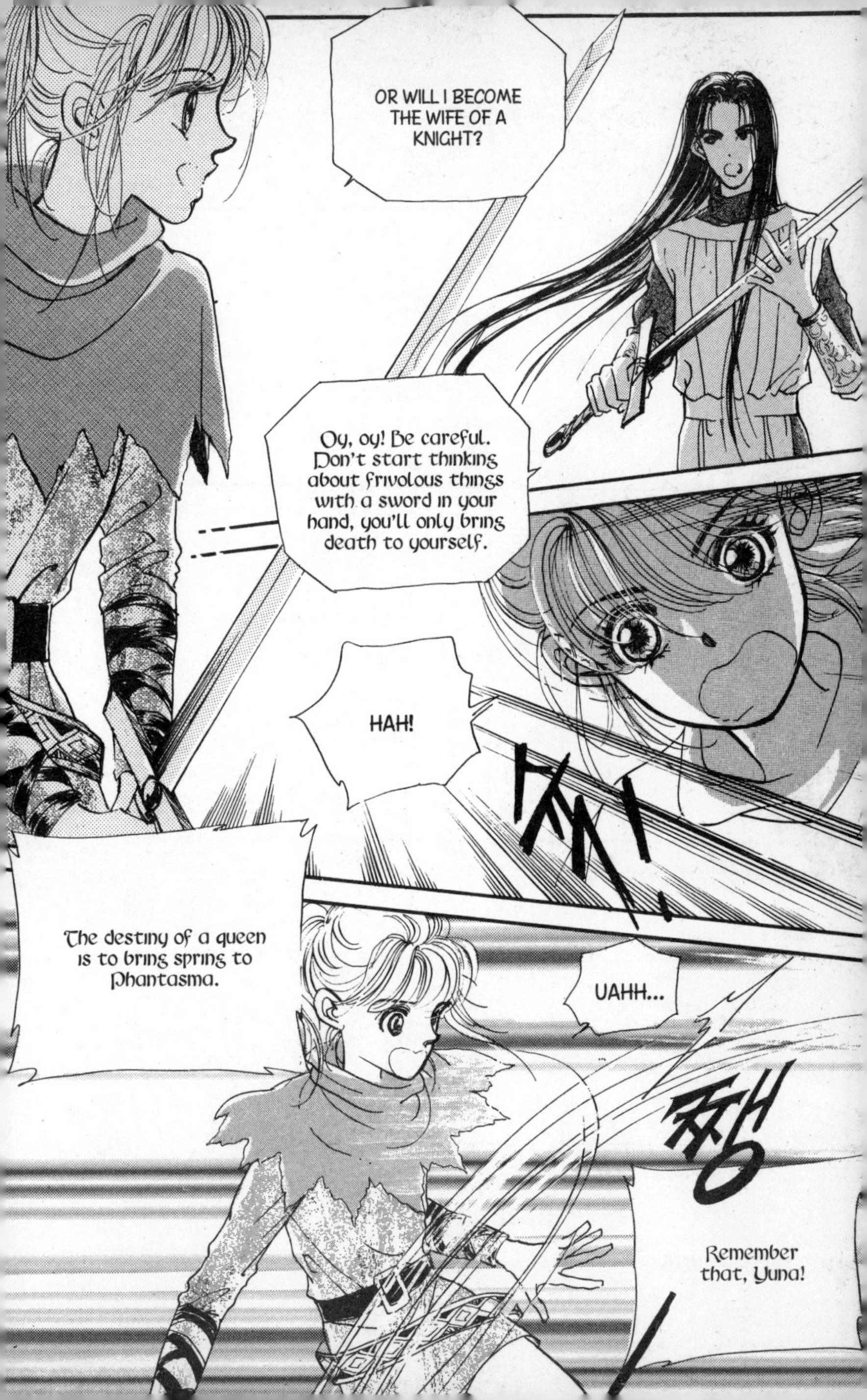
OR WILL I BECOME THE WIFE OF A KNIGHT?
Oy, oy! Be careful. Don't start thinking about frivolous things with a sword in your hand, you'll only bring death to yourself.
HAH!
The destiny of a queen is to bring spring to Phantasma.
UAHH...
Remember that, Yuna!

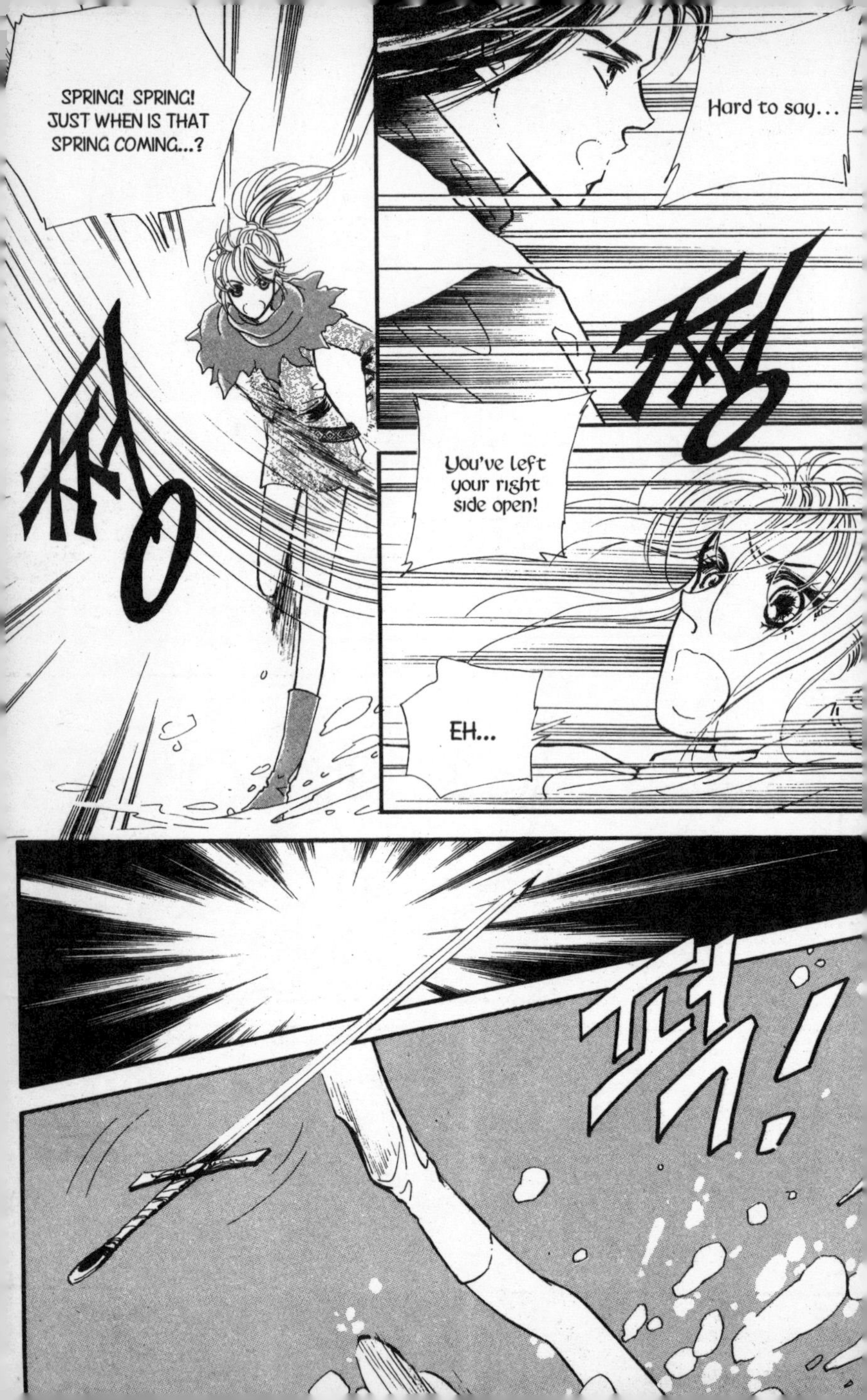
SPRING! SPRING! JUST WHEN IS THAT SPRING COMING...?
Hard to say...
You've left your right side open!
EH...

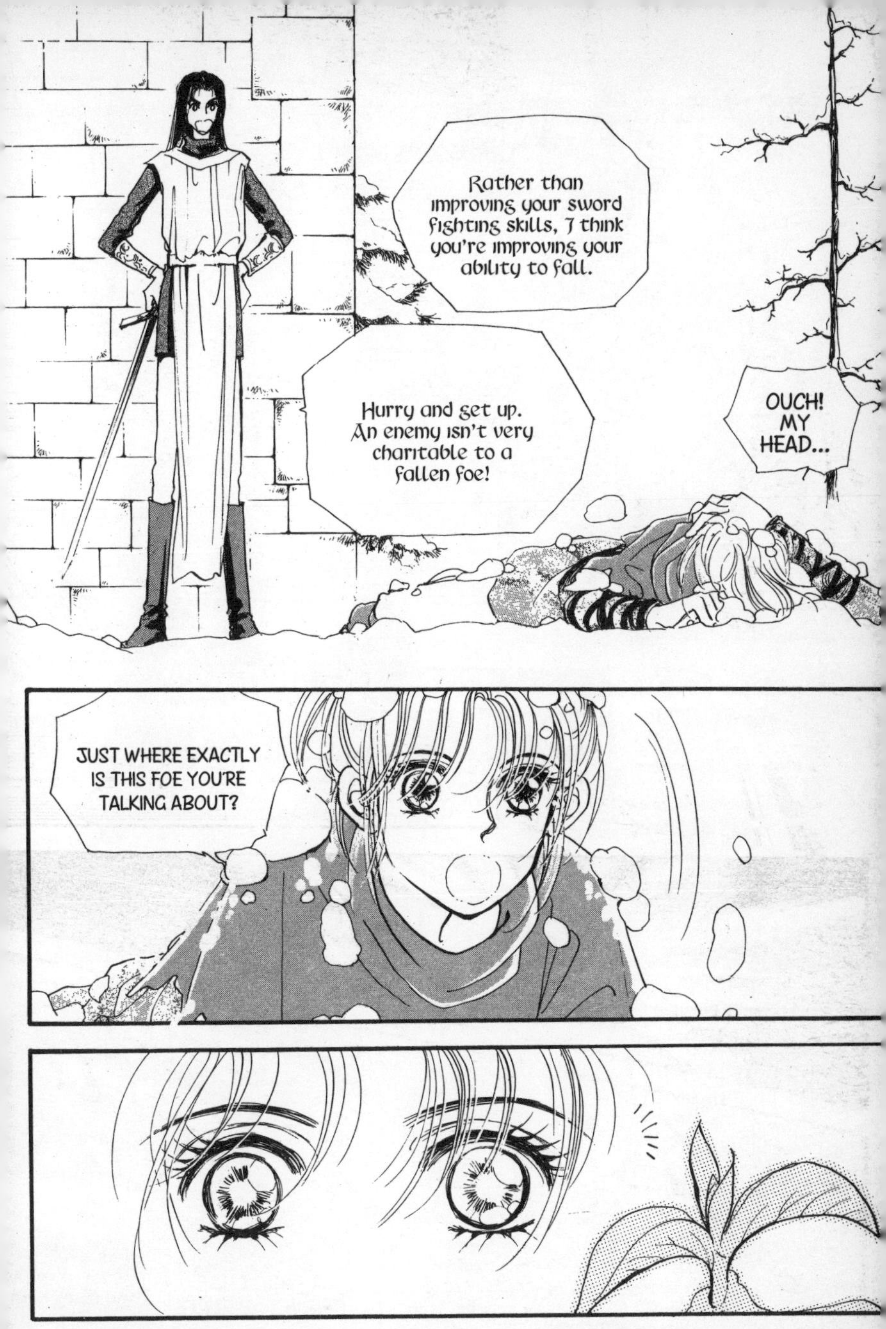
Rather than improving your sword fighting skills, I think you're improving your ability to fall.
Hurry and get up. An enemy isn't very charitable to a fallen foe!
OUCH! MY HEAD...
JUST WHERE EXACTLY IS THIS FOE YOU'RE TALKING ABOUT?

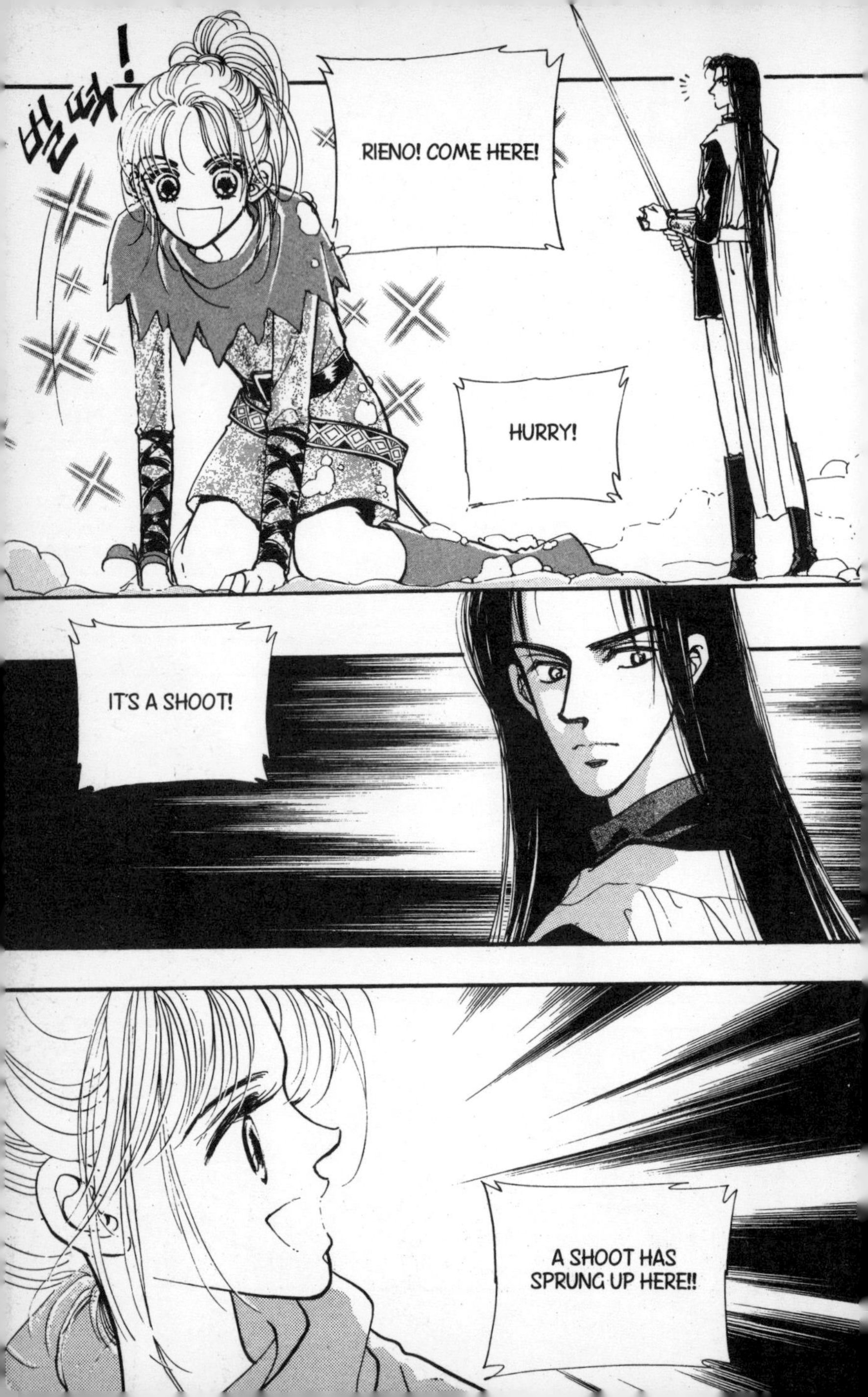
벌떡!
RIENO! COME HERE!
HURRY!
IT'S A SHOOT!
A SHOOT HAS SPRUNG UP HERE!!

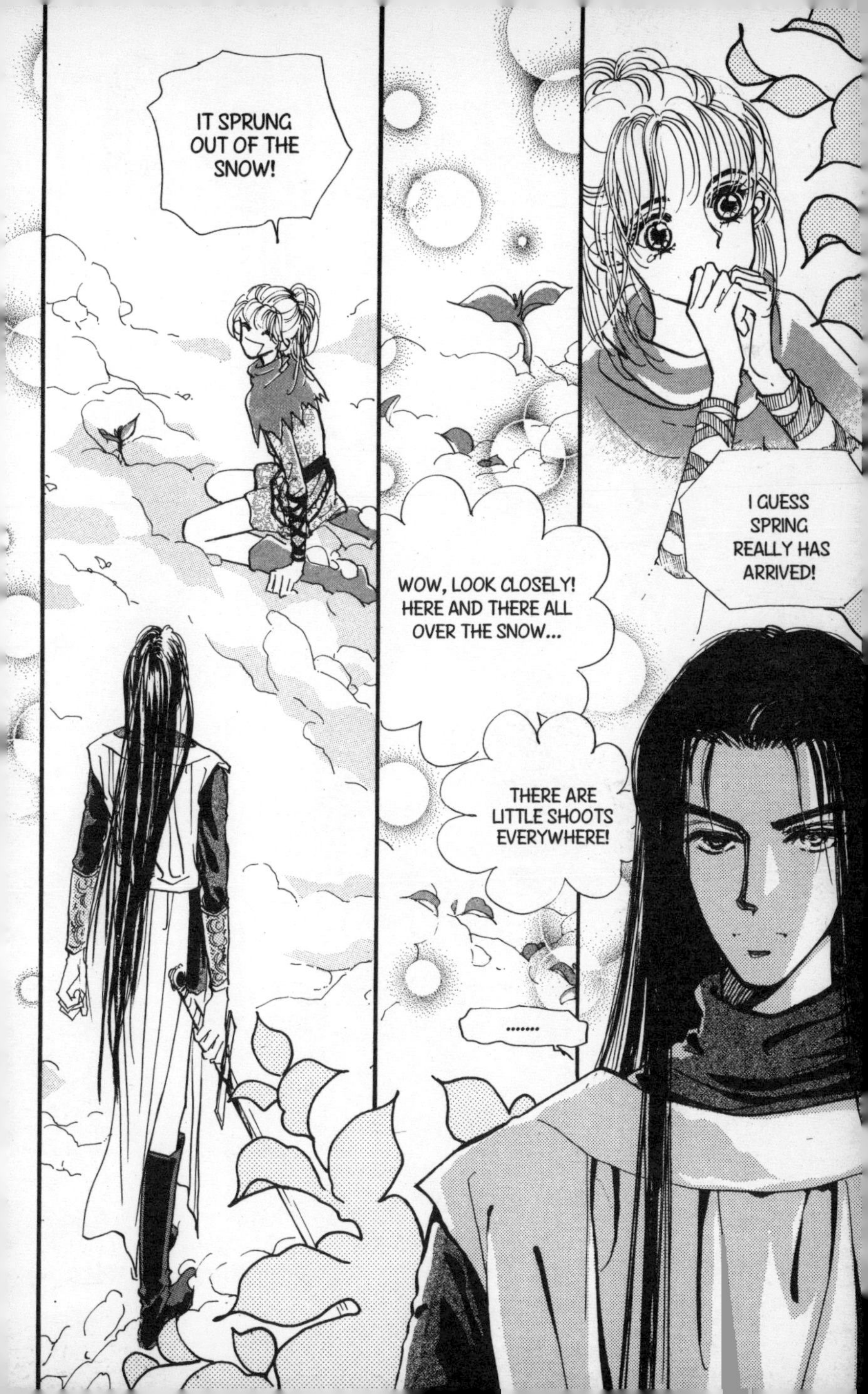
IT SPRUNG OUT OF THE SNOW!
WOW, LOOK CLOSELY! HERE AND THERE ALL OVER THE SNOW...
THERE ARE LITTLE SHOOTS EVERYWHERE!
....
I GUESS SPRING REALLY HAS ARRIVED!

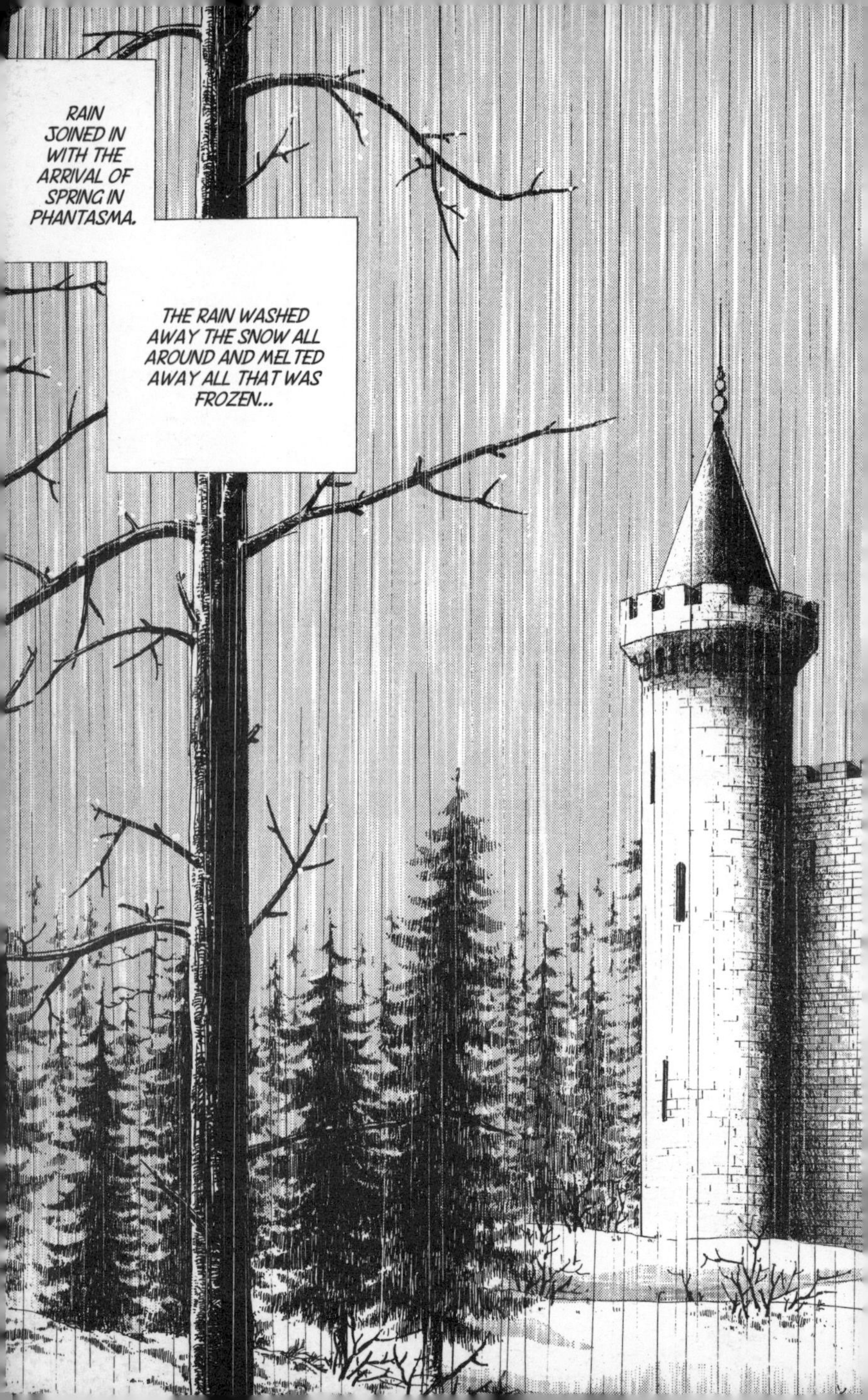
RAIN JOINED IN WITH THE ARRIVAL OF SPRING IN PHANTASMA.
THE RAIN WASHED AWAY THE SNOW ALL AROUND AND MELTED AWAY ALL THAT WAS FROZEN...

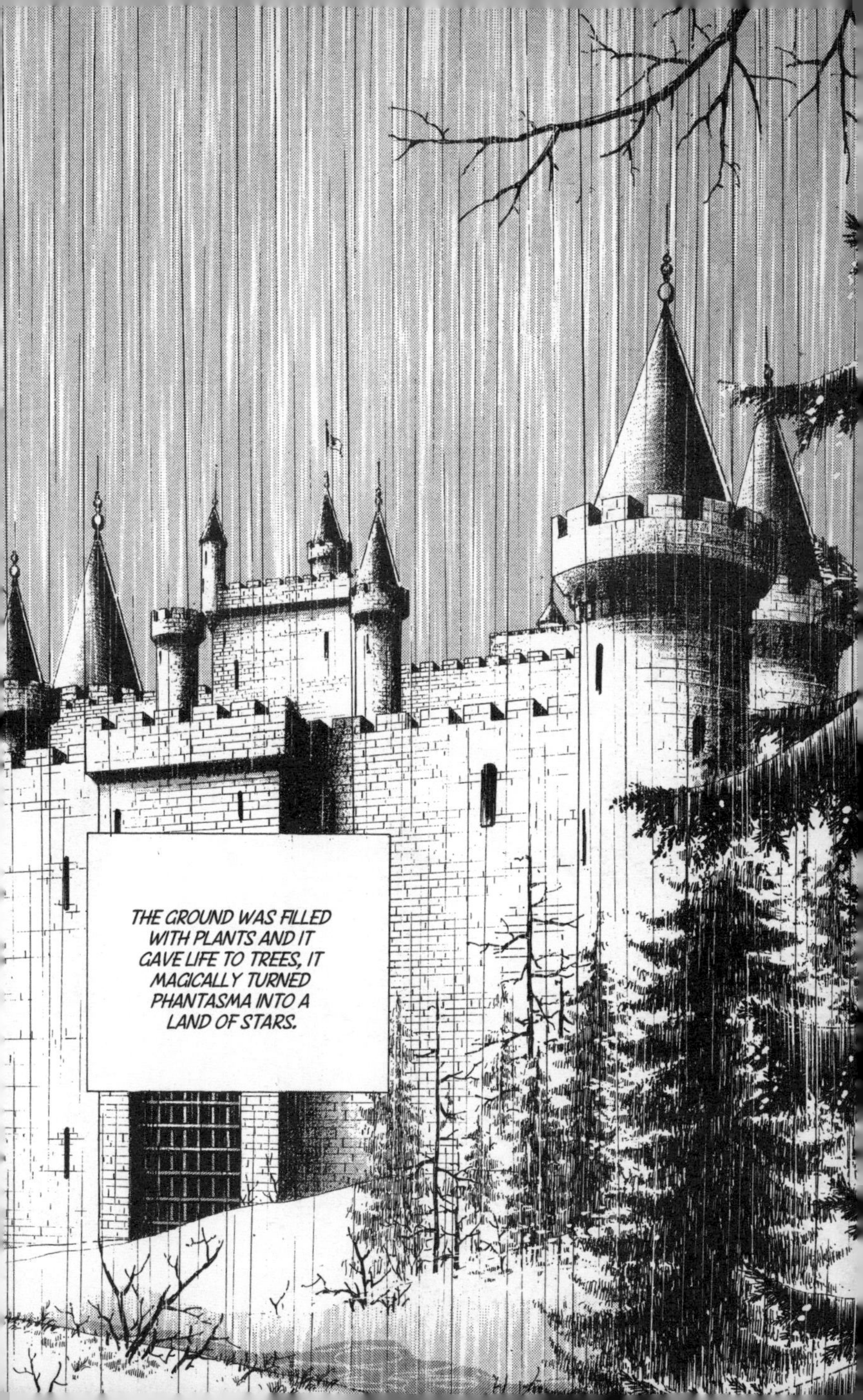
THE GROUND WAS FILLED WITH PLANTS AND IT GAVE LIFE TO TREES, IT MAGICALLY TURNED PHANTASMA INTO A LAND OF STARS.

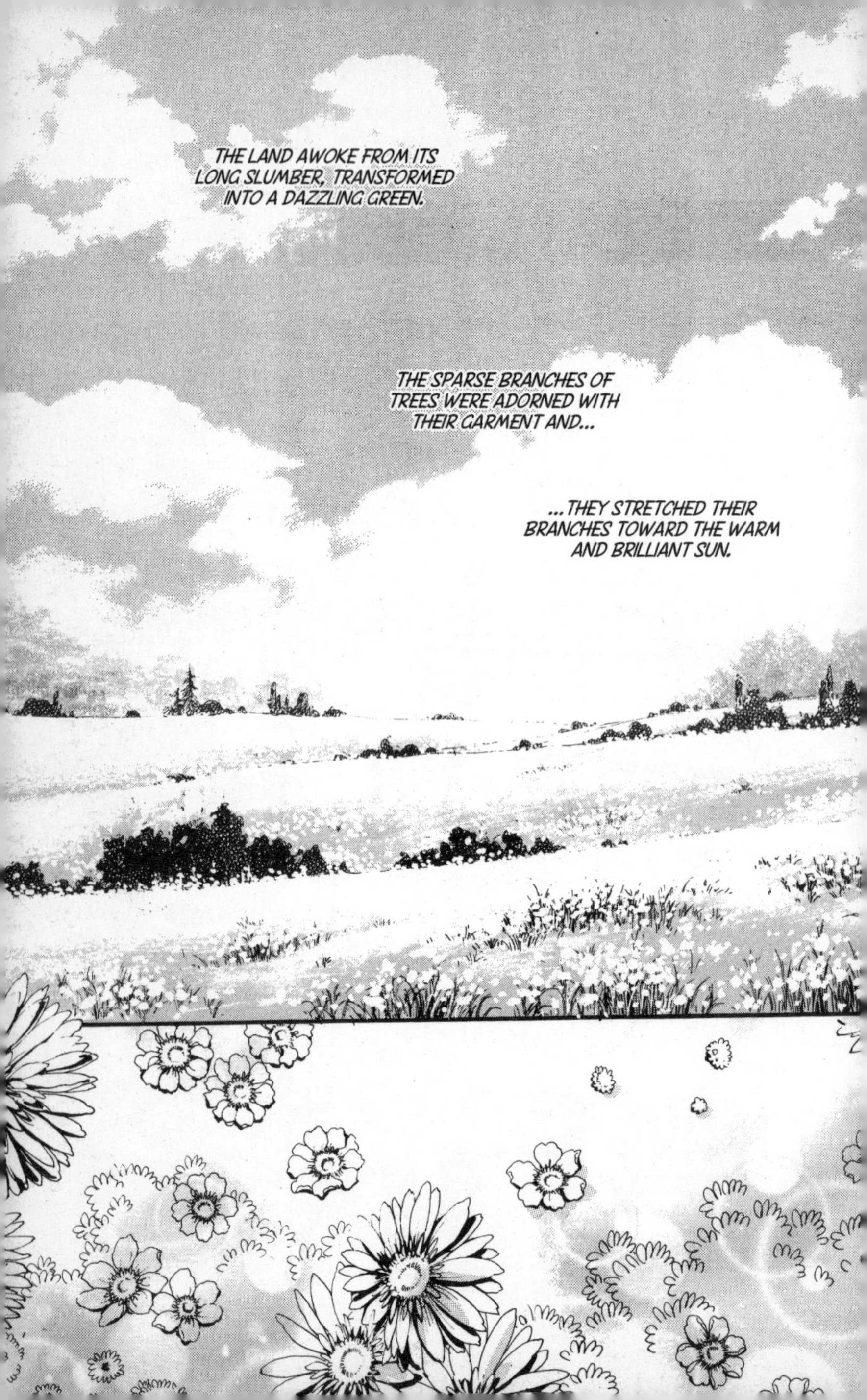
THE LAND AWOKE FROM ITS LONG SLUMBER, TRANSFORMED INTO A DAZZLING GREEN.
THE SPARSE BRANCHES OF TREES WERE ADORNED WITH THEIR GARMENT AND...
...THEY STRETCHED THEIR BRANCHES TOWARD THE WARM AND BRILLIANT SUN.

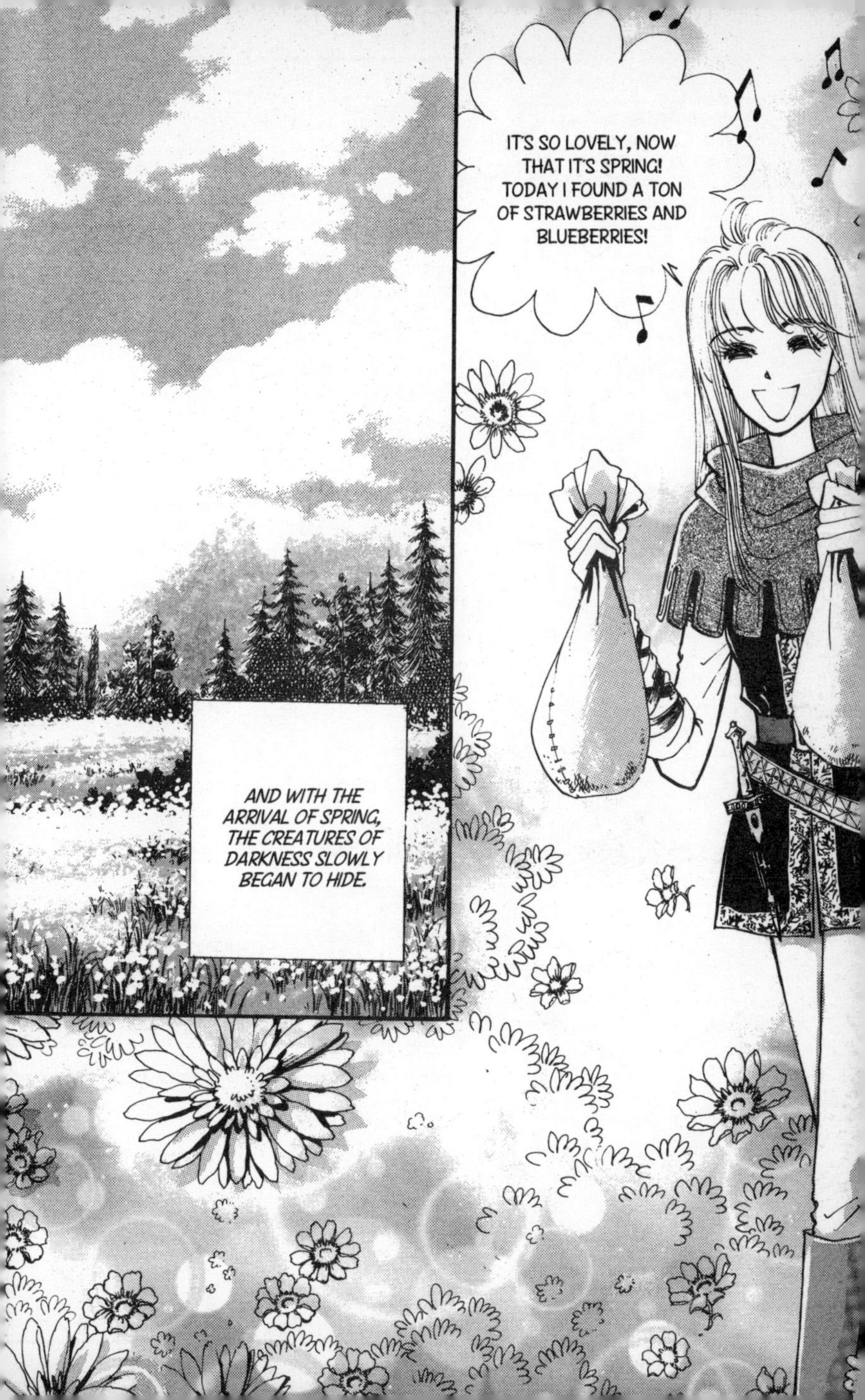
AND WITH THE ARRIVAL OF SPRING, THE CREATURES OF DARKNESS SLOWLY BEGAN TO HIDE.
IT'S SO LOVELY, NOW THAT IT'S SPRING! TODAY I FOUND A TON OF STRAWBERRIES AND BLUEBERRIES!

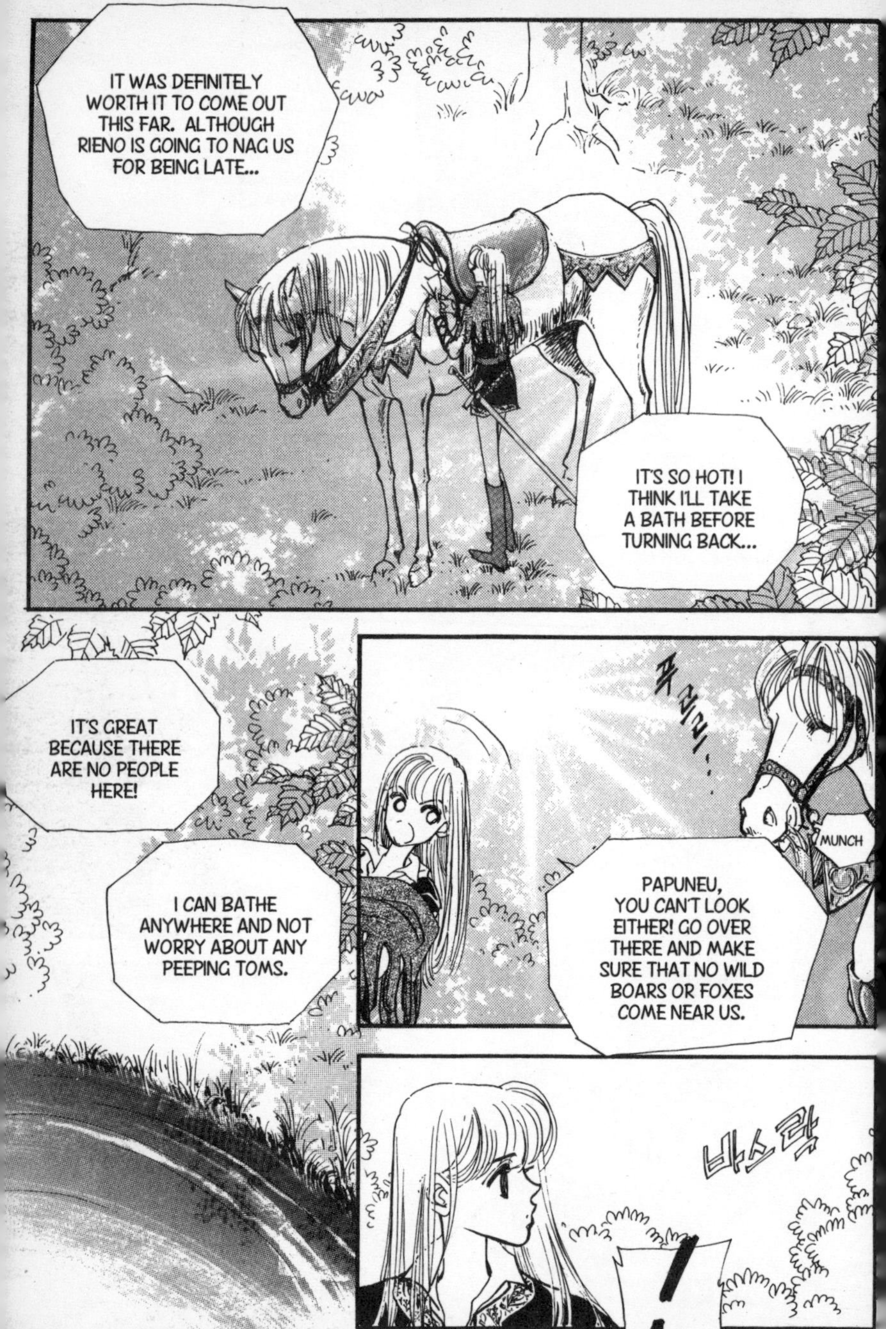
IT WAS DEFINITELY WORTH IT TO COME OUT THIS FAR. ALTHOUGH RIENO IS GOING TO NAG US FOR BEING LATE...
IT'S SO HOT! I THINK I'LL TAKE A BATH BEFORE TURNING BACK...
IT'S GREAT BECAUSE THERE ARE NO PEOPLE HERE!
I CAN BATHE ANYWHERE AND NOT WORRY ABOUT ANY PEEPING TOMS.
MUNCH
PAPUNEU, YOU CAN'T LOOK EITHER! GO OVER THERE AND MAKE SURE THAT NO WILD BOARS OR FOXES COME NEAR US.
!

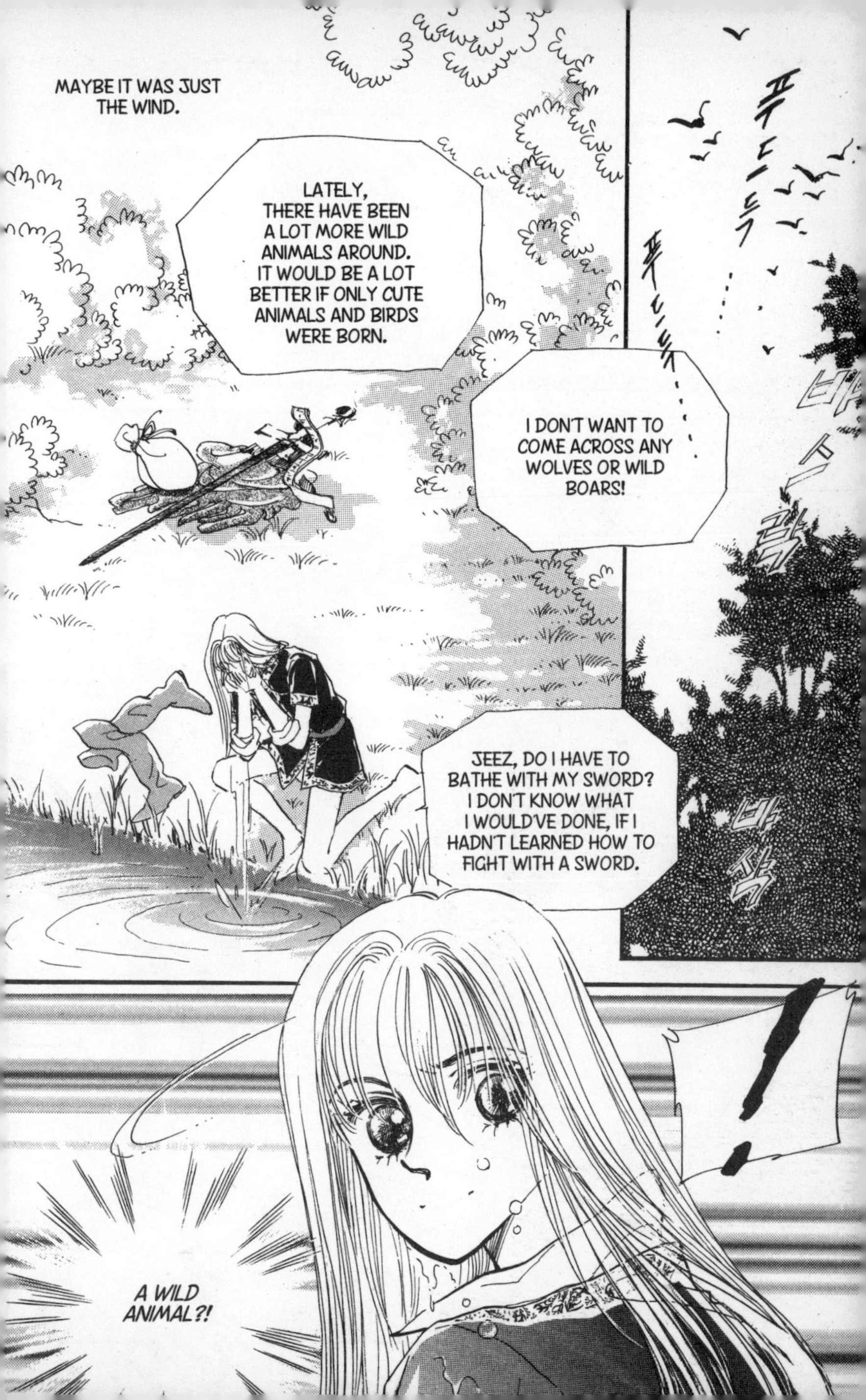
MAYBE IT WAS JUST THE WIND.
LATELY, THERE HAVE BEEN A LOT MORE WILD ANIMALS AROUND. IT WOULD BE A LOT BETTER IF ONLY CUTE ANIMALS AND BIRDS WERE BORN.
I DON'T WANT TO COME ACROSS ANY WOLVES OR WILD BOARS!
JEEZ, DO I HAVE TO BATHE WITH MY SWORD? I DON'T KNOW WHAT I WOULD'VE DONE, IF I HADN'T LEARNED HOW TO FIGHT WITH A SWORD.
!
A WILD ANIMAL?!

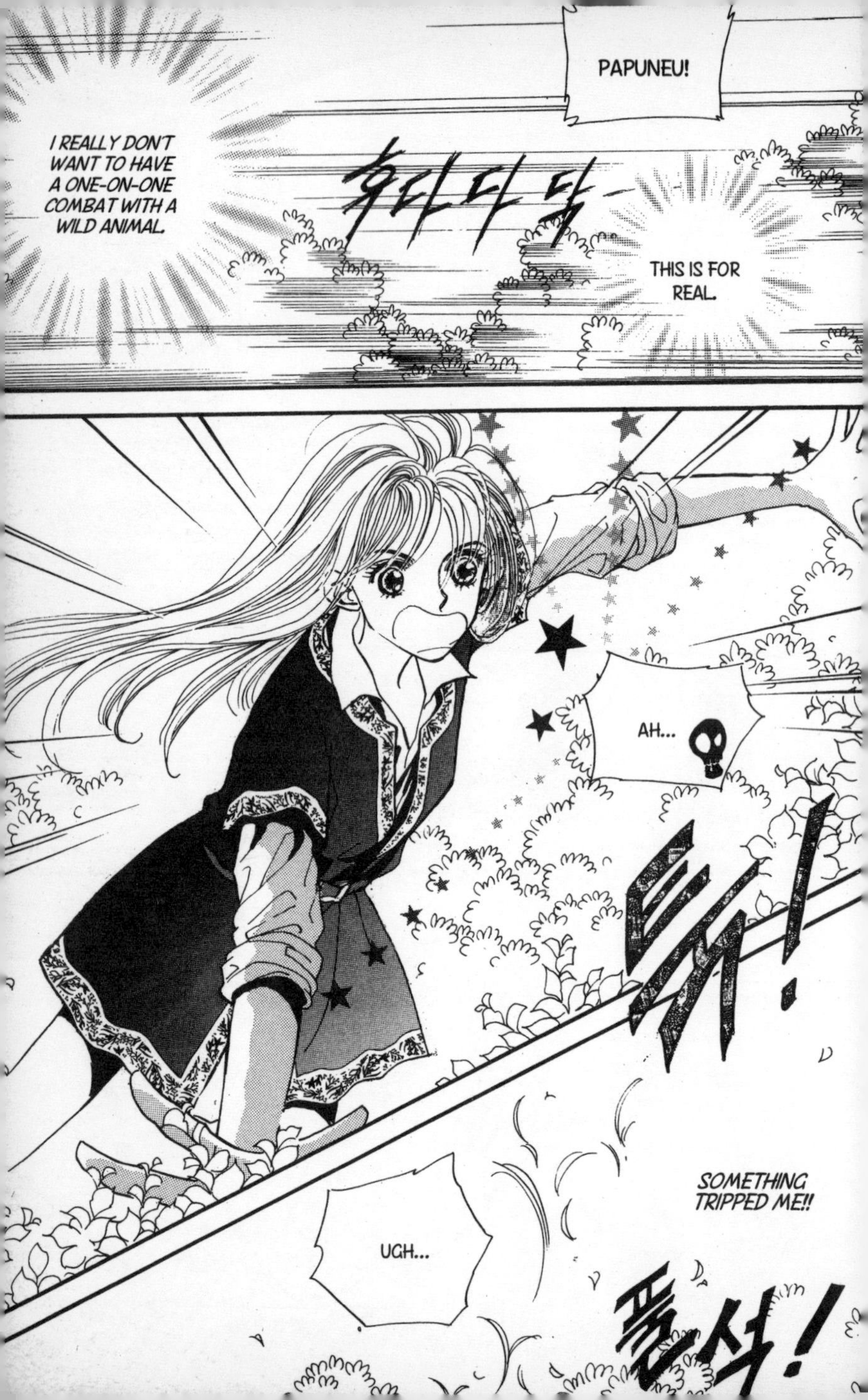
PAPUNEU!
I REALLY DON'T WANT TO HAVE A ONE-ON-ONE COMBAT WITH A WILD ANIMAL.
후다다닥
THIS IS FOR REAL.
AH...
듯!
SOMETHING TRIPPED ME!!
UGH...
풀석!

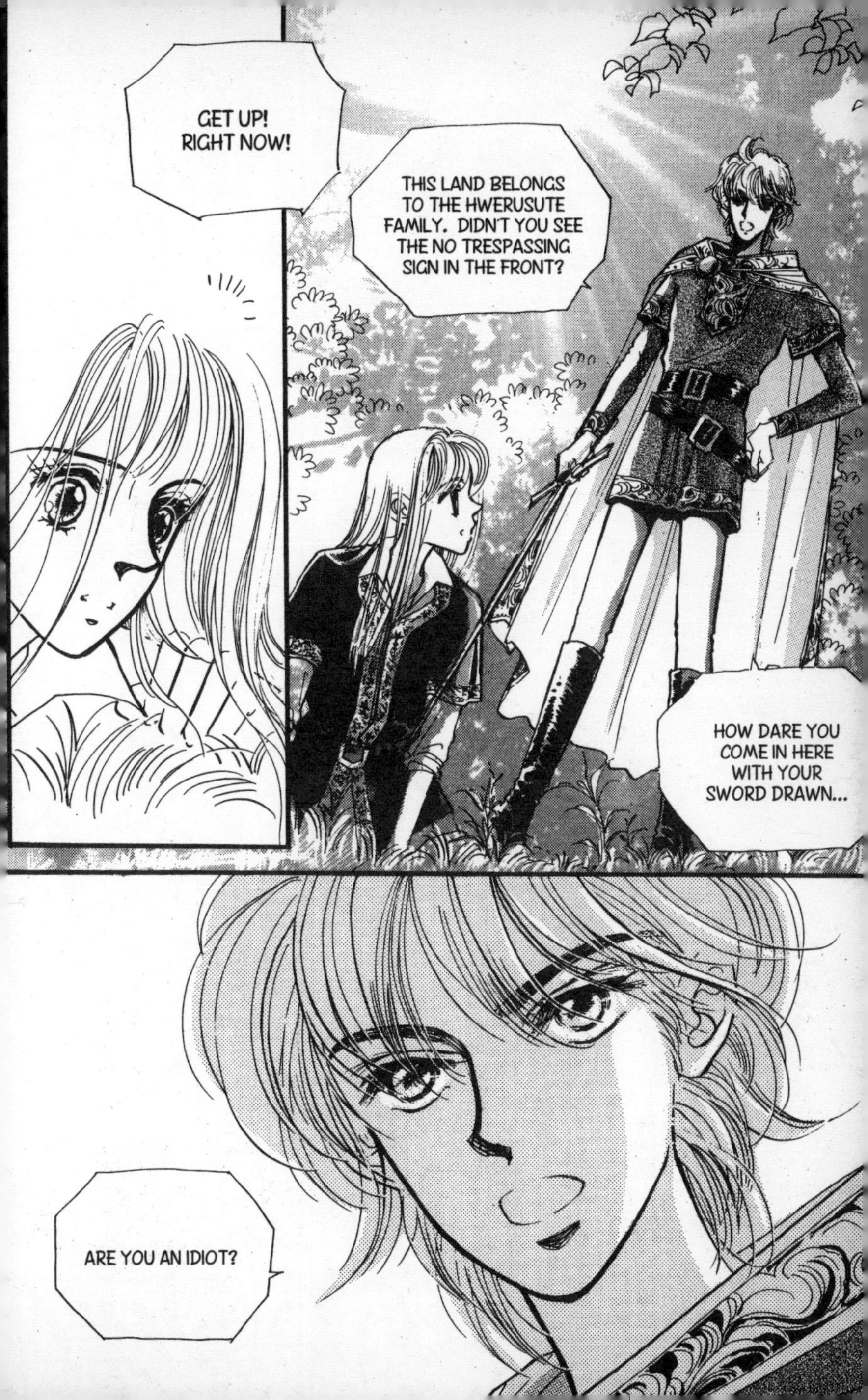
GET UP! RIGHT NOW!
THIS LAND BELONGS TO THE HWERUSUTE FAMILY. DIDN'T YOU SEE THE NO TRESPASSING SIGN IN THE FRONT?
HOW DARE YOU COME IN HERE WITH YOUR SWORD DRAWN...
ARE YOU AN IDIOT?

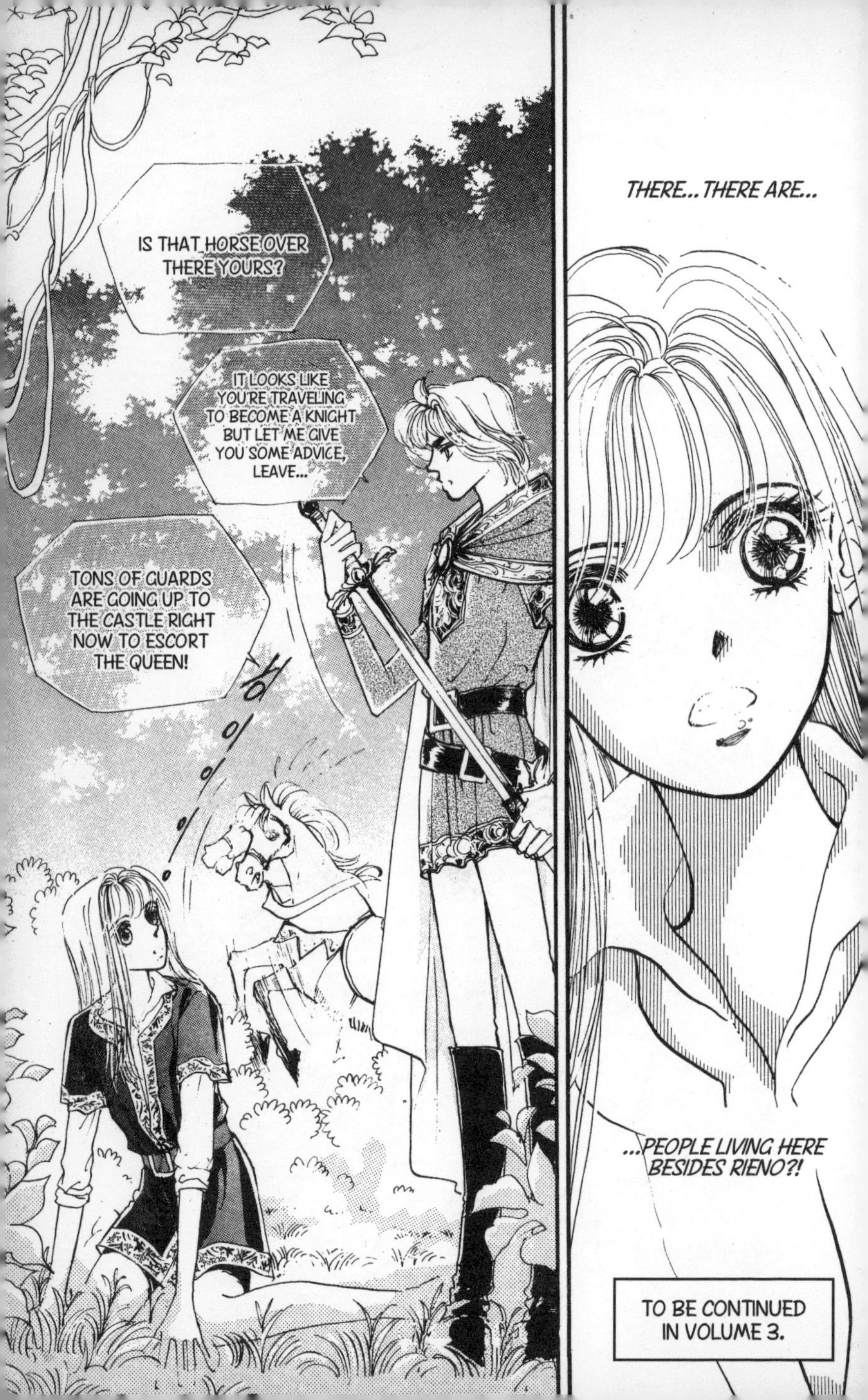
IS THAT HORSE OVER THERE YOURS?
IT LOOKS LIKE YOU'RE TRAVELING TO BECOME A KNIGHT BUT LET ME GIVE YOU SOME ADVICE, LEAVE...
TONS OF GUARDS ARE GOING UP TO THE CASTLE RIGHT NOW TO ESCORT THE QUEEN!
THERE... THERE ARE...
...PEOPLE LIVING HERE BESIDES RIENO?!
TO BE CONTINUED IN VOLUME 3.

IN THE NEXT VOLUME OF...

THE QUEEN'S KNIGHT

YUNA IS ANGRY WITH RIENO AFTER EAVESDROPPING ON HIS DECISION TO SEND HER AWAY FROM HIS CASTLE... BUT THAT DOESN'T STOP HER FROM RECEIVING HIS "DREAMY" KISS. NOW KNOWN AS QUEEN YUNA, SHE AWAKENS AT ELYSIAN AND IS INTRODUCED TO HER THREE GUARDIAN KNIGHTS. WHAT YUNA DOESN'T KNOW IS THAT THE THREE GUARDIAN KNIGHTS ARE PART OF A PLOT DEVISED BY PHANTASMA'S ELDERS. TO MAKE MATTERS WORSE, RIENO HAS ACCEPTED PRINCESS LIBERIA'S REQUEST TO BECOME HER KNIGHT! CAN A JEALOUS YUNA WIN OVER RIENO, OR IS IT A CASE OF UNREQUITED LOVE?

COMING SOON!

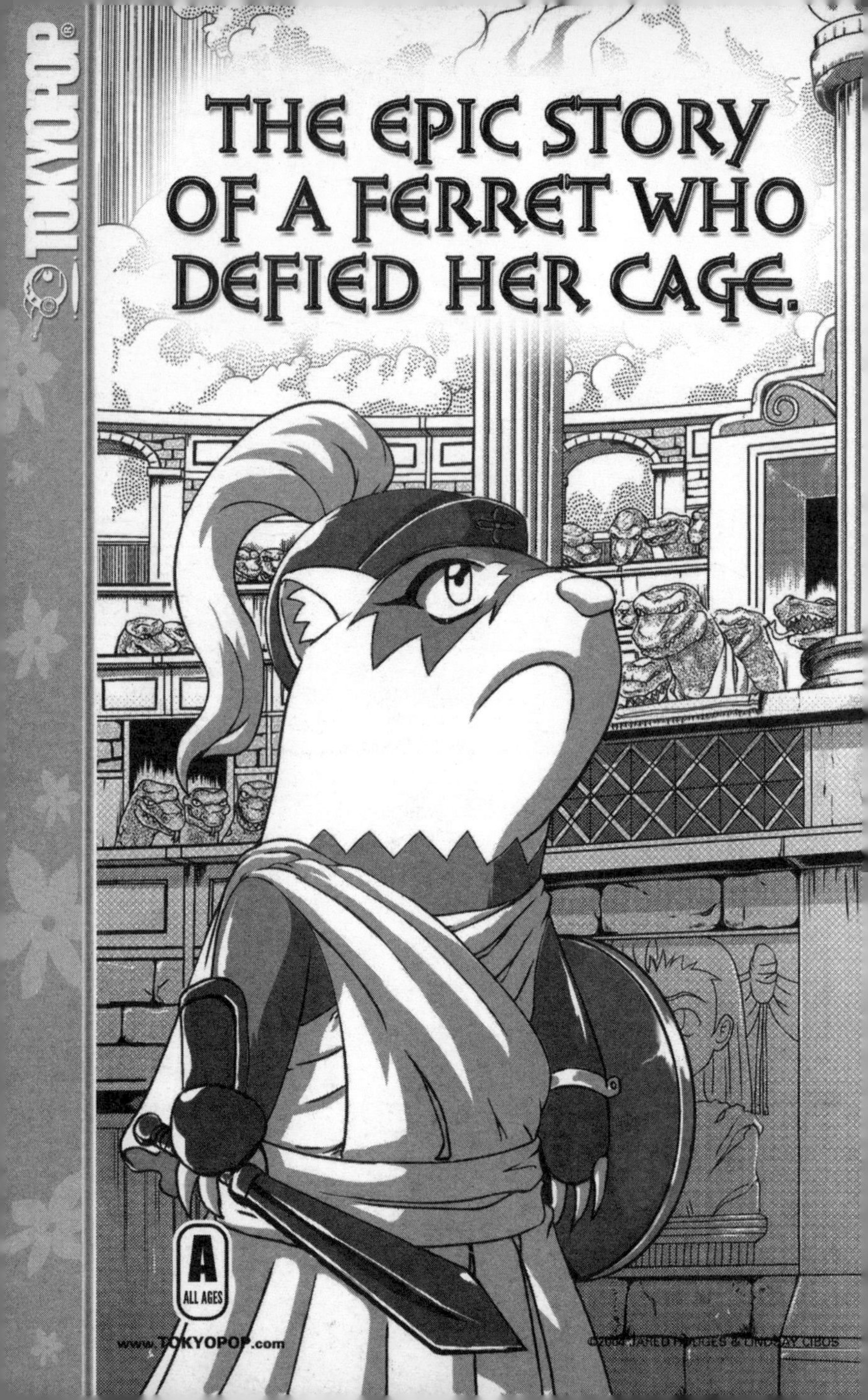
TOKYOPOP
THE EPIC STORY OF A FERRET WHO DEFIED HER CAGE.
A
ALL AGES
www.TOKYOPOP.com

BOYS BE™

A GUY'S GUIDE TO GIRLS

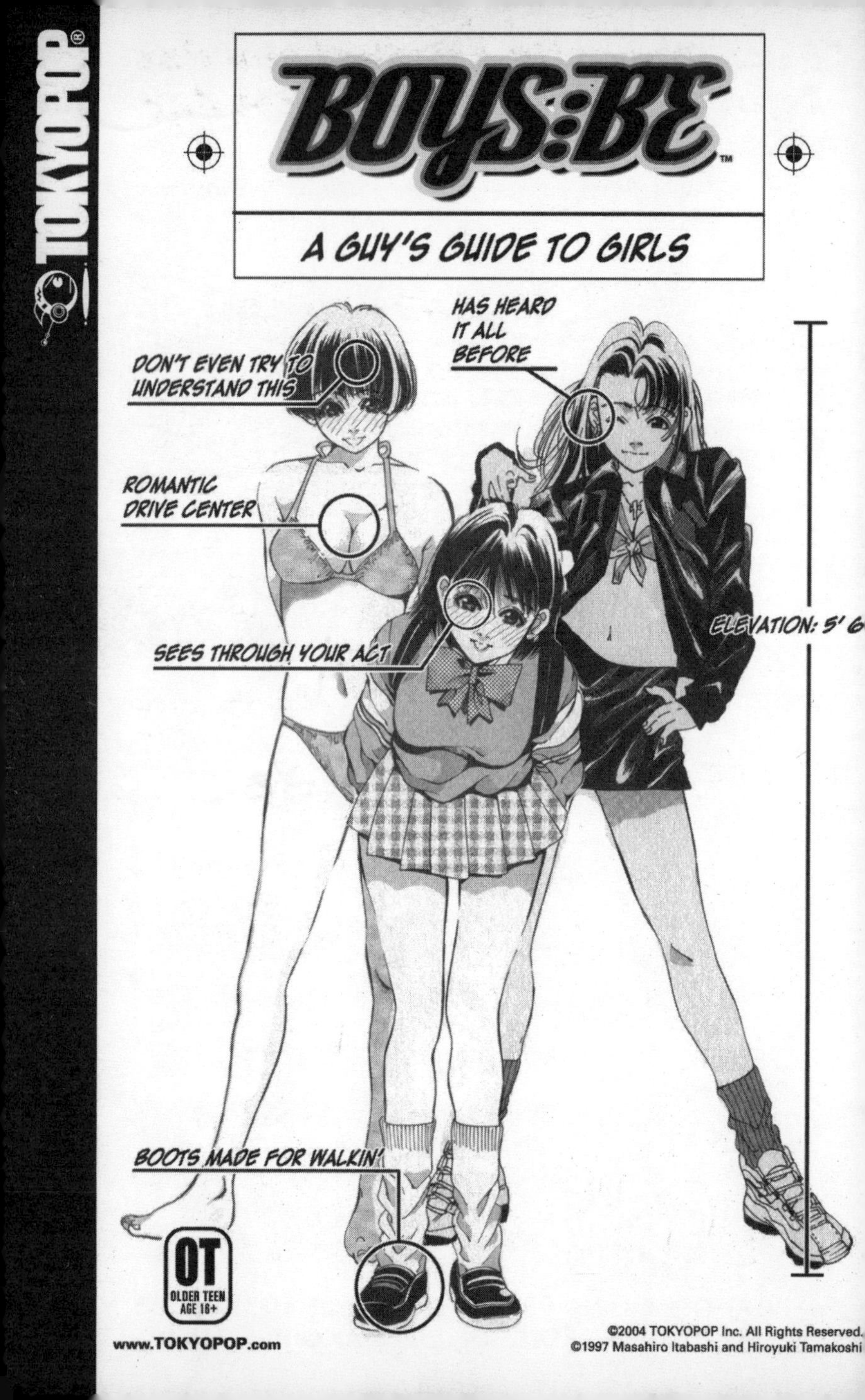

HAS HEARD IT ALL BEFORE
DON'T EVEN TRY TO UNDERSTAND THIS
ROMANTIC DRIVE CENTER
ELEVATION: 5' 6
SEES THROUGH YOUR ACT
BOOTS MADE FOR WALKIN'

OT OLDER TEEN AGE 16+

www.TOKYOPOP.com

10.19.04T

ALSO AVAILABLE FROM ⊗TOKYOPOP®

10.19.04T

A touching story
about a regular guy
with an irregular gift.

HANDS OFF!

T
TEEN
AGE 13+